Diana Dwyer and Jane Scampion

Psychology A Level

MACMILLAN

Acknowledgements

First and foremost our sincerest thanks to both our dads, Doug Ginger and Derrick Scampion, who read the script from cover to cover and made many helpful suggestions: and not a psychology qualification between them. Thanks also to David Horn and Jim Dwyer for their moral and domestic support, to Jeff Baynham for the photographs and Roy Hunt for the cartoons.

The author and publishers wish to acknowledge, with thanks, the following illustration sources, and to state that they have tried to clear copyright, but in any case where they may have failed, the publishers will be pleased to make the necessary arrangement at the first opportunity: Brooks and Cole Figs 3.27, 9.2; Copp, Clark and Pitman Ltd Fig 3.27; Harcourt, Brace & Jovanovich Figs 7.9, 7.13; Harper and Row Figs 2.4, 7.10; HarperCollins Ltd Figs 5.9, 7.1, 7.5, 9.1, 9.4; Hodder and Stoughton Figs 3.36, 7.6; Holt, Rinehart and Winston Figs 3.20, 7.2, 7.7, 7.8, 8.1, 9.3; Macmillam Archive Figs 3.4, 3.5; McGraw-Hill Fig 8.3; Thomas Nelson Figs 3.32, 3.33, 3.34, 3.35, 8.1, 8.2, 8.4; Prentice Hall Figs 3.6, 3.7, 9.5; Radio Times Fig 6.3; Sheldon Press, London Figs 3.14, 3.15, 3.16, 3.17, 6.1, 6.2; Wildcant Fig 4.1.

Grateful thanks are extended, too, to the Associated Examining Board, Northern Examinations and Assessment Board (Joint Matriculation Board and Northern Examining Association), and Oxford and Cambridge Schools Examination Board for questions from previous examination papers.

First published 1995 by
MACMILLAN PRESS LTD
Houndmills, Basingstoke, Hampshire RG21 2XS
and London
Companies and representatives
throughout the world

ISBN 0–333–61171–3

A catalogue record for this book is available from the British Library.

13 12   11   10   9   8   7   6   5
06   05   04   03   02   01   00

Printed in Malaysia

Good design

for effective revision

3

Cognitive Psychology

Syllabus analysis
Ensures you only do the topics you need – no more, no less

Start and completion column Keeps tabs on your progress – see at a glance which areas still need to be worked through

Self assessment For you to note how well you've done or areas which need to be improved

Chapter breakdown Shows you in detail what is covered in the chapters

AEB	NEAB	O & C	Topic	Date attempted	Date completed	Self Assessment
✓	✓	✓	**Models of Memory**			
✓	✓	✓	**Organisation of Information in Memory**			
✓	✓	✓	**Practical Implications of Memory Research**			
✓	✓	✓	**Theories of Forgetting**			
✓	✓	✗	**The Visual System in Humans**			
✓	✓	✓	**Perceptual Abilities**			
✓	✓	✓	**Visual Illusions**			
✓	✓	✓	**Theories of Perception**			
✓	✓	✓	**Development of Perception**			
✓	✓	✓	**Selective Attention**			

Contents

Topic

Topic

List of Core Studies

Exam Board Addresses

For syllabuses and past papers contact the Publications office at the following addresses:

The Associated Examining Board
Publications Department
Stag Hill House
Guildford
Surrey
GU2 5XJ
Tel. 01483 302302

University of Cambridge Local Examinations Syndicate
1 Hills Road
Cambridge
CB1 2EU
Tel. 01223 553311

Northern Examinations and Assessment Board
12 Harter Street
Manchester
M1 6HL
Tel. 0161 953 1170
(Also shop at the above address)

University of London Examinations and Assessment Council
Stewart House
32 Russell Square
London
WC1B 5DN
Tel. 0171 331 4000

Oxford and Cambridge Schools Examination Board
Purbeck House
Purbeck Road
Cambridge
CB2 2PU
Tel. 01223 411211

University of Oxford Delegacy of Local Examinations
Unit 23
Monks Brook Industrial Park
Chandler's Ford
Eastleigh
Hants
S05 3RA
Tel. 01703 266232

Northern Ireland Council for the Curriculum, Examinations and Assessment
29 Clarendon Road
Belfast
BT1 3BG
Tel. 01232 261200
Fax 01232 261234

Welsh Joint Education Committee
245 Western Avenue
Llandaff
Cardiff
CF5 2YX

Remember to check your syllabus number with your teacher!

Introduction 1

AEB	NEAB	O & C	Topic	Date attempted	Date completed	Self Assessment
✓	✓	✓	**A and AS level Syllabuses**			
✓	✓	✓	**Revision**			
✓	✓	✓	**Writing a Psychology Essay**			
✓	✓	✓	**The Exam**			

The aim of this book is to provide a thorough study guide for students studying A and AS level psychology. This book is based on the AEB syllabus but includes a great deal of the NEAB modular syllabus and the Oxford and Cambridge Core studies with exam questions. It is also envisaged that the book will be of use for the growing number of students studying psychology as part of other courses.

1.1 The A and AS level syllabuses and exams

The AEB syllabus

The AEB A level comprises two end of course exams and four pieces of coursework.

Paper 1 (40 per cent)

Four questions must be answered in **three hours**.

This paper is divided into four sections:
Section A is compulsory, **one** out of three questions set must be answered.
Section B, C and D comprise four question each – **one per subsection**. No more than **two** questions from any one section may be answered.

Section A: Perspectives on Psychology (compulsory)
(i)   The nature of psychological enquiry
(ii)   Issues and controversies in psychology

Section B: Cognitive Psychology
(i)   Perception
(ii)   Attention
(iii) Memory
(iv)   Language and thought

Section C: Social Psychology
(i)   Social perception
(ii)   Interpersonal attraction and prejudice
(iii) Social influence
(iv)   Pro- and anti-social Behaviour

Section D: Comparative Psychology
(i)   Genetic and evolutionary determinants of behaviour
(ii)   Learning and behaviour in the natural environment
(iii) Laboratory studies of learning and behaviour
(iv)   Animal communication and social behaviour

Paper 2 (40 per cent)

Four questions must be answered in **three hours**.

Section A is a compulsory methodology and statistics question.
Section B, C and D comprise four questions each – **one per subsection**. No more than **two** questions from any one section may be chosen.

Section A: Experimental Design and Research Methods

Section B: Bio-psychology
(i)   The nervous system and behaviour
(ii)   Awareness
(iii) Motivation and emotion
(iv)   Anxiety and stress

Section C: Developmental Psychology
(i)   Early socialisation
(ii)   Cognitive development
(iii) Social behaviour and individual differences in development
(iv)   Adolescence, adulthood, senescence

Section D: Individual Differences
(i)   Personality and intelligence
(ii)   Normal and abnormal behaviour
(iii) Psychopathology
(iv)   Therapeutic approaches

The AEB AS level comprises one end of course exam and two pieces of coursework.

Paper 1 (80 per cent)

A **three hour** exam comprising **one** compulsory research methods and statistics question and **three** other questions taken from the following sections. No more than **two** questions may be answered from any one section. Four questions are set on each of the following sections:

Section B: Cognitive processes
Section C: Biological Foundations of Behaviour
Section D: Individual Development
Section E: Social Behaviour
Section F: Work and the Individual
Section G: Adulthood: Adjustment and Abnormality

The Oxford and Cambridge Syllabus

The AS and first year of the A level involve a selection of Core Studies most of which are included in this book.

Paper 1 (40 per cent of A level + 80 per cent of AS level)

A **three hour** exam which involves 20 short questions and two stimulus questions on the core studies.

Paper 2 (10 per cent of A level + 20 per cent of AS level)

Two pieces of structured practical work.

Paper 3 (10 per cent of A level)

One piece of practical work and one assignment.

Paper 4 (10 per cent of A level)

A **one and a half hour** paper on research methods. Students will be given a paper to research a week before the exam.

Paper 5 (30 per cent of A level)

A **three hour** exam comprising three stimulus response structured essays on specialist options.

Students will have studied **two** of the following options:

Psychology and Education
Psychology and Health
Psychology and the Environment
Psychology and Organisations
There will be **two** questions set on each of these choices.

The NEAB Modular Syllabus

This syllabus comprises three compulsory and six optional modules.

Compulsory Modules

Perspectives in psychology
Research methods and data analysis
Contemporary Topics in Psychology

Optional Modules

Psychology of Atypical Behaviour
Social Psychology
Child Development
Cognitive Psychology and its Application
Health Psychology
Psychology in Education

Candidates at A level are required to do **all** the compulsory modules and **three** of the optional modules (one of the optional modules can be chosen from another discipline).

AS level candidates are required to do **two** of the compulsory modules (Perspectives in psychology and Research methods and data analysis) and **one** optional module.

Assessment

Modular

One **one and a half hour** test to be taken at the end of each module.

Each module is worth nearly 17 per cent, of which 3 per cent is coursework.

Tests can be taken in December, March and June.

Non-modular

Candidates at A level are required to take a **three hour** exam on the compulsory modules and three separate **one and a half hour** module tests on the chosen options – all in June.

AS level candidates will be required to take two compulsory and one optional module **one and a half hour** tests in June.

1.2 Revision

What to revise

Make sure you revise sufficient material to ensure that you can answer the required number of questions. **Look carefully at the way the exam paper is structured.**

For example, the AEB A level exam is divided into eight sections which, apart from section A on Paper 2, are further divided into subsections. There is guaranteed to be one question on each subsection. Therefore, if you decide you cannot revise everything in a section, it is **NOT** advisable to select topics from each subsection because you may then have an extremely limited choice or even be unable to answer any questions from that subsection. **It is more sensible to omit an entire subsection and learn every topic in the other ones.**

When to revise

Having decided what you are going to revise, make a **revision plan**. Work out how many revision sessions you will have before the exam and decide what you will revise in each slot. You may not stick to it rigidly, but it should be a useful guide and will help you realise if you are way behind schedule.

How to revise

Now you have decided what and when to revise, you must start work in earnest.

Before you even start, decide when you are going to **finish**. Evidence shows that our learning efficiency falls in the middle of a session but picks up towards the end. It is therefore more efficient to do lots of small learning sessions than one long one. For example, if you have a two hour block of time available, you could decide that you will work for four 25 minute blocks with short breaks in between. The breaks must be short, and they must be **planned**.

Few people can revise effectively by simply reading through their work. Most of us have to do something with the material. The most common procedure is to make revision notes, that is, brief summary notes. Use headings and numbered points whenever you can. Try to summarise major theories in one or two sentences. **Understanding** is essential: you are unlikely to remember things you do not understand. Keep testing yourself and make sure you are actually learning the material; just because you have summarised it, this does not mean you know it.

Use the Activity and Exam preparation sections which appear throughout the book to test your knowledge and your ability to apply it to particular questions. The advantage of revising early is that, if you do not understand, you can go back to your teacher for help. Some students worry that if they revise too early, they will have forgotten everything before the exam. Some forgetting is inevitable, but when you go over it again, nearer to the exam, you will remember much more quickly than the last time you revised. Most important of all, you should not be struggling to understand, because any difficulties will have been faced at the earlier revision sessions.

1.3 Writing a psychology essay

Essay questions are designed to test two skills: **description** and **analysis**. Your answers should include both of these.

The AEB marking scheme calls these:
Skill A: knowledge-based and descriptive skills which demonstrate understanding of relevant psychological theories, concepts, evidence and application.
Skill B: analytical and evaluative skills.

No more than 16 marks out of a possible 25 can be obtained if only one of these skills is demonstrated. Essays awarded 17 marks or above demonstrate both skill A and skill B to a high standard.

Definitions of the skill words used in essay titles

Describe (skill A): Outline a theory and/or present evidence
Define (skill A): Explain what is meant by a particular term.
Examine (skill A): Describe a theory or concept in a detailed manner.
Criticise (skill B): Present inadequacies and conflicting views.
Evaluate (skill B): Consider the value of a theory or area of study, with reference to good and bad points, usefulness and applications.
Compare and contrast (skill A and B): Consider similarities and differences between theories or concepts.
Discuss (skill A & B): Describe and evaluate by considering different if not contrasting points of view.

Writing essays under exam conditions

1. **Read the essay title very carefully**, <u>underline</u> the important words. Pay very careful attention to what is being asked and think about how you will **organise** the relevant material to best answer the question. At this stage, try not to worry too much about time: it is much better to read the question thoroughly than to pick out key points and plunge on without proper regard to what is being asked.

2. **Avoid writing everything you know** on a subject or reproducing a previously prepared answer to a different question. The most frequent lament in reports of examiners is that students use 'prepared answers', and do not answer the actual question. This seriously reduces your marks.

3. **Make a plan.** This may take up some of the precious time available but is still worth five minutes. It serves several purposes:
   - It focuses your mind on the actual question rather than simply on the general topic area
   - It helps you organise the material in a logical way. As you write the plan, you may think of additional points you hadn't at first considered, and you can then insert them in the correct place
   - It enables you to relax and concentrate on the actual writing rather than worrying all the time that you might forget to include a certain point.

   Having said all that, plans must be brief and not take up half the essay writing time.

4. The essay should follow a simple **basic structure:**
   Introduction, in which you set the scene by outlining the main points, arguments or theories.
   Main body in which each theory or concept is discussed and evaluated, each in a separate paragraph.
   Conclusion.
   For example, consider the following essay question:

   > 'Discuss two theories of intelligence. What are the implications of these theories for intelligence testing?'
   >
   > **(AEB, 1991)**

   Obviously, you need to decide which two theories you will discuss. When making this choice, bear in mind the second part of the question and try to choose *contrasting* theories which have very different implications for testing.
   - In your *introduction*, start by outlining very briefly what is meant by a theory of intelligence, that is, that it concerns the nature of the relationship between various abilities.
   - In the *main body*, describe and evaluate each theory and then outline its implications for testing. These implications should follow on logically from the theory itself.
   - The *conclusion* should *not* simply be a summary but should be an attempt to answer the question and draw justifiable, but probably tentative, conclusions. In this example, you could reasonably say that there is no universal agreement among psychologists as to the nature of intelligence. Each theory has important far-reaching implications, particularly in terms of how and why tests are used and, even more importantly, the conclusions that are drawn from test results.

5. Think very carefully about what you are writing: is it based on sound psychological theory or simply a tabloid interpretation of an event?

   Do not write your own personal opinions: your conclusions should **always** be based on the **evidence** presented. For example, it is inappropriate to say 'I think Freud was wrong because he was just obsessed with sex' (or, as one student wrote at the end of a well argued essay 'but anyway, I think Freud was just a dirty old man'). On the other hand, provided that you have presented a well reasoned argument, it is reasonable to state that Freud can be criticised for placing too much emphasis on sex while underestimating other social influences.

6. In terms of **style**, avoid the use of the first person. You are probably aware that in coursework you do not write 'I constructed a questionnaire' but 'a questionnaire was constructed'. The same applies in essays.

   Use **psychological language**, but only that which you understand and which is appropriate.

   Never try to learn chunks of textbooks: not only is this time consuming and extremely tedious but unless you understand it you cannot apply it to a particular question. If you do understand it, then put it in your own words.

7. Use **references** to support your arguments. Many students are daunted by the number of researchers' names with which they are presented: if this is a problem, try at least to remember the names of the main researchers in each area.

At the end of every main section of each chapter you will find:

- **Key terms:** make sure you know the meaning of each one.
- **Self-test questions:** the answers to these are all in

the text – if you do not know the answers, go back and reread. All these questions are based on essential information that you will require to answer the longer questions in the exam.

- **Exam questions with guidance notes:** read the question, cover up the guidance notes and try to answer it. Then check your ideas against those in the notes. This will be good practice for when you sit the actual exam. Don't forget that these are guidance notes and that you may use different material. The structure, however, will give you an indication of what is required and whether or not you are on the right lines.
- **Additional exam questions:** so that you are familiar with a wide range of possible questions.

At the end of each Core Study there are questions from, or based on, the Oxford and Cambridge exam papers.

1.4 The exam

Sitting the exam

Make sure that you are familiar with the **structure** of the exam and are aware of exactly how many **questions** you will be required to answer, and from which sections these will come. This is known as the **rubric**. Look at past papers: this is really important because although this book provides you with many past paper questions and information as to the number of questions you need to answer in each section, it is still very useful to be familiar with the appearance of the paper and to consider the rubric with an exam paper in front of you.

Long before the exam, be familiar with how much **time** you have to answer each question. Allow yourself a few minutes to read through the paper and choose your questions and divide your time strictly between questions, including time for planning.

Last minute revision tends to cause panic. If you cannot resist looking at your notes in the last minutes before the exam, look at something you know well. It may seem pointless, but it will help to put you in a confident frame of mind.

Time

We have already advised you that you must be familiar with exactly how long you can afford to spend on each question. The AEB exams are three hours and this gives you about 44 minutes per question allowing for reading time. **DO NOT TAKE LONGER THAN THIS FOR ANY ONE QUESTION**, or you may be very short of time on the last question. Remember that, on any answer, it is much easier to get the first 10 marks than the last 10 marks.

Question choice

Read through the paper carefully. Do not just pick out key words, such as 'play' and think 'I've revised that, I'm OK'. Read the question carefully and consider whether you can answer **all** parts. Complicated questions may be easier than they look: read them carefully and ascertain exactly what is being asked. Some students panic when they see a quotation question. Don't! There are some worked examples of such questions in the book, showing, we assure you, that these questions are often much easier than they at first appear to be.

Having chosen your questions, it's often a good idea to start with the your **most preferred one** (but do not be tempted to spend more than the allotted time on it) and move on to the second most preferred and so on. The feeling of having written one, two or even three good answers will put you in the right frame of mind for tackling that last, not so easy (OK, awful) question. Remember what we said about writing a **plan** on essay questions. Try to keep calm. There is, believe us, no such thing as a 'mind going blank'.

All the best!

Major Approaches In Psychology

2

AEB	NEAB	O & C	Topic	Date attempted	Date completed	Self Assessment
✓	✓	✓	**Theories of learning**			
✓	✓	✓	**Psychoanalytic Theory**			

2.1 Theories of learning

Learning can be defined as a relatively permanent change in behaviour as a result of experience. It is a fundamental process in all animals, enabling an organism to adapt to changing circumstances in order to survive.

Learning theorists propose **two** means by which organisms come to behave in new ways: classical conditioning and operant conditioning.

Classical conditioning

Pavlov investigated salivation in dogs by conducting the following experiment. For several feedings, each time the dog received its food, a bell was sounded and the amount of saliva produced by the dog was measured. After several such 'trials' Pavlov sounded the bell **without** giving the dog any food and the dog still salivated (see Figure 2.1).

We need to know the scientific names for this procedure:

1. The **food** is an **unconditioned stimulus** (UCS), a stimulus that elicits a response automatically or reflexively.
2. **The salivation to the food** is an **unconditioned response** (UCR), that is, a response which is automatically produced.
3. **The bell** is a **conditioned stimulus** (CS) because

it will only set off the reflex action **on condition** that it is presented just before the food.
4. **Salivation to the bell** is a **conditioned response** (CR), a response to the conditioned stimulus.

In situations like the ones Pavlov studied, the CR is very similar to the UCR: the only difference is that the UCR is evoked by one stimulus and the CR is evoked by a different stimulus.

We can summarise Pavlov's procedure in the formula shown in Figure 2.2:

Classical conditioning, therefore, involves **learning by association**: simply learning to associate two events which often occur together.

Principles of classical conditioning

For conditioning to be effective, the conditioned stimulus should occur **before** the unconditioned stimulus, not after it or at the same time. This is because, in classical conditioning, the conditioned stimulus becomes a kind of *signal* for the unconditioned stimulus.

The following are four important principles of classical conditioning.

Extinction

If a conditioned stimulus is repeatedly presented without the unconditioned stimulus, then the conditioned response will disappear.

Spontaneous recovery

If a response is classically conditioned then extinguished, the response may suddenly reappear when the conditioned stimulus is presented after a delay. For this reason, the elimination of a conditioned response usually requires more than one extinction session.

Stimulus generalisation

A dog who has been conditioned to salivate to the sound of a bell of one tone may well salivate to a similar sounding bell or a buzzer. Stimulus generalisation is the extension of the conditioned response from the original stimulus to similar stimuli.

Figure 2.1 A dog strapped into a harness for an experiment on classical conditioning

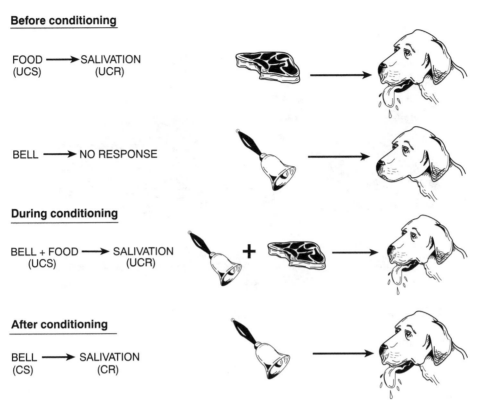

Before conditioning

FOOD ⟶ SALIVATION
(UCS)   (UCR)

BELL ⟶ NO RESPONSE

During conditioning

BELL + FOOD ⟶ SALIVATION
        (UCS)   (UCR)

After conditioning

BELL ⟶ SALIVATION
(CS)   (CR)

Figure 2.2 The classical conditioning formula

Higher-order conditioning

If a dog has learnt to salivate to a bell and then a flash of light is presented regularly before the bell is rung, then the dog will eventually salivate to the light (although it is unlikely to salivate as much as it would to the bell). This is known as **higher-order conditioning**.

Classical conditioning in everyday life

Pavlov's work helps us understand significant everyday behaviour, and can be applied to many other topic areas in psychology as you will see as you read through this book. Two examples of this are fear conditioning and advertising.

Fear conditioning

Classical conditioning has been used to explain how people may acquire exaggerated fear reactions called **phobias**. This was demonstrated in a classic study (which would not be permitted nowadays on ethical grounds, see Chapter 10).

Watson and Rayner (1920) conditioned a fear response in a 11 month old boy known as 'Little Albert', who was fond of playing with a white laboratory rat. Watson made a loud noise by banging

Before higher order conditioning

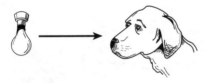

During higher order conditioning

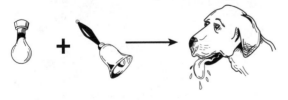

After higher order conditioning

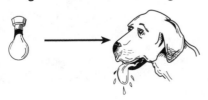

Figure 2.3 Higher-order conditioning

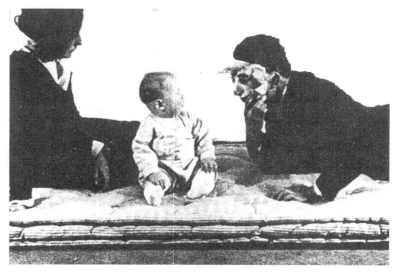

Figure 2.4 John Watson testing 'Little Albert' for stimulus generation with a Santa Claus mask
Source: C. Wade and C. Tavris, Psychology (Harper & Row, 1990, 2nd edn), p. 214.

together two steel bars behind Albert's back when he played with the rat. After 7 trials, Albert showed fear of the rat even though there was now no noise. Albert's fear was **generalised** to objects similar to the rat such as a rabbit, the fur collar of a coat and even a Santa Claus mask (see Figure 2.4).

Activity

In the case of Little Albert:

1. What was the UCS?
2. What was the UCR (a reflex action)?
3. What was the CS?
4. Sue cannot stand the smell or taste of mushrooms. How would learning theorists suggest that taste aversions can arise? How might such a reaction be beneficial to animals?
5. The 'Little Albert' study is a demonstration of how phobias may be acquired. **Behaviour therapy** is a means of using learning theory to treat phobias – this is discussed in Chapter 9. Before reading this, think about how it might be achieved: with what would you now need to pair the phobic object (in Albert's case, the rat)?

Conditioned fear is highly resistant to extinction. When a strong fear is involved, conditioning may take place after only **one** pairing of a neutral stimulus with the UCS.

Advertising

Advertising campaigns often try to take advantage of classical conditioning. Advertisers pair their products with UCSs that produce pleasant emotions, often sexual arousal. Advertisers hope their product will become associated with these positive feelings. Coffee is paired with romantic meetings, soap powder with happy family life and so on (see Figure 2.5).

Figure 2.5 Advertisers use pictures associated with strong UCSs that elicit strong positive reactions

Operant conditioning

Operant conditioning (also called instrumental conditioning) was first described by **Thorndike** in 1911. He devised a 'puzzle box' in which cats were placed and had to solve the problem of how to escape. The more often they were placed in the box, the quicker their escape (see Figure 2.6).

Having conducted several studies with a variety of animals, Thorndike suggested that:

1. Learning did not depend on a sudden flash of inspiration but on **trial and error** and, as such, was a gradual process (see Figure 2.7).
2. The process of learning could be expressed in the **Law of Effect**: a response that is followed by pleasant consequences becomes more probable and a response that is followed by unfavourable consequences becomes less probable.

Activity

Operant conditioning is so named because the conditioning **operates** on the environment to produce an outcome. In classical conditioning, the animal or person's behaviour does not have any environmental consequences. Thus in Pavlov's procedure the dog receives food whether or not it salivates. But in operant conditioning the organism's response produces an **effect on the environment**. What effect did it have on Thorndike's cats? Can you think of any other important differences between operant and classical conditioning?

Figure 2.6 Thorndike's Puzzle Box

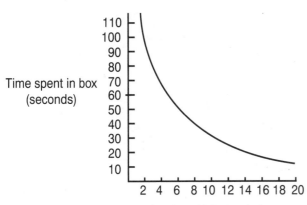

Figure 2.7 The learning curve for Thorndike's Puzzle Box

The work of Skinner

Skinner developed machines for operant conditioning which are named 'Skinner boxes'. Rats and pigeons are most often used (see Figure 2.8).

When placed in a Skinner box the animal has to press a lever to open a food tray and thus obtain **reinforcement** in the form of food. By accident, in the course of exploration, the rat will press the lever and food will be presented. Every time it presses the lever, food is delivered, so pressing the lever is reinforced. The rat will then press the lever more often, and this becomes a **conditioned response**.

Skinner expressed Thorndike's Law of Effect in different terms.

Behaviour which is **reinforced** tends to be **repeated**.

Behaviour which is **not reinforced** tends to be **extinguished**.

Figure 2.8 A Skinner box

Reinforcers and punishers

> **Reinforcement** is anything that increases the probability that the response that preceded it will occur again. In other words it strengthens a response.
>
> **Punishment** is anything which decreases the probability that a response will arise.

There are **two** kinds of reinforcement and **two** kinds of punishment:

1. A **positive reinforcer** is anything pleasurable which increases the probability of a response. Examples are food, warmth, drink, good music.

2. A **negative reinforcer** is the removal of, or escape from, anything unpleasant which increases the probability of a response occurring. Examples are escape from an electric shock or from being shut up in a small room.

3. A **positive punisher** is anything unpleasant that decreases the probability that the event preceding it will occur again. An example is smacking.

4. A **negative punishment** is the removal of something pleasant which decreases the likelihood of a response. Examples are removal of pocket money, no television for a week.

Activity

Having discovered that your daughter is smoking, suggest a

* positive punisher
* negative punisher

that will decrease the probability of her smoking. If you were a parent wanting to increase the probability that your son would do his homework, suggest a

* positive reinforcer
* negative reinforcer

that could be used for this purpose.

The effects of punishment

The work of Skinner has revealed that positive reinforcement is far more effective than punishment in regulating behaviour. There are many problems with the use of punishment, including the fact that it has unpleasant emotional side effects. Nevertheless, it can be effective in suppressing a behaviour if, when used with young children or animals, it **immediately follows the undesirable action**. The most effective way of changing behaviour is to use a combination of punishment for undesirable behaviour coupled with positive reinforcement for desired behaviour, using behaviour shaping if necessary.

Escape learning

Learning which is brought about by negative reinforcement is called **escape learning**. For example, suppose an animal is made to stand on an electrified floor grid and is given a mild electric shock; if it jumps or runs away from the grid, the shock stops. Escape behaviour is therefore reinforced by the cessation of the shock. The problem with this type of learning is that it can deal only with very simple types of behaviour: because the shock produces large emotional responses in the animal it is unlikely to try to do anything more complex or unusual than escape.

Secondary reinforcement and punishment

Any reinforcers which satisfy a biological need (reinforcers such as food, drink, sex) are known as **primary reinforcers**. Similarly, pain and extreme heat or cold are inherently punishing and are therefore known as **primary punishers**. If we pair a primary reinforcer with a second stimulus, then that stimulus on its own becomes a reinforcer because of its association with a primary reinforcer. Money, praise, a smile, applause, good grades are all secondary reinforcers. Criticism, a frown, a telling-off, sharp words are all secondary punishers.

Just because a reinforcer (or punisher) is secondary does not mean it is any less **potent** than a primary reinforcer. Money has an enormous effect on people's behaviour. Not only can it be exchanged for primary reinforcers such as food and shelter, but also it brings with it other secondary reinforcers, such as praise and respect. Similarly, secondary punishers can be very powerful: the sound of the dentist's drill or a hand raised in anger is sufficient to bring about a fear reaction in many of us.

Principles of operant conditioning

Extinction

In operant conditioning extinction occurs when a response is no longer reinforced, so that the response is gradually weakened and disappears.

Spontaneous recovery

A previous reinforced response may suddenly recur even in the absence of reinforcement.

Stimulus generalisation

If a person is reinforced for making a particular response to a certain stimulus, they are likely to make the same response to a similar stimulus. A pigeon that has learned to obtain food by pecking at a white button will also peck at a red or green button.

Schedules of reinforcement

1. **Continuous reinforcement:** reinforcement is provided every time the correct response occurs. Once reinforcement stops, extinction is fairly rapid.
2. **Variable reinforcement:** this involves reinforcement for some responses and not for others on an inconsistent basis, and reflects what happens in real life situations. A very important aspect of variable reinforcement is that inconsistently reinforced behaviour is **very difficult to extinguish**.

In terms of child development, consider a child who whines for an ice-cream every time she passes a particular shop. Every now and again the whining is reinforced as she gets an ice-cream. The whining will continue for a very long time before it is finally extinguished. Ironically, the longer the gap between reinforcements and the more irregular the reinforcements, the longer it is before behaviour is extinguished.

On the other hand, it means that desirable behaviour does not need to be praised every time it is exhibited: occasional praise or other reinforcement will ensure the behaviour is not extinguished.

Behaviour shaping

For a response to be reinforced, it must first occur. Complex behaviour, like a child using a knife and fork properly or a pigeon playing ping pong will never occur spontaneously. In order to teach complex behaviour, Skinner used a system called **shaping**. In shaping you start by reinforcing any behaviour which is even vaguely related to the required behaviour. Once an animal has been conditioned to perform a particular action it tends to generalise and use this as the basis of further behaviour. The responses that you reinforce on the way to the final one are called **successive approximations**.

Parents unconsciously use behaviour shaping techniques. For example, when a child is given a knife and fork he is praised (reinforced) for merely holding it correctly, but as he gets older and more adept he would only be praised for holding it and using it correctly. This applies to a host of human activities. Chapter 8 contains an account of Skinner's theory of language acquisition in children; this depends heavily on behaviour shaping by successive approximations.

Activity

Which of the following expressions apply only to classical conditioning (CC), which to only operant conditioning (OC) and which to both?

1. Stimulus paired with a reflex action
2. Response results in punishment
3. Response can be extinguished
4. Development of phobias
5. Stimulus generalisation
6. Behaviour shaping
7. Response occurs before reinforcement
8. Response occurs after stimulus presentation
9. Variable reinforcement schedule.

Answers: 1. CC **2.** OC **3.** Both **4.** CC **5.** Both **6.** OC **7.** OC **8.** CC **9.** OC

Uses of operant conditioning

Everyday uses

Operant conditioning is used every day in our efforts to influence other people. For example:

- Language acquisition and table manners have already been mentioned
- Parents and peers use an elaborate and often unconscious system of rewards and punishments to encourage sex-appropriate behaviour
- Parents tend to reward their children for expressing attitudes of which they approve and punish or ignore them for expressing attitudes with which they disagree.

Behaviour modification programmes

Carefully designed programmes have been devised which use operant conditioning techniques in order to change behaviour: a technique known as **behaviour modification**. In behaviour modification, a psychologist sets a specific behavioural goal and then systematically reinforces the individual's successive approximations to it.

These techniques have been used in places such as classrooms, mental hospitals, factories and prisons. Specific examples of the use of behaviour modification covered in this book are **token economies** (see section 9.5) and **biofeedback** (see section 7.5).

Behaviourism

Much of our behaviour consists of learned responses to simple stimuli. Can **all** behaviour be analysed into simple units? Some psychologists believe it can: behaviour, they maintain, is the sum of many simple **stimulus–response connections**. Other psychologists maintain that even the simplest responses to simple stimuli involve paying attention to a vast amount of information.

A group of psychologists known as **Behaviourists**, of whom the most famous are **Watson** and **Skinner**, belong to the former group: in fact behaviourism is often referred to as S–R psychology because of its emphasis on these simple stimulus–response connections. The contributions and limitations of behaviourism are discussed in detail in Chapter 10.

Social learning theory

Social learning theory, formulated by **Bandura**, is an offshoot of strict behaviourism which is concerned with human rather than animal behaviour and sees people as **active** manipulators of their own environments, rather than being mere **passive** recipients of experiences. We can manipulate our own environments by, for example, seeking out experiences we enjoy and influencing other people's behaviour.

The main tenets of Social learning theory are:

1. Although classical and operant conditioning are important determinants of learning, they are not the only ones.
2. People also learn by **observation** and **imitation**. You do not have to experience pleasant or unpleasant events directly for them to influence behaviour; you are able to imagine the effects.
3. Vigorous standards of experimentation should be used. The Core Study in section 5.6 on Aggression is a typical example. This has led to a criticism that the behaviour observed lacks **ecological validity**: it does not reflect real-life behaviour.
4. The theory states that imitation is not indiscriminate: people are more likely to copy:

   - Models who are reinforced
   - Models who are liked, admired and respected (including parents, teachers, media heroes and heroines)
   - Models who are similar, especially in terms of sex and age: same sex friends are powerful models.

5. Imitation is only likely to occur if the individual has **self-efficacy**, a belief that they are capable of performing the act.

6. **Cognitive factors** as well as behaviour are important influences on learning. Cognitive factors determining whether imitation takes place are:

   - The amount of **attention** paid to a model; we pay more attention to those models listed in **4**
   - The **knowledge acquired** from watching others, including whether or not they were rewarded
   - **Expectation** about the consequences, depending on past and present experiences
   - The amount of **self-efficacy** we have.

7. Eventually, we are able to a certain extent to guide our own behaviour rather than being dependent on outside influences; we can, for example, reward and punish ourselves, seek out certain experiences while avoiding others. This concept of us influencing our own environment as well as the environment influencing us is known as **reciprocal determinism**, and is discussed in more detail in Chapter 10.

Social learning theory has an important influence in many areas of psychology, including:

- Developmental processes (particularly in the acquisition of gender role and moral behaviour)
- Social behaviour (for example, the effects of the media on aggression and prosocial behaviour)
- Abnormal behaviour (in cognitive behaviour therapy). All of these are dealt with in more detail in later chapters.

Preparing for the exam

Key terms

behaviour modification
behaviour shaping
behaviour therapy
Behaviourism
classical conditioning
conditioned fear
conditioned response
conditioned stimulus
continuous reinforcement
ecological validity
escape learning
extinction
higher-order conditioning
Law of Effect
negative punishment
negative reinforcement
operant conditioning

phobia
positive punishment
positive reinforcement
primary punishers
primary reinforcers
reciprocal determinism
secondary punishers
secondary reinforcer
self-efficacy
Social learning theory
spontaneous recovery
stimulus generalisation
successive approximations
trial and error
unconditioned response
unconditioned stimulus
variable reinforcement

Types of exam question

Most questions are concerned with the principles and practical applications of learning theories. Note that learning theories are on the comparative section of the AEB paper, and that behaviourism is covered in the perspectives section.

Self-test questions

1. In Pavlov's original experiment on dogs, identify the following:
   a the unconditioned stimulus
   b the conditioned stimulus
   c the conditioned response.
2. With reference to classical conditioning explain the meaning of the following:
   a extinction
   b stimulus generalisation
   c higher-order conditioning.
3. How can classical conditioning explain how phobias may be acquired?
4. What is Thorndike's Law of Effect?
5. With reference to operant conditioning explain the meaning of the following:
   a positive reinforcement
   b negative reinforcement
   c punishment.
6. What is a secondary reinforcer? Give an example.
7. What is behaviour shaping? Give an example.
8. Briefly describe *one* application of operant conditioning.
9. What are the main principles of Social learning theory?
10. Under what circumstances is behaviour most likely to be imitated?

Exam question with guidance notes

a Outline the main aspects of Social learning theory, mentioning supporting empirical evidence. **(10 marks)**

b Briefly discuss <u>one</u> way in which Social learning theory differs from Operant Conditioning. **(4 marks)**

c Account for <u>one</u> aspect of social development from a Social learning perspective. **(6 marks)**

JMB (1991)

a

• This is straightforward as you simply need to repeat the points made in the text, although you may have to abbreviate them somewhat. Crucial points are learning by observation and imitation and taking account of cognitive factors. The empirical evidence comes from the Core Study in Chapter 5 (p. 139). Notice the rigorous standards of experimentation that are employed, lending the study to criticisms of lack of ecological validity. There are also *ethical* problems with this study.

b

• Notice that this part of the question requires only *one* difference which should be evaluated. The main difference is that operant conditioning does not take account of *cognitive factors* in learning whereas social learning does. There can be no doubt that thinking influences learning, and the extreme position taken by Skinner that we should only take account of measurable aspects of behaviour rather than the processes going on 'inside our heads' is a source of criticism.

c

• You will need to refer to other parts of the book to answer this question. You could use either aggression, moral behaviour or gender: the social learning position on all of these areas is covered in detail.

• If you choose *aggression*, you can refer to studies of the influence of the media on aggression in children, a major concern of the Social learning theorists.

• With respect to *moral development*, you can briefly contrast this view with the Freudian approach which gives a different account of how rules are internalised. Alternatively, you can contrast it with the stage theories which see moral development as more dependent on cognitive development and maturation rather than reinforcement and imitation. (Don't try to do too much comparison for 6 marks.)

• The social learning theory of *gender* role development is supported by considerable empirical evidence, and can also be contrasted with the Freudian approach or compared with the cognitive development approach of Kohlberg or with gender schema theory. Again, there is plenty to write so don't get too carried away for 6 marks.

Additional exam questions

1. Describe what you consider to be key features of operant conditioning and discuss some practical applications of operant conditioning techniques in educational settings. **(25 marks)**
   AEB, AS (1990)

2. Tony and his mother had been observed interacting many times. The following episode was typical.

   Tony (who is 18 months old) sits in front of the bookshelf pulling books out. He pulls out a book and picks up a piece of paper (his sister's homework) and looks at it. Tony pulls out another book, his mother comes over and says 'Tony, no' and moves away saying 'Don't touch again', and slaps his hand.

   Tony goes back and touches the books. His mother says 'No' again and Tony throws himself on the floor and whines. He gets up and picks up a doll and throws it, then goes to the shelves and pulls out books again. Tony then picks up a framed picture from the shelf. His mother yells 'No, Tony! Don't touch!' Tony laughs. His mother says 'I am not playing with you'. He picks up another picture. His mother tells his sister to get it back from him and she does. His mother pulls him away and says 'Don't touch and stop laughing'. Tony laughs and goes to watch television.

   Analyse Tony's behaviour from the perspective of operant conditioning and discuss why an operant approach to modifying Tony's behaviour may be ineffective. **(14 marks)**
   NEAB (1993)

2.2 The psychoanalytical approach: Sigmund Freud (1856–1939)

The unconscious mind

In the course of his original career as a neurologist, Freud encountered patients suffering from a variety of physical symptoms such as paralysis, amnesia and blindness for which no apparent physical cause could be identified. Freud called these **hysterical symptoms** and believed that the cause could be located in the **unconscious mind**. Freud likened the human mind to an iceberg – the greater part being concealed below the surface.

Ways of investigating the unconscious mind

Freud (with a colleague, Breuer) used the following means of investigating the unconscious mind; these are the main tools of modern-day psychoanalysis:

1. **Free association:** patients are encouraged to lie comfortably on a couch and speak aloud every thought that comes into their head – however disturbing, trivial or shocking.

2. **Dream analysis:** Freud believed that all dreams are significant and if analysed appropriately could give clues as to the contents of the patient's unconscious mind. Freud's theory of dreams and its relation to the unconscious mind is discussed in Chapter 7.

3. **Analysis of 'slips of the tongue' or 'parapraxes':** Freud believed that many apparent accidents or slips were really no such thing, but that they indicated unconscious wishes.

Using these methods on patients, Freud found enough common themes and symbols to begin to construct a theory of the unconscious, personality and development.

Instincts

According to Freud there are two basic instincts which provide the energy to 'run' the personality.

1. **The life instinct: Eros**
   This comprises **two** parts: **self-preservation** and **sex**.

   The energy force for this part of the life instinct is the **libido**. As the child develops, the libido is focused on different organs, known as the **erotogenic organs** of the body. The instinct aims to achieve satisfaction of an erotogenic zone: the mouth, the anus, and the genitals.

   By the time the child is six or seven years the libido is directed into other activities concerned with growing up.

2. **The death instinct: Thanatos**
   The energies of the death instinct propel the individual towards death. Because the life instinct is more powerful, the energies of the death instinct are channelled away from ourselves and into aggression towards others.

Freud believed that the energies of the two instincts must find release and that society needs to provide socially acceptable ways that this can occur in order to avoid a variety of social problems.

The theory of psychosexual development

Personality changes

Freud constructed a theory of development which shows how early experiences affect adult personality. Stimulation of different areas of the body is important as the child progresses through the important developmental stages.

1. **The oral stage (0–2 years)**
   At this stage, the focus of the libido is the **mouth** and the child obtains pleasure from oral stimulation: sucking, biting and so on. The child needs to obtain just the right amount of stimulation: too much or too little can lead to **fixation** (not successfully moving on from a developmental stage) and this will affect adult personality.
   a **Too little stimulation** can lead to an adult personality that is uncaring, self-centred, inclined to treat people as objects and over-dependent on oral habits such as smoking, drinking, excessive eating and nail biting.
   b **Too much stimulation** can lead to a personality which is gullible, unrealistically optimistic and generally over-enthusiastic.

Figure 2.9 'The oral stage can influence behaviour in adult life'.
(Photo courtesy of Jeff Baynham)

2. **The anal stage (2–4 years)**
   The libido is now focused on the anus and children obtain pleasure from the physical sensation of passing faeces and from the power that their parents' sudden concern with when and where this process takes place gives them.
   a **Too little stimulation** (caused by over-strict toilet training) can lead to a personality, known as the **anal retentive** personality which is obsessive about tidiness and cleanliness, generally pessimistic, mean, and excessively self-controlled.
   b **Too much stimulation** can lead to a personality, known as the **anal expulsive** personality, which is over-generous, untidy, messy and disorganised and can even be sadistic.

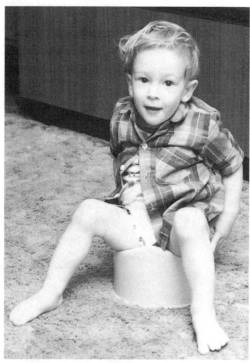

Figure 2.10 The anal stage is closely associated with potty training. (Photo courtesy of Jeff Baynham)

3. **The phallic stage (3–5 or 6 years)**

   The focus of the libido is now the genitals and the pattern of development, which has hitherto been the same for both the sexes, takes a different course for boys than for girls. Freud believed that around the age of three years children begin to have unconscious sexual feelings towards their parent of the opposite sex and sees the same-sex parent as a rival. This he called the Oedipus complex

The Oedipus complex

Boys

During the phallic stage the little boy has intense feelings for his mother and feels hostile towards his father who he considers to be a rival for his mother's affections. At the same time the boy becomes interested in genitals, an interest which both his parents discourage. The boys sees this as proof of his father's disapproval of his desires towards his mother and begins the fear that his father will punish him by **castration**. Everything about his father is bigger and more powerful and the boy feels confused and very frightened. In order to overcome this situation the boy

identifies with his father: this means that he becomes as much like his father as possible. In this way, at least vicariously, the boy can possess his mother. Freud believed that it is through the process of identification that children learn **sex-appropriate** behaviour and their **moral code** of conduct, both of which are based on the father's standards. All sexual desires, including that for the mother, are now repressed.

Activity

The Core Study of 'Little Hans' (p. 21) provides a detailed account of the Oedipus complex. We suggest you read through this and summarise the main points before reading on.

Girls

Small girls realise that they do not have a penis and believe that they have been castrated for their desires towards their fathers. Thus they experience **penis envy** and regard their mother as their rival. However they also fear losing their mother's love and resolve this by identifying with their mother, thus taking on the sex-appropriate behaviour and morality demonstrated by their mother.

(The Oedipus complex in girls is sometimes referred to as the Electra complex, but this was not a term used by Freud.)

Fixation in the phallic stage can lead to a variety of problems: an obsession with power, authoritarianism, lack of feeling for others, an inflated opinion of oneself and a variety of sexual problems.

4. **The latency stage (6 years to puberty)**

   In this stage energies are channelled into other areas of development and all sexual desires remained repressed. The personality doesn't change very much.

5. **The genital stage (12–18 years)**

   The sex organs mature in this stage and hormone levels change. If children have successfully resolved the Oedipus complex, they now begin to take an interest in the opposite sex. This is the beginning of adult sexuality.

Core Study

Analysis of a phobia in a five-year-old boy: Sigmund Freud (1909)

'Little Hans' was the subject of a series of letters from his father to Freud, who made the following interpretations.

Little Hans had a peculiarly lively interest in his 'widdler'. When watching his new-born sister being bathed he was concerned that 'her widdler's still quite small' but added, by way of consolation, the thought that it would get bigger. It is possible that he was unable to accept that she did not have a widdler at this stage as to do so would somehow pose a threat to his own widdler. This fear could be traced back to a threat made by his mother when she found him fingering his penis – 'if you do that, I shall send for Dr A. to cut off your widdler'.

In his attitude to his parents he was a little Oedipus. He wanted his father out of the way so that he could be alone with his mother and sleep with her. Both his baby sister and his father had a claim on his mother's attention and reduced the chances of his being alone with her.

One day Hans experienced a panic attack in the street. The reason was, at first, unclear, but seemed to be connected with wishing to be with his mother. However his fear existed in her presence and he eventually identified it, quite specifically, as being a fear that a white horse would bite him.

Soon after, Hans traced his fear of being bitten by a horse back to something he had overheard a father say to his child, 'don't put your finger to the white horse or it'll bite'. The words 'don't put your finger' resembled the form of words in which his previous warning against masturbation had been expressed. Around this time his father had told him that women do not have widdlers and he remembered his mother's threat to cut his off.

Having partly mastered his complex, Hans was able to communicate his wishes in regard to his mother. He did this by way of fantasy which he recounted concerning two giraffes (representing his mother and father) – a crumpled one and a big one. The big one was calling out because Hans had taken the crumpled one away and sat on it. Hans was now enlightened as to the nature of his horse phobia. The horse represented his father and he was afraid of his father because of the hostility he felt toward him.

Hans also revealed that he was afraid of carts, buses and furniture vans (all heavily laden vehicles), of heavily laden horses, and of horses moving quickly. Hans clarified this by explaining that he was afraid of horses falling down and his phobia extended to everything that might cause them to fall down. He then recalled an event which immediately preceded the outbreak of his condition. He had been out walking with his mother and had seen a bus horse fall and kick about with its feet. He had been very frightened by the event and thought the horse was dead.

His father pointed out to him that he must have wished it was him (father) who had fallen down and died. Hans did not dispute this interpretation.

As his fears and fantasies were made known to him, Hans was able to resolve them.

QUESTIONS

1. a Briefly describe one of Hans' dreams or phantasies **(2 marks)**

    b Say how Freud interpreted his phantasy/dream. **(2 marks)**

    Oxford and Cambridge Specimen Paper

2. a In Freud's case study of Little Hans, how did Hans respond to the birth of his sister? **(2 marks)**

    b According to Freud, what was the connection between Hans' sister and his fear of the bath? **(2 marks)**

    Oxford and Cambridge (1994)

The tri-part personality theory

According to Freud the adult personality comprises **three parts** which come into being during the first three developmental stages.

Id

The id is present at birth, and is the most primitive and egocentric part of the personality, housing the instincts. It operates on the **pleasure principle** and has a basic drive to satisfy all needs and desires immediately, without reference to reality. We never lose this aspect of our personality, but as we grow older we learn to control it.

Ego

The ego deals with the demands of the outside world and arises during the anal stage. As we grow up, and especially as toilet training begins, we learn that we cannot expect to have all our needs and desires met as soon as they arise. The ego operates on the **reality principle** and keeps the demands of the id in check by finding a way of satisfying them in a manner which is socially acceptable.

Superego

The superego tells us what is right and wrong and how we ought to behave. It represents the internalisation of the parents' morality and develops out of the resolution of the Oedipus complex when the child identifies with the parent of the same sex. It operates on the **morality principle**. (The structure of the superego is discussed in section 8.5 on moral development.)

Freud saw personality as a dynamic balance between the three aspects of the personality: hence the term **psychodynamic theory**. It is the difficult job of the ego to find a middle route between the selfish demands of the id and the often unrealistically high moral standards of the superego.

The defence mechanisms

Freud believed that the dynamics between the id, ego and superego are such that anxieties are inevitably experienced. The ego has a number of unconscious defence mechanisms that it employs in order to reduce these anxieties. These include:

1. **Repression:** this involves excluding from consciousness thoughts or memories that provoke anxiety, for example 'forgetting' to turn up for a dental appointment
2. **Displacement:** this involves the transfer of ideas and impulses from one object or person to another, for example, a student may snap at a friend after being criticised by her tutor
3. **Regression:** this involves the return to a form of behaviour characteristic of an earlier stage of development, due to stress; for example a student experiencing anxiety about exams may revert to thumb-sucking.

Activity

Which of the three defence mechanisms just mentioned are being used when:

1. An adult has a temper tantrum in response to frustration?
2. A patient in therapy fails to keep an appointment when sessions begin to provoke anxiety?
3. A teenager cries when his parents refuse to let him go to a party?
4. A salesman gets annoyed with his daughter after failing to secure a big order?

Experimental studies of Freud's theory

1. **Levinger and Clark (1961)**, in an investigation of repression, asked participants to make word associations to 30 neutral and 30 emotional words. Participants were significantly more likely to forget the associations for the emotional words than for the neutral words.

   However an alternative explanation for these results is offered by Eysenck and Wilson (1973), who point out that arousal decreases the effectiveness of memory and the emotional words produce more arousal.

2. **Yarrow (1954)** investigated thumb-sucking which could be a possible consequence of oral fixation. In a study of 66 children he found that those who had spent least time feeding in the first six months of life spent most time sucking their thumbs.

   It is possible, however, that the babies who spent least time feeding had a greater need to suck than the others and that this need was later satisfied by thumb-sucking.

3. **Friedman (1952)**, in an investigation of the Oedipus complex, showed 300 children between the ages of five to 16 years pictures of (**i**) a mother and child, (**ii**) father and child and (**iii**) a father and child standing by some stairs. The children were asked to talk about what was happening in the pictures and their answers were analysed. It was found that children produced more conflict themes with the same-sex parent and girls fantasised that the father figure went upstairs: a psychoanalytic symbol for sexual intercourse.

Evaluation

Strengths

1. In a period of sexual repression, Freud's theory opened the debate on the importance of sexual and aggressive urges.
2. It drew attention to the emotional needs of children and to the possible **long-term effects** of traumatic events in childhood.
3. It showed how people may **conceal** the real motives for their actions, even from themselves. This has intuitive appeal.
4. It resulted in a more **compassionate** attitude to people with mental illness.

Criticisms

1. Freud's theory overemphasises the importance of sexuality and underestimates the role of **social relationships**.
2. It overemphasises the importance of the **early years** in personality formation. Many other theorists, including some following in the psychoanalytic tradition (for example, Erikson), believe that personality goes on changing throughout life.
3. There is no **evidence** for the existence of the id, ego and superego.
4. The theory is **not scientific**. It is not falsifiable nor is it predictive. It works backwards, merely offering an explanation for existing behaviours.
5. The sample from whom Freud obtained his data was very **biased**, being mainly middle class, middle aged women seeking help for neurotic symptoms. He used case studies, from which generalisations should not be made. (See Section 11.1 for a discussion of the use of case studies.)
6. The theory is very **biological** and **deterministic**. (See Section 10.1 for further discussion on determinism).
7. Freud did not take sufficient account of **cultural variations** within society.

Preparing for the exam

Key terms

anal stage	libido
conscience	life instinct (Eros)
death instinct (Thanatos)	morality principle
defence mechanisms	Oedipus complex
displacement	oral stage
dream analysis	parapraxes
ego ideal	phallic stage
ego	pleasure principle
fixation	Psychoanalytic theory
free association	Psychodynamic theory
genital stage	psychosexual development
hysterical symptoms	reality principle
identification	regression
id	repression
latency stage	superego

Types of exam question

Questions on Freud are not limited to any one part of an A level syllabus. Apart from dedicated essays, which are rare, you should consider the Freudian contribution to the following areas:

1. Personality theories
2. Aggression
3. Sex-role development
4. Causes and treatment of abnormal behaviour
5. Play
6. Moral development.

Self-test questions

1. What methods were used by Freud to gain access to the unconscious?
2. Briefly describe the life instinct and the death instinct.
3. List the first *three* stages of psychosexual development.
   In which stage does:
   a Fixation cause self-centredness or habits such as smoking?
   b The ego emerge?
   c Fixation cause fastidiousness and compulsive behaviour?
   d The superego emerge?
4. Briefly describe how the superego emerges in boys.
5. a What are the *three* parts of the personality?
   b Which part is present from birth and operates on the pleasure principle?

    c   Which acts as an internal parent?

    d   Which is concerned with reality?

6.   What is a defence mechanism? Describe *two*.

7.   Briefly describe a study that attempts to test Freud's theory.

Exam question with guidance notes

Describe and evaluate the <u>contributions</u> of EITHER the psychoanalytic OR the behaviourist approach to an understanding of human behaviour.

           (25 marks)

           AEB (1993)

We shall answer this question from the psychoanalytic approach. This is a question from the compulsory 'Perspectives' section of the AEB and, as such, requires an *overview* of the whole syllabus. You therefore need to include a good selection of contributions mentioned earlier: personality, aggression, gender role development, play, moral development and the treatment of abnormal behaviour.

- Introduce the essay with a summary of *Freudian theory*, paying attention to the aspects to which you will need to refer in your chosen contributions.
- Now discuss each contribution in turn. We will cover the main points of each one, but there is no need to mention them all: obviously it is wise to select those in the parts of the syllabus you intend to revise.

    a *Gender role development* depends on satisfactory resolution of the Oedipus complex. It draws attention to a child's sexuality, which certainly exists, but cannot adequately account for typical gender identification in one-parent families. It adequately accounts for the fact that children take on gender roles to the extent that their parents do, but social learning theory provides an alternative explanation.

    b *Play* was seen as a means of expressing anxiety, providing a safe outlet for expressing pent up emotions and repressed wishes. Play therapy, by providing insight into a child's problems, allows the therapist to help the child find ways of coping with these anxieties (see section 8.3).

    c *Moral development*: morality is internalised during the phallic stage, represented by the emergence of the superego, and depends on the successful resolution of the Oedipus complex. This theory implies that women are morally inferior to men, a contention for which there is no evidence. This and other criticisms are covered in section 8.5.

    d *Personality theory*: individual differences in personality depend to some extent on the course of the psychosexual stages and the types of defence mechanisms used to cope with conflict. It is a complex theory which, some would argue, gives a better account of the diversity and complexity of people than does the trait approach. However, it is culturally biased and non scientific.

e *Aggression*: Freud saw aggression as an inevitable part of the human condition since it is part of the id. This aggression requires a safe outlet which society needs to provide. This contrasts strongly with the social learning theory view and many may see the channels through which aggression may be 'safely' expressed as ones which encourage aggression. On the other hand, supporters of the Freudian view would point to the potentially dangerous consequences of allowing no such release.

f *Abnormal behaviour*: Freud offered a much more compassionate view of abnormal conditions than had hitherto been in existence. He helped to dispel the myth of mental illness being caused by evil spirits. You can provide a brief overview of the therapies available and an evaluation of their effectiveness. This is covered in section 9.5.

Additional exam question

a Outline Freud's theory of psychosexual development. **(6 marks)**

b Discuss *one* problem psychologists encounter in empirically investigating Freud's claims about development. **(6 marks)**

c Discuss *one* way, using examples, in which Erikson's theory differs from that of Freud. **(8 marks)**

JMB (1992)

Cognitive Psychology

3

Topic

AEB	NEAB	O & C		Date attempted	Date completed	Self Assessment
✓	✓	✓	**Models of Memory**			
✓	✓	✓	**Organisation of Information in Memory**			
✓	✓	✓	**Practical Implications of Memory Research**			
✓	✓	✓	**Theories of Forgetting**			
✓	✓	✗	**The Visual System in Humans**			
✓	✓	✓	**Perceptual Abilities**			
✓	✓	✓	**Visual Illusions**			
✓	✓	✓	**Theories of Perception**			
✓	✓	✓	**Development of Perception**			
✓	✓	✓	**Selective Attention**			

3.1 Memory

Memory can be viewed as the capacity to store and, later, recall or recognise events that were previously experienced. Memory is an **active** process, a system that receives, encodes, modifies and retrieves information. People usually refer to memory as if it were a single ability, but the term 'memory' covers a complex collection of abilities, processes and mental systems.

The information processing view of memory

Psychologists do not view memory as an entity (as a 'thing') but rather as **a process**. They use the language of computer programming to describe the processes involved in remembering. This helps to emphasise the fact that the brain does not passively record information but actively **alters** and **organises** it. The information processing model views remembering as consisting of three stages: **encoding**, **storage** and **retrieval**:

1. **Encoding** involves converting information into psychological formats that can be represented mentally. To do so, we use mainly visual, auditory and semantic codes:
    *   **Visual codes** would be used when we remember a face, a picture or a scene
    *   **Auditory codes** involve sounds and are used when we remember spoken language or a tune
    *   **Semantic codes** represent input in terms of their meaning: when we hear a story we do not remember (encode) it word for word but we retain its essential meaning.

Other forms of encoding are possible: for example, memories for specific motor skills like swimming, driving or riding a bike.

2. **Storage** is the second process of memory, and involves retaining information over a period of time.

3. **Retrieval** involves the recovery of stored material, known in the language of computers as 'accessing' of information. With well known information, like your name and address, retrieval is effortless and instantaneous. But with large amounts of information, information not properly understood or information not recalled for a long time, retrieval is far more difficult and not always successful.

Models of memory

The multistore approach: Atkinson and Shiffrin (1968, 1971)

This is the most prominent information processing model of memory and proposes that there are **three** memory stores:

1. A **sensory** memory store
2. A **short-term** memory store (STM)
3. A **long-term** memory store (LTM).

According to this model, information from the environment must pass through the sensory store and the short-term store (both of which are temporary stores) before it can be transferred into the long-term store and thereby become part of long-term memory (LTM). This model can be represented by the diagram in Figure 3.1.

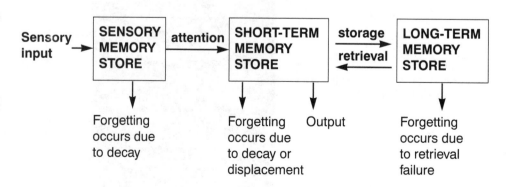

Figure 3.1 Atkinson and Shiffrin's multistore model of memory

Sensory memory

This holds information until it is recognised and passed on for further processing. Important characteristics of the sensory store are that:

1. It takes fleeting impressions of sensory stimuli (sights, sounds, smells, touches and so on) and preserves them for a second or two; just long enough for them to be **recognised** and passed on for further processing. For example, if you were to hear a sound outside, you would retain this sound in your mind just long enough to recognise what it is: maybe the sound of someone shutting their car door.

2. Atkinson and Shiffrin argue that there are different sensory registers or **modality-specific** stores for each of the senses. Visual information is stored in the iconic memory, auditory stimuli in the echoic memory and so on. The iconic memory lasts only about half a second, the echoic memory for several seconds or even longer. This is demonstrated by the fact that if you close your eyes, the scene in front of you is gone almost immediately but if you have just heard something, for instance, a clock striking, the sound of it echoes in your mind for a few seconds.

    Without sensory memory we could only hear and see stimuli (or feel, taste or smell them, as the case may be) at the moment they were **physically present**, which would not be long enough for them to be recognised.

3. Most information that enters the sensory registers is **lost**. The capacity of the sensory store is quite large, but the capacity of the short-term store is very limited, so little is passed from the sensory memory into short-term memory. This is demonstrated by the fact that, at any one time, there are countless events and objects surrounding you at all times, yet only a very small amount is kept in mind at any one time. Only that which we **attend to** is retained and moves on to the next stage of memory.

Short-term memory

Information which has been attended to is then passed to a short-term memory store. Important characteristics of the STM are that:

1. It can retain **unrehearsed** information for about 20–30 seconds.

2. It can hold **rehearsed** information for considerably longer. Material can be rehearsed by, for example, repeating it to yourself, as you might do if you had just been given someone's address and didn't want to forget it.

3. It can hold very few items at once. Miller (1956) suggested that its capacity is 'The Magical Number Seven, Plus or Minus Two'. That is, only between **five and nine items** can be retained at any one time.

4. However, if information is **chunked** – in other words several items are stored as a single unit – then the capacity of STM increases.

Activity

Read and try and recall the letters TU–CFB–IB–BCA–A. It is unlikely that you remembered them all because there are eleven items to recall, thus exceeding the capacity of the STM. Now try to remember TUC–FBI–BBC–AA. Now you will probably have no trouble at all in retaining this information as there are now only **four** items to remember.

Think of examples of how advertisers 'chunk' their telephone numbers to make them easier to remember.

5. Once the capacity of the short-term store is exceeded, then new information **displaces** the old: the more recent information 'pushes out' the less recent information.

6. Information in STM is stored **acoustically**. Items are transferred from short-term to long-term memory by rehearsal. Atkinson and Shiffrin suggest that rehearsal has **two functions**:
    - It can keep items in STM (as occurs when you repeat a telephone number to keep it in your memory until you dial it or write it down)
    - It can serve to transfer these items from STM to LTM.

Long-term memory

The important points concerning LTM are:

1. The long-term store has **unlimited capacity** and can hold information for an indefinite period of time.
2. Atkinson and Shiffrin argue that nearly all forgetting from LTM is due to failure of **retrieval** rather than the trace having decayed (this is covered in more detail in 'Theories of forgetting' later in the chapter).
3. Information that is being held in STM through rehearsal is gradually **absorbed** into long-term memory.

Activity

Now that you have read the whole account of the multistore model, we'd advise you to do the following:

Go back to the diagram which represents it (Figure 3.1, p. 28) and make sure you understand it. Now try to **learn** it. Draw the three empty boxes and then try to complete them without looking at the book. Make sure you understand and know this model.

There is a useful table in the Core Study (p. 32), giving the difference between the three stores. Learn this before going on any further.

Evaluation of the multistore approach

Atkinson and Shiffrin were by no means the first psychologists to suggest a distinction between STM and LTM, and this distinction is, of course, central to the theory. Evaluation of the model therefore depends on the validity of this distinction and we will consider arguments both for and against it.

Evidence for a dual memory system

Evidence to support the concept of two different types of memory comes from **three** main sources:

1. **Amnesiacs:** some amnesiacs retain a LTM for events prior to brain injury and retain STM for events currently taking place, but have no ability to **transfer** information from STM to LTM. Other amnesiacs have shown more impairments in LTM than STM, suggesting there are two memory systems located in different areas of the brain.

2. **Brain waves:** there is evidence that a unique type of brain wave is found when people recall very recent events within the STM period. Researchers interpret this as evidence for a memory storage system that holds incoming information for a short time. There is also evidence that different biochemical processes seem to operate in temporary as opposed to permanent storage.

3. **The serial position effect:** when lists of words (or other items) are presented and people are asked to recall them in any order, those at the **beginning** and **end** are remembered better than those in the middle. This could be explained in terms of a dual memory system: items at the beginning of the list have been transferred to LTM, those at the end are still in STM. However, some psychologists see no reason to interpret these findings in terms of different memory stores.

Problems with the dual memory model

These are covered in the Core Study (p. 32). Read them carefully and make notes on them.

Levels of processing model: Craik and Lockhart (1972)

To understand the levels of processing model, you need to read the Core Study in this section.

According to this model, the memory is seen as **a single dimension** rather than as a **series of separate stores**. A word can be processed at three levels:

*   Physical (in terms of appearance)
*   Acoustic (in terms of sound)
*   Semantic (in terms of meaning).

Activity

Think about the word 'SHEEP'.

*   You can process it by **physical** means; one physical feature is that it is written in capital letters. Think of two more physical features.

- You can process it by **sound**, for example, it rhymes with 'heap'. Think of **two** other acoustic features you can use.
- You can process the word **semantically**, according to meaning. It is a type of animal. What other semantic features does it have?

These processes differ in depth: the physical level is the most superficial, with acoustic deeper and semantic the deepest of the three. The more deeply an item is processed, the more cognitive effort is put into storing it. The more effort that is put into storage, the more likely the memory is to endure. It follows that the **more deeply a word is processed**, the **more likely it is to be remembered**.

Within any of these three levels of processing there can be variations in depth. The more concepts and associations that are made, the deeper the processing. Enduring memory is not therefore dependent on transfer from STM to LTM.

This model corresponds to the common sense observation that we are more likely to remember something we have learnt and understood thoroughly than something we have simply 'mugged up' for an examination.

Many experiments have been conducted to test this model: an example is given in the Core Study (p. 32).

Evaluation of the Levels of Processing Model

1. The main problem with the levels of processing model is that there is no objective way of measuring the **depth** to which items are processed (Baddeley, 1978). If a person were asked to draw a picture by each word in a list and then tested for recall, how it is possible to assess the depth of processing of those words? Because there is no objective measure of depth of processing, the theory is, according to Baddeley, circular and therefore untestable because any events which are well remembered are assumed to be 'deeply processed'.

2. The main contribution of this model is that it does account for the fact that some long-term memories are relatively easy to recall while others are comparatively difficult: in other words,

it distinguishes between **levels** of LTM instead of lumping them all together.

Additions and alternatives to these models

Working memory: Baddeley (1976, 1989)

This proposes a more complex model of STM. Baddeley does not reject the concept of STM as a means of rehearsing incoming information ready for transfer into LTM, but he does believe that this view of STM is too limited. He takes a more functional approach, using the term **'working memory'** in preference to short-term memory.

Working memory is an **active** store used to hold information which is being manipulated: information about which you are consciously thinking. At any one time this may include where you parked your car, what you need to get done at work that day, what time you arranged to meet your friend for lunch and that you must pick up some bread on the way home but that's the only shopping that's necessary.

According to Baddeley, working memory consists of **three** components:

1. A **rehearsal loop**, which is the equivalent of the STM of the original model. This is the component used when we recite a phone number to hold it temporarily.
2. A **visuospatial sketchpad**, which allows us to hold visual images temporarily. This is the component used when we visualise our route home or imagine what our bearded friend would look like if he were clean-shaven.
3. An **executive control system**, which handles the limited amount of information that people can judge at one time, as they make decisions. This is the component used when we weigh up the pros and cons of buying a particular outfit.

Baddeley's model allows for the fact that STM does **not** only encode phonetically, as in the original model, and that it has a greater variety of functions than those in the original model.

Core Study

Levels of processing: a framework for memory research: F. Craik and R.S. Lockhart (1972)

Multistore models

The case in favour

According to multistore models, memory can be classified into **three** levels of storage: sensory stores, short-term memory (STM) and long-term memory (LTM).

The differences between these stores are represented in Table 3.1.

The different characteristics of these stores has intuitive appeal, with information following a well-regulated path between stores. Nevertheless there are problems with these models.

The case against

1. **Capacity:** one hypothesised difference between STM and LTM is the difference in capacity, specifically that whereas capacity in LTM is limitless, the capacity in STM is relatively small. Yet in terms of the computer analogy (the information processing model) on which the multistore model is based, it is not clear whether the limited capacity refers to storage capacity or to the rate at which the processor can perform certain operations.

   Attempts to measure this capacity have tended to concentrate on storage and use number of items recalled as a means of measurement. Research has shown a great variation in range of values: the typical findings are five to nine items (Miller's Magical Number Seven, Plus or Minus Two) but some studies have a range of only two to four items (Baddeley, 1970; Murdock, 1972), while others show a capacity for up to 20 items if the items to be remembered are words which form a sentence (Craik and Masani, 1969). These differences are explained in terms of **chunking**, but a 'chunk' cannot be defined independently of how easy it is to recall, and there is, therefore, no objective definition of a 'chunk'.

2. **Coding:** most multistore models maintain that coding of verbal material is acoustic in STM and predominantly semantic in LTM. However, even with verbal material, coding can be visual in STM and some theorists even believe that it can be semantic (Schulman, 1970, 1972). Coding no longer seems to be a satisfactory basis for distinguishing between STM and LTM.

3. **Forgetting:** according to this model, rates of forgetting from STM should be similar regardless of different designs and experimental conditions. Yet there are wide variations in number of items recalled and in the length of time information is retained.

Levels of processing

When a stimulus is perceived, it is analysed in a series of stages.

1. **Physical** or sensory features such as brightness or loudness are noted
2. This is followed by a deeper analysis in which the input is **matched against previously learned concepts**
3. Once the stimulus has been recognised it may be further processed by **enrichment** or **elaboration** – for example, a word, smell or sight may trigger associations or images based on past experience.

The deeper that stimuli are processed, the more persistent is the memory trace that is formed. Stimuli with which a person is already familiar will already have connections with existing schemata and will therefore be more deeply processed and remembered better than unfamiliar material.

As well as this basic memory system, there is a second way of retaining information, referred to as 'keeping the items in consciousness' or 'retention of the items in primary memory'.

Table 3.1 Commonly accepted differences between the three stages of verbal memory

Feature	Sensory registers	Short-term store	Long-term store
Entry of information	Preattentive	Requires attention	Rehearsal
Maintenance of information	Not possible	Continued attention Rehearsal	Repetition Organisation
Format of information	Literal copy of input	Phonemic Probably visual Possibly semantic	Largely semantic Some auditory and visual
Capacity	Large	Small	No known limit
Information loss	Decay	Displacement Possibly decay	Possibly no loss. Loss of accessibility or discriminability by interference
Trace duration	¼–2 seconds	Up to 30 seconds	Minutes to years
Retrieval	Readout	Probably automatic. Items in consciousness Temporal/phonemic cues	Retrieval cues Possibly search process

Craik and Lockhart accept Moray's (1967) concept of a **central processor** which is limited in its capacity but may be used in several different ways. This central processor can operate at all levels. At deeper levels a person can make greater use of previous knowledge and schemata and therefore the central processor can handle more material. At less deep levels, its capacity is more limited. Some types of information, such as the sounds of words, are very easy to retain within primary memory but others, like exact physical features, are virtually impossible to retain.

Experiments conducted to test the levels of processing model measure the amount of incidental learning which occurs when subjects are required to carry out orienting tasks requiring different levels of processing. For example, Tresselt and Mayzner (1960) required subjects to carry out three different orienting tasks: crossing out vowels, copying the words, and judging how far the word was an instance of the concept 'economic'. They were then tested on incidental learning and found that under the last condition four times as many words were recalled than under the first, and twice as many as under the second. Several other similar studies are cited, all supporting the view that the deeper the level of processing required in the orienting task, the better the memory performance.

Concluding comments

It is important that future research in this area investigates the effects on memory of various types of perceptual operations. One of the major problems of such research is that deeper analysis usually involves longer processing time, and it is therefore important to try and separate variables such as time and amount of effort from the actual depth at which processing occurs.

Multistore models of memory have been useful but are often taken too literally. The levels of processing model is not a theory as such, it is speculative and incomplete in that it does not, for instance, concern itself with organisation or retrieval. Nevertheless, it is presented as a conceptual framework within which research might proceed and within which issues like organisation and retrieval can be understood.

QUESTIONS

1. What are the *three* basic levels of processing according to Craik and Lockhart, and how do these levels apply to the recognition of words?
    (4 marks)
    Oxford and Cambridge Specimen Paper

2. **a** What is meant by the levels (depth) of processing? **(2 marks)**
    b Select and describe *one* piece of evidence that supports the levels (depth) of processing hypothesis. **(2 marks)**
    Oxford and Cambridge (1994)

Activity

In terms of working memory, which of the three components above is used in:

1. Recalling the position of furniture in your bedroom.
2. Deciding whether it is more important to do your psychology coursework, geography essay or clear up your room (this is dependent on remembering the various threats made and assessing their relative severity).
3. When first being introduced to a group of people, remembering their names long enough to say: 'Pleased to meet you, Mary, Yasmin, Asad.'

Storage in long-term memory

Atkinson and Shiffrin (1968) claim that all knowledge is held in the same long-term store, but **Tulving (1965)** suggests that it is probable that different types of memories are stored differently. Tulving draws a distinction between:

-   **Procedural** knowledge: knowing **how**. This involves all knowledge of how to perform activities and therefore includes how to ride a bike, how to book an airline ticket, and how to use a pencil.
-   **Declarative** knowledge: knowing **that**, which can be subdivided into:
    a **Episodic** memories, which are memories of personal events and, unlike semantic memories, often involve a particular time and place. Episodic memories may include your first day at school and what you did last Sunday.
    b **Semantic** memories, which consist of knowledge about the world, independent of any particular context, and includes facts, rules and concepts. There are literally thousands of pieces of knowledge in semantic memory, a lot of which can be effortlessly used. You know

that 3 + 3 = 6, that a mouse is a small furry animal, that there are 60 seconds in a minute.

Activity

Classify the following memories/information as either procedural, episodic or semantic:

1. Mexico is in South America
2. How to make a cup of tea
3. Henry VIII had six wives
4. How to mend a puncture
5. How you celebrated your last birthday
6. How to spell psychology.

It is not yet clear whether the distinction between these three types of memory corresponds to different brain systems or whether they simply provide a convenient way of categorising different types of learning and memory.

One Case Study, that of a man known as KC who became amnesic as a result of a motor accident, is of interest in this debate. KC has virtually no episodic memory: he does not remember anything that has ever happened to him. He shows relatively little impairment in semantic memory and his procedural memory is largely undamaged: he has retained a good deal of knowledge about the world and his skills are virtually intact. This does indicate that different brain systems are responsible for different types of long term memories, but research in this area is still in its infancy.

Activity

You may find it useful to make a note of this study to use as an example of the usefulness and limitation of the Case Study method.

Organisation of information in memory

Our memory houses a vast amount of information, and without some organisation that information would be virtually useless since we simply would not be able to recall it.

We organise material to make it meaningful but in doing this we **reconstruct** the information, in other words, we add details or change it to make it fit into our own personal memory store and conform to our existing values and beliefs. There is, in fact, one main principle which operates during reconstruction: **how and what you remember is determined by who you are and what you already know**. The information which is added may or may not be an accurate reflection of what really occurred.

Schemata, stereotypes and scripts

1. A **schema** is an organised cluster of knowledge about a particular object or sequence of events. Information stored in memory is often organised in the form of schemata (schemata is the plural of schema) and this means that recall of events or objects will be influenced not simply by what was actually observed but by the person's particular schemata.

    Bartlett (1932) carried out one of the earliest studies of the effect of schemata on memory. He investigated the way in which British undergraduates remembered and retold stories whose words and themes were taken from another culture. His most famous story 'The War of the Ghosts' was a tale from the Native American (American Indian) culture and was confusing to the undergraduates because of their lack of understanding of this culture. When they retold the story most of them omitted place names, did not mention ghosts and altered other details.

The tendency to change information so that it becomes more meaningful to our own culture or personal experience is known as **semantic substitution**. To a British person these reconstructions made more sense than the original since there are, for example, few ghosts in Western culture.

In everyday life, schemata are useful because they help us to make sense of separate pieces of information and thus remember them better. The advantages of organising memory around a schema has been demonstrated in many studies.

Bransford and Johnson (1972) found that passages were much easier to recall if given a suitable **title** which activated a well-known schema that provided a meaningful context for material, especially material presented in an ambiguous form. Bransford and Johnson also investigated the effect of providing an inconsistent title, such that one or two elements of a story were difficult to put into context. In this case, material that did not fit was simply not recalled.

2. A **stereotype** is a particular type of schema, one which is concerned with **people**. Stereotypes are assumptions about the personality traits or physical attributes that we assume apply to a whole group of people. Stereotypes are discussed in detail in Chapter 4, so they will only be mentioned briefly here, but they do have an important influence on memory. When we meet or hear about someone for the first time, we combine the information presented with that of our stereotype and make assumptions which then become part of memory. For example, if someone is described to you as being Italian, you may well remember them having been described as dark-haired even when no such description was given.

3. A **script** is also a particular type of schema which, rather like the script of a play, organises what people know about common activities. Bower, Black and Turner (1979) showed that people have similar scripts for many common activities such as going to the supermarket or visiting a doctor.

Since we have expectations based on scripts for many activities, we often make assumptions and then incorporate those assumptions into our memory as if they were actual happenings. For example, if someone were relating an incident and said 'and as they left the restaurant, she put some money on the table' this may well be remembered as her having left the waiter a tip, because in the usual 'restaurant script' that would be the obvious reason why a person would leave money on the table.

In everyday life we constantly 'fill in the gaps': we would hardly be sensible if we didn't. For instance, if you heard someone say, as they got out of a driving school car 'OK, five o'clock, Thursday, then' you may well remember this as the person having made

arrangements for the time of their next lesson, even though they could have been referring to a doctor's appointment.

Clustering, conceptual hierarchies and semantic networks

1. **Clustering** is the tendency to remember similar or related items in groups. Even when people memorise lists of unrelated items that cannot be divided into clear groups, they still tend to use clustering. In this case, individuals tend to use their own idiosyncratic or subjective systems of organisation. The fact that people automatically cluster items demonstrates that they need to impose some **organisation** on material stored in their memory.

2. **Conceptual hierarchies** involve classifying items on several different levels according to properties they have in common. Bower (1970) demonstrated that organising information into a conceptual hierarchy dramatically improves recall. He asked participants to recall lists of words which were either presented randomly or in the form of a conceptual hierarchy, for example that shown in Figure 3.2.

3. **Semantic networks** consist of sets of pathways that link together different concepts.

Not all material can be conveniently stored in hierarchies; nevertheless it is organised into some sort of framework even if this is less systematic. These frameworks are known as semantic networks. A simple semantic network could be like that shown in Figure 3.3.

The lines between the words (or concepts) are **pathways** connecting them. Some pathways are shorter than others: shorter pathways imply stronger associations. The length of the pathways can be termed the semantic distance (Collins and Loftus 1975). The more closely two words are related, the shorter the semantic distance and the more likely one item is to lead to recall of another. Taking an example from Figure 3.3, for the majority of people the distance between **cold** and **hot** would be shorter than the distance between **cold** and **sneeze** or between **cold** and **winter**.

Organisation in memory can occur either at storage

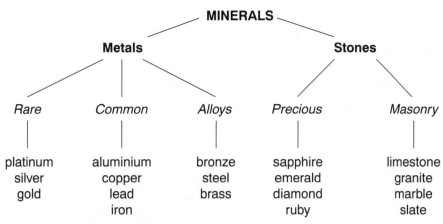

Figure 3.2 A conceptual hierarchy

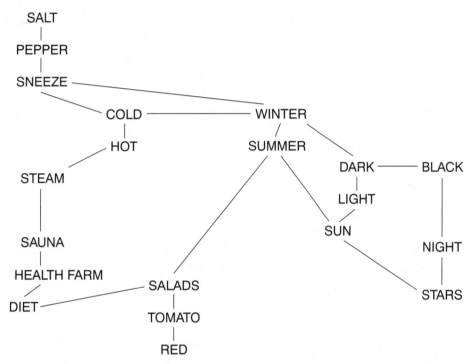

Figure 3.3 A simple semantic network

or at recall, as shown by experimental studies. Weist (1972) tape recorded participants rehearsing out loud a list of words which had been presented in random order. These recordings showed that participants categorised the lists during rehearsal, in other words at storage. At this stage, organisation helps to reduce the amount of material that needs to be remembered by chunking it, categorising it or arranging it hierarchically. At retrieval, organisation helps by increasing the number of associations and therefore the number of retrieval routes available.

Theories of forgetting

Is memory permanent?

There is disagreement among psychologists as to whether memory is permanent and forgetting simply due to an ability to recall information or whether some memories are, in fact, lost forever.

Evidence that memories may be permanent

1. **Penfield and Perot (1963)**, before brain surgery on epileptics, electrically stimulated parts of the brain and found that patients reported vivid experiences from the distant past which they had previously long forgotten.

However, Loftus (1980) questions the value of this type of evidence. She points out that electrically stimulated memories occurred in only a very small number of patients and, in those in whom it did occur, the memories may well have been reconstructive rather than accurate. In addition, even if some memories can be recalled, it does not mean that all memories can be.

2. Work on **hypnosis**, the hypothesis being that under hypnosis people can clearly remember events from the past. However, Putnam (1979) has shown experimentally that people under hypnosis may well remember more details, but these details are less accurate than those given by people who have not been hypnotised.

   In the light of these findings, Loftus argues that there is no reason to believe that long-term memory is permanent. Nevertheless, it is in fact a hypothesis that is almost impossible to disprove since there is simply no way of knowing whether any items which appear to have been forgotten could, under certain conditions, be recalled.

   Regardless of whether or not memory may be permanent, students reading this book hardly need to be told that there are times when we simply cannot remember something, however much we want to! We will now consider some theories put forward to account for this.

Theory 1: decay or fading of the memory trace

This theory states that forgetting is caused by the fact that **memory traces decay over time** if they are not recalled every now and again.

Problems with this theory

- Motor skills are remembered for many years, even if they are not practised (you never forget how to swim or to ride a bicycle).
- Some trivia also seems to persist for no reason and despite not being recalled for many years.

Theory 2: failure of retrieval

Some memory traces do last a lifetime and in some cases forgetting may be due to **failure of retrieval**

rather than a true loss of memory. As everyone knows, some forgetting is temporary. Klatzky (1980) suggests that when the conditions of encoding and recall are the same, then remembering is much easier. This accounts for why returning to childhood haunts brings back vivid memories previously long forgotten.

Activity

Why do the police stage reconstructions?

Material which is part of a semantic network is far less likely to be forgotten than episodic memories simply because they are part of a much larger framework, whereas episodic memories are not. It is episodic memories which may be on the 'tip of your tongue' and may suddenly 'pop up' when something of which you may not even be aware triggers the memory for which you were searching.

Activity

How does the work on semantic networks relate to revision techniques?

Theory 3: interference

This theory proposes that people forget information because of **competition from other material**.

   There are two kinds of interference:

- **Retroactive interference** occurs when new learning interferes with the retrieval of old learning.
- **Proactive interference** occurs when old learning interferes with new learning.

   For example, suppose you learn to drive in a manual car with a conventional gearstick and later drive an automatic which has no gearstick and no clutch. When you first drive the automatic your driving is jerky because you keep mistaking the brake for the clutch and putting your hand down to change gear. This is **proactive** interference because driving the manual car (old learning) has interfered with driving the automatic (new learning). You then go back to the manual but now you don't drive it as well as you did in the first place. You forget to get into the correct gear whilst waiting at traffic lights and you stall the car much more than you did when you first drove it. This is **retroactive** interference because driving the automatic (new learning) has interfered with driving the manual car (old learning).

Activity

Invent your own mnemonic or other memory aid to distinguish between retroactive and proactive interference.

Many studies have shown that interference certainly affects recall, but it is unlikely to be the only reason why we forget. Since most evidence comes from experimental situations it is difficult to ascertain the extent to which interference contributes to forgetting in ordinary everyday life.

Theory 4: repression or motivated forgetting

Freud proposed that we forget because **we do not want to remember**. Certain memories which are frightening, painful, embarrassing or degrading, in other words, associated with great anxiety, are forced into our unconscious mind. They are, in Freud's terminology, **repressed**. Repression is the means by which we protect ourselves from unacceptable or painful memories, thereby maintaining our sense of self-integrity.

As mentioned in Chapter 2 there are considerable problems with testing Freud's theory. Experiments have been conducted in which recall of words learnt under anxiety and non-anxiety conditions have been compared, but no experimentally induced situations could, or indeed should, equate to the traumatic incidents of childhood involved in some clinical cases.

We have considered four separate theories of forgetting but Tulving (1974) states that there are only **two** major reasons for forgetting:

- trace-dependent forgetting
- cue-dependent forgetting.

This goes back to the argument about whether or not memory is permanent. Trace-dependent forgetting involves permanent loss of some memories and is covered in Theory 1. Cue-dependent forgetting involves failure of retrieval, a failure to have the right cues to bring back memories. This is covered in Theory 2 and Theory 4. Theory 3 involves a change in what is remembered, with some consequent forgetting occurring during this change.

Practical implications of memory research: methods for improving memory

Rote learning

Some basic information simply has to be learned by rote and will then hopefully become as automatic as knowing the alphabet or counting, both of which were originally learnt in this way.

Elaboration: relating old information to new

Simple rote learning is fine for very basic information but it is unlikely to help us remember more complicated concepts. For this, elaborative rehearsal is much more effective. Elaboration involves associating new items of information with items that have already been stored, or with other new items.

Activity

Think back to theories of learning and the definition of positive and negative reinforcement. If you first learn that **all** reinforcers **strengthen** a response, then you can relate the concept of positive and negative reinforcers back to this definition. You will not then make the common mistake of confusing negative reinforcement with punishment because you will already know that **all** reinforcement, whether negative or positive, strengthens a response, whereas punishment weakens it.

Fitting new information into existing schemata helps enormously in retrieval, probably because you have to attend carefully to the information and understand it before it can be assimilated into existing memories.

Organisation

This is very closely related to elaborative rehearsal. We have already seen from the work of Bower and others how much easier it is to recall information which is organised either hierarchically or in some other way which provides meaningful associations between individual items.

Making notes

Making notes from a book or from your lecture notes is an extremely effective way of remembering the information, and is greatly superior as a revision technique to simply reading the material. This makes sense both in terms of the multistore model and the levels of processing model. In terms of the multistore model, in the process of making your own notes you are rehearsing the material, thereby making it more likely to enter LTM. In terms of the levels of processing model, in order to make the notes you have to understand the material, in other words, you have to process it at the semantic level, again making it more likely to be retained.

Mnemonic devices

A mnemonic is a strategy for **helping the memory**. Some simple mnemonic devices with which you may be familiar are:

1. Inventing a sentence with the same **initial letters**, in the correct order, as the items to be remembered. For example, 'Never Eat Shredded Wheat' for points of the compass
2. **Rhymes** such as 'Thirty days hath September, April, June and November . . .'
3. **Method of loci**, in which an individual thinks of a familiar place or walk and forms a mental image which links what they wish to remember with a familiar place. So you may imagine a bag of sugar sitting on the couch and a jar of coffee hanging in the doorway.

Activity

In relation to revision, there are considerable individual differences in how useful people find mnemonics: some students use them a great deal, some hardly at all. They certainly can be useful when learning lists. For example, think about the evidence for and against the distinction between STM and LTM. This can be summarised as amnesiacs, brain waves, serial position effect, capacity, coding, forgetting. You might therefore find it useful to invent a mnemonic connecting these words, or their initial letters. Similarly, it may be helpful to invent one for Piaget's stages of cognitive development, Kohlberg's stages of moral development and so on.

Eyewitness testimony

As previously mentioned, memories are often reconstructed rather than being an accurate recall of actual events.

Loftus (1979, 1984) has done extensive research in this area and has demonstrated many times the ease with which we can be misled into 'remembering' false information. The design of much of her research involves two groups of participants viewing exactly the same filmed or videotaped material and then being questioned about it. All the questions are concerned with the same events, but the actual wording of the questions varies. For example, one film sequence involved a traffic accident in which two cars collided. One group were asked 'How fast were the cars going when they **smashed into** each other?', while the other group were asked 'How fast were the cars going when they **contacted** each other?' When 'smashed into' was used the estimates were around 40 mph, whereas with 'contacted', estimates were about 30 mph. One week later all the participants were asked if they had seen any broken glass. In fact there was no broken glass, but of the 'smash' group 33 per cent reported seeing glass whereas only 14 per cent of the 'contact' group said they had seen it (Loftus, 1974, Loftus and Palmer, 1974). Loftus has also shown that witnesses can be affected by what other witnesses supposedly reported seeing: that, for example, a man had a moustache when he was clean-shaven and that a 'stop' sign existed when it did not.

The research done by Loftus clearly shows that the wording of questions of police and lawyers undoubtedly influences a witness's recall, as does the testimony of other witnesses. Considering how much weight is given to eyewitness testimony in courts of law, the fact that this type of reconstruction occurs should be of considerable concern to us all.

Preparing for the exam

Key terms

clustering
conceptual hierarchies
cue-dependent forgetting
declarative knowledge
echoic memory
elaborative rehearsal
encoding
episodic
executive control system
eyewitness testimony
iconic memory
information processing
long-term memory
mnemonic devices
modality-specific stores

proactive interference
procedural knowledge
rehearsal loop
repression
retrieval
retroactive interference
schema
script
semantic networks
sensory memory store
short-term memory
storage
trace-dependent forgetting
visuospatial sketchpad

Types of exam question

Essay questions from the AEB tend to concentrate on:

1. Models of memory
2. Theories of forgetting
3. The organisation of information in memory
4. Practical applications of memory research.

Self-test questions

1. Why is memory considered to be an active process?
2. What are the *three* stages involved in the information processing model of memory?
3. What are the *three* stores involved in the multistore approach?
4. What is meant by 'a modality-specific store'?
5. Why is most information lost from the sensory memory store?
6. What is meant by Miller's 'Magical Number Seven', and how does this relate to the capacity of STM?
7. In what ways do studies of amnesia support the distinction between STM and LTM?
8. Briefly describe *three* pieces of evidence against this distinction.
9. According to the levels of processing model, what are the *three* levels at which a word may be processed?

10. What is the main problem with this model?
11. What are the *three* components of Baddeley's working memory?
12. Give an example of each of the following:
    a A procedural memory
    b an episodic memory
    c a semantic memory.
13. What is meant by 'constructive memory'? How has the work of Bartlett and of Loftus contributed to our understanding of the constructive processes involved in recall?
14. Name *four* theories of forgetting. In each case, *briefly* summarise the hypothesised cause of forgetting.

Exam questions with guidance notes

Discuss applications of psychological research on memory and describe the studies upon which these applications are based. **(25 marks)**
AEB (1992)

The examiners' report commented that, though this was the most popular question in the cognitive section, it was the one which was least well answered: 'Many candidates wrote excellent answers on models of memory which did not actually fit either part of the question (applications or research).'

When you have spent weeks learning material in a certain format, it is difficult, under exam conditions, to be faced with having to organise this material in a way which answers the questions. But you must! Start with a *plan*.

• Introduce the essay with brief reference to memory being an *active process* and the fact that memory research can be usefully applied to improving memory and to checking on its accuracy.

• For the main body of the essay, you could use the last part of our discussion (from 'Practical Implications of Memory Research' onwards) (p. 39) and elaborate this with information from earlier sections.

    For example, when writing about elaborative rehearsal, use the levels of processing model as support: evidence indicates that material which is more deeply processed is better remembered: this is obviously relevant to practical applications, and you have research evidence to support this in the Core Study.

• Then we come to *organisation* of information; the better organised, the more likely it is to be remembered, so this is a related application. Go back to the subsection on Organisation of Information in Memory (p. 36) for supportive research evidence: Bower's work (and that of Collins and Quillian, not covered in this text, but with which many of you may be familiar).

    Mnemonic devices can be mentioned briefly (no long details, though!) and Loftus' work on eyewitness testimony (plenty of research evidence here) is obviously important in its implications.

• You could also briefly introduce some theories of *forgetting*, since they provide an insight into how we might be able to reduce forgetting. Klatzky

(1980) is useful for research evidence and any studies you may know on retroactive and proactive interference, with a view to preventing it.

- As you can see, there is plenty of material with which to answer *both* parts of the question. The most important thing to remember is: *keep calm* and make a plan, so you do not end up with a totally irrelevant essay or simply a disorganised confusion of studies.

a **Describe psychological explanations of forgetting.**   **(10 marks)**

b **Discuss practical applications which have developed from such explanations.**   **(15 marks)**
AEB (1994)

a Introduce the essay with reference to the disagreement amongst psychologists as to whether memory is *permanent*. There are four theories covered in the text; you need to cover them briefly as this is only worth 10 marks (allow 15–17 minutes only). You can include biological explanations (work on forgetting caused by brain damage) if you are familiar with this research.

b Each theory implies different practical applications:

- *Decay theory*: this implies that material needs to be well learnt initially and rehearsed every so often.

- *Failure of retrieval*: Klatzky's work is relevant here: previously forgotten material is more likely to be recalled when conditions are as similar as possible to those when the material was remembered (encoded). Police reconstructions are based on this, as is the more everyday fact that when you've mislaid something, you try to think back to what you were doing when you last had it!

- *Interference*: both retroactive and proactive interference can often prevent accurate recall. Again, it is necessary to learn information thoroughly so that interference is less likely. Advertisers are understandably concerned that one product advertisement may interfere with another and that you need additional cues at point of sale so that you can relate the product to the particular advertisement.

- Loftus's work on *reconstructive memory*, in as much as it clearly demonstrates how certain facts are forgotten or distorted, can legitimately be included here.

Additional exam questions

1. Discuss models of memory in relation to duration of storage and mode of representation.   **(25 marks)**
AEB (1990)

2. a Describe and evaluate **two** psychological explanations of forgetting from long term memory.   **(15 marks)**

b What practical advice, based on **either** or **both** of these explanations could you offer someone preparing for an examination?   **(10 marks)**
AEB AS (1993)

3. a What is meant by a mnemonic? Select *one* example to illustrate your answer. **(5 marks)**

   b What is meant by 'context effects' in the study of memory? **(5 marks)**

   c What advice might a psychologist give to people who believe they have a poor memory? Justify your answer by reference to theory and research in psychology. **(10 marks)** **(Total 20 marks)**

NEAB (1993)

3.2 Visual perception

Ours senses provide us with the raw data about our environment, but it is the brain that actually helps us to make sense of this confusion of information. The brain actively **interprets** and **organises** our sensory input, going beyond the basic data to create an understanding of our surroundings. Most of the time this occurs so effortlessly and automatically that we take it entirely for granted. The ability to perceive the external world accurately is absolutely essential to our survival and usually our perceptual system succeeds admirably in this task.

Perception applies to information received from all our senses, but we will concentrate on visual perception, not least because vision is probably the most important sense for human beings.

The visual system in humans

The stimulus for vision is light and this enters the eye through the **cornea**, a transparent protective coating at the front of the eye. The cornea bends the light rays so that they pass through the **pupil**, an opening in the **iris**. The iris is the coloured part of the eye and it makes the pupil dilate or constrict to control the amount of light entering the eyeball. The greater the amount of light, the smaller the pupil becomes. But psychological factors can also affect pupil size: positive emotional reactions, such as looking at someone you find sexually attractive, cause the pupil to dilate; negative emotions constrict it.

Light then passes through the **lens** which focuses it onto the **retina**, the light-sensitive inner lining at the back of the eye. The lens achieves this focusing by changing shape, thinning to focus on distant objects and thickening to focus on near ones. The lens not only focuses light on to the retina but reverses and inverts the light pattern, so that the image on the retina is upside down and side to side in relation to the actual object being viewed (see Figure 3.4).

The retina consists of photosensitive cells or **photoreceptors**, called rods and cones. There are about 120 million rods and 7 million cones.

- **Cones** are sensitive to colour and need plenty of light to respond, thus they are primarily involved in day vision; they are not a great deal of use on a dark night or in a dark cinema. Cones are mainly concentrated near the centre of the retina. In the most central area, called the fovea, there are only cones; the **fovea** is the area where vision is sharpest. Towards the edges, the density of cones decreases sharply and there are virtually none on the very periphery. There are three types of cones, each sensitive to a different region of the colour spectrum. One type is mainly sensitive to red/orange, another to green and a third to blue/violet.

- **Rods** respond only to varying degrees of light and dark, not to colours. They are very sensitive to light, 500 times more so than cones, allowing us to see in dim light or at night. Rods are most densely present in the outer part of the retina and their great sensitivity enables them readily to detect movement in the periphery of vision, a useful survival mechanism.

Activity

Now check that you can answer the following questions:

1. What is the stimulus for vision?
2. Complete the diagram showing the sequence in which light passes through the eye:
   cornea → _____ → _____ → **retina**

3. Fill in the gaps in the table below:

Part of eye	Location	Function
cornea		
pupil		
iris		controls size of pupils
fovea	centre of the retina	
lens		focuses light onto retina

4. If you were viewing a moving cat at dusk, which type of receptor cells in the retina would be involved?

The eye–brain connection

Although the eyes receive information from the outside world and the retina does a great deal of information processing, visual input is meaningless until it is **processed in the brain**. Connections between the eye and brain are quite intricate and we will consider only the main ones.

Information from the retina passes to the **optic nerve** which carries messages from each eye to the brain: information from the left eye travels first via the left optic nerve and information from the right eye travels via the right optic nerve.

As shown in Figure 3.5, at an intersection called the **optic chiasma** the fibres that make up each optic nerve separate and some of them cross to the side opposite from that of the eye they came from. This arrangement means that signals from both eyes go to both hemispheres of the brain. However, stimuli in the right half of the **visual field** are registered by

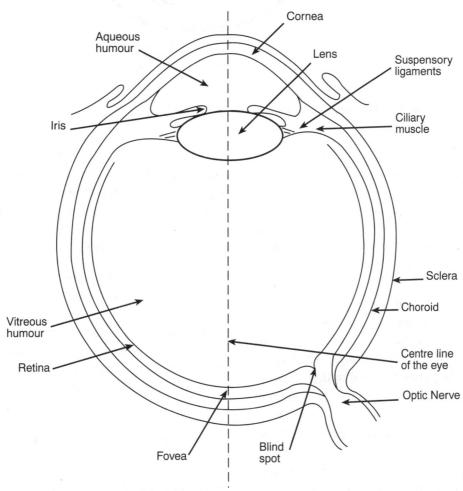

Figure 3.4 The human eye
Source: R. Davies and P. Houghton, Mastering Psychology (Macmillan, 1991), p. 85.

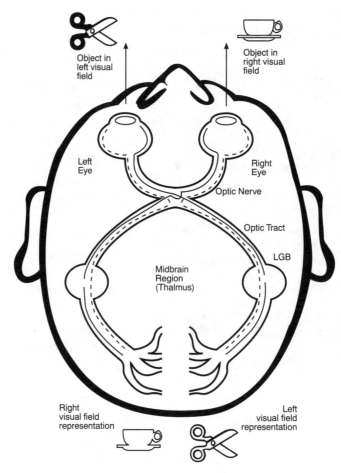

Figure 3.5 The visual pathways from the eyes to the brain
Source: R. Davies and P. Houghton, Mastering Psychology (Macmillan, 1991), p. 87.

receptors on the *left* side of each eye. This means that objects in the right visual field travel to the left hemisphere of the brain (via the left side of the retina) and objects in the left visual field travel to the right hemisphere. The importance of this can be seen in the Core Study in Chapter 7. The nerve fibres from the right side of each retina travel to the right hemisphere of the brain while those from the left side of each retina travel to the left hemisphere.

Beyond the optic chiasma, the optic nerve is known as the optic tract. The nerve fibres in each of the two optic tracts diverge along two pathways. The larger of these, known as the **primary visual pathway**, goes into the thalamus which is the main 'relay station' of the brain. In an area of the thalamus known as the **lateral geniculate nucleus (LGN)**, these messages are processed and then sent on to the areas of the occipital lobes comprising the **primary visual cortex.** Any damage to the primary visual pathway causes severe damage to vision.

The second pathway from the optic tract passes via a different route to the **secondary visual cortex**, located in a different part of the occipital lobe at the back of the brain. The primary and secondary visual pathways appear to have different functions, each using information from the same visual input:

- The primary visual pathway perceives form, colour, brightness, contrast and depth (Livingstone and Hubel, 1988).
- The secondary visual pathway perceives the location of objects in space and coordinates visual input from the other sense organs (Meredith and Stein, 1983; Sparks, 1988).

Information processing in the visual cortex

Hubel and Wiesel (1959, 1979) conducted pioneering work into how individual cells in the visual cortex respond to particular visual stimuli. They inserted micro-electrodes into individual cells of the visual cortex of cats and monkeys and recorded the impulses from these cells while the animals were sitting in front of a screen onto which different patterns and lines were projected.

Hubel and Wiesel found three types of neurons in the visual cortex:

1. **Simple cells**, which are most responsive to lines or bars presented in a certain orientation in a specific part of the retina. In the real world, such features make up the boundaries and edges of objects.
2. **Complex cells**, which are most responsive to moving lines in a particular orientation but only if they are moving in a particular direction, for example, from left to right.
3. **Hypercomplex cells**, which respond mainly to lines of a particular length.

This is a greatly over-simplified account of Hubel and Wiesel's work, but it does help to illustrate important features of our visual perceptual system. It suggests that the brain responds more readily to certain stimuli than to others and is designed to extract certain simple features from a complex stimulus. It appears to be most responsive to lines, edges, angles and corners. Frisby (1980) suggests that each individual neuron registers certain basic features of a stimulus which then serve as building blocks that the brain somehow builds up into a complete and coherent picture. Other researchers, however, believe that this is too simple an explanation for such a complex system.

Our perceptual powers

As mentioned earlier, perception is an active process involving organisation and interpretation of sensory information. We will look first at how perception is organised and then at how we interpret the visual input.

Principles or organisation

The guiding principle of **Gestalt** psychologists, writing earlier this century, is that 'the whole is greater than the sum of its parts'. In other words, when we perceive the world we impose an order and structure which cannot be found in any of its particular units or components. The processes by which we impose order or structure on our sensations, making them into coherent whole, are referred to as processes of perceptual organisation.

Laws of organisation

The **Gestalt** psychologists put forward a set of **laws of organisation:** rules by which we perceive shapes and forms and which the Gestalists believe are innate.

1. **Figure/ground:** one of the most important laws of organisation is that we perceive things in terms of figure and ground. If you look out of the window or around the room, you may see cars, houses, books on a table, a clock on the mantlepiece. All of these are **figures** which have a definite location in space. These figures stand out against the **background** which has no definite shape and seems to continue behind the figures. Occasionally, usually in specially designed pictures, we have difficulty in separating figure from ground. In the famous picture of the Rubin vase (Figure 3.6) the figure can be either a vase or two faces seen in profile. Similarly, in the Escher picture (Figure 3.7) the figure can be white angels or black devils. Many camouflage techniques work because they make the figure indistinguishable from the ground.
2. **The Law of Proximity:** things that are close together tend to be seen as a group rather than

Figure 3.6 The Rubin vase
Source: C.G. Morris, Psychology: An Introduction (Prentice-Hall, 1988, 6th edn), p. 107.

Figure 3.8 The Law of Proximity

Figure 3.7 Devils and Angels, by Escher
Source: C.G. Morris, Psychology: An Introduction (Prentice-Hall, 1988, 6th edn), p. 107.

Figure 3.9 The Law of Closure: 1

Figure 3.10 The Law of Closure: 2

separately. Figure 3.8 is seen as three pairs of lines and a single one rather than seven lines.

3. **The Law of Closure:** we tend to see figures as a complete whole even though there are gaps. Figures 3.9 and 3.10 are seen as a circle and triangle respectively.

4. **The Law of Similarity:** things that are in some way alike, in terms of shape, colour or size, are usually perceived as belonging together as part of a pattern. Figure 3.11 is seen as consisting of noughts and crosses grouped together in horizontal lines, not as noughts and crosses alternating with each other in vertical columns.

5. **The Law of Continuity:** lines and patterns tend to be continued in space. In Figure 3.12, you are more likely to perceive a single line partially covered by a circle rather than a circle and two separate lines.

6. **The Law of Common Fate:** when single elements are moving in the same direction at the same speed they are seen as a whole. Thus a flock of birds flying overhead is seen as one element, not as a group of individual birds.

These laws or organisation can essentially be reduced to two: **the law of Pragnanz** or 'good form' and **the law of 'belonging'**. The law of Pragnanz

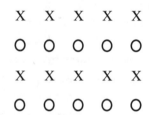

X X X X X

O O O O O

X X X X X

O O O O O

Figure 3.11 The Law of Similarity

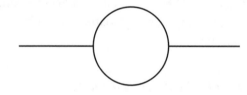

Figure 3.12 The Law of Continuity

refers to the fact that we tend to see things as a coherent whole, thus we close gaps and make objects more symmetrical. The law of belonging specifies the ways in which we group certain elements within a stimulus pattern. The laws of organisation are not hard and fast rules which always apply, neither are they explanations; but they do provide us with a reasonably accurate description of how we usually perceive the world.

Activity

Which laws of organisation are involved in the perception of:

a A stimulus consisting of one or more distinct regions and the remainder having no clear shape?

b A stimulus consisting of pairs or sets of phenomena which are similar?

c A stimulus which is perceived as a complete figure even though it is incomplete?

d A stimulus which is perceived as a single object even though its contours (edges) are broken by another object?

Distance and depth perception

It is essential for our survival that we can locate objects in space and perceive depth. In order to do this, we need to be able to translate a two dimensional retinal image into a three dimensional picture, something we can do with remarkable accuracy.

We use many cues to determine depth and distance; some of the cues depend on us having two eyes and are known as **binocular** cues, others depend on cues from one eye only and are known as **monocular** cues.

Binocular cues

- **Convergence:** the closer an object is to us, the more our two eyes have to move inwards or converge in order to fixate on it. Our brain uses information from the eye muscles in order to provide us with information about how far away the object is. Convergence only works for objects which are closer than about 10 feet away, after that the difference in convergence is too slight to provide useful data (see Figure 3.13).
- **Retinal disparity:** since our eyes are about $2\frac{1}{2}$ inches apart, each one receives a slightly different image of any object we are observing. The difference between the two images is known as retinal disparity. The nearer the object, the greater the retinal disparity. The brain is able to use the amount of retinal disparity as an indication of depth and distance.

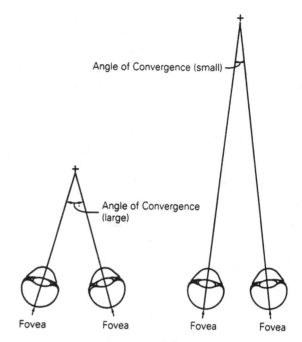

Figure 3.13 Convergence cues to depth
Source: P.G. Zimbardo, Psychology and Life (HarperCollins, 1992, 13th edn), p. 285.

Monocular cues

- **Interposition:** when an object overlaps another, then it is seen as being in front of the one it covers (Figure 3.14).
- **Linear perspective:** when you look at two lines which you know to be parallel, such as the edges of a ceiling or the sides of a straight road, they appear to converge in the distance. This convergence is another cue to depth: the greater the convergence, the farther away any object in the scene appears to be (Figure 3.15).
- **Relative size:** we are familiar with the size of everyday objects, so the smaller they appear, the farther away we assume them to be (Figure 3.16). We also compare their size with other objects in the scene. An elephant which appears smaller than a dog will be perceived as being much farther away than the dog.
- **Height in the visual field:** as we look into the distance along a flat plane, objects farther away are seen as higher in our visual field (Figure 3.17).
- **Texture gradient:** when something has an even texture, that texture appears to be finer in the distance than in the foreground (think of a sandy or pebbly beach). This change of texture is another cue to distance or depth (Figure 3.18).

- **Atmospheric perspective:** the farther away an object is, the more blurred its edges become; this is yet another cue to distance. On a misty day a hill seems farther away than when the mist clears.

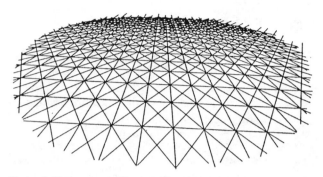

Figure 3.18 Texture gradient

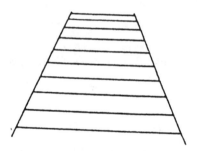

Figure 3.14 Interposition
Source: J. Radford and E. Govier (eds), A Textbook of Psychology (Sheldon Press, 1980; 1982), p. 263.

These and other cues to distance (such as shadowing and motion parallax) mean that our perception of distance and depth is remarkably accurate.

Perceptual constancies

The sensory information we receive from the environment is constantly changing as we move around, as the elements which we are looking at move and as light intensity varies. Yet on the whole we form a stable perception of an object regardless of the position from which we view it or whether it is seen in bright daylight or at dusk.

The ability to perceive objects as relatively stable and unchanging despite changes in sensory information is referred to as **perceptual constancy** and is another means by which we obtain accurate information about the world.

Figure 3.15 Linear perspective
Source: J. Radford and E. Govier (eds), A Textbook of Psychology (Sheldon Press, 1980; 1982), p. 263.

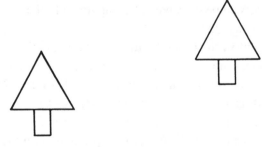

Figure 3.16 Relative size
Source: J. Radford and E. Govier (eds), A Textbook of Psychology (Sheldon Press, 1980; 1982), p. 263.

1. **Shape constancy** is the ability to perceive objects as having a constant shape despite changes in the shape of the retinal image. A door is perceived as rectangular even when viewed from the side when the retinal image is no longer rectangular (see Figure 3.19).

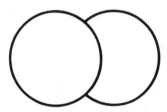

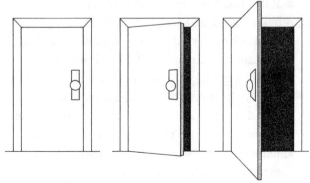

Figure 3.17 Height in the visual field
Source: J. Radford and E. Govier (eds), A Textbook of Psychology (Sheldon Press, 1980; 1982), p. 263.

Figure 3.19 Shape constancy

2. **Size constancy** is our ability to see things as being the same size even when the size of the retinal image changes, as it does when objects are viewed from different distances (Figure 3.20).

   In order to achieve size constancy and shape constancy, the perception of depth or distance is obviously crucial. Once these depth and distance cues are removed, as they are if we view an unfamiliar object through a very small aperture, then our assessment of size and shape becomes much less accurate.

3. **Location constancy** refers to our ability to see things as being stationary even when the retinal image is constantly moving. When driving fast, we see telegraph poles 'fly by' but we know that they are not really on the move.

4. **Brightness constancy** means that despite changes of illumination, the perceived brightness of familiar objects hardly varies at all. What appears to matter in terms of perception is not the absolute brightness of an object but how bright it is in comparison to its surroundings.

Up to now we have been considering how our perceptual powers provide us with a representation of our immediate environment which is sufficiently accurate to meet our survival needs. But our perception of the world is not always accurate, as we see in the next subsection

Visual illusions

An illusion is any figure which produces a **false interpretation** of **reality**. Psychologists are interested in such figures because they provide us with a better understanding of the processes of perception in everyday circumstances.

Theories of visual illusions

Misapplied perceptual constancy

Gregory (1963) suggests that some visual illusions can be explained in terms of misapplied perceptual constancy. Within the diagram of the Ponzo illusion (Figure 3.21a), there are cues which indicate that this represents a three dimensional scene (Figure 3.21b). The lines at the side could be parallel lines disappearing into the distance. One horizontal line above another could represent different height in the visual field. Both of these, as we have seen, are depth cues. These two cues, then, suggest that the top line is further in the distance than the line beneath it. Since the retinal image of both is the same size, the principal of size constancy encourages us to perceive the top line as being longer than the bottom one.

With respect to the Muller–Lyer illusion (Figure 3.22a), Gregory has suggested that, in the absence of other cues, the figure with the fins diverging represents an inside corner and the one with the fins converging represents an outside corner (Figure 3.22b).

"Excuse me for shouting, I thought you were further away."

Figure 3.20 Size constancy
Source: S.A. Rathus, Essentials of Psychology (Holt, Rinehart & Winston, 1991, 3rd edn), p. 111.

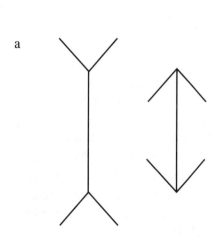

Figure 3.21
a The Ponzo illusion
b Cues of a three dimensional scene

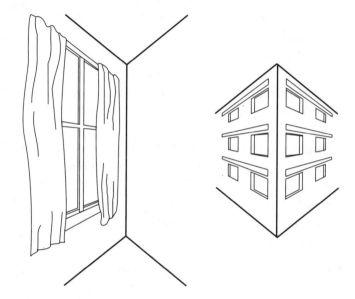

Figure 3.22
a The Muller–Lyer illusion
b Cues of an inside and outside corner

Past experience indicates that a vertical line between diverging arrowheads is farther away than the ceiling and floor lines represented by the arrowheads. Conversely, converging arrowheads suggest that the vertical line is closer than the lines receding from it. Since the two lines appear to be at different distances but are the same retinal size, the one which appears to be farther away is perceived as longer.

Evaluation

Gregory's theory of misapplied constancy can easily be applied to the Ponzo illusion but it is more problematic when applied to the Muller–Lyer illusion.

Evidence in favour

1. When viewed on a dark background, the Muller–Lyer configuration of lines is seen as **three dimensional**.

2. This illusion is barely experienced by people who have lived in an environment which has given them little experience of **linear perspective**: people such as the congenitally blind who have restored sight and Zulus whose environment consists of rounded buildings and who have little experience of objects with straight edges and right-angled corners.

Limitations

There are several versions of the Muller–Lyer illusion for which this theory cannot account:

1. The illusion still persists if the lines are **horizontal**, yet this is not the way we perceive the edges of buildings.

2. If the lines are removed altogether and only the fins left in place, the distance between the fins with the points facing inwards appears greater

than the distance between the fins with the points facing outwards.

3. The illusion remains very strong when the fins are replaced by circles, squares or several other shapes, as shown in Figure 3.23. These obviously cannot be accounted for by architectural features providing misleading depth cues.

Gregory's theory of misapplied constancy can thus account for some geometrical illusions, but it is not an adequate explanation for all of them.

Day's theory

Day (1972) has put forward a more general theory which accounts for the types of illusions shown in Figure 3.24a and 3.24b. As already mentioned, we simultaneously use many cues, such as texture gradient, relative size and interposition, to judge distance and depth. According to Day, when some of these cues are so strong that they override others, they can mislead us so that our judgment of depth, distance and size become distorted. Thus, in Figure 3.24a, we compare the size of the inner circle with those around it and are deceived into judging the one surrounded by large circles as smaller than the one surrounded by small circles.

Other theories

Figure 3.25 illustrates another type of visual illusion in which lines appear distorted. The most plausible explanation offered to account for such illusions is concerned with the way in which certain components of the stimulus are coded in the visual system. For example, acute angles are usually judged as being less acute than they really are. Since the illusion shown in Figure 3.25 involves the perception of acute angles, this could explain the apparent distortion of the lines.

Activity

1. Why are psychologists interested in visual illusions?
2. How has the size–distance principle been used to explain some visual illusions?
3. Which illusions can it not explain?

There is, then, no universally accepted explanation of all types of illusion. We'll end this topic by inviting you to look at a fascinating and powerful illusion for which there is as yet no convincing explanation: the Fraser illusion, in which, despite the evidence of your own eyes, there is no spiral, simply a set of concentric circles (see Figure 3.26).

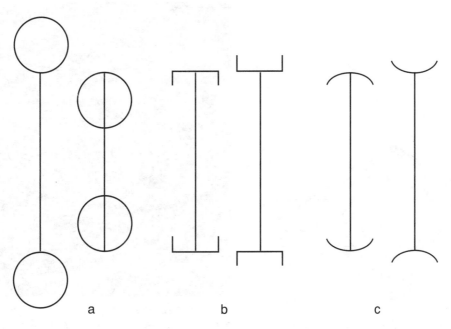

a   b   c

Figure 3.23 Alternative versions of the Muller–Lyer illusion

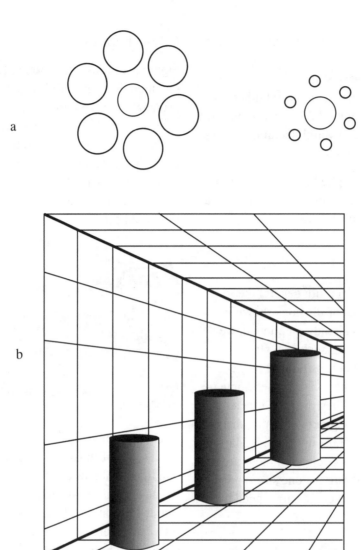

Figure 3.24 Visual illusions explained by Day's theory

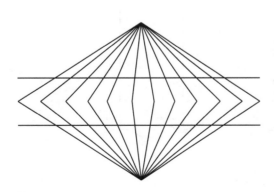

Figure 3.25 A visual illusion which may be caused by coding in the visual system

Figure 3.26 The Fraser illusion
Source: J.E. Grusec, R. Lockhart and G. Walters, Foundations of Psychology (Copp Clark Pitman Ltd, 1990), p. 277.

Cognitive processes in perception

Schemata

Perception is not a process carried out in isolation from other thought processes. One of the main influences on our perception is simply what we expect in particular circumstances. These expectations are based, in turn, on information stored in our memory: these clusters of information are known as **schemata**.

> Schemata are cognitive structures that provide us with a general framework in which to organise everything we know about a type of stimulus, its attributes and features and its relation to other stimuli. For example, we have a schema about a human face: that it has two eyes, a nose and a mouth. So, when viewing a person in profile, we assume that they have two eyes, even though only one is visible.

Schemata, then, lead us to have certain **expectations** about the world. These expectations have a powerful influence on the way we interpret information; interpretations are made so quickly and automatically that most of the time we are completely unaware of them.

Activity

You will come across references to schemata in several areas of psychology, especially memory, perception and Piaget's theory of cognitive development. In all these areas, the meaning is the same. Think about why schema is such a pervasive and important concept in cognitive psychology.

Important influences on perception

1. **Perceptual set: set** is a temporary predisposition or readiness to perceive or react to a stimulus in a particular way, because we are mentally prepared for it to arise. This mental preparation can be triggered by various cues:

   a **Labels:** look at Figure 3.27. What do you see? This ambiguous picture can be viewed as the face of a young woman or as a saxophone player. You were given no clue as to what to expect, so you may have seen either one. But if a label, either 'a young woman' or 'a saxophone player' had been placed under the picture, then the likelihood is, you would have seen it as such. Labels, then, can influence perception.

   b **The immediate context** in which a stimulus is viewed can also act as a perceptual set. A very simple example of this effect was demonstrated by Bruner and Minturn (1952). They presented people with the stimulus shown in Figure 3.28, either as one of a series of numbers or one of a set of capital letters. Seen in a context of numbers, it is likely to be perceived as a number thirteen; seen together with letters, it is likely to be perceived as the capital letter B.

Figure 3.27 How labels influence perception
Source: J.W. Kalat, Introduction to Psychology (Brooks/Cole, 1993, 3rd edn), p. 161.

B

Figure 3.28 Context and perception

2. **Expectation:** Perceptual set involves expectation, but usually refers to a temporary readiness to perceive stimuli in a certain way. **Perceptual familiarisation**, that is, expectations set up over a lifetime, can also affect the way in which we interpret stimuli. For instance, there is a spelling mistake in the previous sentence. Now that it's been pointed out to you, you'll probably spot it quite easily, but the likelihood is that you did not notice it when you first read the sentence because you expect words in books to be spelt correctly.

Lachman (1984) demonstrated the effect of expectation on perception of a stimulus by asking people to read the phrases shown in Figure 3.29. If you have seen these examples before, or if by now you are **expecting** some trickery, you will not have been fooled, but naive subjects often misperceive these stimuli because they breach our expectations about the way sentences and phrases are structured.

sixteen hours previously. Again, the hungrier participants were more likely to see the pictures as food-related than the participants whose stomachs were reasonably full.

The value we put on a stimulus can also affect perception. **Bruner and Goodman (1946)** presented coins to children who either came from poor or from well-off families. When asked to estimate the size of the coin by adjusting a circle of light so that it was the same size as the coin, children from poorer homes estimated it to be larger than did those children from the richer families.

Lambert, Solomon and Watson (1949) conducted an interesting variation of this study by changing the value of a poker chip during the course of the study. They first asked nursery school children to estimate the size of the chip which, to them, was worthless. They were then given the opportunity to use the chips to obtain sweets from a machine. On retesting, the children now perceived the chips as larger than they had before.

Figure 3.29 The effect of expectation

3. **Motivation:** Needs and values motivate us to perceive stimuli in a certain way. **Sanford (1937)** presented hungry participants with vague and ambiguous pictures and found that they invariably interpreted them as representing items of food.

McClelland and Atkinson (1948), in a similar type of study, presented blurred images to participants who had either eaten one hour or

Activity

In the following lists, some words are incomplete. Fill in the gaps to make the first word you think of. Work as quickly as you can:

dog, rabbit, c–t   wolf, badger, –ox
hat, beret, c–p   run, sprint, d–sh

Now look at the words you have chosen and consider what you have put if the lists had been:

rattle, baby, c–t   carton, container, –ox

mug, saucer, c–p   bowl, plate, d–sh

This is a demonstration of perpetual set. How was it established in this instance?

Theories of perception

Bottom-up and top-down models

When we perceive a scene, we have **two** sources of information:

1. The actual sensory information which we receive from the scene itself
2. The non-visual information stored in our brain about what we expect the world to look like.

In line with this, we can distinguish two processes involved in perception: **bottom-up processes** and **top-down processes**:

- The **bottom-up processes** involve information travelling 'up' from the stimulus, via the senses, to the brain which then interprets it, relatively passively.
- The **top-down processes** involve the brain 'sending down' stored information to the sensory system as it receives information from the stimulus, enabling a plausible hypothesis about the scene to be made without the need to analyse every feature of the stimulus.

Bottom-up models, then, are **data-driven** and emphasise the importance of the stimulus itself, the raw data of direct experience.

Top-down theories, on the other hand, are **hypothesis-driven** and stress the importance of such higher mental processes as expectation, beliefs, values and social influences.

The interactive approach

A middle ground is occupied by **interactive models** which state that perception involves both the bottom-up process of interpreting the actual stimulation received as well as the top-down process of selecting from all possibilities those which our past experience tells us to expect in certain situations.

Most theorists agree that both bottom-up and top-down processes have a role to play, but the relative importance they put on these two processes is very different.

Bottom-up: Gibson's direct perception theory

J.J. Gibson (1979) claims that our main source of information comes from the **sensations received** from the scene we are viewing: a scene rich in information involving texture, comparative size, colours, shadowing and a host of other cues. With all this rich and varied information at our disposal, we simply do not need to carry out a continuous process of hypothesis testing based on non-visual factors like memory and expectation.

Hubel and Wiesel's work (p. 46) demonstrates that we are wonderfully equipped with built-in systems for the reception of information important to our survival. For Gibson, then, perception is direct: it works like a radio receiving signals from outside. The radio is specially built to receive certain signals and does not need to interpret them. Gibson felt that too much theorising about perception was based on work done in the artificial situation of the psychology laboratory when people are presented with static, limited stimuli in isolation from most of the cues they would receive in the real world.

Evaluation

Contribution In many circumstances, this theory seems to provide a plausible explanation of perceptual processing and Gibson must be given credit for having drawn our attention to the rich array of the visual information available to the perceiver.

Limitations There are some aspects of perception for which Gibson's theory has difficulty accounting.

1. Few cells have been found to pick up complex features of the world: we have no cells which, for example, respond to 'mouse' in the same way they may respond to lines of a certain length. Some cognitive, **interpretative** processes must be taking place when we catch sight of a mouse.
2. The theory cannot adequately account for the fact that the same stimulus means different things to different people: it ignores the role of **assumptions**.
3. Let us consider visual illusions in everyday life. If we do indeed have so many cues in our optic array, why do we make so many mistakes? For example, we regularly perceive vertical lines to

Figure 3.30 A common visual illusion

be longer than horizontal lines, as shown in Figure 3.30.

4. What we perceive about objects includes many factors other than their physical properties and relative position in space. Think about what you may perceive if looking at a pair of trousers in a shop window: whether they will be comfortable, keep their shape, be the kind of style that will flatter your figure and so on. All these inferences require higher mental processes that go beyond the physical properties of the trousers.

Top-down: constructive theories

Gregory (1972) and Bruner (1957), amongst others, favour the top-down model of perception. They see perception as an active, interpretative, hypothesis-testing process in which our visual sources are enriched by non-visual ones. Perception is not a passive response to external stimuli but a response of the whole person, a process of constructing reality according to our assumptions about how the external world probably is or should be. We don't simply receive information, we **process** it, **analyse** it and **draw inferences** from it. We are not aware of such constructive processes: they are automatic and immediate.

Evaluation

Contributions   We have already discussed how Gregory accounts for visual illusions in terms of hypothesis-testing: we make mistakes because we receive inadequate information from stimuli; information which leads us to the wrong interpretation. We have simply used an incorrect hypothesis, such as assuming depth cues are present when they are not, as in the Ponzo illusion (Figure 3.21a and b).

Limitations   This approach has been criticised for

ignoring the fact that evolution has equipped us with a means of selecting what is important from the stimulus array. As already mentioned, Hubel and Wiesel's work demonstrates that we have a 'wired in', innate system which selects, refines and extracts information from the stimulus. We have no need to invent perceptual constancy every time we look at a view; we have a ready-made receiver to do this.

Neisser's analysis-by-synthesis theory

Both direct perception and constructive theories, then, can account for some aspects of perception, but neither fully explains it. In fact, evidence indicates that both bottom-up and top-down processes play a part in perception, but not always to the same extent in different situations. When we are familiar with the environment and know what to expect, we use a top-down approach which saves us from having to analyse stimulus features in detail and is therefore cost-effective. In a strange and unfamiliar situation, we are more likely to adopt a bottom-up approach. In most situations, we use both.

Neisser (1976) has put forward an interactive model that seeks to integrate the two approaches. This model, known as analysis-by-synthesis, emphasises the importance of **three** processes in perception:

*   the features of the stimulus itself,
*   the use of schemata
*   perceptual exploration (a search for expected features).

According to this model, when we look at something, say a face, certain features of the stimulus and certain expectations from past experience lead us to hypothesise, say, that it is the familiar face of our friend Jim. We use our schema of Jim's face to search for expected features and if there is a match, our hypothesis is confirmed and the stimulus is recognised. If, however, the features do not fit (the jaw is too square, the face is too lined) then we will work on a new hypothesis and so the process continues until we find an hypothesis which fits the bill and can therefore be confirmed (see Figure 3.31).

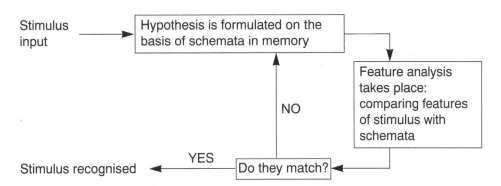

Figure 3.31 Neisser's analysis-by-synthesis model

Activity

1. Insert 'bottom-up' or 'top-down' into the following:

   a _____ theorists emphasise the importance of the stimulus.

   b _____ emphasise the importance of expectation and beliefs.

   c Gregory is a _____ theorist.

   d J.J. Gibson is a _____ theorist.

   e _____ processing involves hypothesis-testing.

2. Decide whether the following statements correspond to the views of Gibson, Gregory or Neisser:

   a Expectation has a powerful effect on what we perceive.

   b Most of the time we receive enough information from the outside world not to need to construct hypotheses about what they are.

   c We sometimes perceive things incorrectly because we make incorrect assumptions.

   d Our senses are the equivalent of excellent receivers: in most circumstances, we don't need to interpret the data provided.

   e An important aspect of perception is the search for expected features.

The development of perception: learned or innate?

One of the most explored aspects of perceptual processes is the extent to which they are learned or innate.

The **Gestaltists** believe that the basic organisational processes involved in perception are innate, wired into our brains from the start. The work of Hubel and Wiesel appears to support this view: we are physiologically equipped, probably from birth, to respond to certain perceptual stimuli.

Other psychologists believe that we are born with very limited perceptual powers, that all we see at birth is a chaotic swirl of colours, shapes and shades and that we learn perception through our experiences in the world around us.

Evidence

There is an enormous body of work relevant to the nature–nurture controversy as it applies to perception. We will consider a relatively small sample of evidence from four sources:

1. Studies of congenitally blind people whose sight has been restored
2. Studies of very young children
3. Studies of animals reared in perceptually deprived conditions
4. Studies of people from various cultures.

1. **Studies of congenitally blind people whose sight has been restored**
   Von Senden (1932) studied the perceptual abilities of patients who, having been born blind, had undergone surgery to restore their sight. These patients could
   - distinguish figure from ground
   - detect objects and fixate on them
   - follow moving objects with their eyes.

   This suggests that some aspects of visual perception may be innate. However, we must be cautious in jumping too readily to definite conclusions based on this type of evidence. It is doubtful whether the perceptual abilities of those with restored vision are much like that of a newborn infant. Congenitally blind adults have had many years' experience of the world during which time they will have come to rely on other senses. It is also possible that parts of their visual system may have deteriorated from birth.

2. **Studies of very young children**

Adams (1987) found that infants in only the fourth day of life spent more time looking at green, red or yellow squares than at grey squares of equal brightness, indicating that some colour discrimination is present very early in life, probably at birth.

Fantz (1961) presented infants of between one and fifteen weeks with pairs of visual stimuli and measured the amount of time they spent looking at each. He found that they preferred complex figures to plain ones, for example a checkerboard to a plain square. Fantz also measured how long babies aged between four days to six months fixated on a schematic drawing of a face (Figure 3.32(A)), a scrambled 'face' (with the same features rearranged) (B) and a face outline with the same proportion of black and white but in a block (C). Babies preferred the schematic face, followed by the jumbled face. The plain face was virtually ignored.

Fantz concluded that the perception of form is innate and that very young babies are preprogrammed to respond to a human face.

Michael Eysenck (1993) has questioned these conclusions. He points out that there was relatively little difference in the time spent looking at the 'real' face as compared with the jumbled one, and that other researchers have found no such differences. Even if these differences do exist, it is possible that the schematic face is preferred not because it represents a face but simply because it is a complex, symmetrical visual stimulus.

Bower (1964) studied size constancy in infants between 75 and 85 days of age. By using reinforcement, he first taught infants to respond to a 30 cm cube. He then tested them to see if they would respond to different sized cubes at different distances, arranged so that the size of the retinal image was the same (see Figure 3.33). He also used 30 cm cubes at varying distances. He found that overall these babies preferred the 30 cm cube, although not exclusively so. Bower concluded that young babies have fairly good size constancy but that it is not as fully developed as in adults. He concluded that within the first few months of life, infants use depth cues to achieve size constancy.

Gibson and Walk (1960) used the now famous 'visual cliff' apparatus to study depth perception in infants old enough to crawl. This apparatus consists of a sheet of glass covering both a deep and shallow surface with a checkerboard pattern beneath it (see Figure 3.34). Babies are placed in the centre of the apparatus just on the shallow side and are encouraged to crawl to their mother who stands, with open arms and an encouraging smile, at one end of the glass top. Babies do not hesitate to crawl across the shallow side but cannot be induced across the deep side. This indicates that human infants over the age of six months can perceive depth and are aware of the dangers involved. But we cannot conclude that this ability is innate since much perceptual learning has taken place between birth and the time of testing.

Studies using neonate animals which are mobile very soon after birth indicate that depth perception, at least in those species in which it is essential for survival, may be innate. Chicks less than 24 hours old never hop to the deep side,

Face A   Face B   Face C

Figure 3.32 Diagrammatic faces used by Fantz
Source: N. Hayes, A First Course in Psychology (Nelson, 1984),
p. 180.

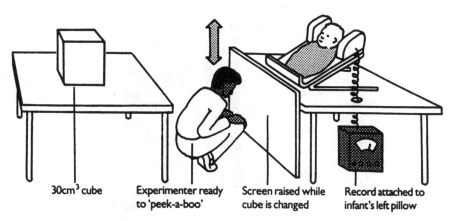

| 30cm³ cube | Experimenter ready to 'peek-a-boo' | Screen raised while cube is changed | Record attached to infant's left pillow |

Figure 3.33 Bower's 'peek-a-boo' experiment
Source: N. Hayes, A First Course in Psychology (Nelson, 1984), p. 181.

Figure 3.34 Gibson and Walk's 'visual cliff'
Source: N. Hayes, A First Course in Psychology (Nelson, 1984), p. 183.

neither do goat kids and lambs which are tested as soon as they can walk. These animals also show great fear if placed on the deep side of the apparatus.

Studies previously cited indicate that certain visual perceptual abilities, especially those essential for survival, are innate. But that obviously does not mean that **all** perception is inborn and there is considerable evidence that experience does affect perception.

3. **Studies of animals reared in perceptually deprived conditions**

   Blakemore and Cooper (1970) reared kittens in total darkness except for a few hours each day when they were only exposed either to horizontal or to vertical lines (Figure 3.35). When they were eventually placed in a normal environment they were unable to respond to lines to which they had never been exposed. For example, kittens reared with no experience of horizontal lines could avoid table legs but would walk straight into a horizontally stretched piece of string. There are two possible interpretations of these findings:
   - Normal visual experience is essential for perceptual abilities to develop, or
   - Perceptual abilities present at birth deteriorate if not used.

   Research indicates that the second interpretation is the more plausible one since physiological evidence indicates that cells sensitive to lines in a particular orientation deteriorate when they are not stimulated early in life.

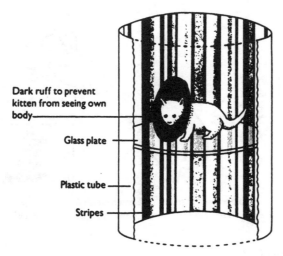

Dark ruff to prevent
kitten from seeing own
body

Glass plate

Plastic tube

Stripes

Figure 3.35 Blakemore and Cooper's kitten in a 'vertical world'
Source: N. Hayes, A First Course in Psychology (Nelson, 1984), p. 187.

4. **Studies of people from various cultures**
    The Core Study in this section demonstrates that visual perception varies from culture to culture.
        Segal *et al.* (1966) found that people living in environments in which the buildings are not predominantly rectangular are less susceptible to the Muller–Lyer illusion than those reared in a more 'carpentered' environment.

Activity

There are a lot of studies to learn for the nature–nurture debate on perception. You may find it helpful to draw up a table like Table 3.2, inventing key phrases for each study and then learning the association between the researchers and what they did **very thoroughly** so that you avoid confusion when answering questions. We've done a couple of the easy ones for you.

Table 3.2 Studies in the nature–nurture debate

Researcher	Study	Innate/learned?
Von Senden (1932)		
Adams (1987)		
Fantz (1961)	Faces	Innate
Bower (1964)		
Gibson and Walk (1960)	Visual cliff	
and so on		

So what conclusions can we draw about the influence of inborn factors and learning in perceptual processes? It seems that both nature and nurture play a part, and that some perceptual abilities are more susceptible to the effects of learning and experience than are others. Some of the most fundamental perceptual processes, especially those necessary for survival, are probably present, if not at birth then at least very soon afterwards. But the child's perceptual world is not the same as the adult's. Certain of the more subtle perceptual abilities certainly appear to be significantly influenced by experience. Perception is probably best regarded as a competence derived initially from basic, inborn, physiological mechanisms which is then moulded and modified by experience.

Core Study

Pictorial perception and culture: Jan B. Deregowski (1972)

Cross-cultural studies have shown that there are persistent differences in the way pictures are interpreted by people of various cultures.

Conventions for depicting three dimensional objects in two dimensional pictures give perceivers depth cues which indicate that some objects are further away than others. In some cultures, these depth cues are not interpreted as cues to distance, leading to misinterpretation of the picture as a whole. In order to study pictorial perception, William Hudson devised a test consisting of series of pictures in which there are various combinations of three dimensional depth cues:

1. **Familiar size**: the larger of two familiar objects is drawn much smaller to indicate that it is further away
2. **Overlap**: a hill is partly obscured by another hill
3. **Perspective**: the convergence of lines which are recognised as being parallel in real life.

In all but one of the pictures, Hudson omitted density gradient as a perceptual cue. See Figure 3.36 for an example of such a picture.

Hudson's test has been used in many parts of Africa. Subjects were asked to name the objects and then certain questions were posed, such as: 'What is the man doing?' 'What is closer to the man?'

Those who interpreted the depth cues were classified as having three dimensional perception. If depth cues were not taken into account, they were classified as having two dimensional perception. The results from African tribes were clear: both children and adults found it difficult to perceive depth in the pictorial material. There were variations in the extent of this difficulty, but it appeared at most educational and social levels.

It may be that people find pictures of the perspective type difficult to interpret because they prefer pictures that depict the essential characteristics of an object even if all these characteristics cannot be seen from a single viewpoint. (For example, one unsystematic observation indicated that pictures of faces in profile are not liked because both eyes cannot be seen.)

Hudson investigated this by using the two drawings shown in Figure 3.37. The one on the left is known as a 'split style' drawing (as the legs are unnaturally split to the side). The picture on the right is a view like a photograph of an elephant seen from above. Hudson found that, with only one exception, subjects from Africa preferred the drawing of the split elephant. The one person who did not prefer the drawing said that it was because the elephant was jumping about dangerously.

Deregowski's research has led him to postulate that in all societies children have an aesthetic preference for drawings of the split style; in most societies this preference is suppressed because the drawings do not convey information about the depicted objects as accurately as perspective drawings do. Some societies, however, have developed the split drawing to a high artistic level; these pictures are intended to serve primarily as ornaments and, being highly stylised, are not understood outside a specific culture. Thus, the same psychological processes, when influenced by culture, result in widely different artistic styles.

Drawings, then, do not offer us a universal lingua franca; there are significant differences in the way pictures can be interpreted and the mapping of these cultural differences has only just begun.

Figure 3.36 Test items used by Hudson
Source: R.D. Gross, Key Studies in Psychology (Hodder & Stoughton, 1990), p. 23.

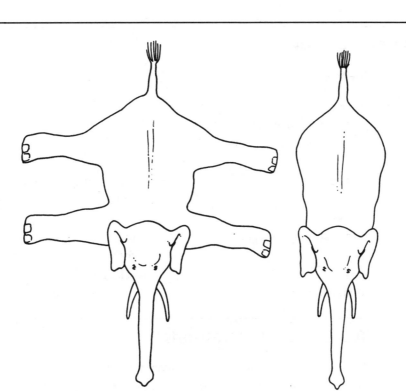

Figure 3.37
a 'Split-elephant' drawing
b Top-view perspective drawing
Source: R.D. Gross, Key Studies in Psychology (Hodder & Stoughton, 1990), p. 29.

QUESTIONS

1. Describe some of the cultural differences that have been observed in the interpretation of pictures.

2. How did Hudson set about studying picture perception?

3. **a** What is meant by a 'split style' of drawing?
   (2 marks)

   b Give *one* explanation of why this might have developed in some cultures. **(2 marks)**

   Oxford and Cambridge Specimen Question

Preparing for the exam

Key terms

binocular cues
bottom-up processes
carpentered environment
cones
cornea
Gestalt
illusion
information processing
iris
lens
monocular cues

optic chiasma
optic nerve
perceptual set
photoreceptors
photosensitive cells
Pragnanz
pupil
retina
rods
schemata
top-down processes

Types of exam questions

1. The ways in which sensory processes relate to perception.
2. Description and evaluation of theories of perceptual organisation.
3. Development of perception.
4. Explanations of visual constancies and illusions.
5. The nature–nurture debate as applied to perception

Self-test questions

1. Hubel and Wiesel found three types of neurons in the visual cortex. Name each one and briefly describe their function.
2. Explain the meaning of the Gestaltist claim that 'the whole is greater than the sum of its parts'.
3. Name and describe *three* laws of perceptual organisation suggested by the Gestaltists.
4. In the perception of distance and depth, what is a binocular cue and what is a monocular cue? Give an example of each and explain how it operates.
5. What are perceptual constancies? Describe *two*.
6. How does Gregory account for visual illusions? Can his theory account for all types of illusion?
7. Describe a study that illustrates the effect of motivation on perception.
8. Describe a study that illustrates the effect of expectation on perception.
9. Briefly describe the difference between bottom-up and top-down theories of perception. Give an example of each.
10. Whose theory combines bottom-up and top-down theories?
11. What methods have been used to investigate whether perception is innate or learned?
12. Briefly describe *two* studies investigating the nature–nurture debate, one using children and one using animals, and state the conclusions of each.

Exam questions with guidance notes

1. **'There is more to visual perception than meets the eye'.**
   Discuss the above statement in relation to theories of perceptual organisation. (25 marks)
   AEB (1992)

First, let's consider the examiner's report: 'Answers describing a whole range of visual illusions and constancies were quite common ... Such approaches are no longer acceptable given that the requirements of this question are clear from the wording. A high proportion of candidates seemed unable to write a critical essay on the theories chosen ...'

Now you know what *not* to do, let's consider what to do.

- Start by a brief consideration of the active nature of perception.
- Distinguish between *bottom-up* and *top-down* theories.
- The theories of organisation you could use are Gestalt, J.J. Gibson, Gregory, Neisser.
- Write about the ones you select, at least one top-down and one bottom-up, and *evaluate* each one.
- Supporting evidence and criticisms of J.J. Gibson's and Gregory's theories are clearly laid out in the section on Theories of Perception.
- You could finish with a consideration of Neisser's interactive model.

2. **a Describe the findings of any *two* different areas of research in the study of perceptual development.** (10 marks)
   b Describe and evaluate the methods used in such research.
   (15 marks)
   AEB (1994)

   a   The areas of research you can choose for part (a) are those listed at the beginning of the subsection on Development of Perception, that is:
- studies of the sight restored congenitally blind
- studies of neonates
- studies involving perceptually unusual experiences
- studies from other cultures.
   Describe the research findings from any *two* of these areas, not forgetting to *interpret* the results.
   b   Describing the methods themselves is fairly straightforward (although not something you may be used to doing, so give it some thought).
   Evaluation of the methods requires you to put forward the *advantages* and *limitations* of each one. For example:
- Use of neonates is useful because they have virtually no perceptual experience so it taps inborn abilities. However, in practical terms it is limited: young humans are not mobile, so crawling and walking cannot be used as a means of investigating inborn perceptual capacities. Obviously this can and has been done using some animals, and the results are useful in their own right, but they cannot be generalised to humans.
   There are also problems of *interpretation* of data, as illustrated by Michael Eysenck's criticism of Fantz's conclusions.

- As done above, go through each method, pointing out its uses and limitations, many of which are mentioned in the text (don't forget that the Core Study is relevant here).
- It is appropriate, in an evaluation, to mention the ethics of such studies, but only *briefly*. Resist the temptation to write at great length about the ethics of raising animals in perceptually deprived conditions, not because this argument is not valid but simply because it is a very small part of the answer to this particular question. A sentence will suffice.
- Conclude with an overview of the methodology and emphasise the fact that, given the limitations of the methodology and the complex nature of the topic area, a variety of methods is required.

Additional exam questions

1. 'Perception is a developmental process.' To what extent does psychological evidence support this statement? **(25 marks)**
   AEB (1989)

2. Critically discuss explanations of visual constancies and illusions.
   (25 marks)
   AEB (1990)

3. a Describe what is known about how information is processed in the retina. **(8 marks)**
   b What do visual illusions tell us about perception? **(12 marks)**
   JMB (1988)

4. a Using evidence from experimental studies, describe what psychologists have discovered about the development, in human infants, of
      i   pattern perception **(6 marks)**
      ii depth perception **(6 marks)**
   b Discuss *two* difficulties of investigating the development of perception in human infants **(8 marks)**
   (Total 20 marks)
   (JMB 1991)

5. Discuss, using appropriate empirical examples, how perception may be influenced by a person's expectations about the stimuli presented.
   (20 marks)
   JMB (1989)

3.3 Attention

'PAY ATTENTION!' When teachers say this, what they really mean is that you should pay attention to **them**, in order that you might understand and remember what is going on in the lesson since, in any situation, there are many stimuli competing for your limited capacity to attend. But what exactly is meant by attention?

Some psychologists believe that the term 'attention' is too vague to be useful. Others believe that there are several kinds of attention, each with its own mechanisms and functions. Michael Eysenck (1993) suggests that it is most frequently used to refer to **selectivity of processing**.

Selected or focused attention

The 'cocktail party' effect

Cherry (1953) was interested in answering two questions concerned with situations like parties:

1. How do we successfully follow one conversation when there are many others going on around us?
2. How much of the surrounding conversations do we actually absorb?

Cherry investigated the problem by using **two** types of listening tasks:

1. **Binaural tasks**, which involve hearing two different messages at the same time through both ears and being required to follow one message while ignoring the other. In experimental studies involving this task, participants found it extremely difficult; some parts of the tape had to be played up to twenty times before each message could be deciphered. It soon became clear that, in the 'cocktail party' situation, this cannot be the method we use to focus attention on one particular conversation.
2. **Dichotic tasks**, which involve hearing two messages at the same time, but presented through separate ears, and then being required to follow or 'shadow' just one of the conversations.

The results of Cherry's research and that of more recent investigators were as follows:

1. The dichotic task was much easier than the binaural one.
2. We take in very little of any conversation to which we are not attending (in technical terms, the non-shadowed message). In one study, participants assumed that the non-shadowed conversation was in English when it was in fact in German and, in another study, did not even notice when the unattended message consisted of English words pronounced backwards (although they did feel that there was something a bit strange about it).
3. Nevertheless, certain characteristics of the non-shadowed message were detected. Participants noticed when the speaker changed from male to female and they were able to detect a pure tone that was inserted in to the middle of the message.

Activity

Before you read any further, think about what is different between the situations in which the non-shadowed message is noticed and those in which it is not noticed (compare items **2** and **3** above).

Cherry suggested that at an event like a cocktail party we are good at focusing on physical aspects of speech, such as the direction from which it is coming or whether or not it is being spoken in a male or female voice. We do not, however, absorb much of the meaning.

It seems that it is **physical properties** of unattended speech which are noticed, but **not the semantic content**.

Theories of selective attention

Broadbent's filter theory

This theory states that we are unable to analyse all incoming information and so there is a 'filter' limiting the amount of information that requires higher-level analysis. This filter prevents the higher-level information processing systems becoming overloaded. Information not selected for higher-level processing remains only briefly in the filter and is then lost.

In the dichotic listening task, we are able to select the appropriate message by means of its most obvious physical characteristic, that is, the particular ear it enters. This represents the lowest level of processing. The non-shadowed task is rejected by the filter and is not therefore processed at a higher level, so we know nothing of its meaning.

Activity

Before we evaluate Broadbent's theory consider the following question. There are occasions, at parties or in a busy public house, when, although we are 'engrossed' in an interesting conversation, we may suddenly be distracted by something said in another conversation. What type of 'message' may this entail, and why does this contradict Broadbent's theory?

Evaluation

The following research findings cannot be accommodated by Broadbent's filter theory.

1. Moray (1959) demonstrated that when people are presented with their own name in an unattended message, they detect it on approximately one third of the trials. This implies that analysis for meaning has taken place **before** selection occurred.
2. Treisman (1964) asked bilingual participants to shadow a message in one channel whilst the same message was presented to the unattended channel in their second language. Participants were aware that the second message was the same as the first, indicating that they must have been analysing the **meaning** of the unattended message.

Despite these criticisms, Broadbent's theory has formed the basis for the later theories considered below, so he must be credited with the basic theoretical model.

Treisman's attenuation theory (1964)

Treisman has proposed a modification of the filter theory. She argues that information in the unattended message is **attenuated**, in other words, it is reduced in intensity. According to Treisman, an unattended message, identified on the basis of physical characteristics, is not entirely excluded from further analysis but is 'toned down' so that it does not interfere with the attended message. It does, however, receive some higher-level meaningful analysis but this often does not reach the threshold level necessary to reach consciousness. After analysis in terms of physical characteristics, analysis of words takes place. If the words in the unattended message present a sufficiently strong signal (if, for example, they have emotional importance to the individual), they will receive attention. This accounts for the fact that participants in Moray's and Treisman's studies noticed certain of the words that were presented in the non-attended channel. It also explains why we are liable to hear our own name being uttered in cocktail party conversations and why we notice emotionally charged messages such as 'help'.

Evaluation

1. Treisman's model can account for the data both from experimental studies and from everyday situations.
2. Treisman does not, however, provide any details of how the process of attenuation actually operates.

Deutsch and Deutsch's late selection model (1963)

Deutsch and Deutsch proposed that all stimuli are fully processed before any filtering takes place. We can only respond to the limited number of stimuli at once, since survival depends on selecting the most important stimuli and responding to them quickly. But this does not mean that we have not noticed the other stimuli. If a message, even an unattended one, is pertinent to us it will pass into our attention. This model suggests that we need attention not because we cannot process all incoming stimuli, but because we cannot **respond** to them all. The fewer stimuli we see or hear, the more likely we are to process all of them completely.

Evaluation

Some critics feel that it is implausible that we analyse **all** information before any selection is made. This would involve a huge amount of unnecessary processing.

The three theories can be summarised as follows:

Broadbent: unattended messages are blocked before analysis for meaning.
Treisman: unattended messages are attenuated before analysis for meaning.
Deutsch and Deutsch: unattended messages are analysed for meaning before any selection occurs.

Activity

Many questions on attention, perception and memory ask you to consider whether these processes can be considered as **information processing**. Before you go any further, consider this in the context of attention. What exactly do we mean by 'information processing'? How are we processing information when we, quite unconsciously, pay attention to some stimuli while seeming to ignore others? At the end of this subsection, the Question with guidance notes considers this issue, but it's well worth your while to think about it before you read the discussion. Make sure you can understand it in the context of **perception** and **memory** as well.

A compromise position

There is still no agreement amongst the theorists as to when selection of input occurs, but the following concept offers a compromise between the late selection and the attenuation theory.

Johnston and Heinz (1978) argue that selection can occur at a number of stages during information processing and that the exact timing of selection depends upon the demands of the task. For example, if you are told to attend only to a female voice, a task which depends only on the physical properties of the stimulus, selection will occur very early in the processing. If, however, you are required to attend to certain words or meanings, selection will take place much later.

Johnston and Heinz (1979), in a study investigating timing of selection, presented target and non-target words to both ears of participants. Target words were those which participants were required to repeat, non-target words were those to which they were not required to attend. In one condition, the target words were presented in a male voice and the non-target words in a female voice. In the other condition, all words were presented in the male voice. In the first condition, non-target words should be discarded at an early stage of processing, as the individual only has to pay attention to the physical aspects of the message. Conversely, in the second condition selection should take place later, as the participant has to pay attention to meaning before discarding the non-target words. Findings indicated that participants in the second condition had greater recall of non-target words than the participants in the first condition, presumably because they had processed non-target words to a higher level. This supports Johnston and Heinz's proposal that the timing of selection depends on the **type of task** required. Nevertheless, it is not clear how this relates to everyday situations in which we are not provided with target and non-target words.

Preparing for the exam

Key terms

attention
attenuated
binaural tasks

dichotic tasks
information processing
semantic

Types of exam question

1. A consideration of studies of selective attention.
2. An appreciation of how information processing can be used to explain attention.

Self-test questions

1. What problem was Cherry investigating?
2. Briefly explain what is meant by:
   a a binaural task
   b a dichotic task.
3. What aspects of an unattended message are we likely to notice?
4. According to the following theories, how much do we process information before we attend to it?
   a Broadbent's filter theory
   b Treisman's attenuation theory
   c Deutsch and Deutsch's late selection model
   d Johnston and Heinz's compromise suggestion.

Exam question with guidance notes

Many cognitive psychologists interpret attention as information processing. Use experimental evidence to consider this approach.

(25 marks)
AEB (1989)

Information processing simply means going through a series of stages in order to select, organise and interpret incoming information. As mentioned earlier, it can apply to the way we *memorise* or *perceive* or *attend to* information. So, in terms of this particular essay, you are simply being asked to consider the theories which attempt to account for the stages we go through when we attend to certain incoming information while discarding the remainder.

• This essay could be introduced with reference in Cherry's 'cocktail party' effect as this sets the scene for the problems which need to be addressed. The question is the *extent* to which we process peripheral information: some argue that we process it at a very minimum level, others that we process it to a high level in order to know what is worth discarding and what is worth responding to.

• Go through the experimental evidence and then describe and evaluate each theory in turn – Broadbent, Treisman, Deutsch and Deutsch.

- All the theories explain attention in terms of information processing – they differ in their view of the *stage at which* information processing of peripheral (unattended) material occurs.

Additional exam questions

1. Discuss the contribution that research on information processing has made to an understanding of attention. **(25 marks)**
   AEB (1992)

2. **a** Describe techniques used in the experimental study of selective attention. **(5 marks)**
   b Describe and evaluate *two* theories or models of selective attention. **(20 marks)**
   AEB (1993)

3. **a** What is meant by attention? **(5 marks)**
   b Discuss ways in which attention has been investigated. **(15 marks)**
   JMB (1989)

4

Social Cognition

AEB	NEAB	O & C	**Topic**	Date attempted	Date completed	Self Assessment
✓	✓	✓	**Interpersonal Perception**			
✓	✓	✓	**Attribution Theory**			
✓	✓	✓	**The Social Self**			
✓	✓	✓	**Attitudes and Attitude Change**			
✓	✓	✓	**Prejudice and Discrimination**			

4.1 Interpersonal perception

The study of interpersonal perception is concerned with the processes we use to form impressions of other people. Because we receive so much complex information, we all have to be selective in what we notice, learn and remember and we need to simplify by using mental short-cuts; these short-cuts have been called **heuristics**. This simplification is absolutely necessary: we could not possibly cope with all the social information with which we are bombarded without some simplification and organisation, but the strategies we use can encourage bias and inaccuracies in person perception. We use many heuristic strategies when processing information; we will consider **four** main ones:

1. **Implicit personality theory**
2. **The halo effect**
3. **Stereotyping**
4. **The primacy effect.**

Implicit personality theory

Implicit personality theory refers to the notion that we all carry around with us an idea about **which personality characteristics are likely to go together**. For example, it may be considered that a humorous person will also be good natured, generous and sensitive. So if somebody displays humour on an initial meeting, other aspects of their personality can be **inferred**. Such a process allows a little information to go a long way and enables us to form impressions quickly.

Asch (1946) argued that some personality characteristics are more important than others in impression formation. He presented a control group of participants with a list of these words to describe an imaginary person:

intelligent, skilful, industrious, determined, practical, cautious.

Four other groups received the same list but with the addition of one word from these four:

warm, cold, polite, blunt.

When the list included 'warm', the general impression was one of a generous, humorous, sociable, popular person. When 'cold' was included, the overall impression was quite different. However, the inclusion of 'polite' or 'blunt' appeared to make little difference to the overall impression. Asch concluded that 'warm' and 'cold' are **central traits**, traits likely to have an important effect on how someone is perceived, whereas 'polite' and 'blunt' are not very influential and are referred to as **peripheral traits**.

Kelley (1950) experimented to see how a 'warm' or 'cold' description might influence the behaviour of student participants toward a person said to possess one of these characteristics. Before the arrival of a lecturer who had been invited to speak to them, students were told a little about him. Some were told that he was 'rather warm', others that he was 'rather cold'. In a discussion following the lecture, Kelley noted how often students interacted with the lecturer. It was found that the participants who had received the 'warm' description engaged in more interaction with the lecturer and described him in more favourable terms than did those who had received the 'cold' description.

Activity

How do the methods used by Asch and Kelley differ? Which do you consider to be more 'true to life'? There are obvious advantages in trying to make a study reflect a real-life situation; are there any drawbacks in this method? Include this in your evaluation of the studies.

The halo effect

The halo effect is a form of implicit personality theory. If our initial impression of a person is generally positive there is a tendency for this to influence the way we perceive their subsequent behaviour: we view everything they do in a favourable light. A similar process occurs if our initial impression is negative.

Wilson and Nisbett (1977) arranged for participants to watch an interview with a Belgian professor who adjusted his personality to appear likeable or unlikeable. Not surprisingly, the participants preferred the likeable professor, but they also preferred his appearance and accent though these aspects obviously did not alter.

The halo effect probably occurs because people like to have a **consistent** view of others. It is easier to view other people as either good or bad rather than a mixture of the two: we know how to respond to them, and what to expect from them.

Activity

There are many examples of the halo effect in the media: it should perhaps be a cause for concern that some children's books and television programmes portray a world conveniently divided into 'goodies' and 'baddies', with the 'baddies' being singularly ugly and the 'goodies' extraordinarily beautiful. Can you think of any such examples?

Stereotypes

A stereotype is a widely held belief that all members of a particular group share certain important characteristics (which may be negative, positive or neutral). Thus our judgement of an individual can begin when we can identify them as belonging to a particular group – be it a grouping based on sex, race, age, religion or sexual orientation – and does not require any personal knowledge.

Katz and Braly (1933) conducted a classic of ethnic stereotyping. Students were asked to choose five or six personality characteristics from a list of 84 trait words to describe various ethnic groups (Americans, Turks, Jews, English, Japanese, Irish, Germans, Italians, Chinese and Negroes). The results showed that there was considerable agreement about which traits befitted each ethnic group. Negroes were described as 'superstitious', Germans as 'stolid' and Italians as 'musical'.

Gilbert (1951) repeated the study and found far less agreement among the participants. Karlins *et al.* (1969) repeated the study again and discovered a higher level of stereotyping than in 1951, but the stereotypes were far less extreme than those expressed in 1933, and more likely to be positive.

In interpreting the results, we must take into account the fact that in 1951 and 1969 the students were more aware of the issues surrounding racial

stereotypes and prejudice and more likely to give socially acceptable answers.

Stereotypes allow us to make a little information about a person go a long way, but they do represent a serious social problem because they are often ill-founded. They distort judgements, determine the amount of contact that will be made with members of a particular group and do not necessarily disappear with familiarity.

The primacy effect

The **first information** that we receive about another person tends to have more influence over the impression formed than does later information: this is known as the primacy effect.

Asch (1946) presented two groups of people with lists of six adjectives describing another person. Group **A** were presented with the following list:

intelligent, industrious, impulsive, critical, stubborn, envious.

Group **B** were presented with the same list but in the opposite order. Participants were asked to choose adjectives which they felt best described the imaginary person. A primacy effect was observed. Group **A**, whose list had begun with positive characteristics, described the person much more positively than did group **B**, whose list began with negative characteristics.

Jones *et al.* (1968) presented participants with a film of a student answering multiple choice questions. They were not told how many of the 30 questions had been answered correctly; in fact it was 15. All of them saw the entire film, but it was adjusted so that one group saw most of the correct responses being made at the start of the film, while the other group saw most being made near the end. The former group gave an average estimate of 20.6 correct answers, whereas the latter group estimated just a 12.5 average. Once again, the primacy effect is clearly illustrated.

Evidence suggests that the primacy effect is particularly strong if a negative first impression is made.

Activity

Think about why a negative first impression may be harder to change than a good first impression. How do you feel when a person you haven't met before is overbearing or rude? What may happen if you, after meeting them a few more times, decide that they are quite nice after all and make some friendly overtures to them?

The primacy effect may be due to several factors:

* We pay more attention to information when we are first presented with it
* Having formed an impression we are reluctant to alter it, and tend to ignore or reinterpret conflicting information.

The primacy effect can be reduced or even avoided if:

* People are forewarned about the biasing effect of first impressions
* People are asked to pay close attention to all available information
* After an unrelated activity has taken place, contradictory information is presented. In this case the **recency effect** is likely to occur; that is, the most recent information is taken into consideration.

Self-fulfilling prophecies

Most of the research on interpersonal perception which we have considered so far is concerned with the one-way process of how we form impressions of other people. However, it is important for us to recognise that these impressions can have a significant effect on how people then **respond to us**. Sociologists refer to 'labelling theory' to describe the effect which being labelled or stereotyped (for example as 'car mechanic' or 'troublemaker' or 'divorcee') can have on how others react to you. These labels can operate as **self-fulfilling prophecies** in that, once we have labelled someone, our behaviour towards them may make them behave in such a way as to confirm our original impression.

Word, Zanna and Cooper (1974) showed how subtle and serious the effect of self-fulfilling

prophecies can be. These researchers carefully trained black and white confederates to behave in the same way when being interviewed for a job. It was found that the interviewers, all of whom were white, behaved differently towards the black and white applicants; for example, white applicants were interviewed for longer and received more eye contact. The researchers then carefully analysed the way in which the two groups of confederate interviewees had been treated and then trained interviewers to behave towards applicants in two different ways – ways which precisely matched how the black and white applicants had previously been treated. They then interviewed white participants, treating one group in the way the previous white applicants had been treated and the other group in the manner in which the previous black applicants had been treated. The performance at interview of all the applicants was assessed by independent judges. Those who were treated as 'black' performed worse than those who had been treated as 'white'. These results obviously suggest that interviewers behave towards black applicants in such a way as to elicit a poor interview performance from them in comparison to white applicants.

Activity

Describe how the self-fulfilling prophecy can explain why certain children, especially girls and members of certain ethnic groups, may underachieve in education. You can use this in an essay on various other parts of the syllabus: intelligence, gender, and prejudice.

Importance of bias

It should be clear from this research that, essential though mental short-cuts such as stereotyping are, they can lead to bias. The tendency to respond in routinised, unthinking ways has been appropriately labelled mindlessness (Langer, 1989). It is important that we attempt to consider carefully the way in which stereotypes and other short-cuts can be damaging, in order that we live more meaningful lives in relation to the people around us.

Preparing for the exam

Key terms

central traits
halo effect
heuristics
implicit personality theory

interpersonal perception
primacy effect
self-fulfilling prophecy
stereotyping

Types of exam question

1. What psychologists have learned about the process of interpersonal perception.
2. The role of stereotypes in impression formation.

1. Why do we need to use heuristics in interpersonal perception?
2. What are 'central traits'?
3. What is the halo effect?
4. Briefly describe the Katz and Braly (1933) study of ethnic stereotyping.
5. The Katz and Braly study was repeated in 1951 and 1969. How did results change and what are the likely reasons for this?
6. Suggest *two* possible reasons why the primacy effect occurs.
7. How can the primacy effect be reduced?
8. What is meant by the term 'self-fulfilling prophecy', and how does it relate to the heuristics used in interpersonal perception?

Exam question with guidance notes

Critically consider the role played by stereotypes in how we perceive other people.

(25 marks)
AS level AEB (1991)

- Begin by *defining* stereotypes and mention their purpose in reducing cognitive overload.
- Describe how they influence our perceptions of other people: it is very important here to make reference to *research*.
- The other heuristics are relevant: the halo effect is a form of stereotyping (into good and bad); first impressions are based on stereotypes, as is the implicit personality theory. All of these processes have an important influence on our *perception* of the social world.
- Mention that stereotyping can be the basis of *prejudice*.
- Finally, it is crucial to include the *self-fulfilling prophecy*: our stereotypes influence the way we treat other people which, in turn, affects the way they react to us. Again, include research to support your argument. You do not have to restrict this to research mentioned in this chapter: the Core Study of Rosenhan (1973) in section 9.3 is a striking example of the operation of

self-fulfilling prophesies based on stereotypes of the 'mentally ill'.
*   Conclude with reference to the uses and drawbacks of stereotyping.

Additional exam question

How do we form impressions of other people? Refer to both theory and empirical research in your answer. **(20 marks)**

NEAB Specimen Question

4.2 The process of attribution

Humans constantly and unthinkingly speculate on the possible causes of happenings, and especially on those that directly concern them. Thus, we ponder on the way we or others have behaved, and try to find logical reasons for such behaviour. Why did my boyfriend break off the relationship? Why did I fail that exam? Why was Azima so nice to me earlier on?

Fritz Heider, the founder of attribution theory, suggested that people often try to decide whether someone's behaviour is the result of either

(a)   internal causes: the person's disposition or personality, or

(b)   external causes: situational, outside factors.

For example, suppose somebody snaps at you: you may attribute this to the fact that they are a bad tempered, unpleasant person, thus making an **internal** attribution; or to the fact that they must have had a particularly bad day, an **external** attribution.

Activity

1.   Are the following attributions internal or external?
    a   I'm late because the 8.30 bus was cancelled.
    b   Paul didn't revise because he's lazy.
    c   Mary cleaned her room because her brother was due to visit.
2.   Sometimes, when people have extra-marital affairs, they say that they did not mean it to happen, it was in no way planned. By making this comment, what type of attribution are they encouraging the listener to make and why?

Theories of attribution

Theories of attribution are concerned with understanding and explaining how people attribute causes to their own and other people's behaviour.

Correspondent inference theory: Jones and Davis (1965)

When someone behaves in a certain way, what helps you determine whether the behaviour **corresponds** to the disposition of the person? When do we feel confident that a person's actions tell us something about his or her personality characteristics? Jones considers that, although many factors are taken into consideration, **expectations** are particularly important.

When people behave in a way that is expected: by crying at a funeral or dressing smartly for an interview, for instance, we draw few conclusions about them as a person. We assume they are behaving in that way because the situation demands it.

On the other hand, if their behaviour is unexpected, for example, they are crying in class or have dressed in their best suit to attend a football match, then we are far more likely to attribute their behaviour to personality characteristics.

There are many factors on which we base expectations. Some of the most salient are:

1.   **Social desirability:** we expect people to behave according to social norms (dressing appropriately, queueing and so on)
2.   **Roles:** we expect nurses to be sympathetic to patients and deferential to doctors
3.   **Particular settings:** we expect people to be cheerful at parties and distressed at funerals.

To sum up, we tend to attribute behaviour to personality when that behaviour is unexpected because it violates social norms or simply because it is unusual.

Activity

What kind of attributions are you likely to make of the following unexpected behaviour, and what consequences might the attributions have for the actor?

a   A politician, during a prominent campaign, loses his temper and tries to thump the journalist who is questioning him

b   Your psychology teacher bursts into tears when reading your essay

c   At an interview for a job which is described as 'requiring a person who enjoys working in a busy, hectic atmosphere', the candidate announces that she feels most comfortable when working alone in a quiet atmosphere.

Kelley's covariance theory

Covariation is nothing more than the tendency for two things to occur at **the same time**. According to Kelley, we look at how events **go together** or **covary** and then we tend to assume that if two events often occur together, one causes the other. For example, if you get a headache every time you eat chocolate, then headaches and chocolates covary, and you blame the chocolate for the headache, even though you may be wrong.

According to Kelley, we rely on **three** kinds of information in an effort to draw conclusions about the causes of behaviour:

- consensus
- consistency
- distinctiveness.

We will explain these by examples.

Imagine we are interested in explaining why a particular student (Phil) is asleep in a psychology lesson. In deciding why this has happened, we rely upon the following information sources:

- **Consensus** refers to the extent to which other members of the psychology class behave in a similar way. If they all sleep through the class, we can say there is a high consensus. If Phil is the only one asleep, then there is low consensus.
- **Consistency** refers to the regularity of Phil's psychology slumbers. If he falls asleep in all his psychology lessons, then there is high consistency, but if it has occurred on only one occasion, there is low consistency.
- **Distinctiveness** refers to how Phil behaves in other similar situations. If he sleeps in all his classes, then there is low distinctiveness (because his behaviour is not distinct to psychology). If, however, he is wide awake in his other lessons, then there is high distinctiveness.

According to Kelley, certain patterns of consistency, consensus and distinctiveness information lead us to make external attributions, whereas other patterns encourage internal attributions. For example, a combination of:

- High consensus (everybody is asleep in the lesson)
- High consistency (Phil always sleeps in these lessons)
- High distinctiveness (Phil is wide awake in other lessons)

leads us to make an **external** attribution – either the lesson is extremely dull or it takes place in the middle of the night.

If there is:

- Low consensus (no one else sleeps in the lesson),
- High consistency (Phil regularly falls asleep in psychology)
- Low distinctiveness (Phil sleeps in all his lessons)

then we would be led to make an **internal** attribution – Phil is not interested, lazy or has some condition that renders him very tired.

Activity

Consider the following example: you are walking down the local high street when a man rushes up to you with a bunch of flowers and declares his undying love for you; not an event that has ever happened to you before. You have seen him do this on several other occasions: the object of his passion has been a 70 year old woman, an ice cream man, a nun and a famous football player. Is this behaviour towards you displaying:

- High or low consistency (has he shown this behaviour to you before?)
- High or low distinctiveness (is this behaviour distinct towards you or shown to others?)
- High or low consensus (do other people behave like this towards you?)

What kind of attribution would you make?

Evaluation

Although laboratory studies offer some support for Kelley's theory, his model does not take account of all aspects of the attribution process:

- People do not draw on the three types of information equally, as covariation theory would suggest. Research indicates that distinctiveness is seen as the most important source of information, consistency is the second most important and least attention is paid to consensus.
- Some research indicates that people do not just seek information from the three sources suggested by Kelley but look for additional information about the personality of the actor (Garland and White, 1975).
- Kelley's model tends to assume that we are all logical, rational and systematic in the way we decide causes of behaviour, but often we are not.

Kelley has recognised some of the limitations of his theory and put forward an additional model which covers most situations in which we do not consider consensus, consistency and distinctiveness.

Causal schemata theory: Kelley (1973)

In order to use consensus, consistency and distinctiveness, you have to be reasonably familiar with the person. Nevertheless, we do not hesitate to make attributions of cause based on only one observation. Kelley suggests that we have preconceived notions about the most likely causes of

behaviour based on our ideas about how people in general behave and why. He calls these ideas **causal schemata**. One important causal schema is the tendency to jump to the most obvious conclusion and discount all others. If a plane crashes in fog, we assume the crash was caused by fog, even though it could have been due to other factors. The tendency to discount any other possible causes of behaviour once we have identified the most obvious one is known as the **discounting principle** and demonstrates the urge we all have to simplify social perceptions.

Attributional biases

Our attempts to arrive at an accurate and logical attribution of behaviour are not always successful. Under some circumstances, the attributional process will be biased. The following represent some of the more common forms of attributional bias or error:

The fundamental attribution error

Evidence indicates that we are much more likely to decide that a piece of behaviour is due to a person's disposition rather than to situational factors. This tendency to **overestimate dispositional causes and underestimate situational ones** is such a common and pervasive error that it is known as the **fundamental attribution error**.

Ross *et al.* (1977) arranged a study in which confederates in a general knowledge quiz were assigned the role of either questioner or answerer, the former being allowed to devise the questions. Participants, acting as the audience, were later asked to compare and assess the general knowledge of those who asked and those who answered questions. Even though they were aware of the arrangements, they invariably rated the questioner as having the greater knowledge. The assessors failed to take into account the advantage given to questioners by the structure of the game, and attributed the questioners' abilities to set posers which others could not answer to their superior general knowledge.

The actor–observer effect

As we have seen, when we attribute a cause to the behaviour of others, we tend to make dispositional attributions. However, when we attribute cause to our own behaviour, we are likely to make a situational attribution.

For an experimental demonstration of the actor/observer effect see the Core Study of this section (p. 83). ·

The self-serving bias

We tend to make dispositional judgements for our successes and situational ones for our failures. In other words, we take credit for successes and blame circumstances for our failures.

Zuckerman (1979), in an analysis of many studies, found that people tended to claim that success was due to ability or effort while failures were attributed to outside factors.

The seriousness of the consequences

The more serious, drastic or important the consequences of an action are, the more likely we are to attribute the cause to dispositional factors.

Walster (1966) presented participants with an account of an incident in which a parked car rolled down a hill; they were told it had one of three consequences:

(i) Little damage was done
(ii) The car collided with another and caused some damage, but only to property
(iii) The car crashed into a shop injuring the shopkeeper and a small child;

Participants were then asked to indicate how responsible they felt the car owner was for the incident.

It was found that as the seriousness of the consequences increased, so did the extent to which the owner was held responsible.

The ways in which we attribute causes to our own and others' behaviour has very wide ranging implications: the way individuals make attributions concerning the way others treat them, about their successes and failures and about such feelings as depression, all affect how well they function in the social world, and how happy they are in it.

Core Study

Behaviour as seen by the actor and as seen by the observer: R.E. Nisbett, C. Caputo, P. Legant and J. Marecek (1973)

Jones and Nisbett (1971) proposed that actors (people themselves) are likely to attribute their behaviour to situational factors. On the other hand, observers are inclined to attribute it to **dispositional** qualities (stable attitudes and personality traits). This study presents three separate demonstrations of the different views of behaviour taken by the actor and the observer.

Study 1

The study used female students who were divided into 33 groups of four people. Each group consisted of two genuine subjects and two confederates. The confederates and one of the subjects (the actor) were asked to volunteer to serve as weekend hosts to the wives of potential financial backers for the university. They were offered payment of either $.50 per hour or of $1.50 per hour for their work. The second real subject in each group was assigned the role of observer.

The two confederates always volunteered, serving as models and agents of social pressure. After the real subject (the actor) had indicated whether or not she would volunteer, both she and the observer were asked to indicate, on a scale of 0–8, the extent to which each of the following motives applied to her:

1. I wanted to help the university and the Human Development Institute.
2. The activities sounded as if they would be interesting.
3. It was a chance to earn some money.
4. I thought that meeting the people would be fun.
5. The other girls seemed interested in it and that made me think it would be worthwhile.
6. There was a lot of social pressure to volunteer.

The actor (the subject who had been asked to volunteer) was then also asked: 'On a scale of 0–8, how likely do you think it is that you would also volunteer to canvass for the United Fund?'

Similarly, the observer was asked: 'On a scale of 0–8, how likely do you think it is that the girl you watched would also volunteer to canvass for the United Fund?'

Expectations

Observers were expected to attribute an actor's compliance or non-compliance to dispositional factors rather than situational ones and to expect the actor's behaviour to generalise to other situations.

Results

Money was an important incentive. Of the 17 actors offered $.50 per hour, only 4 volunteered, whereas of the 16 offered $1.50, 11 volunteered. However, in their ratings, the importance of money was underestimated by both the actor and the observer – putting it below the desire to help, interest of the activities and fun of meeting people.

The results show that the observer is more likely than the actor to make dispositional attributions. If the actor volunteered as a weekend host, observers saw her as more likely to volunteer to help with the United Fund than those who did not volunteer. Actors were less likely to make this prediction.

In conclusion, it appears that observers are inclined to make dispositional inferences from behaviour in circumstances when the actors infer nothing about disposition.

Study 2

This study was concerned with the differences in actor/observer perceptions when the actor is well known to the observer.

30 male student subjects were asked to write about why they liked their present girl friend and why they had chosen their college major. They were also asked to write a similar account of their best

friend's choice of girlfriend and major.

External reasons included: 'She's a relaxing person; chemistry is a high-paying field.' Dispositional reasons included: 'I need someone I can relax with; I want to make a lot of money.'

As before, subjects were significantly more likely to give external reasons for their choices and dispositional reasons for their friend's choices.

Study 3

In this study, it was found that people ascribe more personality traits to other people than to themselves.

Conclusion

All three studies provide evidence in support of the hypothesis that actors attribute cause to the situation while observers attribute cause to the disposition of the actor.

The researchers suggest that this is because we prefer to see ourselves as free agents, able to control events. If our actions are dictated by traits and overriding dispositions, we would have less flexibility and freedom. Our own control and freedom is enhanced if we see others as possessing traits which will make their behaviour more stable and predictable.

QUESTIONS

1. a   In the Nisbett study on attributions, who were the subjects and how were they chosen?

    (2 marks)

    b   How did the experimenter assess the 'perceived reasons for volunteering'?

    (2 marks)

    Oxford and Cambridge Specimen Paper

2. Briefly summarise the findings of Study 1.

3. What reasons did subjects give for their choice of girl friend and college major? How did this differ from the reasons they attributed to the choices made by their best friends?

Preparing for the exam

Key terms

actor-observer effect

attribution

causal schemata theory

consensus

consistency

correspondent inference theory

covariation

discounting principle

dispositional factors

distinctiveness

external causes

fundamental attribution error

internal causes

self-serving bias

situational factors

social desirability

Types of exam question

1. Evaluation of the main theories or approaches.
2. A knowledge of attributional errors and biases with research evidence.
3. Practical applications of attribution theory.

Self-test questions

1. Heider claimed that we try to determine if behaviour is due to internal or external attributions. What does this mean?
2. According to Jones and Davis, what is the role of expectation in attribution?
3. Kelley's covariation model argues that we use *three* kinds of information to make attributions. What are they?
4. Briefly outline *two* criticisms of Kelley's theory.
5. What is the discounting principle? Illustrate your answer with an example.

Exam question with guidance notes

How has knowledge of attribution theories helped psychologists to understand human behaviour? (25 marks)

AEB (1989)

The examiners' report commented that candidates failed to focus on the crucial element of this question, that is, how theories have helped psychologists understand human behaviour.

You need to answer this with reference to the specific *theories*:

Jones – we use knowledge about how we expect people to behave.

Kelley – we use consistency, consensus and distinctiveness *but* not on every occasion, for example, we often use the discounting principle.

It is very important to include the *biases* we make in attributions, each one of which serves a purpose.

- The fundamental attribution error (examples of this can be drawn from research in various areas of psychology, such as Milgram, Zimbardo and studies on helping, see Chapter 5): people are more predictable and more accountable for their actions if behaviour is caused by disposition.

- Self-serving bias: protects our self-esteem.
- Actor/observer effect: when accounting for our own behaviour, we are fully aware of situational factors.
- Seriousness of consequences: makes the world appear fair.

The functions served by these biases all shed light on understanding human behaviour.

Additional exam question

Critically discuss attributional approaches in social psychology.   **(25 marks)**
AEB (1990)

4.3 The social self

Murphy (1947): suggests that 'The self is the individual as known to the individual.'

It includes what we know about ourselves and how we evaluate ourselves physically, morally, spiritually, materially and in relation to family, friends and work associates.

The self-concept

The self-concept is generally considered to comprise **three** components:

Self-image

This refers to our perception of ourselves, that is the kind of person **we think we are**. Kuhn (1954) asked people to describe themselves by providing twenty responses to the question, 'Who am I?' Responses could generally be categorised into **three** types:

- Those describing social roles: 'I am a mother'
- Those describing personality characteristics: 'I am conscientious'
- Those describing physical characteristics: 'I am fat'.

Evidence suggests that young adults provide more descriptions concerned with body image than do older people.
   Arnhoff and Damianopoulos (1962) showed men, aged either twenty or forty, a set of photographs of men dressed only in their shorts with blanked-out faces, one of which was their own. The twenty year olds were much more successful at identifying their own photograph than were the forty year olds, indicating a greater concern amongst the younger group with body image (see Figure 4.1).

Self-esteem

This is the evaluative aspect of the self-concept and refers to the degree to which **we like and value ourselves**. The development of self-esteem is considered in Chapter 8.

The ideal self

This represents the kind of person **we would like to be**. If our self-image and ideal self are close, then we are likely to have a high self-esteem. If, on the other hand, our self-image is quite different from our ideal self, our self-esteem will be low.

Sources of self

Self-information comes from a wide variety of sources, of which **three** of the most important are:

1. Reaction of others

The term **symbolic interactionism** has been used to express the fact that our self-concept is, at least in part, created by our interpretations of the symbolic gestures (words, actions, facial expressions and the like) expressed by others during our interactions with them.

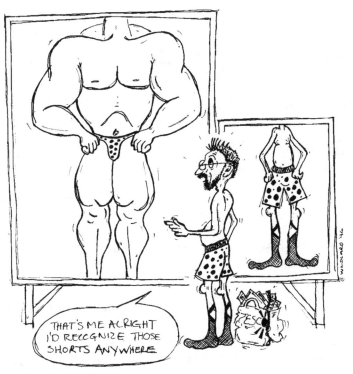

Figure 4.1 A deluded sense of self (cartoon drawn by Roy Hunt)

Cooley (1902) coined the term 'looking glass self' to express the idea that our self-concept is significantly influenced by what we believe **others think of us**. We build up our self-concept by interpretation of the gestures, words, actions and expressions of others as we interact with them on a daily basis.

Mead (1934) believed that because we are anxious to be positively evaluated we learn to anticipate the reactions of others by **imagining ourselves in their position**. In this way, behaviour and the self-concept are guided by society even in the absence of others, because internal control is based on how we expect others to react.

Goffman argued that in any given social situation we endeavour to fulfil the role which is **expected of us**. Goffman's work is discussed later in this section.

2. Social comparison

Many aspects of self are only meaningful in **comparison with others**. For example, if you get 50 per cent in an exam, you immediately want to know how other students have performed, in order to evaluate your own performance. Festinger (1954) argued that those whom we choose for comparison are likely to be similar to ourselves on relevant attributes, such as age and experience.

3. Observing our own behaviour

Bem (1970) suggests that, in certain circumstances, mainly when we are uncertain about how we feel, we understand our self by observing our **own behaviour**. If we observe ourselves behaving in a cool, calm manner in an emergency, we can conclude that we are a calm, level-headed person. Thus, we attribute causes to our behaviours in much the same way that we attribute causes to the behaviours of others: we do not always have 'inside knowledge'. Bem recognises that people do not always base their self-concept on their actions.

Lepper *et al.* (1973) offered some children a reward for drawing with felt-tip pens whilst others were simply given an opportunity to use them. Several weeks later all the children were observed in a situation where they had the opportunity to use felt-tips if they wanted to, but no reward was given. The group who had been rewarded showed less interest than the other group in the pens. The children may have attributed their earlier enjoyment of the pens to the fact that they were rewarded for using them rather to any intrinsic pleasure.

Activity

What sources of information do we rely upon for the following:

1. Deciding whether we are tall or short for our age?
2. Estimating how popular we are?
3. Deciding how we feel about spiders?

The accuracy of the self-concept

Greenwald (1980) identified **three** ways in which the information about the self can be biased:

Egocentricity

We tend to think that others see, think and feel in the same way as we do, and that we ourselves are more important in **influencing** others than we really are. Most people give themselves more credit than they are due for tasks achieved in group work (Thompson and Kelley, 1981).

Cognitive conservatism

We are reluctant to change our self-concept, so we tend to avoid information that may cause us to **re-examine** ourselves.

The self-serving bias

Markus argues that we will go to great lengths to view ourselves positively and protect our self-esteem. There are a wide range of self-enhancing processes including:

- **Downward social comparison**: we tend to compare ourselves with others who have in some way achieved less than we have, be it exam marks, marital happiness or weight loss
- **Selective forgetting**: we tend to forget our failures and remember our successes
- **Selective acceptance of feed-back**: we tend to regard the source of negative feedback as invalid in some way
- **Self-handicapping**: we may set up 'excuses' to help cope with failure, should it happen.

Impression management and self-presentation

In almost every social situation, we are concerned with how other people perceive us and we endeavour to establish a positive image through a process known as impression management or self-presentation. Self-presentation has several goals: we may at times like to appear competent, powerful, demure, helpless or in need of sympathy.

Goffman (1959) argued that, in the course of our social interactions, we take on different roles and perform them in a way similar to that of actors on a stage. We put on a performance appropriate to the particular audience and the impression we wish to make. In order to do this, we have a variety of means at our disposal, including the actual words we use, the tone of voice, the movements and the facial expression.

Self-presentation techniques refer to methods by which we try to create a certain impression. Table 4.1 describes and gives examples of some such strategies:

Table 4.1 Self-presentation techniques

Tactic	Description	Example
Self-promotion	Emphasising the positive aspects of oneself	'At school, I was in the top set in maths'
Ingratiation	Promises and flattery	'John really fancies you, you know'
Basking in reflected glory	Associating with successful, well-liked people	'One of my students was in the Olympic games'
Intimidation	Presenting an image of power and competence	'I won't mark your essay if you give it in late'
Supplication	Emphasising a weakness in order to elicit help or sympathy	'I'm terrified of electricity: can you please wire this plug for me?'

Activity

In Figure 4.2a–e, match the self-presentation tactic to the appropriate cartoon

Figure 4.2 Self-presentation tactics (Cartoons by Roy Hunt)

Core Study

Extended self: rethinking the so-called Negro self-concept: W. Nobles (1976)

Nobles suggests that social scientists exercise power, domination and oppression over the people they study in a manner comparable to the colonial masters and their subject people. Table 4.2 provides a comparison of political and scientific colonialism.

Psychology, particularly, has dominated and oppressed people from non-Western cultures. It presents itself, its conceptions and formulations as the standard by which all peoples of the world are to be understood.

Western psychology as a tool of oppression is clearly shown in the study of 'Negro' intelligence and self-concept. This study focuses on the so-called 'Negro' self-concept.

The Negro self-concept and scientific colonialism

Western psychology's study of the 'Negro' self-concept qualifies as scientific colonialism in the following ways:

1. Data is extracted from the community to be transformed into goods (books and articles)
2. The so-called 'Negro' self-concept is being studied by people who are not 'Negroes'
3. Researchers assume unlimited right of access to data and creation of information
4. The research produces profits for the researcher, not shared with the people being researched.

Table 4.2 Comparative colonialisms

Colonialism manifested by	Political colonialism	Scientific colonialism
1 Removal of wealth	Exportation of raw materials and wealth from colonies for the purpose of 'processing' it into manufactured wealth and/or goods.	Exporting raw data from a community for the purpose of 'processing' it into manufactured goods (i.e., books, articles, wealth, etc.)
2 Right of access and claim	Colonial Power believes it has the *right of access* and use for its own benefit anything belonging to the colonised people	Scientist believes he has unlimited *right of access* to any data source and any information belonging to the subject population
3 External Power Base	The centre of power and control over the colonised is located outside of colony itself	The centre of knowledge and information about a people or community located outside of the community or people themselves

Source: Journal of Black Psychology, 2(2) (February 1976). Reprinted with permission.

Nobles' chief concern, however, is that the view of the black self concept will be filtered through a Euro–American perspective and thus present an invalid view of black reality.

The European world is tempered by some guiding principles including (1) 'survival of the fittest' and (2) 'control over nature'. This translates to values and customs emphasising the rights of individuals, competition, independence and individuality.

The African World has different guiding principles:

1. 'Survival of the tribe' and
2. Being at 'one with nature'.

This is reflected in cooperation, interdependence, collective responsibility and groupness. It is also reflected in the concept of self. African philosophy leads to an extended view of self, centred on the identity of the people. This view is summed up by Mbiti (1970): 'I am because We are, and because We are, therefore I am.'

The effect of these different values on the understanding of the black self-concept is **critical**. The black self-concept has been understood from a European perspective. Nobles believes that it should be African based.

The black self-concept

Black people find themselves dominated by a European system of reality. Nobles argues that this leads to psychological confusion because it denies the most important aspect of the African conception of self – as an extended view encompassing the people they belong to.

Nobles suggests that this situation produces the pseudo-entity referred to as the 'Negro' – referring to an African person who denies the philosophical confusion. This means that the black person is made to believe, falsely, that their natural temperament and spirit is wrong and uncivilised, and that the Euro–American way is right and should be followed.

Without an acknowledgement of the African in black people, their self-concept cannot be fully understood.

QUESTIONS

1. In what ways does Nobles criticise the Western idea of self concept?   **(4 marks)**
    Oxford and Cambridge Specimen Paper
2. According to Nobles, what are the guiding principles of the European world and of the African world?
3. How do these principles relate to the differing concept of self held by Europeans and Africans?
4. What is the main conclusion of the paper?

Preparing for the exam

Key terms

basking in reflected glory
body image
cognitive conservatism
downward social comparison
egocentricity
ideal self
impression management
ingratiation
intimidation
'looking glass' self
selective acceptance of feedback
selective forgetting
self-concept

self-enhancing processes
self-esteem
self-handicapping
self-image
self-information
self-presentation
self-promotion
self-serving bias
social comparison
social roles
supplication
symbolic interactionism

Types of exam question

The types of questions asked fall into the following categories:

1. How the self forms as a result of interaction with others.
2. A consideration of impression management strategies.

Self-test questions

1. Give a definition of self.
2. Briefly describe the *three* components of the self-concept.
3. Identify three sources of self-information
4. What does the Arnhoff and Damianopoulos study suggest about body image?
5. What is symbolic interactionism?
6. Briefly describe Bem's theory of self-perception – use an example to illustrate your answer.
7. Briefly outline *two* reasons why our self-concept may be inaccurate.
8. Describe *two* impression management tactics, and give an example of each from your everyday experiences.

Exam question with guidance notes

Critically consider the view that the self is a social construct, formed on the basis of our interaction with others. (25 marks)

AEB (1992)

- First present the arguments and evidence that the self is a *social construct*.
- Make reference to *symbolic interactionism* and to the theories of Cooley, Mead and Goffman.
- Mention the need for *social comparison* and Festinger's argument that we have a need to see how we measure up to 'social reality'. Reference to

Schachter and Singer's study is relevant here (this is the Core Study in section 7.3).

- Describe the *alternative* view of self provided by Bem, using the study by Lepper to support this theory.

Additional exam question

Describe and evaluate psychological research concerning the strategies of self-presentation which people may use in social encounters. **(25 marks)**
AEB (1991)

4.4 Attitudes

1. **Bem (1979).** 'attitudes are likes and dislikes.'
2. **Allport (1935).** 'an attitude is a mental and neural state of readiness organised through experience, exerting a directive or dynamic influence upon the individual's response to all objects and situations with which it is related.'

The three components of attitudes

1. The **cognitive** component: what a person 'knows' and believes about the attitude object – for example, that snakes are dangerous and vicious (even though this is not necessarily true).
2. The **affective** component: what a person feels about the attitude object – horror and revulsion at the sight of snakes.
3. The **behavioural** component: concerned with the action taken by the person towards the attitude object – avoidance of contact with snakes, hysterical reaction if one is close.

Activity

Suggest appropriate affective, cognitive and behavioural components of the attitude: 'The benefits of exercise are greatly exaggerated.'

Attitudes and behaviour

People generally assume that attitudes and behaviour go together in a consistent manner, and that attitudes cause behaviour. However, behaviour is constrained and shaped by more than just attitudes, and is **by no means always consistent with them**.

1. **La Pierre (1934)** travelled around America with a young Chinese couple requesting service at 251 hotels, motels and restaurants. The oriental couple were discriminated against only once in the establishments visited. Nevertheless, a questionnaire circulated to all these establishments some time later revealed that 91 per cent of replies received indicated that they would not serve Chinese people. La Pierre suggested that this reflected a major inconsistency between behaviour and attitudes.
2. **Corey (1937)** found almost no relationship between attitudes towards cheating (as measured by questionnaire) and actual cheating behaviour.
3. **Wicker (1969)**, in a major review of studies looking at the relationship between attitudes and behaviour, concluded that attitudes were rarely related to behaviour.

Reasons why behaviour cannot be predicted from attitudes

1. **Behaviour depends on many factors other than attitudes:** in the La Pierre study, influential factors other than the attitude are likely to include:

- The money to be made by serving the Chinese couple
- Their respectability
- The possibility of an unpleasant encounter if they were refused service.

There are many occasions when situational pressures are strong and swamp the effect of the attitude.

2. **Inappropriate measurement of attitudes and behaviour:** La Pierre attempted to relate general attitudes (feeling towards Chinese people) to specific behaviours (serving this particular well-dressed, affluent, polite Chinese couple). Other studies have tried to relate specific attitudes to specific behaviours and have found greater correspondence.

3. **The personal relevance of the attitude:** only on issues which affect us directly are our attitudes likely to dictate behaviour. Sivacek and Crano (1982) asked college students their opinion about a proposal to raise the legal drinking age from 18 to 21 years. 80 per cent of the students were against the proposal, but it was only the students under 19 years of age, those who would have been affected by the new law, who were willing to campaign against the proposal.

4. **Social norms:** norms have an important influence on behaviour and may, on occasions, override an attitude. Minard (1952), in a study of race relations in a West Virginian mining town, found a great deal of prejudice and discrimination towards black people in ordinary social settings, but not in the mines, where black and white men worked alongside one another in friendship. Different social norms existed above and below ground and these norms had a stronger influence on behaviour than did attitudes.

Resolving the attitude/behaviour dilemma

If attitudes and behaviour are so inconsistent, then can we predict behaviour from attitude questionnaires? **Fishbein and Ajzen (1977)** suggest that this is possible if we are careful in our questionnaire construction; they make the following suggestions:

1. It is attitudes towards **behaviour** that should be measured, rather than attitudes towards objects. This is not a trivial distinction. Your attitude towards voting for John Major may not be the same as your attitude to John Major.

2. Attitudes towards specific behaviours (using a bottle bank) will provide the best predictor of

single acts (taking the bottles to the bottle bank); whereas more general attitudes (attitudes to ecology) are more useful predictors of **multiple behaviour** (buying recycled loo rolls, reducing the thermostat and so on).

Activity

1. Think about how Migram's work on obedience (section 5.3) and Ross *et al.*'s study demonstrating the fundamental attribution error (section 4.2) can be used to illustrate the point that behaviour does not always depend on attitudes. Can you think of other studies which demonstrate the same effect?

2. Think of an example from real life when attitudes and behaviour do not correspond. For example, we often pretend to be delighted with an unwanted and hideous gift – pink fluffy slippers, perhaps. Why? (This can be useful to **briefly** include in an essay to illustrate a point.)

Theories of attitude change

Cognitive dissonance theory

Festinger maintains that when people hold inconsistent beliefs, or if they act in a way which is contrary to their attitudes, they experience a feeling of psychological tension known as cognitive dissonance. This is unpleasant, and one way of reducing it is to undergo a change of attitude. If you apply for a job and don't get it, you have two dissonant cognitions (pieces of knowledge which are inconsistent):

- I liked that job
- I didn't get it.

You cannot change the fact that you didn't get the job so you change your **attitude to it**, for example:

- it wasn't that good
- it would have involved a lot of travel
- I'm not sure I would have got on with the people there, and so on.

Activity

A twenty year old student, who does very little work on his course because he thinks he can revise it all at the last minute, hears that his friend, whose attitude he has copied, has just failed his degree.

1. What are the two dissonant cognitions in this example?
2. Suggest how dissonance might be reduced.

There are many situations in which dissonance is aroused; two principal ones are:

Counter-attitudinal behaviour

This involves doing something which goes against our attitudes, so we justify it by changing our attitude. This is the essence of the Core Study in this section which, as it is a little complicated, we will summarise very briefly. People agree to tell others that a job they know to be extremely boring is actually interesting. Some are paid a reasonable fee to do this, which justifies the behaviour. Others are paid a pittance and can only justify their behaviour by convincing themselves that the job wasn't really that boring after all.

Activity

Now read the Core Study of Festinger and Carlsmith (p. 96) carefully; summarise it in such a way that you can include it in an essay on cognitive dissonance.

Post-decisional dissonance

Dissonance is also likely following a difficult decision between two objects or activities. Brehm (1956) asked women to rate the desirability of a number of household appliances on a scale from 1 to 8. They were then able to choose from two of the appliances as a 'reward' for taking part in the study. Afterwards items were rated again and the women showed an increased liking for the object they had chosen and a decreased liking for the object they had rejected.

Activity

You are applying to University. You have been offered exactly the same points at Sheffield and Birmingham and, having visited both, you find it extremely difficult to choose between them – but choose you must, and you opt for Birmingham. According to cognitive dissonance theory, once this decision has been made, how is your attitude to Sheffield likely to change and how are you likely to react to opinions from others that Sheffield is a wonderful University or that Birmingham leaves something to be desired?

Evaluation

Strengths

1. Cognitive dissonance theory has provided some interesting, often counterintuitive, predictions which have been experimentally supported.
2. It can explain attitude change under many circumstances.

Criticisms

1. Bannister and Fransella (1980) argue that the 'theory' is so simplistic and vague as not to constitute a theory at all.
2. Dissonance theory is based on the assumption that we strive towards consistency. However Katz (1968) argued that people are able to tolerate a high degree of inconsistency among their attitudes and between attitudes and behaviour, not allowing themselves to examine the logic connecting certain attitudes. If people do not acknowledge inconsistency, then they do not experience dissonance.
3. Alternative explanations for the supporting evidence have been offered. The **self-perception theory** offer such an alternative.

Core Study

Cognitive consequences of forced compliance: L. Festinger and J.M. Carlsmith (1959)

In this study Festinger and Carlsmith set out to test two derivations that logically follow from the theory of cognitive dissonance:

1. If a person is forced to do or say something which is contrary to their private opinion, he/she will tend to **change the opinion** to bring it into line with what was done or said.
2. The **greater** the pressure used to elicit compliant behaviour the **weaker** the tendency to change the original attitude will be.

Procedure

Subjects comprised 71 male psychology students from Stanford University. They were asked to take part in a study of 'Measures of Performance'. For a whole hour, they were given an extremely boring task to do. The 'experiment', though meaningless, was carried out in a very convincing manner.

After completing the task, all subjects, except a group of controls, were requested to tell another waiting subject that the task they would do was enjoyable and interesting. Subjects were either paid one dollar or twenty dollars to do this.

Finally, all the subjects were interviewed and asked a number of questions, including whether or not they had found the task interesting. They were also asked if they had any suspicions about the true nature of the experiment and, on the basis of this, results from 11 of the subjects had to be discarded.

Results and conclusions

Table 4.3 summarises the results:

The most significant result is the rating concerned with how enjoyable they found the task. Those receiving payment for telling another person that the task was enjoyable experienced dissonance because their behaviour was counter to their attitudes. However, the twenty dollar group did not feel the need to reduce dissonance by changing their attitudes because the twenty dollar payment provided ample justification for their counterattitudinal behaviour. The one dollar group, however, did not provide a justification for their behaviour and they were forced to reduce dissonance by changing their view of the task.

The results therefore support Festinger's theory of cognitive dissonance.

Table 4.3 Average ratings on interview questions for each condition

Questions (rated from −5 to +5)	Control	1 dollar	20 dollars
How enjoyable were the tasks	−0.45	+1.35	−0.05
Would be willing to participate in similar experiment	−0.62	+1.20	−0.25

QUESTIONS

1. **a** What type of method was used for the study?
   b Discuss whether the study was ethical and should have been performed.
   c Consider how the study may have been altered to be more ethical and consider how such changes might have altered the results.
   Based on Oxford and Cambridge Specimen Question

2. In the study by Festinger and Carlsmith:
   a How did the psychologists measure dissonance? **(2 marks)**

---

b In the two conditions of the experiment, the subjects (participants) were offered either one dollar or twenty dollars to tell a lie. Which condition provoked more dissonance, and why? **(2 marks)**

Oxford and Cambridge (1994)

3. In what way is the sample used in this study a biased one?

Self-perception theory

Bem (1967) argues that self-perception, rather than dissonance, explains why people come to believe in their own lies (as occurred in Festinger and Carlsmith's experiment). Bem's theory is discussed in section 4.3 on the Social self. Briefly, he argues that, under certain circumstances, we observe ourselves behaving in a certain way and we infer our attitudes from that behaviour. In the case of the participants in the Core Study who received only one dollar to tell an untruth, they infer that one dollar is not enough to lie and therefore infer that they were not lying and the task must have indeed been enjoyable and interesting. Twenty dollars, on the other hand, is sufficient to warrant a lie. The two theories propose very similar patterns of thought, but for different reasons: dissonance theory suggests that people change their attitudes because they need to reduce the tension that dissonance causes and self-perception theory suggests that people are merely finding a reasonable explanation for their own behaviour.

Evaluation

Bem acknowledges that it is unlikely that all attitude change is dependent on behaviour rather than the other way around. Nevertheless, the approach does offer insight into how some attitudes may be acquired and changed. If you can get people to change their behaviour, then their attitudes will follow. For example, if a company can persuade consumers to buy their product, perhaps by offering an irresistible discount, the consumer may come to think that if they buy it they must like it and buy it again.

How can we decide between these two theories? Dissonance theory, unlike self-perception theory, predicts that when people act in a way which is counter to their attitudes, they will become aroused because of the feeling of tension they experience. Evidence suggests that arousal occurs when people act in a way which is very objectionable in terms of their attitudes but not when the discrepancy is small. So both theories may, on occasions, be applicable, but in different circumstances.

Preparing for the exam

Key terms

affective component
attitudes
behavioural component
cognitive component
cognitive dissonance

counterattitudinal behaviour
post-decisional dissonance
self-perception
social norms

Types of exam questions

The types of question asked fall into the following categories:

1. The relationship between attitudes and behaviour.
2. Evaluation of theories of attitude change.

Self-test questions

1. What is an attitude?
2. Name the *three* components of attitudes.
3. In the La Pierre study suggest *three* reasons why the Chinese couple were served.
4. What situational influences are likely to have a greater influence on behaviour than attitudes?
5. What is meant by the term 'cognitive dissonance'?
6. Give an example of a situation which is likely to arouse cognitive dissonance, and suggest how dissonance might be reduced.
7. How would Bem's theory of self-perception account for the findings of the Core Study?

Exam question with guidance notes

Discuss whether attitudes predict behaviour accurately and consistently.

(25 marks)

AEB, AS level (1989)

The introductory paragraph should indicate the fact that most people assume attitudes and behaviour are *consistent*, but that studies show otherwise.

- Give an account of La Pierre's classic study. Mention the reasons why, in this case, attitudes did not predict behaviour.
- Give general reasons why attitudes do not predict behaviour – with references to research where appropriate.
- Conclude with reference to Fishbein and Ajzen's ideas on when attitudes can predict behaviour.

Additional exam question

Describe and evaluate any *one* theory of attitude change. **(25 marks)**

AEB (1994)

Extra Note

Make sure you learn cognitive dissonance theory, as this is the major theory of attitude change. Self-perception theory, while being a theory in its own right, is also a criticism of cognitive dissonance theory, since it offers an alternative explanation for the findings of the Core Study and other similar research.

4.5 Prejudice

Secord and Backman (1974) define prejudice as 'an attitude that predisposes us to think, feel, perceive and act in favourable or unfavourable ways towards a group or its individual members'.

Discrimination refers to the unequal treatment of individuals or groups based on arbitrary characteristics such as race, sex, ethnicity and cultural background. It often takes the form of limiting or restricting their **access** to privileges or resources.

Discrimination involves **behaviour**
whereas
Prejudice is an **attitude**.

Theories of the origin of prejudice

Theories advanced to explain the origins of prejudice fall into two broad categories:

1. **Personality theories**, which place the emphasis on the personality dynamics of the individual.
2. **Social psychological theories**, which focus on the ways in which social systems, group dynamics and institutional factors within a society can produce prejudice.

The major personality theory

The authoritarian personality

Adorno, Frenkel-Brunswik, Levinson and Sanford (1951) argue that certain personalities, in particular the authoritarian personality, are predisposed to be prejudiced. Some important characteristics of an authoritarian personality are:

1. A rigid adherence to very traditional, conventional values
2. A belief in harsh punishment for violation of these traditional norms
3. An extreme need to submit to those in higher authority, together with enormous admiration for 'strong' leaders
4. An expectation of unquestioning submission by those perceived to be lower in the social hierarchy
5. A generalised hostility, especially to minority groups.

Adorno *et al.* developed a number of scales designed to measure, by questionnaire, facets of prejudice and racism. The best known of these scales is the 'F' Scale, a scale designed to measure fascist personality tendencies. A high score on the 'F' scale indicates anti-democratic tendencies and a propensity to be prejudiced. Adorno *et al.*, by interviewing members of a highly prejudiced group as measured by the 'F' scale, found that they had parents who tended to be overstrict and highly punitive, especially where sex or aggression were involved. These parents also had unrealistically high expectations of their children: success, and being 'seen' to do well, seemed to be of paramount importance. Although the prejudiced individuals rarely criticised their parents, they did express considerable underlying hostility towards them.

Adorno *et al.* offer a Freudian explanation of how these childhood experiences are translated into a personality syndrome. The hostility felt towards the parents is repressed and finds release through various defence mechanisms, for example, through **displacement** of hostile feelings onto minority groups who cannot fight back, or through **projecting** their own inadequacies and weaknesses onto these minority groups.

Activity

Go back to Chapter 2 and make sure you understand the concept of defence mechanisms. How does the Freudian interpretation of the origins of this personality type fit in with the fact that people with an authoritarian personality prefer a very rigid, hierarchical society? Why might authoritarian personalities be intolerant of groups such as homosexuals and teenagers who dress unconventionally?

Evaluation

1. All the scales are worded so that agreement with almost every statement indicates authoritarianism. With this kind of design there is always the danger that people simply agree with all the statements (they fall into an 'acquiescent response set').
2. Hyman and Sheatsley (1954) argue that authoritarianism can be explained in terms of poor education and low socioeconomic status rather than in terms of a personality dynamics.
3. Some researchers question the fact that authoritarianism is always associated with right-wing political views, never with left-wing attitudes. A number of researchers argue that authoritarianism can also be a feature of extreme left-wing views but this is still a matter of controversy.
4. Some researchers argue that prejudice may not be the result of a personality disorder but the product of straightforward socialisation practices.
5. The theory cannot explain how entire societies or groups within societies become prejudiced, neither can it explain why prejudice is more prevalent in times of economic hardship.

This theory, then, may be useful to explain the origins of some instances of prejudice, but not all. For these we will turn to the socioeconomic interpretations.

Social psychological theories

Prejudice and group membership

Allport (1954) argues that prejudice is an **intergroup** phenomenon. He believes that humans show a basic tendency to form groups and to have a preference for their own group above all others.

Realistic group conflict theory

Sherif (1966) believes that **conflict of interest between groups** is a sufficient cause of prejudice.

Sherif's summer camp studies

In one of two field experiments, Sherif brought together 22 white, middle class boys for a two-week summer camp at the Robber's Cave State Park in Oklahoma. The boys were randomly assigned to two separate groups each with eleven members. For the first week, the two groups were totally separated while each undertook activities aimed at fostering group cohesion and identity; during this time they labelled themselves the 'Eagles' and the 'Rattlers'. It was only at the end of this week that they became aware of each other's existence. The staff then set up a series of competitions between the group, offering valued prizes for all members of the winning team. Very strong 'ingroup' and 'outgroup' feelings were manifest, leading to the emergence of ridiculous stereotypes. As the games progressed, fights and other visible displays of hostility became frequent occurrences. Eventually, after many assaults and counterassaults, the Eagles won the competition and the Rattlers stole their prizes. Sherif had succeeded not only in inducing prejudice but also physical conflict and cheating as a result of it.

It would be inappropriate not to mention the fact that the researchers at the Robber's Cave site later successfully reduced the hostility by getting the boys to work cooperatively to solve a common problem; we will consider the implications of this later in the section.

Social Identity Theory

Tajfel (1978) argues that intergroup discrimination can occur even in the absence of competition or threat. We refer you to the Core Study in this section.

Tajfel and Turner (1979) argue that discrimination occurs because, in order to perceive themselves in a positive light and boost their own self-esteem, people overestimate the good qualities of the group of which they are a member and overestimate the bad qualities of the outgroup.

Activity

One of the two theories above emphasises **social** competition as a cause of prejudice, whilst the other emphasises **realistic** competition. Which is which?

Why, according to social identity theory, may people with low self-esteem be very dependent on belonging to a group and be prone to prejudiced attitudes?

Conformity to social norms

In some sections of society, certain prejudices are the norm. The extent to which members of a society conform to such a social norm depends on the need they have, because of deep-rooted insecurity, to belong to and to be accepted by others in the conforming group, and on the consequences of nonconformity.

A number of studies support the idea that a cause of prejudice is conformity to norms.

Minard (1952) studied a West Virginian mining community and found that different norms operated for miners below and above ground. In the mines 80 per cent of white miners were friendly with black miners, yet only 20 per cent continued their friendship above ground.

The scapegoat theory

This theory states that prejudice is inevitable because it is caused by **frustration**, and that within any society there are innumerable sources of frustration, the most apparent being lack of decent jobs and housing. Frustration usually results in aggression and, when the source of the frustration cannot be attacked or even identified, the aggression is displaced onto other targets such as ethnic minority groups.

The social psychological causes of prejudice we have considered indicate a number of possible reasons why prejudice is implanted, and it may be that every reason has some validity.

Reduction of prejudice

Attitude change

Attitudes are usually important to those who hold them and important attitudes are the hardest to change. Indeed, if you accept Adorno's explanation for the authoritarian personality, changing prejudiced attitudes would threaten the very integration of such people's personality.

Changing group categorisation

- Tajfel has stated that categorisation of people into distinct groups is sufficient to arouse bias against other groups (see the Core Study).
- Gaertner *et al.* (1989) showed that encouraging members of separate groups to consider them all as one big group, thereby perceiving everyone as individuals rather than group members, can reduce bias.

As Tajfel says, 'Perhaps those educators in our competitive societies who from the earliest schooling are so keen on 'teams' and 'team spirit' could give some thought to the operation of these side effects'.

Core Study

Experiments in intergroup discrimination: H. Tajfel (1970)

Intergroup discrimination is a feature of most modern societies. Tajfel believes that whenever we are confronted with a situation to which some form of intergroup categorisation appears relevant, we are likely to act in a manner that discriminates against the outgroup and favours the ingroup. If this is so, it should lead to the following consequences:

1. There may be discrimination against an outgroup even if there is no reason for it in terms of the individual's own interests.
2. There may be such discrimination in the absence of any previously existing attitudes of hostility or dislike towards the outgroup.
3. This generic norm may manifest itself directly in behaviour toward the outgroup before any attitudes of prejudice or hostility have been formed.

Study 1

The subjects were 64 boys, aged 14 and 15 years, from a Bristol comprehensive school. They came into the laboratory in groups of eight. Each group was from the same class and were well acquainted with each other prior to the experiment.

They were told that the study concerned visual judgements and were asked to estimate the number of dots in each of 40 dot-clusters that were flashed on to a screen. They were told that some people tended to overestimate the number of dots whilst others tended to underestimate them. After their judgements had been made, they were classified as either 'underestimators' or 'overestimators' supposedly on the basis of these judgements, but in reality, they were randomly allocated to groups.

The boys were then asked to complete a second task in which, in complete confidence, they assigned real money rewards or penalties to other subjects. They did not know the identity of the other subjects, but it was made very clear whether or not they belonged to the same group. The boys could never assign money to themselves.

In order to make their allocations, the boys were shown a matrix like the one in Figure 4.3 and asked to choose a pair of figures, one from the top row, the second from the same position in the bottom row. Each row was clearly labelled to indicate whether the subject was choosing between two members of his own group, two members of the other group, or one member from each.

In their choices, the boys could have used one of three strategies:

1. **Maximum joint profit**, so that the boys as a whole would get most money out of the experimenters
2. **Maximum fairness**, giving each of the pair approximately the same amount of money
3. **Maximum discrimination** in favour of the ingroup.

Results

When the choices involved two ingroup or outgroup members, the boys did choose maximum fairness. However, as soon as the pair was a mixed one, they chose to discriminate against outgroup members and in favour of the ingroup. The results were at a high level of statistical significance. Thus, an ingroup–outgroup mentality had been created merely by association with others on the basis of

1	2	3	4	5	6	7	8	9	10	11	12	13	14
14	13	12	11	10	9	8	7	6	5	4	3	2	1

Figure 4.3 Example of matrix used by Tajfel

supposed estimations of numbers of dots. Furthermore, though it could not benefit themselves in any way, boys discriminated in favour of the ingroup.

A second study, in which boys were divided on the basis on supposed preference for paintings, but in reality, at random, gave similar results.

Tajfel concludes that intergroup conflict is extremely easy to trigger. He created it without the introduction of conflicting interests or competition but merely by creating a situation in which subjects could clearly categorise an ingroup and outgroup. This soon resulted in discriminatory behaviour.

QUESTIONS

1. **a** In the Tajfel study, who were the subjects of the experiments? **(2 marks)**
   b How were the subjects divided into groups? **(2 marks)**
   Oxford and Cambridge Specimen Paper
2. On what basis did Tajfel create an ingroup/outgroup mentality?
3. What are the main conclusions of these studies?

Think how the concept of deindividuation, mentioned in section 5.6 on Aggression, may contribute to increase of prejudice and discrimination.

Equal status contact

In the 1930s there was a belief, called the contact hypothesis, that prejudice could be reduced simply by increasing the contact between different groups of people, but this was a very naive assumption since contact alone can actually increase prejudice and discrimination. There are other important variables which determine whether contact will reduce or increase prejudice. **Cook (1978)** outlines **five** conditions, other than merely increased contact, which are liable to reduce prejudice:

1. The most important condition is that the people are of **equal status** with each other. If members of different groups continually meet on an unequal basis, stereotypes and prejudiced attitudes are reinforced.
2. The situation should be structured to encourage **mutual interdependence** and **cooperation**.
   Let's return to the Robber's Cave field study.

After the acriminious competitions, Sherif arranged ways in which that the two groups of boys could work towards a common goal. This was achieved by staging a series of 'emergencies', one of which was the breakdown of the camp van which was carrying food supplies. Getting it moving required the cooperation of all the boys.

3. **Personal interaction** must occur.
   Deutsch and Collins (1951) showed that when black and white housewives who lived in the same apartment buildings were brought together in circumstances in which they got to know one another as individuals, then prejudice was reduced.
4. **Exposure to non-stereotypic individuals:** when we meet people who break our usual stereotypes, especially when they appear very similar to us, then traditional stereotypes begin to disappear.
5. **Norms** surrounding the situation **must encourage helpful, egalitarian attitudes**.
   Gerard and Miller (1975), in a study of desegregation in Californian schools, found that children still continued to mix predominantly with their own racial groups. This may well have been because desegregation had been opposed by school officials and parents and did not therefore reflect the general ethos and attitudes of the community.

Cook (1985) devised an experimental situation in which these five criteria were met. He selected a group of highly prejudiced white women, half of whom were hired on the pretence of developing a training exercise to be used in industry while the other half served as controls. Over a period of 20 days, for two hours a day, these women worked alongside two female confederates, one black, one white, on a complicated task that required full cooperation. The conditions were designed to satisfy each of the conditions above in the following way:

- All the women were of equal status, since they were working together on the same task, being paid the same, and all had similar educational attainment levels
- A lunch break was placed into the session so that there was an opportunity for personal conversation, which was encouraged by the confederates
- The confederates discussed racial prejudice and equality in the lunch hour so that the white confederate could express non-prejudiced attitudes
- The task required was sufficiently complex to require close cooperation and interdependence in order to complete it.

When tested several months later, 40 per cent of the women showed a significant reduction in prejudice as opposed to only 12 per cent in the control group.

Activity

Cook's work is a good demonstration of how **in theory** prejudice and discrimination can be reduced. But he would probably be the first to agree that it is quite another matter to satisfy the necessary conditions for this reduction in everyday situations. Go through each of Cook's conditions and make brief notes on why each one could be difficult to satisfy in real life situations.

There is no easy answer to prejudice reduction. The conditions laid down by Cook need to occur repeatedly over an extended period of time, because it is the tendency of people to dismiss new information or simply to reinterpret it to fit existing views. The broader cultural framework cannot be ignored. Repeated equal-status contact situations will only be possible in societies that have norms of tolerance and do not stress social categorisation according to race or gender (Pettigrew, 1986).

Preparing for the exam

Key terms

attitude
authoritarian personality
conformity
contact hypothesis
deindividuation
discrimination
egalitarian
fascism
group cohesion

mutual interdependence
non-stereotypical individuals
prejudice
realistic group conflict theory
scapegoat theory
social categorisation
social identity theory
social norms

Types of exam questions

1. Evaluation of main theories.
2. Consideration of reduction of prejudice and discrimination, and why this is problematic.

Self-test questions

1. Define the terms 'prejudice' and 'discrimination'.
2. Describe some attributes of an authoritarian personality.
3. What explanation for the existence of authoritarianism is provided by Adorno *et al.*?
4. Can personality theories fully account for prejudice?
5. In the Robber's Cave State Park study, how did Sherif create prejudice between two groups of boys? What does this tell us about the nature of prejudice?
6. In the Minard (1952) study, what explanation can be given for the difference in the white miners' attitudes towards their black colleagues above and below ground?
7. Briefly describe the scapegoat theory of prejudice.
8. What is the 'contact hypothesis'?
9. Why is contact insufficient to reduce prejudice? What else is required?

Exam question with guidance notes

a   **What do psychologists mean by the terms prejudice and discrimination?**   (4 marks)

b   **Describe and evaluate** *one* **psychological study of prejudice** *or* **discrimination reduction.**   (8 marks)

c   **Critically consider why many attempts to reduce prejudice or discrimination have failed.**   (13 marks)

                    AEB (1992)

a   Make sure you clearly state that discrimination is actual *behaviour* and that prejudice is an *attitude*. The examiners' report indicates that 'most candidates were able to offer clear definitions of prejudice but were less than clear on the meaning of discrimination. Some candidates suggested that it was a less severe form of prejudice'.

Note: This part of the question is only worth 4 marks and therefore only a *brief* description is required.

b   The examiners' report indicated that some candidates spent too long describing studies on the origins of prejudice. Ensure that the study you choose concerns prejudice *reduction*, for example, Cook or Sherif. But do not forget that Sherif's study is concerned with demonstrating how prejudice is *built up* as well as broken down.

c   There are several points to be made here:

- Social norms are difficult to change
- The authoritarian personality is self-perpetuating
- Frustration is suggested as a cause of prejudice. A great deal of frustration is rooted in conditions which are difficult, if not impossible, to change.
- Tajfel points out that simply dividing people into groups, or merely implying the existence of groups, is enough to give rise to prejudice, and grouping is almost impossible to *avoid* in human societies.
- Refer to *Cook*'s work (this is very important): most attempts to reduce prejudice fall short of his recommendations in some way.

Additional exam question

Describe and evaluate psychological insights into the origins of prejudice.

(25 marks)
AEB (1993)

Note

Do not be tempted to omit the section on reduction of prejudice and discrimination as it is an increasingly popular area for questions.

5

Social Interaction

AEB	NEAB	O & C	Topic	Date attempted	Date completed	Self Assessment
✓	✓	✗	**Affiliation and Interpersonal Attraction**			
✓	✗	✓	**Audience and Coaction Effects**			
✓	✓	✓	**Conformity and Obedience**			
✓	✓	✓	**Leadership**			
✓	✗	✓	**Prosocial Behaviour**			
✓	✓	✓	**Aggression**			

5.1 Affiliation and interpersonal attraction

Affiliation refers to the desire to seek out the company of other people. There appear to be **two** main reasons why people choose to be with others:
1. Certain **situations** encourage affiliation.
2. Certain **personalities** are more inclined than others to affiliate.

Affiliation and the situation

Research suggests that **two** main situations encourage affiliation:

* Being afraid
* Needing to gain a means of measuring ourselves when we are uncertain of how to act.

Schachter (1959) requested participants to take part in a research project concerning the physiological effects of electric shocks. Half of the participants were advised to expect intense and painful shocks as part of the experimental procedure. The others were assured that they would receive only a mild and painless shock. Before the experiment, each participants was offered the choice of waiting alone or in a room with several people.

* In the high anxiety condition, 63 per cent chose to affiliate
* In the low anxiety condition, 33 per cent elected to wait with others.

Further studies reveal that anxious participants are not interested in waiting with others unless they are in the same experiment, that is, in the same anxiety-provoking situation. Variations on this study reveal that:

* Though people prefer to wait with others, they choose to do so only where companions are slightly less fearful than they themselves are, since this offers them some reassurance together with a lessening of their own fears
* In embarrassing situations people do not seek out others, even if they are uncertain or afraid.

Morris *et al.* (1976) studied the responses of participants who were shown to a waiting room prior to supposedly taking part in a study of sexual attitudes. In one condition, fear was induced by the presence of electric shock devices and information about receiving shocks in an experiment. In the other condition, embarrassment was induced by the presence of contraceptive devices, pictures of nudes and literature on sex and venereal diseases. In the fear situation the participants affiliated a great deal, but in the embarrassing situation they left the room almost immediately.

Affiliation and individual differences

It seems that some people are more inclined than others to seek out company. Variables include:

* **Birth order:** Schachter (1959) found that first-born participants were more likely to seek out company when anxious than were later born participants
* **Personality:** some people claim to enjoy being alone and choose not to seek company
* **Lack of confidence in social skills:** some people long for human companionship but find that social situations bring stress and anxiety; in many cases, people believe that they lack the skills needed for mixing with others and feel that they will make a fool of themselves and be judged negatively.

To sum up, it seems that the extent to which we seek the company of others depends on the nature of the situation and facets of our own personalities.

Attraction

Factors affecting attraction

A number of factors influencing liking and attraction have been identified by psychologists.

Familiarity and proximity

Probably the best single predictor of whether two people are friends is how far apart they live.

Newcomb (1961) examined friendship development among college students. He found that second year students tended to be friends with their first year room mate, regardless of other factors.

Priest and Sawyer (1967) found that students were

more likely to be friends with a student who lived one door away rather than with one living two doors away, even though the difference was only 8 feet.

These and many other studies indicate that the well known saying 'familiarity breeds contempt' is not an accurate adage.

Similarity

There is much research to suggest that we tend to like and feel attracted to people who are similar to us, in terms of attitudes and values, age, ethnicity, economic background, personality and self-esteem. Intimate relationships are also more likely to form and be maintained if the couple are similar.

Hill *et al.* (1976) found that couples who stayed together were similar in age, intelligence and attractiveness than were couples whose relationships broke down.

We prefer people similar to us for several reasons:

- They are likely to share our interests and enjoy the same activities
- They validate our attitudes and general view of the world, thereby enhancing our self-esteem
- They are easy and relaxing to communicate with.

Complementarity

A very different idea from the previous one was advanced by Winch (1958), who argued that 'opposites attract'. He proposed that people choose partners who possess qualities they themselves lack; in this way a couple can complement each other, each fulfilling the other's needs. For example, a bossy person is best suited to a submissive partner, thus providing them with a willing person to boss. Winch did provide some support for this view, but his concept of complementarity has certainly not been universally supported by evidence. It may be that some relationships are based on this principle, but by no means all.

Perceived competence

Although evidence shows that we like people who are competent and intelligent, we like them best if they are not too perfect. A study by Aronson *et al.* (1966)

indicated that we prefer brainy people to be fallible, perhaps because it makes them more human, but we don't like too much incompetence.

Physical attractiveness

Physical attractiveness is not only a major determinant of sexual attraction but also of friendship. There is a considerable body of research suggesting that we view more positively and behave more favourably towards people whom we consider to be attractive.

Dion (1972) showed a group of adults the record cards of seven year old children detailing some kind of misbehaviour, either mild or severe, accompanied by a photograph of either an attractive or unattractive child. Participants shown the unattractive child tended to consider the misdeed as more serious and as more typical of that child's usual behaviour than when they were shown an attractive child.

Walster *et al.* (1966) assigned people to a single evening date on an entirely random basis. They were then asked to indicate how much they liked their partners. Regardless of differences in personality, the more attractive the date the better they were liked. This applied to both men and women.

The matching hypothesis

Sexual relationships tend to be formed between couples who are equal in terms of levels of attractiveness.

Walster *et al.* (1966) followed up the 'blind date' couples six months later, and enquiries revealed that it was the couples with the more similar levels of attractiveness who were most likely to have continued seeing each other.

Activity

1. Recap in your mind the most important determinants of the formation of friendships. Think of **three** of your closest friends:
   - Where did you first meet them?
   - In what ways are they similar to you?
   (Don't forget the most obvious similarities such as age and sex.)

Do the factors identified by psychologists apply to you?

2. Before reading the next section, think of someone with whom you used to be friends but with whom you no longer keep in touch. Why is this? Bear these reasons in mind as you read the theories concerned with why some friendships survive longer than others.

Theories of attraction

Learning theory

This is a very straightforward theory of interpersonal attraction based on classical and operant conditioning. **Byrne and Clore (1970)** suggest that we like those people with whom we associate pleasurable feelings (classical conditioning) and those people who reward us in some way (operant conditioning). Conversely, we dislike those with whom we associate unpleasant occurrences or those who punish us.

Most of the factors discussed in this section can be understood in terms of learning theory:

- Physical proximity gives us many opportunities to engage in rewarding **interaction**
- Attractive people are good to look at and we gain **prestige** by being with them
- People with similar attitudes to ourselves offer the very valuable reward of endorsing our opinions, thereby bolstering our **self-esteem**.

The learning perspective implies that relationships begin to break down if excitement and novelty are replaced by boredom, and being taken for granted.

Evaluation

Learning theory can quite easily explain the importance of factors which determine whether or not a relationship will form in the first place, and to some extent whether or not it will continue, but it is more limited in this latter aspect.

Social exchange theory

Social exchange theory and equity theory are in some senses extensions of learning theory. **Homans (1961,**

1974) argues that in all relationships we assess the rewards that can be gained and balance these against the costs: the profits are simply the rewards *less* the costs. Not surprisingly, people tend to stay in relationships that show an overall profit and withdraw from relationships which are perceived as too costly. People do not necessarily evaluate the profits (or outcomes as they are usually known) very consciously or systematically, but this assessment certainly takes place.

Thibaut and Kelley (1959) have extended the basic assumptions of social exchange theory to consider in greater detail the means by which we evaluate outcomes. We do not assess rewards and costs in absolute terms: we compare them with what we had expected and with what alternatives are available.

- **The comparison level** is the actual outcome as compared to what we had expected and thought we deserved. This, in turn, depends on past experiences of relationships and our level of self-esteem.
- **The comparison level for alternatives** involves comparing what we have with other relationships which are currently available to us. Although we can be friends with many people at once, we only have a limited amount of time to spend with each and we will assess alternatives. In sexual relationships, we are usually permitted only one openly acknowledged relationship and costs therefore take account of any **alternative** relationship we may desire but cannot acknowledge.

The result is, then, that even if a relationship is profitable in absolute terms, we may leave it if a more advantageous one becomes available. On the other hand, we may stay in a relationship which offers little reward if we think this is the best available.

Evaluation

1. This theory is intuitively convincing and explains the **dynamic** qualities of a relationship: since rewards and costs are constantly changing, relationships are by no means stable. It can explain why friendships don't usually end due to

a single argument but because people 'drift apart' as rewards, costs and comparison levels change, partly because people themselves change.

2. Social exchange theory offers a very plausible explanation of how and why people move through the various **phases** of relationships.

3. For criticisms, see the discussion at the end of the subsection on Equity theory below.

Activity

Imagine the following situation which may well apply to you. You have been friends with Chris throughout your school life and now you are going to separate Universities. You meet up as soon as you get back home for the first Christmas break. In terms of social exchange theory (SET), how have the rewards and costs changed since you last met? What are going to be the likely topics of conversation, and how will they differ from previous chats?

Now think about the future for you and Chris. You will probably both get jobs away from the area in which you went to school. You are both likely to eventually live with a partner and maybe have children. How will the costs and rewards of your relationship change over time and what factors will determine whether or not it will survive?

Equity theory

Walster, Walster and Berscheid (1978) derive this theory from social exchange theory but introduce an extra dimension, that of **investment**. Whereas costs and rewards are consequences of a relationship, investments are goods or abilities that one person brings with them to the relationship, such as the capacity to earn a large salary. According to this theory, profits should be in proportion to the investment made, even if this means that benefits are not equally divided. This may account for the fact that an unattractive, older man who commands a large salary is far more likely to marry a younger attractive woman than a similar man with a much lower income.

Greenberg and Cohen (1982) found that partners who feel they are getting less than they deserve, a 'raw deal' as it were, feel aggrieved and angry; partners who are overbenefited feel uncomfortable and guilty.

Considerations of fairness may be more important in the early stages of a relationship. If the relationship endures, people seem to monitor the relative inputs less closely.

Evaluation

Social exchange and equity theories have been criticised for viewing people as essentially selfish and unwilling to give more than they get. The theories tend to ignore evidence suggesting that people are capable of unselfish and altruistic acts, as we see in the section on prosocial behaviour.

To sum up: most factors which influence whether a relationship will form in the first place, factors such as proximity and similarity, are adequately covered by the simple learning theory model. However, for consideration of the active interaction which takes place within relationships we need to turn to social exchange and equity theories. These two theories take greater account of both sides of a relationship and offer a deeper insight into the causes of how and why relationships change.

Preparing for the exam

Key terms

affiliation
classical conditioning
comparison level for alternatives
comparison level
complementarity
equity

investment
matching hypothesis
operant conditioning
proximity
social exchange theory

Types of exam question

1. Psychological theories of interpersonal attraction.
2. Formation, maintenance and breakdown of friendships.

Self-test questions

1. What aspects of a situation are likely to encourage a person to seek out the company of others?
2. What did Schachter (1959) discover about affiliation?
3. What aspects of personality are likely to influence affiliation?
4. Briefly describe studies which illustrate how the following factors can effect liking and attraction:
   • familiarity
   • proximity
   • similarity
   • physical attractiveness.
5. What is the matching hypothesis?
6. How can classical and operant conditioning explain attraction?
7. Some people stay in unrewarding relationships, other people leave relationships which are rewarding. How can social exchange theory explain both of these possibilities?
8. What is the difference between equity theory and social exchange theory?

Exam question with guidance notes

How do psychologists explain the formation and maintenance of friendships?

(25 marks)
AEB (1988)

Note that this question clearly asks you to explain the factors affecting BOTH the *formation* and *maintenance* of friendships.

• Begin by identifying the factors involved in determining the *formation* of a relationship: proximity, similarity and so on. Be careful not to spend too long on this section, but do include some research evidence.
• The maintenance part of the question demands a knowledge of the theories of interpersonal attraction.
• Learning theory suggests that, in order to maintain a relationship,

reinforcements must be given and received. Once reinforcement reduces or ceases, the relationship is likely to end.
- Social exchange theory states that, on both sides, *rewards* must outweigh *costs*. If they do, the relationship is maintained; if not, it breaks down.
- Equity theory states that relationships must be *equitable* or they are liable to break down.
- In each case, ensure that you *evaluate* the theory.
- Conclude with a brief *comparison* of the main theories as a means of summing up.

Additional exam questions

1. Discuss psychological explanations of the process of affiliation.

    (25 marks)
    AEB (1994)

2. Describe and evaluate psychological theories of and investigations into **either** the formation **or** breakdown of relationships   **(25 marks)**
    AEB AS (1993)

3. Describe and evaluate *two* psychological theories of interpersonal attraction.   **(25 marks)**
    AEB (1991)

5.2 Audience and coaction effects

An **audience** is a group of listeners or spectators who do not participate in the activity; a **coactor** is a person who works alongside another person at a similar task. This section is concerned with the effect that being observed by an audience or having others performing alongside has on another person's performance.

Social facilitation is the tendency for people to perform **better** on tasks when others are present than when they are alone. A number of studies carried out at the beginning of this century showed that the presence of others enhances an individual's performance on certain tasks.

Triplett (1898) investigated the effects of competition on the time it took children to make 150 winds of a fishing reel. He observed that the children, when asked to wind the reels as fast as they could, performed faster in pairs than when alone.

It is not clear whether the superior performance of the children who worked in pairs was due to the element of competition involved or to the mere presence of others.

Allport (1924), having requested participants not to compete one with another, found a social facilitation effect on a number of tasks including crossing out the vowels in a page of writing and carrying out simple multiplications.

Dashiell (1935) showed that there is a similar effect even when participants are simply told that others are performing the task in another room.

Social inhibition is the tendency for people to perform **less well** in the presence of others than when alone. In contrast to the research findings previously cited, the presence of others can sometimes have an adverse effect on performance.

Dashiell (1935) found that participants faced with an audience often worked faster at solving mathematical problems, but tended to make more errors.

Allport (1924) found that although social facilitation was apparent during the performing of simple tasks, when the participants were required, without conferring, to refute seemingly logical arguments, they produced a higher quality of work when alone than when in a room with others.

Explanations for social facilitation and social inhibition

Zajonc (1966)

Zajonc argued that well-known, well-practised tasks are facilitated by the presence of others but new or difficult tasks are performed less well when others are present. He suggests that the presence of others increases the performer's **arousal level**. Arousal is known to facilitate performance on well-learned tasks but to inhibit performance on complex or new tasks except those which are extremely simple. This corresponds to the **Yerkes-Dodson law** which is explained in Chapter 7.

Zajonc *et al.* (1969) put cockroaches in a situation in which they had to run down a straight corridor in order to escape a bright light. It was found that they reached their goal more quickly when in pairs or in the presence of other cockroaches than when they were alone. However, if the task was made more difficult by their having to make a right angled turn in order to reach their goal, those in pairs or with an audience performed less well than those who were alone.

Activity

Are the following activities likely to be facilitated or inhibited by the presence of others?

1. Learning to ride a bike
2. Dealing cards to a group of very experienced and sophisticated poker players on your first night doing the job
3. The same task after three months' experience with less serious poker players
4. Participating in an important race after months of intense practice
5. Being asked to give a short paper on learning theory to a group of fellow psychology students after only three weeks of studying the subject in a new college.

Cottrell (1972)

Cottrell agreed with Zajonc that we perform easy and well-practised tasks better and difficult tasks less well when we are aroused. However, he argues that other people only become a source of arousal when we consider them to be evaluating us. It is not therefore the mere presence of others that matters, but the belief that they are, in some way, judging us. Under these circumstances we experience **evaluation apprehension**. On simple tasks we work harder when being evaluated, but on difficult tasks the pressure of being judged has a detrimental effect on performance.

Paulus and Murdock (1971) noted the effects of an audience on student participants. The effect was stronger if the participants thought they were being watched by 'experts' than if they thought the audience comprised only other students.

Baron (1986)

Baron offers an explanation known as the **distraction–conflict model**. He argues that the presence of others is distracting because we divide our attention between the task and the reaction of the audience. This distraction means that we are less able to concentrate on the task in hand and experience conflict as we try to attend to both the task and the others present. This conflict increases our motivation and makes us work harder to overcome the distraction. If a task is relatively easy, the increase in motivation outweighs the negative effects of the distraction caused by the presence of others and social facilitation takes place. However, with difficult tasks the negative effects of distraction cannot compensate for the positive effects of increased motivation, and the performance of the task suffers.

These theories are not necessarily contradictory. They all agree that the presence of others can cause arousal but offer different explanations as to the **source** of this arousal. It is quite possible that all these processes (the mere presence of others, evaluation and distraction) can all affect human performance depending on the particular situation.

Preparing for the exam

Key terms

coactor

distraction–conflict model

evaluation apprehension

social facilitation

social inhibition

Yerkes–Dodson law

Types of exam question

Questions tend to be straightforward. They expect you to know the effects of an audience and coactors and the theories that explain these effects.

Self-test questions

1. Define the terms 'social facilitation' and 'social inhibition'.
2. In what circumstances will the presence of others facilitate performance and in what circumstances will the presence of others inhibit performance?
3. Briefly describe *one* research example of social facilitation and *one* of social inhibition.
4. When learning to juggle you are likely to perform better when you practice alone. What explanation for this is provided by the following theorists:
   a. Zajonc?
   b. Cottrell?
   c. Baron?

Exam question with guidance notes

Discuss what psychologists have learned from their research into audience and coaction effects.

(25 marks)

AEB (1988)

This is a straightforward question.

- You should distinguish between audience and coaction effects, discuss the meaning of social facilitation and social inhibition and outline the circumstances under which each is likely to occur. Use *research evidence* to support your arguments.
- Cover each of the *three* theories that seek to explain the research findings: Zajonc, Cottrell and Baron. Again, use research to support each one.
- Conclude by saying that no one theory has received universal acceptance and that it is quite possible that they are *complementary* in that each may explain the effects of an audience and coactors under different circumstances.

5.3 Conformity and obedience

Conformity

> **Conformity** can be defined as yielding to perceived group pressure.

Sherif (1935) studied conformity by using the 'autokinetic effect', a visual illusion in which a spot of light in a dark room appears to move when it is still. Participants were asked to estimate how much the spot of light moved. When they were alone, the estimations given by different participants were very variable but when they were tested in groups of three, their estimates became very similar: a **norm** for each group emerged. This happened despite the fact that no one had been instructed by the experimenters to reach a group agreement and, when questioned afterwards, participants could not be convinced that they had been influenced by the group.

The autokinetic effect represents an **ambiguous task** for which there is no correct answer and, for this reason, some researchers considered it an inappropriate task to use in conformity studies.

The work of Asch

Asch (1951, 1952, 1953) devised a simple and completely unambiguous task involving estimation of line length. Participants were presented with a line and asked to match it, for length, with one of three other lines. When 36 people in a control condition were asked to make the estimation, no one was incorrect. Each participant was asked to judge line length in a group comprising at least six other people, all of whom were confederates of the experimenter. The group members sat around a table and gave their answers aloud, one by one, with the 'stooge' seated such that he was always the second from last to answer. The first two judgements were correctly made by everybody but on the third trial the confederates deliberately gave the same wrong answer and henceforth they continued to do this on most of the other trials. Over 76 per cent of the stooges conformed at least once, 5 per cent doing so on every trial. Overall, 37 per cent of all judgements were incorrect.

People offered a number of reasons for conforming

* They did not want to 'spoil' the results of the experiment
* They misunderstood the instructions in some way
* If they answered differently from the majority they might be considered 'peculiar'.

Activity

> Imagine you had been a participant in this study. Whether or not you conformed, think about how you might feel: uncomfortable, embarrassed, challenged, happy, stressed? Consider carefully the ethics of conducting such a study.

Variations on the original study

Asch performed a number of variations on his original study, resulting in the findings shown in Table 5.1.

Table 5.1 Asch's later findings

Variation	Result
1. **Group size 2–15**	Conformity increased up to group size around 7. Henceforth remained steady
2. **One confederate answered correctly**	Conformity rate dropped to 6 per cent
3. **Confederate answered incorrectly but still differently from the majority**	Conformity still considerably reduced
4. **Task made more difficult**	Conformity rose

Replications of the Asch study

1. **Perrin and Spencer (1980)**, using British students, found conformity rates of less than 1 per cent. They argued that the results of Asch's study were due to the fact that it took place in the 1950s when people were a great deal more conforming than they were in the 1980s.

2. **Doms and Avermaet (1981)**, however, point out that for their study, Perrin and Spencer used medical and engineering students who may have been particularly confident in their ability to judge line length and therefore less likely to conform. Using students from different disciplines, they found much higher conformity rates.

Activity

Another major study showing the influence of both conformity and obedience is the Core Study by Zimbardo. Read it and summarise the main findings.

Reasons for conformity

1. **Informational influence:** in situations in which we feel uncertain as to how to behave, we may look to others to provide information.
2. **Normative influence:** most of us want to be accepted and liked, which encourages us to do as other people are doing in order to gain their acceptance.
3. **Social pressure:** in any situation there is a lot of pressure to go along with others and much conformity seems to be due to conceding to these pressures.
4. **Fear of appearing foolish:** although people like to display a degree of individuality, they usually do so within certain parameters. If we do or say things which conflict with the general view, we risk ridicule and disapproval.
5. **Mindlessness:** numerous examples of conforming behaviour in everyday life are performed with very little thought at all.

Activity

Usually, conforming behaviour is motivated by a variety of reasons but one of the previously stated causes may predominate. What do you think is the main cause of the following conformist actions:

1. Wearing jeans to college
2. Agreeing to meet at a certain pub you don't particularly like but most of your friends do
3. Not talking to yourself when others are around
4. Having cereal for breakfast
5. At a formal dinner with a bewildering array of cutlery, looking around to see which pieces others are using for their fish course.
6. When asked to fill in a sponsor form, writing down an amount of money at least as much as most other people?

Individual differences in conformity

There is not a great deal of evidence for the existence of a conforming personality. Some research suggests that people with an authoritarian personality (as discussed in section 4.5 on Prejudice) have an 'unquestioning respect for convention' and are therefore likely to be extremely conformist. Conformists tend to have low self-esteem, a generally negative self-concept (Santee and Maslach, 1982) and be of low intelligence (Nord, 1969).

However, all these individual differences are swamped by situational factors. Generally people are more likely to conform if they want to be accepted by the majority group, for whatever reasons. They are also more likely to conform if non-conformity carries a **penalty**, particularly if they have been punished for not conforming in the past.

Obedience

Obedience can be defined as complying with the demands of a perceived authority figure.

History has shown that the pressure to obey authority is such that people will act in a way that goes against common sense, common humanity and self interest.

The work of Milgram

In an attempt to understand obedience, **Milgram** conducted a series of provocative and enlightening experiments. His original study is the second Core Study of this section which you need to study and summarise before reading further.

Core Study

A study of prisoners and guards in a simulated prison: C. Haney, C. Banks and P. Zimbardo (1973)

The study investigated the effects of playing the role of 'guard' and 'prisoner' in the context of a simulated prison.

Subjects

24 stable and mature subjects were chosen from 75 respondents to an advertisement asking for male volunteers to take part in a psychological study of 'prison life'. They did not know each other prior to the study.

Procedure

Physical aspects of the prison: the prison was built in the basement of Stanford University.

Role instruction: subjects were randomly assigned to the role of 'prisoner' or 'guard' and voluntarily agreed to play the role in return for fifteen dollars a day for up to two weeks.

Guards were instructed to 'maintain a reasonable degree of order within the prison necessary for effective functioning'. They were not given specific instructions as to how they should achieve this but they were told that on no account could they use any form of physical punishment or aggression.

Uniforms: in order to promote anonymity the following uniforms were administered. Guards wore plain khaki shirts and trousers and reflecting glasses. Prisoners wore a smock, no underclothes, a hat made from a stocking and had an ankle chain.

Induction procedure: the prisoners were arrested at their homes by police, charged and taken to the police station. Once at the prison they were stripped, deloused and given a uniform. They were then put in a cell and ordered to remain silent.

Results

All encounters tended to be negative, hostile and dehumanising. Prisoners were generally passive.

Guards initiated most of the interaction, much of which was in the form of commands or verbal affronts.

Five prisoners had to be released before the others. Four showed extreme emotional depression, crying, rage and acute anxiety. The fifth developed a psychosomatic rash on his body. Of the remaining prisoners, only two said they were not willing to forfeit the money they had earned in return for being 'paroled'.

The experiment was terminated prematurely after only six days.

Reality of the simulation

For practical and ethical reasons the simulated prison was not totally realistic. Many particularly unpleasant aspects of prison life were absent, such as involuntary homosexuality, racism, beatings and threats to life. Also, the maximum anticipated sentence was just two weeks. It is therefore possible that the study does not serve as a meaningful comparison to real prison environments.

The pathology of power

Being a guard carried with it a status and freedom to exercise an unprecedented degree of control over others. This control required no justification and many of the guards clearly found the sense of power it gave them exhilarating. After day one, all the prisoners' rights were redefined as privileges and used as rewards to elicit obedience.

Pathological prisoner syndrome

Prisoners' first response was disbelief, followed by rebellion and finally by acceptance. As the days wore on the model prisoners' behaviour was passive, dependent and emotionally flat.

The processes involved in bringing about these reactions were:

1. Loss of personal identity.
2. Arbitrary control exercised by the guards.
3. Dependency and emasculation. The prisoners were made to be totally dependent on the guards for commonplace functions such as going to the toilet, reading and lighting a cigarette. The smocks, worn without underwear, lessened their sense of masculinity.

Conclusions

If this mock prison could generate such pathology in such a short time, then the question of what is happening in real prisons has to be posed. It suggests that guards and prisoners are locked into roles which are enormously destructive to their human nature. The research provides a starting point for further research into the training of guards and the operating principles of prisons.

QUESTIONS

1. **a** In the prison simulation study, describe how the behaviour of the 'guards' changed during the study   **(2 marks)**
    b What does Zimbardo mean by the term 'pathology of power'?   **(2 marks)**
    Oxford and Cambridge Specimen Paper

2. How were the participants chosen for this study?

3. Discuss whether the study was ethical.

Core Study

Behavioural study of obedience: S. Milgram (1963)

Milgram set out to investigate the nature of obedience in order to understand the inhumane acts carried out by the Nazis in Hitler's Germany, acts which were made possible by obedience on a grand scale. In experimental conditions, he set out to see if subjects would administer painful electric shocks to another person simply because they were instructed to do so.

Method

Subjects

40 males between 20 and 40 years of age, obtained by a newspaper advertisement asking for volunteers for a study on learning and memory at Yale University. They were paid 4.50 dollars for agreeing to take part.

Location

The experiment took place in a smart, well-appointed laboratory in Yale University.

Procedure

One naive subject and one victim (a confederate) were used in each trial. They were told that they were to take part in an experiment on learning in which one of them would be the 'learner' and the other would be the 'teacher'. The naive subject was asked to draw a slip of paper from a hat to determine which role he would play. The draw was rigged so the subject was always the teacher.

The learner was strapped to an 'electric chair' appliance and electrodes were attached to his arms; cream was applied 'to avoid blisters and burns'. He was also told that 'although the shocks can be extremely painful, they cause no permanent tissue damage'. The teacher was taken into a separate room next door to administer the punishment.

The learning task

The task of the learner was to complete sets of word pairs. The subject read a series of word pairs to the learner and then read the first word of each pair together with four alternatives. The learner had to indicate which of the four was correct by pressing one of four switches.

The shock generator

This was a panel with 30 levers, each clearly labelled with voltage ranging from 15 to 450 and a description of the seriousness of the shocks, ranging from 'slight shock' to 'danger severe shock' and finally to 'XXX'. When a lever was pressed a light came on and a buzzer sounded.

The subject was instructed to give a shock each time the learner gave a wrong answer and to increase the intensity by one level with each wrong answer.

In all trials the learner gave a predetermined number of correct and incorrect answers. Nothing was heard from the learner until the 'shocks' reached 300 volts, at which point he pounded on the wall. After this he ceased to respond to the questions. When 315 volts were given, the learner once again pounded on the wall, but after this nothing was heard from him and no responses were made to any questions. (In other variations, the victim yelled to be let out and shouted that he refused to carry on, but not in this original study.)

Experimental feed-back

At any point in the experiment when the subject turned to the experimenter for advice or to object to the procedure, the experimenter responded with the following verbal 'prods':

1. 'Please continue.'
2. 'The experiment requires that you continue.'
3. 'It is absolutely essential that you continue.'

4. 'You have no choice, you must go on.'

Debriefing

Afterwards the subjects were reunited with the victim, debriefed and interviewed.

Results

Of the 40 subjects involved in the original study, 26 went to 450 volts.

This represents a staggering 65 per cent of the sample. Of the remaining 14, five stopped at 300 volts, four at 315 volts, two at 330 volts and one each at 345 volts, 360 volts and 375 volts.

Most of the subjects displayed signs of severe stress and discomfort and were clearly relieved when the experimenter finally stopped the procedure.

Discussion

The extent of obedience

The following features of the experiment are considered by Milgram to explain the findings:

1. The fact that the experiment took place at the prestigious Yale University lent the study and procedure **credibility** and **respect**.
2. The subject believed that the experiment was for a **worthy purpose** – to advance knowledge and understanding of learning processes.
3. The subject believed the victim had **volunteered** to be in the study and therefore has an obligation to take part even if the procedures become unpleasant.
4. The subject felt himself to be similarly **obligated** to take part in the procedure as planned.
5. Being **paid** increased the sense of obligation.
6. As far as the subject was concerned, the roles of learner and teacher had been allocated fairly, by drawing lots. Thus the learner could not feel **aggrieved** that he had been unfairly assigned his role.
7. As most subjects had never been a subject in a

psychology experiment before, they had little idea about the rights and expectations of experimenter and subject. The situation was novel and there were no **norms** operating and nobody with whom to discuss ambiguities and doubts.

8. The subject had been assured that the shocks were 'painful but not dangerous'. This short-term pain was balanced with the possibility of **long-term scientific gain**.
9. The victim responded to all the questions without apparent discomfort until the 300 volt level was reached. They had thus indicated their **willingness** to take part.

QUESTIONS

1. **a** Give a psychological definition of obedience. **(2 marks)**
   b In Milgram's study, describe the distinguishing features of the way in which the obeying subjects behaved. **(2 marks)**
   Oxford and Cambridge Specimen Paper

2. **a** State features of the procedure in the Milgram study that made it appear very 'scientific'. **(2 marks)**
   b The subjects (participants) in the Milgram study were deceived in a number of ways. Identify *two* examples of these deceptions.
   (2 marks)
   Oxford and Cambridge (1994)

3. **a** How did Milgram obtain his sample of subjects (participants) in this study?
   (2 marks)
   b What is the name for this method of sampling? (Refer to section 11.3 if in doubt.)
   (2 marks)
   c Why is this procedure likely to result in a biased sample? **(2 marks)**

> **d** In what other ways was Milgram's sample not typical of the general population?
>
> **(2 marks)**
>
> **4 a** How was the extent of obedience measured in this study? **(2 marks)**
>
> **b** What were the main findings? **(2 marks)**
>
> **5** Name *five* factors which Milgram considers contributed to the staggering level of obedience shown by the subjects (participants). **(10 marks)**
>
> **6** The term 'ecological validity' refers to the extent to which behaviour shown in a psychological study corresponds to its
>
> equivalent in an everyday, real life setting.
>
> **a** Name *two* ways in which this study may not be considered to be ecologically valid.
>
> **(4 marks)**
>
> **b** Suggest a way in which the study could be made more ecologically valid. **(2 marks)**
>
> **c** Evaluate what the study tells us about how people behave in real life situations.
>
> **(4 marks)**

Activity

After reading this Core Study, make sure you know:

1. What percentage of participants stopped *before* reaching 300 volts.
2. What percentage went to the 450 volts (the highest value).
3. The reasons put forward by Milgram to account for these results.

Variations on Milgram's original study

Milgram carried out a series of additional studies in the attempt to identify more precisely the aspects of the study that induced obedience.

1. The learner and participant were placed in the same room. The number continuing to 450 volts dropped to 40 per cent.
2. The participant had to force the victim's hand on to a metal shock plate in order to receive the shock. 30 per cent went up to 450 volts.
3. The experiment took place in a run down office building in Bridgeport, rather than at the

prestigious Yale University. 50 per cent went to 450 volts.

4. Women were used as participants. The results were identical to those obtained using men: 65 per cent went to 450 volts.
5. The participant was only required to read the word pair and another teacher (a confederate) administered the shock. 95 per cent went up to 450 volts.
6. The experimenter left the room after giving the initial instructions, giving all further instruction by telephone. The obedience rate dropped to 20 per cent.

Milgram sums up his considerable research into obedience in the following way: 'A substantial proportion of people do what they are told to do, irrespective of the content of the act and without limitations of conscience, so long as they perceive that the command comes from a legitimate authority.' (Milgram, 1974).

Evaluation

1. The most important criticism of Milgram's work is concerned with its **ethics**. There are several considerations here:

- Participants were **deceived** as to the exact nature of the study for which they had volunteered. However, Milgram could not have found results that truly reflected the way people behave in real situations if he had not deceived his participants, all of whom were thoroughly debriefed afterwards.
- Baumrind (1964) argued that Milgram did not take adequate measures to protect his participants from the **stress** and **emotional conflict** they experienced. Milgram's defence was that he did not expect the results he obtained. He asked a group of students and psychiatrists to predict what would happen prior to the first experiment and all agreed that people would not continue once the victim began to protest. Of course, this defence is only true of the first obedience study he conducted.
- It is possible that being involved in the experiment may have had a long term effect on the participants **self-concepts**. Before the experiment they might have considered themselves incapable of inflicting harm on another person unless the circumstances were extreme. Afterwards, this view of themselves was shattered. Milgram argued that such self-knowledge was valuable. A year after the experiments an independent psychiatrist interviewed 40 of the participants and found no evidence of psychological harm or evidence of trauma.

2. The sample of participants used by Milgram was not very **representative**. It was limited to those people who read the newspaper advertisement and were prepared to participate in a laboratory experiment.

3. Some critics claim that Milgram's work was carried out in an artificial setting and has little relevance to the real world; in other words, it lacked **ecological validity**. Milgram himself believes that the processes involved in obeying authority figures are the same in any situation. Certainly other studies have demonstrated destructive obedience in naturalistic settings, as Hofling's study (discussed next) shows.

Activity

1. What type of sampling method did Milgram use to select his participants? Why does this sampling method invariably result in a biased sample? If in doubt, read section 11.3 on Sampling.
2. Read the ethical guidelines documented in Chapter 10 and consider which, if any, of these guidelines were violated in this study (which was conducted many years before such guidelines were issued).
3. How did Milgram defend his studies?

Hofling's study in a real-life situation

Hofling (1966) performed an obedience study in 22 wards in a range of psychiatric hospitals in the USA. A nurse on duty in each ward was telephoned and ordered by a mythical doctor whom she had not met to give a patient 20 mg of a drug called Astroten. If nurses obeyed the request they would be contravening a number of rules:

a The maximum daily dosage of the drug was 10 mg; this was clearly stated on the label
b Drugs should not be given to patients without written authority from the doctor
c Orders should not be taken from unknown doctors.

Despite this, 21 out of 22 of the nurses involved were ready to administer the drug before being stopped by an observer.

Since 1966 the role of nurses has changed considerably and they operate with a great deal more autonomy than used to be the case. Nevertheless, Hofling's study demonstrates the power that goes with certain **social roles** – doctors, regardless of any personality characteristics, demand respect and obedience from other professionals and patients. The power of social roles is also clearly demonstrated in Zimbardo's Stanford Prison Study (see the first Core Study in this section, p. 118), in which people conformed alarmingly to the roles assigned to them.

Zimbardo's prison study is relevant to both **conformity** and **obedience**; make sure you bear this in mind when answering exam questions.

Implications of obedience studies

The implications of these studies are very far reaching. The main ones, put forward by Milgram, are as follows:

1. In any society, normal people can act in a callous and inhumane way as a result of social pressure. It doesn't take an evil person to serve an evil system; ordinary people are easily integrated into malevolent systems.

2. Nevertheless, although we may be puppets of the system, we are puppets with perception, and we should not abdicate responsibility by saying 'I was only obeying orders'.

3. These studies clearly show that we need to be aware of the dangers of blind obedience so that we are not overtaken by an evil system, as happened in Hitler's regime in Germany.

4. Our obligation, according to Milgram, is to place in positions of authority those people most likely to use it wisely and humanely.

Preparing for the exam

Key terms

autokinetic effect
conformity
ecological validity
informational influence
mindlessness

normative influence
obedience
social pressure
social roles

Types of exam question

The types of questions asked fall into the following categories:

1. Evaluation of the major studies of conformity and obedience, including the ethical considerations.
2. The reasons why people conform and obey.
3. Implications of the findings.

Self-test questions

1. Summarise and criticise *two* major studies of conformity
2. List and briefly describe *five* reasons why people conform.
3. Summarise Milgram's study of obedience.
4. What are the main methodological and ethical criticisms of the study?
5. Use Milgram's variations to discuss why people obey authority.
6. Who were the participants in Hofling's study, and what were they asked to do?
7. The participants in Hofling's study who were prepared to obey were contravening *three* rules. What were they?

Exam questions with guidance notes

1. **Critically evaluate studies of conformity.** **(25 marks)**
   AEB (1987)

Being asked to 'critically evaluate' requires you to
- Briefly describe the *findings* (remember, though, that an essay simply describing the studies and their findings will be awarded very few marks)
- Outline the *strengths*
- Discuss the *weaknesses* and *limitations*
- Discuss the *implications* – you need to be familiar with the ethics of conducting studies, as considered in Chapter 10.
- Go through the important studies one at a time and evaluate each one. Bear in mind the following:
  a **Sherif** used an ambiguous task which is always likely to elicit conformity. The ecological validity of the study is questionable since such a setting is not closely related to everyday conformity.
  b **Asch**'s study particularly shows just how surprisingly high levels of conformity can be. Use the variations of his study to discuss the reasons why people conform. Problems include ethical considerations (since participants suffered much stress and embarrassment as well as possible loss of self-esteem), ecological validity and debate as to whether the study is a 'child of its times'.
  c **Zimbardo**'s study demonstrates the power of *roles* in shaping behaviour. It is obviously important to discuss the ecological validity and the ethics of this study, as well as the problems of using such a relatively small and biased sample (all male, white, middle class students).

2. **Discuss psychological studies of obedience in humans and consider the implications of this type of research.** **(25 marks)**
   AEB (1989)

- Introduce the essay with a *definition* of obedience and a statement as to why it is such an important area of study in psychology.
- When discussing *Milgram*'s study, address the question of ecological validity, methodological weaknesses and ethics, including Milgram's defence.
- Mention that *Hofling*'s study has ecological validity but also subjects participants to deception and stress – though, arguably, not unnecessarily.
- You can use *Zimbardo*'s study to discuss the ease with which ordinary individuals become cruel and sadistic when taking on the role of guards and did not consider the implications of their actions until after the research project had ended.
- *Implications* are dealt with in the text. Above all, Milgram shows that people are capable of committing terrible acts when instructed by an authority to do so. Hofling's study is also disturbing because of its undeniable ecological validity. It is easy to see how the nurses could have behaved as they did and to imagine how similar situations could arise in other working environments.

- You could conclude with reference to the dangers of *blind obedience*, and the advice given by Milgram about ways to reduce the risk of atrocities caused by such obedience.

Additional exam questions

1. Discuss some of the problems involved in the experimental study of conformity and/or obedience **(25 marks)**
   AEB AS (1994)

2. 'Milgram, in exploring the external conditions that produce ... destructive obedience, the psychological processes that lead to such attempted abdications of responsibility, and the means by which defiance of illegitimate authority can be promoted, seems to me to have done some of the most morally significant research in modern psychology' (Elms, 1986). Discuss. **(25 marks)**
   AEB AS (1991)

5.4 Leadership

Leaders may be defined as particularly influential members of a group, who act to guide, direct and motivate the group to achieve its goal (Hollander, 1985).

Leaders certainly fulfil an important function and are often said to be the cause of a group's success or failure.

Theories of leadership

These are concerned with what makes a **good leader**.

The trait approach or 'great person' theory

Thomas Carlyle (1841–1907) was the first to argue that leaders possess certain personality characteristics which distinguish them from non-leaders. In other words, he considered that leaders are **born**, not made.

Stogdill (1974) and Mann (1959) reviewed a large number of such studies and found only a few consistent traits. It seems that, compared to non-leaders, leaders are:

- Slightly more intelligent
- More extrovert
- More sociable
- More dominant
- More self-confident
- More concerned with achievement.

There is also evidence that suggests leaders are taller, older and more experienced than non-leaders.

However, despite identifying a number of leadership tendencies, the research concludes that no reliable or coherent pattern of characteristics can be identified.

Evaluation

One of the imperfections of early studies was their failure to distinguish between the qualities involved in the **emergence** of leadership and the qualities involved in the **effectiveness** of leadership. Later studies which have made this distinction have had more success in identifying significant characteristics. Lord *et al.* (1986) found three traits strongly related to the **emergence** of leadership – intelligence, dominance and masculine personality characteristics – the stereotype of masculinity being one who is aggressive, decisive and unemotional. Lord believes that people have a stereotyped view of what constitutes a good leader and will select leaders who fit this stereotype, but that does not necessarily mean that they will be effective leaders.

Many of the studies which have found a relationship between traits and leadership have been based on self-report personality questionnaires. Respondents may not be realistic in their responses.

The situational approach

This view of leadership maintains that the nature of the **group**, its goals, communication networks and other aspects of the situation are important in determining who emerges as leader and how effective he or she will be. Even factors like seating arrangements can effect who emerges as a leader.

Strodtbeck *et al.* (1958, 1961) studied the group dynamics of juries and noted that the jurors who sat at the ends of the tables were significantly more likely to be chosen as foremen than were members sitting elsewhere.

Bales (1958) showed that the more a group member talked and participated in events, the more likely he or she was to be perceived as a leader.

There is evidence to suggest that **crisis situations** influence who emerges as leader and the extent of their power. Hamblin (1958) deliberately imposed a crisis situation on three out of six teams of students who were competing to discover the rules of a game. After each of six trials they were given clues as to whether their guesses were correct, but for those in the 'crisis' situation these rules were changed after the third trial so all their previous hypotheses were incorrect. Group members who had been influential prior to the emergency became far more influential when in crisis and their suggestions were less often challenged or criticised by other group members. It seemed that the crisis made the group more in need of directive, autocratic leadership.

This could explain the tendency for very strong political leaders to emerge in times of crisis. Hitler came to power at a time when Germany was in economic crisis and Winston Churchill is usually referred to as a great wartime leader whose greatness diminished in peacetime.

The interactionist view: Fiedler's contingency theory

Fiedler (1971) proposed a theory of leadership effectiveness that combines the trait and situational approach, taking into account both personality characteristics and aspects of the situation. Based on the work of **Bales (1970)**, Fiedler identified **two** types of leader:

1. The **task-orientated** leader is concerned with such factors as defining the problems of the group and establishing a plan of action: in essence, with 'getting on with the job'
2. The **relationship-orientated** leader tends to concentrate on establishing cohesiveness, reducing conflict, boosting morale and providing emotional support.

In order to ascertain into which category a leader falls, Fiedler developed the **'Esteem for the Least Preferred Co-worker (LPC) Scale'**. Leaders are asked to describe their least preferred co-worker. A leader who gives a negative description is believed to be mainly concerned with success, suggesting a task-orientated style. A leader giving a positive assessment is judged to be relationship-orientated.

According to Fiedler, the nature of the situation determines which type of leader will be most effective and he identifies **three** important situational variables:

1. The **quality** of the relationship between the leader and the other group members
2. The nature of the **task** to be undertaken: how complex it is and how clearly goals are defined
3. The extent to which the leader has **legitimate authority** over the group.

Fiedler puts forward the following arguments:

1. In **favourable** situations, in which leader–group relations are good, goals are clearly defined and the leader has legitimate authority, the leader does not need to be concerned about relationships. In these circumstances, a task-orientated leader is more effective.
2. Conversely, the task-oriented leader is also preferable in very **bad** situations, since undue concentration on side issues means there is less time to consider the main task.

3. In moderately good or bad situations, where **morale and group relations** need to be improved, the relationship-orientated leader is likely to be more effective.

Evaluation

Criticisms

1. A number of researchers have questioned Fiedler's method of ascertaining whether a leader is task- or relationship-orientated. The LPC score does not show great reliability since it is liable to **change over time**.
2. It is unclear if the LPC score is actually related to the behaviour of a leader towards followers.
3. A further problem with establishing the validity of the theory is the difficulty experienced with measuring the **favourability** of situational factors.

Contribution

Despite the criticisms, this approach has been useful in training people in authority to analyse their own leadership style, carefully to assess important situational factors and to consider ways in which they can adapt their leadership style to suit these situational factors.

Activity

Which leader is more effective in the following situations, a task-orientated or a relationship-orientated one?

1. A small, friendly firm in which the workforce have to strive to meet an unusually large order in a very short time
2. A large, strife-ridden company which has to find a way to fill order books if it is to avoid liquidation
3. A large office comprising many different sections, not all totally harmonious, responsible for mailing goods ordered from a catalogue; it is necessary to speed up the mailing

4. An amateur dramatics group who don't take themselves too seriously and put on the occasional, light-hearted public performance
5. A group of mountain walkers who find themselves in serious trouble when they misjudge the weather and the ease of their chosen route back to base.

The effectiveness of leadership styles

Lewin, Lippitt and White (1939), in a classic study, compared the effectiveness of different styles of leadership on groups of ten year old boys involved in model-making activities. They trained graduate students in **three** leadership styles:

1. **Autocratic:** leaders made all the decisions and assigned tasks without consultation
2. **Democratic:** leaders consulted fully with the group before taking any decisions and offered constructive advice
3. **Laissez-faire:** leaders interacted very little with the group, leaving them very much to their own devices.

The groups assigned autocratic and democratic leaders produced a comparable quantity and quality of models, far better than the group with the laissez-faire leader. The democratic leader had a more positive impact on the boys, who, having been given the opportunity to experience all three styles of leadership, much preferred this style.

Evaluation

There are several problems with the study itself and the conclusions drawn from it.

1. The situation was very **artificial** with leaders acting as instructed rather than responding to the individuals in the group and to the situation as it developed
2. The sample of **participants**, being teenage boys, limits the extent to which the findings can be generalised
3. Few **real-life** situations involve such a limited and specific task

4. Brown (1985) argues that the success of the democratic style may have been due to the fact that it reflected the **ethos** of American society at the time, rather than because the style was more effective *per se*.

Fiedler's argument is that different types of leader are effective in different types of situation. It seems reasonable to conclude that the best leaders are those who can **adapt** their leadership style to the situation. Morley and Hosking (1984) argue that good leadership is a skill which can be developed. Skilful leaders produce the best results possible in any given circumstance, and this requires good negotiation skills together with a thorough understanding of the group concerned, the organisation and the nature of the task.

Preparing for the exam

Key terms

autocratic

crisis situations

democratic

laissez-faire

legitimate authority

relationship-orientated leader

self-report personality questionnaires

situational approach

task-orientated leader

trait approach

Types of exam question

1. Evaluation of the main theories of leadership.
2. Description and evaluation of studies of leadership.

Self-test questions

1. According to research, what characteristics are leaders likely to have?
2. Briefly summarise the main theories of leadership: the 'great person' theory, the situational approach and the interactionist view.
3. Describe and evaluate *one* study related to each theory.
4. Identify which studies are related to leadership emergence and which are related to leadership effectiveness.

Exam question with guidance notes

Describe and evaluate studies of leadership which focus on the emergence and effectiveness of leaders.   **(25 marks)**

AEB (1990)

Essays on leadership tend to be quite demanding and require careful reading; this is no exception. Notice that you are being asked for *studies* and you therefore need to include as many as possible; theories alone will gain you very few marks.

- Introduce the essay by pointing out that there are a number of theories seeking to *explain* leadership: the 'great person' theory, the situational approach and the interactionist view. The first two approaches deal mainly with the *emergence* of leaders whereas the interactionist view, as expressed by Fiedler's contingency theory, discusses *effectiveness* in detail.
- Discuss the 'great person' theory, using Stogdill (1974) and Mann (1959) as sources of evidence. The studies they quote are limited because of the

failure to distinguish between emergence and effectiveness. Lord *et al.* (1986) addresses this problem and does find significant traits related to emergence of leaders, but points out that these may be more related to how others choose particular people to lead them rather than the fact that traits such as intelligence, dominance and masculine personality characteristics equip someone to be an effective leader. The Hamblin study shows how leader and follower relationships can *change* as circumstances change. The studies are, however, limited not only in their failure to address the question of effectiveness (although the Hamblin study touches on this), but on the artificial nature of the situation. Not all of them are laboratory studies but most of them inevitably sample leadership in a limited context.

- Research specifically targeted at *effectiveness* of leadership styles is the classic study of Lewin, Lippitt and White which is described and evaluated in the text.
- Fiedler's work is concerned with *effectiveness* of leadership and you need to describe his theory and research in some detail. Evaluate it with reference to the criticisms of the LPC scale, the difficulties in determining the nature of group relations and, on the positive side, the value of the training programmes developed from the studies and theory.
- You can then conclude with Fiedler's argument that both the situation and the characteristics of the leader are important, and that the most effective leaders are those who can *adapt* to changing circumstances.

Additional exam questions

1. 'Power and leadership arise from the interaction of social influences.' Describe and discuss psychological research which focuses on this statement.   **(25 marks)**
AEB (1991)

2. a Examine research evidence on the emergence of leaders.   **(10 marks)**
   b Discuss psychological insights into leader effectiveness.   **(15 marks)**
AEB (1994)

5.5 Prosocial behaviour

Prosocial behaviours are those which involve putting the needs or interests of others before our own, and include helping others in emergencies and donating time to charity. **Altruism** refers to behaviours which are unselfish and motivated by another person's needs.

People sometimes risk their lives to help others, yet in other situations they do nothing. Research has shown that the reason for this is complex: whether someone will help in an emergency depends on the nature of the situation and the nature of the individuals involved.

The situation

The number of bystanders

Latane and Darley believe that, ironically, the larger the number of potential helpers, the less likely it is that they will help. They carried out a number of experiments to ascertain the truth of this hypothesis.

Latane and Darley (1968) invited female students

to discuss with other students the personal problems of college life. Supposedly to avoid embarrassment, they each sat alone in a small room and conducted the discussion over an intercom. One person, a confederate of the experimenters, mentioned that she was epileptic and during the course of the discussion she feigned a fit.

- When the participants thought that they were the only witness, 85 per cent summoned help
- When they believed there were two other witnesses, 62 per cent requested assistance
- When they thought there were five other witnesses, only 31 per cent helped.

The ambiguity of the situation

Some situations are clearly emergencies, others are open to interpretation, that is, they are **ambiguous**.

Clark and Word (1972) placed participants in a room to complete questionnaires either alone, in pairs or in groups of five. As they worked, a confederate, wearing a maintenance uniform and carrying a ladder and a venetian blind, walked through into an adjoining room. A few minutes later, the participants heard a loud noise as the confederate staged an accident: the blind was pulled off the window, the ladder and the man fell. In one condition, the situation was ambiguous since no other information was provided and the participants could not see what was happening in the room. In the other condition, the situation was made quite clear and unambiguous when the confederate groaned, grunted and yelled out: 'Oh my back. I can't move.' Regardless of the group size:

- All participants went to his aid when the situation was unambiguous.
- In the ambiguous condition only 30 per cent helped.

This reinforces the finding that, in situations in which there is a clear-cut emergency, people will react even when there are plenty of other people present; it is only when we are uncertain that the presence of others inhibits helping.

Location

Psychological investigations indicate that people who live in small closely-knit communities are more inclined to help others than are those who live in large cities.

Milgram (1970) carried out a study in which 'wrong numbers' were rung in Chicago, New York and Philadelphia and in small towns outside each of these cities. Apparently distressed experimenters explained that, having called the wrong number, they now had no money and requested that a call be made to a friend of theirs in order to explain the predicament. In all cases, people were more helpful in the small towns than in the cities.

Suggested causes of the bystander effect

Latante and Darley hypothesise that the following influences may contribute to non-intervention in emergency situations (see the Core Study, p. 133 for more detail).

Diffusion of responsibility

In emergency situations, the more bystanders present, the less responsibility each individual bystander feels. They may believe that someone else will probably assist and that the responsibility for providing help does not lie on their shoulders. Put simply, the responsibility to act is **shared**, or **diffused**. Diffusion of responsibility is greater if we feel that others present are better equipped than we are to deal with an emergency, but on occasions when we feel we are the most competent person present, we will take on the responsibility to act, no matter how many people are present.

Pluralistic ignorance

Bystanders to an emergency may interpret the situation as a non-emergency if others around them are acting in an apparently calm manner. The clarity of the situation is a very important determinant of helping. In circumstances in which we are unsure how to act, we typically look nervously around at others to provide clues as to which behaviour is most appropriate. Since everyone is responding in a similar way, it is possible for everyone to come to the same wrong conclusion: that no action is necessary.

Evaluation apprehension (audience inhibition effect)

People may be inhibited from helping in ambiguous situations in which others are present because they do not wish to look foolish and suffer embarrassment. The greater the audience, the more inhibited we feel. This especially applies to people who do not feel confident of their ability to make an appropriate and useful response to the situation.

As for the reason why people in urban areas are less likely to help than those in a rural community, it is possible that in areas of high density, pluralistic ignorance and diffusion of responsibility are more likely to occur. Perhaps an even more plausible explanation is that the stress involved in living in such close proximity to others encourages people to withdraw from personal involvement and 'mind their own business' as a means of protecting their own and others' privacy.

Students often confuse the **factors** which influence helping with the reasons for this behaviour. Factors which affect helping include:

a number of bystanders
b ambiguity of the situation
c location

Among the suggested reasons why these factors are influential are:

a diffusion of responsibility
b pluralistic ignorance
c evaluation apprehension.

The individuals involved

Research shows that certain people are more likely than others to help than to be helped.

The victims

1. People are more inclined to help those who are **smartly dressed** than those who are unkempt (Bickman, 1974).
2. Victims are more likely to be helped if they are seen as **deserving causes** rather than the source of their own misfortune. (Piliavin *et al.*, 1969; the Core Study, in this section.)

3. We are more likely to help people whom we see as being **similar to ourselves**. This may account for the racial bias that has been observed in a number of studies concerning helping.

West *et al.* (1975) found that when a black person pretended to be a stranded motorist whose car had broken down, 97 per cent of the people who offered help were black. Conversely, when the victim was white, 94 per cent of the helpers were white.
Piliavin *et al.* (1969) also noted a slight racial bias, particularly if the victim was thought to be drunk.

The helpers

1. **Men** are more likely than women to help. Piliavin *et al.* (1969) found that women were more likely to ignore a collapsed man on the subway; Bickman (1974) found they were less likely to give a dime to a stranger; many other studies report a similar female reluctance to offer assistance.
2. Psychologists have been largely unsuccessful in pinpointing a **personality 'type'** most likely to give help, although helpers do tend to be:
    *   empathic (Archer, 1984)
    *   deeply committed to moral standards (Fogelman and Weiner, 1985)
    *   self-confident (Aronoff and Wilson, 1985).

Activity

In which of the following situations is help likely to be provided?

1. A woman faints in a nearly empty railway carriage.
2. A man in a pub starts staggering and lurching about and eventually falls over.
3. A man in a theatre foyer acts in a similar manner.
4. A man and woman are standing screaming at each other in a car park; he is holding her roughly and she is yelling at him to let her go and that she wishes she'd never met him.
5. Your car breaks down on a busy road in central Manchester.
6. The same happens in a small rural village.

Core Study

Good samaritanism: an underground phenomenon?: I. Piliavin, J. Rodin and J. Piliavin (1969)

Aims

The focus of this study is the effect on helping behaviour of:

a   The victim's **problem** (whether or not it appears self-inflicted)

b   The **race** of the victim

c   The presence of a **model** (someone who offers help first)

d   The **size** of the group.

Method

Subjects

People travelling on a particular stretch of the New York underground system between 11 a.m. and 3 p.m. on week-days.

Situation

In order to have a captive audience, a $7\frac{1}{2}$ minute journey, without stops, was used. The study took place in the end section of a carriage in which there were 13 seats and some standing room in the 'critical area' chosen.

Procedure

There were four teams of four experimenters, two females, who observed and recorded the responses of subjects, and two males, who played the roles of victim and model.

In each of the 103 trials the victim stood near a pole in the centre of the critical area and, 70 seconds into the journey, staggered forward, collapsed and then remained on the floor until he was helped.

The victims were male, aged between 26 and 35 years. Three were white and one was black, all were dressed identically in a casual manner.

In 38 trials, they appeared drunk by smelling of alcohol and carrying a bottle in a brown bag.

In the other 65 trials, they carried a black cane and appeared to be sober.

Apart from this, they behaved identically.

Models were all white and informally dressed. There were four model conditions:

1.   Critical area/early helpers, who were close to the victim and helped after about 70 seconds

2.   Critical area/late helpers, who helped after 150 seconds

3.   Adjacent area/early helpers

4.   Adjacent area/late helpers.

In all cases, the model helped by raising the victim to a sitting position and staying with him until the next stop.

Results

Table 5.2 shows the percentage of trials in which help was given, by race and condition of victim, and total number of trials in each condition.

Table 5.2 Percentage of trials in which help was given

Trials	White victims		Black victims	
	Cane	Drunk	Cane	Drunk
No model (%)	100	100	100	73
Model trials (%)	100	77	–	67

As shown in Table 5.2, helping was very high, more than indicated by previous studies of helping behaviour. All the cane carrying victims and a high percentage of the drunken victims were helped. The race of the victims made no significant difference to helping behaviour, but there was a tendency for same-race helping in the drunken condition.

On 60 per cent of the 81 trials where help was given, more than one person offered help. The race of the victim made no difference to the numbers who were involved in helping.

Characteristics of first helper

1. 90 per cent of helpers were male. Although there were more men present, this percentage was statistically significant
2. 64 per cent of helpers were white; this was what would be expected based on the racial distribution of the carriage.

Effect of the model

On the majority of trials, the model did not get the opportunity to act, so no extensive analysis was made of the effect of the model.

Other responses

1. In 21 of the 103 trials a total of 34 people left the critical area, particularly when the victim appeared to be drunk
2. Discomfort of onlookers was visible, especially on occasions when no one helped after 70 seconds.

Diffusion of responsibility

After careful analysis of data it was found that people help more quickly in large groups (seven and more) than in small groups. This does not support findings made by other researchers (for example, Latane and Darley, 1968) but the two studies are not strictly comparable. It is possible that the more people present, the more likely it is that at least one person will help.

Conclusions

The researchers present the following model of response to emergency situations:

- Observation of an emergency creates an **emotional arousal** in onlookers which will be interpreted as fear, disgust or sympathy, depending on aspects of the situation.
- Arousal can be **reduced** by either: helping, seeking help from another source, moving away, or deciding the person doesn't need or deserve help.

The researchers argue that the chosen response depends upon the relative costs and rewards involved:

- **Costs of helping** include effort, embarrassment and possible physical harm
- **Costs of not helping** include self-blame and perceived censure from others
- **Rewards of helping** include praise from self, onlookers and the victim
- **Rewards of not helping** include getting on with one's own business and not incurring the possible costs of helping.

All conclusions can be interpreted using this model:

1. The drunken victim is helped less often because the perceived cost is greater – helping a drunk is more likely to cause embarrassment or harm. The cost of not helping is less because nobody will blame another for not helping a drunk.
2. Women help less often than men because the cost to them in terms of effort and danger is greater and, since it is not seen as a woman's role to offer assistance under these circumstances, the cost of not helping is less.
3. The cost of not helping members of one's own race is high because of censure by one's own racial group, therefore same-race helping is far more likely to occur. The cost of helping a drunken member of another race is comparatively high because the reaction of that person is likely to be less predictable than that of a member of one's own race.
4. Diffusion of responsibility is not found in the cane carrying situation because the cost of not helping is high and the cost of helping is low.
5. As time without help increases, so does arousal level of the onlookers. A late model is not copied because people have already chosen an alternative way of reducing arousal; they leave the area or engage in conversation with others in order to justify their lack of help.

QUESTIONS

1. In the study on Samaritanism in the subway, give TWO independent variables that were studied and briefly report their effect on the behaviour of the bystanders. **(4 marks)**
   Oxford and Cambridge Specimen Paper

2. What type of method was used for the study?
3. a Discuss whether the study was ethical and should have been performed.
   b Consider how the study may have been altered to be more ethical, and suggest how such changes might have altered the results.
   Based on Oxford and Cambridge Specimen Paper

Helping and emotion

It seems that in many emergencies people do not stop to consider the costs of intervention but act spontaneously with little regard for their own welfare.

Clark and Word (1972) arranged an experimental situation in which participants witnessed an electrician apparently receiving a severe shock. The degree of danger to potential helpers was varied by having the 'victim' either still in contact with electricity or having fallen away from the wires. The ambiguity of the situation was also varied.

In the unambiguous conditions, the victims were always helped, even though this could have been extremely dangerous. Many participants grabbed the victim's legs, which would have caused them to receive the shock as well. Afterwards, many of the participants said that they were aware of the potential injury which such action could have caused them but, at the time, they did not think about the possible danger to themselves.

Piliavin, Piliavin and Rodin believe that **arousal** is the key to understanding impulsive behaviour. Rapid helping usually occurs in very serious emergencies when the victim's injuries are severe and getting worse with each passing second. Bystanders become very aroused and help without considering the costs to themselves.

Activity

Don't forget to read the Core Study carefully and make notes on the cost/reward theory put forward by Piliavin, Rodin and Piliavin. This is essential to the topic.

Preparing for the exam

Key terms

altruism

ambiguity of the situation

bystander effect

diffusion of responsibility

evaluation apprehension

pluralistic ignorance

prosocial

Types of exam question

1. Identification of factors involved in determining whether help is offered.
2. Consideration of the implications of research.

Self-test questions

1. List *three* aspects of a situation which are likely to influence helping behaviour.
2. Briefly describe *one* piece of research to illustrate each of the above.
3. Outline suggested causes of the bystander effect.
4. Describe the characteristics of people who are most likely to be helped and people who are most likely to help in an emergency.

Exam question with guidance notes

Analyse the situational determinants of altruism and helping in humans. What are the implications of research in this area? **(25 marks)**

AEB (1991)

- The first part of this question is straightforward. Situational determinants include: the numbers present, ambiguity of the situation, location, seriousness of the situation, characteristics of the individual needing help. Use *research* evidence to support your arguments.
- The reasons why these determinants may be important are: diffusion of responsibility, pluralistic ignorance, evaluation apprehension. You could, if you wish, mention deindividuation (discussed in section 5.6 on Aggression) to help explain some of these effects, such as location and similarity of the victim to the potential helper.
- The implications part of the question requires a little insightful thinking. Having considered the determinants, it is obvious that help is not received just because it is required and there are a number of measures that can be taken by the victim and potential helpers to *maximise* helping behaviour:
  - **a** If you are a victim in situations which may appear ambiguous, it is advisable to make it clear that help is needed.
  - **b** In situations where several people are present, pinpoint individuals to take responsibility for specific tasks: (you – call the police; you – phone for an ambulance).
  - **c** If you are a potential helper, make sure you check whether or not a person needs help rather than pass on for fear of embarrassment or because no one else is helping. Always check whether someone else

has called an ambulance and so on rather than assume that, because there are so many people around, someone must have.

- Finally, bear in mind that you can draw on research from other areas. There is evidence to suggest that watching prosocial television programmes increases helping and cooperation. This suggests that people can be 'programmed' to help.

Additional exam question

Using psychological theory and evidence, discuss some of the determinants of altruism and helping in humans. **(25 marks)**

AEB AS (1993)

5.6 Aggression

A working definition of **aggression** is that it is behaviour intended to bring harm, psychological or physical, to another.

It is probable, however, that such a definition fails to include all aggressive acts.

Theories of aggression

The psychodynamic approach

Freud argued that all human beings possess **two** important instincts, the life and death instincts (see Chapter 2). The conflict between the life and death instincts results in self-destructive tendencies being displaced as aggression towards others or sublimated into sport or some other physical activity.

Freud believed that the instinctual energies must find release in some way or they will build up and cause unbearable pressure, possibly to be eventually released by an uncontrolled display of aggression. There is some evidence that particularly brutal crimes are often committed by very controlled individuals with no history of violent crime, and they are often 'triggered' by a seemingly trivial incident (Megargee, 1966). Freud argued that all of us, without displacement and self-control, could become uncontrollably violent.

Activity

Freud's work is covered in Chapter 2. Make sure you have read and learnt it as it is integral to many parts of the syllabus. Use appropriate criticisms and contributions from this section to evaluate Freud's theory of aggression.

1. According to Freud, is aggression innate or learnt?
2. What is meant by a defence mechanism?

Figure 5.1 Photo courtesy of Jeff Baynham

3. With reference to aggression, how can defence mechanisms provide a safe outlet for aggressive urges?
4. Give examples of **two** defence mechanisms which might be used to control aggression.

The motivational approach

Motivational theorists argue that aggression is a response to **frustration**. **Dollard** *et al.* **(1939)** formulated **the frustration–aggression hypothesis** which states that frustration always leads to aggression and that aggression is always caused by frustration. According to these researchers, aggression is a drive motivated by external, social factors such as prolonged queueing, failure to achieve an important goal and overcrowded living conditions. Aggression is either expressed directly, as an attack on the source of the frustration, or it is displaced onto another person or object.

Critics of this hypothesis point out that:

1. Frustrating experiences do not inevitably lead to feelings of anger; they may lead to feelings such as **depression** or **exhaustion**
2. Aggression can be caused by factors **other** than frustration.

To take account of these problems with the frustration–aggression hypothesis, a more generalised hypothesis, the **arousal–aggression hypothesis**, has been advanced. This suggests that frustration leads to aggression because it causes general arousal which may or may not be expressed as aggression, depending upon the environmental cues available. The classic study of Schachter and Singer (the Core Study on p. 206), shows that when we feel aroused, we need to attribute a **cause** to this arousal and we look for cues in the situation. If the arousal has been caused by frustration, then there will often be situational cues which stimulate a feeling of anger within us. Nevertheless, these cues will sometimes produce other emotions.

The social learning theory approach

Bandura (1973) argues that people learn to behave aggressively through reinforcement and observation. There are numerous examples of reinforced human aggression: controlled aggression in sport is usually what is required to win, aggressive children often get their own way with other children and in many societies male dominance and aggression is respected and prized.

Bandura particularly stresses the power of **observational learning**. He and two colleagues carried out a number of experiments, of which the Core Study in this chapter provides a classic example, demonstrating that children imitate behaviour that they have observed, particularly if it is rewarded. Social learning theory places great emphasis on the influence of the mass media which has now become such a powerful force in modern Western society (this is discussed later in the sub section).

Again, social learning theory is covered in Chapter 2 and is integral to the syllabus, so make sure you have read and learnt it. Evaluation is also covered in that chapter.

The Core Study is also essential reading: a summary of this is invaluable in many essays on aggression.

The normative approach

Some aggression is a reflection of **social norms** within a society or of a subgroup within a society.

In subgroups such as urban youth gangs, the norm is for toughness, strength and aggression, and members are obliged to conform to these norms in order to be accepted and, in extreme cases, to survive.

Deindividuation

Many norms within society actually keep a check on aggression but there are circumstances in which these social constraints are loosened. **Zimbardo (1969)** argues that, under certain circumstances, people lose their sense of identity and become uncharacteristically aggressive. Zimbardo coined the term **deindividuation** to describe this loss of personal identity, in which the individual surrenders his or her own independence and sense of responsibility and simply becomes part of a crowd. When people become deindividuated they cease to act in accordance with social norms and lack their usual self-control, often resulting in such anti-social behaviour as rudeness, aggression and vandalism.

The social learning theory and normative approach are in broad agreement, both suggesting that aggression is learnt from those around us; they simply focus on different **influences**.

Core Study

Transmission of aggression through imitation of aggressive models: A. Bandura, D. Ross and S.A. Ross (1961)

Subjects

36 boys and 36 girls, aged 3 years to 5 years 9 months. 2 adults (1 male, 1 female) acted as models.

Experimental design

8 Experimental groups, each of 6 subjects. 1 control group, of 24 subjects. The experimental groups were subdivided: 4 exposed to aggressive model: 2 groups of girls, 2 of boys

- 2 of these exposed to same-sex model
- 2 of these exposed to opposite-sex model.

4 exposed to non-aggressive model: 2 groups of girls, 2 of boys

- 2 of these exposed to same-sex model
- 2 of these exposed to opposite-sex model.

The control group never encountered the model. All children were rated for physical and verbal aggression. Subjects with similar scores were then arranged in threes and allocated randomly to the aggressive, the non-aggressive and the control conditions. Thus, subjects in each condition were matched on levels of aggression.

Experimental conditions

Subjects were brought individually into a room within the nursery school and sat in one corner to play with toys specially selected to be of high interest value. The model was seated on the opposite corner with tinker toy set, a mallet and a 5 foot Bobo doll. The experimenter explained to the child that these were the model's toys and then left the model and the child alone together.

In the **non-aggressive** condition, the model assembled the tinker toys in a quiet manner and ignored the Bobo doll.

In the **aggressive** condition, the model played briefly with the tinker toy and then aggressed towards the Bobo doll. The model deliberately used novel, distinctive aggressive acts which the subject was extremely unlikely to have encountered before. The sequence was as follows:

- In addition to punching the doll, the model laid it on its side, sat on it and punched it repeatedly on the nose. The model then raised the doll, picked up the mallet and struck the doll on the head, tossed the doll in the air aggressively and kicked it around the room. This whole sequence was repeated three times and accompanied by verbally aggressive responses such as 'Sock him in the nose', 'Kick him', 'Pow' ...
- The whole session lasted 10 minutes. The subjects could only play with their designated toys, so any learning was observational.

Test for delayed imitation

Subjects were taken individually to another room, quite separate from the first. The experimenter stayed with them (because otherwise many children refused to stay), but remained as inconspicuous as possible. There was a selection of attractive toys, both aggressive and non-aggressive, including a 3 foot Bobo doll and a mallet. This session lasted 20 minutes, during which children were observed through a one-way mirror.

Results

Subjects in the aggression condition reproduced a good deal of physical and verbal aggressive behaviour resembling that of the models and their mean scores differed markedly from those of subjects in the non-aggressive and control conditions. Many children in the non-aggressive and control groups showed no aggression at all, and there was no difference in their results (see Table 5.3).

Table 5.3 Mean aggression scores for experimental and control subjects

Response Category	Experimental groups Aggressive		Non-aggressive		Control groups
	F model	M model	F model	M model	
Imitative physical aggression:					
Female subjects	5.5	7.2	2.5	0.0	1.2
Male subjects	12.4	25.8	0.2	1.5	2.0
Imitative verbal aggression:					
Female subjects	13.7	2.0	0.3	0.0	0.7
Male subjects	4.3	12.7	1.1	0.0	1.7

Influence of sex of model and sex of subject on imitation

The hypothesis that boys are more prone than girls to imitate aggression exhibited by a model was only partially confirmed. Boys reproduced more imitative physical aggression than girls, but there was no difference in their imitation of verbal aggression. Boys exhibited much more aggressive imitation (and more non-aggressive imitation) after being exposed to the aggressive male model than did the female subjects. In contrast, girls exposed to the female model performed considerably more imitative verbal aggression and more non-imitative aggression than did the boys.

Discussion

Verbal comments made by young children showed that they considered aggressive behaviour inappropriate for a female model ('That's not a way for a lady to behave') but not for a male ('Al's a good socker, he beat up Bobo').

The results of this study provide strong evidence that observation of behaviour of others is one effective means of eliciting responses which are extremely unlikely to have been produced otherwise. In other words, it explains the **acquisition of new responses** in a way which reinforcement and punishment alone cannot.

QUESTIONS

1. Outline the controls used by Bandura *et al.* in their study on the transmission of aggression.

    (4 marks)
    Oxford and Cambridge Specimen Paper

2. What type of method was used (design, choice of subjects, where it was carried out)?

3. Discuss whether the study conflicted with ethical guidelines.

4. Evaluate whether the study should have been performed.

Activity

The Core Study by Zimbardo in section 5.3 on conformity and obedience demonstrates the effect of deindividuation. It may well be useful to use a very brief summary of this study in certain essays on aggression. With reference to this study:

1. How were the guards deindividuated?
2. How were the prisoners deindividuated?
3. In what ways was unnecessary and unprovoked aggression shown by the guards to the prisoners?

Try to think of an example of deindividuation leading to spasmodic outbreaks of violence in everyday life.

The influence of the mass media on aggression

A large number of studies analysing the content of television programmes indicate that the overall content is very violent. For example:

1. **Gerbner *et al.* (1986)**, in a study of American television, found that the level of violence, especially in cartoons, was very high and had been for the previous twenty years.
2. A British study carried out by **Cumberpatch (1987)** showed somewhat less violence, but cartoons, aimed primarily at an audience of young children, were among the most violent programmes shown.
3. **Parke *et al.* (1977)** conducted a study in which institutionalised delinquent boys were split into two groups, each equivalent in aggressiveness. One group was shown violent films each night for five nights, while the other group acted as a control and were shown non-violent films. Observers found that the boys who had a violent television diet were significantly more aggressive than the control group.

We must bear in mind that this study was very short-term and that delinquent boys may be particularly susceptible to the effects of televised violence. Nevertheless, these findings are a cause for concern.

4. In a review of 230 studies, **Hearold (1986)** noted consistent evidence that television violence is related to aggressiveness in children. She also noted that the effects of violence viewed increases with age for boys but decreases for girls, and that television violence encourages real-life violence, particularly when it is realistic and presented as being justified. Evidence also suggests that people may become desensitised to real-life violence after extensive exposure to television violence.

Although some social psychologists have questioned the evidence, (for example, Freeman, 1984), on the whole it does suggest that television violence does lead to increased aggression in children.

Problems with research on the effects of television violence

The methodological problems of these studies are considerable:

1. Most studies are correlational, seeking to discover if there is a relationship between amount of violent television viewed and levels of aggression. Correlational studies are **not** studies of cause and effect. It is possible that aggressive children select violent programmes to view. It is also possible that aggressive parents have aggressive children and also choose to watch violence on television, thus the children may also watch it but it is not the cause of their aggressive behaviour.
2. Those studies which use an experimental design (such as Parke *et al.*, cited earlier) not only have serious ethical problems but can inevitably only study the effect of television violence over a relatively short period of time with a limited sample of children, usually in very controlled conditions.
3. Accurate measures of aggression are difficult to obtain.

Controlling aggression

Different theories of aggression lead to very different implications for controlling, reducing or even eliminating aggression.

The Freudian approach: catharsis

According to Freud, aggression is instinctive and builds up so that a **release** must be found. Freud did not consider it necessary for the means of release to be directly aggressive. Aggressive tendencies can be released through such means as hard physical activity, verbal expression or redirection away from the initial cause of hostility and onto a more socially acceptable target.

The idea of catharsis, or 'letting off steam', often expressed as a commonsense way of reducing aggression, is one with which many people agree, but research offers little evidence to support the notion.

Hokanson *et al.* (1961, 1962) showed that although physiological arousal could be reduced if participants were given the opportunity to give an electric shock to the person who had angered them, aggression expressed verbally or in fantasy was not successful in lowering arousal.

Patterson (1974) found that high-school football players were more aggressive after a season than before it, hardly supporting the idea that physical activity drains off aggressive urges.

In conclusion, catharsis may make people feel better, but there is little evidence that it leads to a reduction in aggression. On the contrary, it may well escalate it.

Punishing aggression

Skinner argued that punishment was not an effective technique with which to eradicate unwanted behaviour. Children punished for hitting another child are likely to desist from this activity while the arousal caused by the punishment is high, but once it has died down they are likely to return to their old habits. Punishment is often **aggressive in itself** and therefore serves to model aggression. Nevertheless, Baron (1983) suggests that it can be effective if it is strong, consistent and clearly connected with the bad behaviour it seeks to eliminate.

Normative influence

Most Western cultures stress the importance of achievement, competition and success; aggression, in one form or another, is a means by which to achieve these goals, especially in boys. Eron (1980) suggests that if boys were treated more like girls then the levels of aggression in society would be considerably reduced.

Few would doubt that aggression remains a major problem in society. If we wish to reduce aggression, we have to question our implicit acceptance of violence. Many types of aggression are not simply condoned but expected, even demanded, as a means of achieving personal ambitions.

Preparing for the exam

Key terms

aggression	displacement
arousal–aggression hypothesis	frustration–aggression hypothesis
catharsis	psychoanalytic approach
deindividuation	social norms
desensitised	

Types of exam question

1. Evaluation of theories of aggression.
2. Consideration of the implications theories have for the control of human aggression.
3. Discussion of factors which elicit aggression.
4. Evaluation of the influence of the media on aggression.

Self-test questions

1. How does psychoanalytic theory account for aggression?
2. What is the difference between the arousal–aggression hypothesis and the frustration–aggression hypothesis?
3. Describe how deindividuation can be responsible for aggression.
4. Briefly state the conclusions of Parke's study of delinquent boys and TV violence.
5. What is catharsis? Does it reduce aggression?
6. What problems are involved in using punishment to eliminate aggression?

Exam question with guidance notes

Discuss social psychological factors which tend to elicit aggressive behaviour in people. **(25 marks)**

AEB (1990)

The danger with this essay is that there may be a temptation to produce a disorganised list of factors that elicit aggression with little or no reference to psychology. What you must do is *link factors to theories*:

- Introduce the essay with a *definition* of aggression and a statement to the effect that there is no universal agreement as to the causes of aggression and that different theories have different implications for factors which tend to elicit aggressive behaviour in people.
- The *motivational* approach states that aggression is caused by frustration. Give examples of factors causing frustration (this can be linked to the *scapegoat theory* of prejudice). The more generalised arousal–aggression hypothesis suggests that you need anger provoking cues as well as arousal before aggression is displayed (you could make *brief* reference to Schachter and Singer's findings that arousal is likely to result in aggression only when environmental cues encourage it).
- The *social learning approach* links aggression to *reinforcement* and *modelling*; it provides a good explanation of why aggressive parents produce aggressive children, and of gender differences in aggression. The effects of the *media* should be discussed here; don't forget to include some *studies*.
- The *normative* approach shows how aggression is encouraged in certain subgroups within society and by some societies more than others. You could also discuss *deindividuation* and the factors which produce it: anonymity, crowding, uniforms and so on.

Additional exam questions

1. Discuss theories that seek to account for human aggression and their implications for the control of human aggressive behaviour. **(25 marks)**

   AEB (1989)

2. Describe and assess evidence from psychological research into the effects of media violence on children. **(25 marks)**

   AEB AS (1989)

3. Discuss some of the social–psychological factors that give rise to aggressive and violent behaviour. **(25 marks)**
   AEB (1987)

4. Critically consider the view that the media might contribute to the development of aggressive behaviour. **(25 marks)**
   AEB (1994)

6

Comparative Psychology

Topic

AEB	NEAB	O & C		Date attempted	Date completed	Self Assessment
✓	✓	✓	**Evolutionary Determinants of Behaviour**			
✓	✗	✓	**Ethology**			
✓	✗	✓	**Imprinting**			
✓	✗	✗	**Animal Communication**			
✓	✗	✓	**Teaching Language to Primates**			
✓	✗	✓	**Social Behaviour in Animals**			

6.1 Evolutionary determinants of behaviour

Comparative psychology is concerned with the investigation of the behaviour of various species of animals with a view to drawing comparisons (similarities and distinctions) between them. It therefore involves studying animal behaviour in order to give a better understanding of human behaviour.

It was due to the influences of the ideas of **Charles Darwin** that the study of animal behaviour became of interest to psychologists. Darwin showed that all species were biologically related to each other through evolution, so **behaviour patterns** were also likely to be related.

The work of Darwin

Darwin believed that all living things originated from the earliest, very simple, life-forms and are therefore all related. They changed by means of **evolution**, which is a gradual process over millions of years whereby one species emerges from other species by a series of linked steps. Darwin's theory of evolution states that the better an animal is **adapted** to its environment, the more likely it is to survive and produce offspring. An animal is well adapted if it is well suited to its environment and the precise environment to which it is adapted is called its **ecological niche**. Evolution depends on the fact that when there is competition for resources those animals who are best adapted or **fit** will survive longer than those who are less well adapted. This process is known as **natural selection**.

Behaviour is as important as structure in contributing to an animal's survival. A mouse that does not attempt to escape from predators is less likely to survive than one that does. Thus, it is quite easy to see how **behaviour patterns**, as well as the biology of animals, helps them to survive. The **balance** between behaviours is also important: a mouse that pays too much attention to food may not escape from a predator whilst one that is too fearful of predators may miss good feeding places by being too frightened to venture into them.

Genetic determinants of evolution

Offspring inherit discrete particles, called **genes**, from their parents, half from the male parent and half from the female parent. Put very simply, offspring of the same parents will be different from each other and from their parents because they all inherit different combinations of genes. This causes **variations** between individuals. But this is not the only means by which variation can occur. Sometimes, genes change their chemical structure, they **mutate**. This means that some offspring inherit **mutant genes** which are not like those that either parent originally had. Most of these mutant genes are harmful, often lethal, but occasionally they are helpful to survival. The important point is that they also cause variation in offspring.

Natural selection depends on variation. After all, if all organisms are exactly the same, they will all have the same chance of survival. The variation means that those individuals whose genes make them most fit are those most likely to survive longer and pass their genes on to the next generation.

Natural selection operates upon the physical characteristics or **phenotype** of the individual. This is true not only of the physical structure but also the **behaviour** of a species. Genes affect behaviour, and animals have long been bred for specific behavioural traits such as docility or aggression.

Sociobiology

Sociobiology is a new behavioural science, defined as the systematic study of the biological basis of all social behaviour.

It attempts to understand all types of social behaviour, including altruism, aggression, dominance and sexual behaviour, in evolutionary terms. The founder of sociobiology was **E.O. Wilson**.

Sociobiologists argue that the basic unit of evolution is not the species or even the individual, but the **individual's genes**. In other words, it is not as important for individuals to survive as for their genes. Hamilton (1964) was the first to suggest that natural selection tends to maximise not individual fitness but **inclusive fitness**: that is, an animal's fitness depends upon the extent to which its genes or identical copies of these genes can survive. The inclusive fitness of an individual therefore depends upon the survival of its descendants and other genetically related individuals. So, even if an animal has no offspring, its inclusive fitness may not be zero, because its genes will be passed on by nieces, nephews and cousins.

In this way, sociobiology explains some behaviours, such as actions which are beneficial to other animals while putting the actor at risk, which are difficult to explain in terms of original Darwinian principles.

Activity

1. Why are psychologists interested in animal behaviour?
2. In the text you are given **one** example of how behaviour can be adapted to suit a particular environment: try to think of another example.
3. Describe **two** ways in which genetic variation occurs. Why is variation important in evolutionary theory?
4. Other than genetics, what is a major determinant of behaviour? (Think of the work of Pavlov and Skinner.)

Coevolution: It is important to recognise that natural selection is not a one-way process and that alterations in one species have effects on the environment including other plants and animals. So evolution involves **mutual changes** in different species at the same time: this is a phenomenon known as **coevolution** and is especially important when considering social behaviour in animals.

Culturally transmitted behaviour

In many species, evolution depends solely on genetics because in these species only genes can be passed from one generation to the next. However, in species in which there is a complex system of communication, as in humans, evolution of behaviour also depends on **cultural transmission** of information. Remember that natural selection depends

on variation. Suppose one animal learns a completely new behaviour pattern which proves more successful for some purposes than previously typical behaviour. This pattern may be passed on to successive generations and gradually replace the old behaviour without any genetic changes being involved.

Examples of culturally transmitted behaviour

1. Chimpanzees obtaining a meal of insects by pushing a stick into an ants' or termites' nest and withdrawing it when some insects have crawled onto the stock. Infant chimpanzees copy this behaviour from their mothers; it is not genetically programmed into them.
2. The use of simple tools is certainly learnt afresh when each new generation of young chimps copies its parents.
3. Pigeons who, after observing an experienced pigeon, soon learn new and complicated food-finding behaviour.
4. The plundering of milk bottle tops by titmice is a familiar behaviour transmitted culturally from one generation to the next.

These are examples from a very wide array of traditional behaviours which are passed from one generation to another, and it is quite possible that cultural transmission among animals is much more widespread than was originally thought. In human society, one of our most important behaviours, that of spoken language, is obviously culturally transmitted from one generation to the next. Indeed, some would argue that almost everything of importance in human behaviour is culturally transmitted from one generation of a society to the next and that genetic transmission is relatively unimportant as far as human behaviour is concerned.

Selfish and altruistic behaviour

Behaviour that does not immediately benefit the individual while benefiting others is called **altruistic** behaviour, and this type of behaviour is sometimes shown by animals. It is important when discussing altruistic and selfish behaviour in animals that we don't attribute human motives or emotions to this behaviour. Animals are not altruistic in any conscious or deliberate way. Badcock defines altruism as 'an activity which promotes the fitness of the recipient at the expense of that of the provider'.

Activity

Before you read on further, try to think of examples of animal behaviour which benefits the recipient while either putting the provider at risk or at least causing it to expend a great deal of effort on another animal's behalf. Why is this difficult to explain in terms of Darwinian theory? Think about it, then check your ideas with the notes that follow.

Animals sometimes draw a predator's attention to themselves to divert it from their mate, nest or offspring. Finches make alarm calls, cranes feign injury and rabbits make conspicuous escape bids. In many insect colonies, some of the insects die protecting the colony; army ants sacrifice their own lives to form bridges across small streams so that others may cross in safety. These examples of behaviour provide a problem for Darwin's evolutionary theory, a problem which Darwin himself recognised, because they would each lessen the survival chances of the individual behaving like this. Individuals showing this altruistic behaviour would produce fewer offspring than those who behave selfishly, who would in turn leave offspring who behave selfishly and so on. Therefore altruism would diminish still further with each successive generation because all individuals displaying this behaviour would be selected against.

The sociobiological explanation

Altruistic behaviour has, however, been explained by the sociobiologists and is discussed at length in **Dawkin**'s book *The Selfish Gene*. They point out that most offspring produced by sexual reproduction have a 50 per cent chance of carrying the genes of one particular parent. Siblings have a 50 per cent chance of sharing genes and some animals which reproduce asexually all have the same genes, that is 100 per cent chance of shared genes. The greater the chances of there being shared genes, the more probable it is that altruistic behaviour will be demonstrated. The general

rule, put forward by **Hamilton**, is that natural selection will favour altruistic acts if the risk to self is outweighed by the probability of shared genes.

So, according to the sociobiologists, animals act to preserve their own kin, as this protects their own gene pool. But not all altruistic behaviour involves altruism towards kinship groups: we will consider three types of altruism.

- **Parental care** is a form of altruism which is easy to explain in terms of inclusive fitness. If the parent abandoned its young, it would have more time and opportunity to mate and produce more young, but this doesn't make sense in terms of evolution unless those first offspring can survive. So parents invest in their offspring at the expense of their own survival and chances of future reproduction, the benefit being an increase in inclusive fitness.
- **Co-operation** or **mutualism**, in which animals work together to achieve a goal, often involves some form of altruism. For example, animals which hunt in packs are usually altruistic because they share the kill with their offspring and with those animals who stay behind to protect the young. These social groups usually consist of genetically related individuals and therefore this cooperative behaviour is easy to explain in terms of kin selection.
- **Reciprocal altruism** is a form of altruism which is more difficult to explain since it often involves one animal benefiting another to whom it is no way related. However, this type of altruism could be adaptive if the animal was guaranteed to be helped at a later date by the animal it has already helped; that is, if altruism is reciprocal.

Packer (1977) provides an example of reciprocal altruism. When a female olive baboon comes into oestrus, a male consort guards her from other males. However, a rival male may sometimes enlist the help of a third male in order to mate with the female. The third male challenges the consort and while they fight, the rival male gains access to the female for a 'sneak' copulation. Packer showed that altruism is often reciprocated. Those males that most often gave aid were those that most frequently received aid. Therefore, once again, the altruistic act increases the gene survival chances of the individual.

Activity

Sociobiology has been accused of selecting behaviour which can be explained in terms of its theory while ignoring behaviour which does not fit the theory. Can you think of examples of altruistic behaviour which might be difficult to explain to these terms?

For criticisms of the sociobiological approach, see section 10.2 on Reductionism. It is important to be aware of these.

In addition to this, don't forget that behaviour can be **culturally transmitted**, so sociobiology cannot explain *all* types of behaviour in terms of genetic transmission.

In summary, kin selection and reciprocation are two ways in which altruism can be explained in terms of sociobiological theory. If altruistic behaviour involves promoting one's own gene pool, then it is also selfish behaviour at the gene level.

Preparing for the exam

Key terms

altruism

coevolution

comparative psychology

ecological niche

evolution

genes

inclusive fitness

individual fitness

kin selection

mutant genes

mutualism

natural selection

phenotype

reciprocal altruism

sociobiology

Types of exam question

1. The functions of seemingly altruistic and selfish behaviour.
2. Evaluation of theories which explain behaviour in terms of evolutionary concepts.

Self-test questions

1. How do evolutionary factors account for behavioural changes in non-human animals?
2. What is sociobiology?
3. Explain the difference between individual fitness and inclusive fitness.
4. Describe *two* examples of culturally transmitted behaviours.
5. What is meant by the term 'coevolution'?
6. What is altruistic behaviour? Give an example of altruism in non-human animals.
7. How do sociobiologists explain altruism?

Exam question with guidance notes

Describe and critically assess the role of evolutionary concepts in understanding the behaviour of non-human animals. **(25 marks)**
AEB (1993)

For the 'describe' part of the question, give an account of *Darwin*'s theory as it applies to behaviour, and then cover the work of *Hamilton* and *Dawkins* in modifying this theory. One of Darwin's important contributions is in showing how behaviour has been adapted to each ecological niche, and behaviours must combine to form a *balance* (as in the example, used in the text, of the mouse which must not be too retiring or inquisitive).

- Discuss the sociobiological explanations for social behaviour, including the central concept of inclusive fitness. Mention briefly the sociobiologists' explanation for the altruism paradox, but do not be tempted to spend too long on this, it is only a relatively small part of the answer.
- You can include the idea of evolutionarily stable strategies (although it's by no means essential). These are discussed at the beginning of section 6.4 on Social behaviour in animals.
- You may also like to consider the work of the *ethologists* mentioned in section 6.2: they have contributed to our understanding of how genetics and the environment interact. The work on fixed action patterns and sign stimuli would be relevant.
- Now for the 'critically assess' part (which many candidates ignored). Useful points are:
  1. Genes may influence the processes of development in various ways, but these processes are also affected by environmental factors. (Again, this is discussed in more detail in section 6.2.) Behaviour is always an *interaction* between *genes* and *environment*, never purely genetic. The further an animal is up the phylogenetic scale, the more its behaviour is determined by experience. Thus, evolution can only provide a limited understanding of behaviour.
  2. Behaviour is also *culturally transmitted*, even in non-human animals.
  3. Sociobiology *cannot yet account* for all forms of supposed altruistic behaviour, even in the animal kingdom.
- Conclude by returning to the point that although genes, and therefore evolution, are an important influence on behaviour, there is no way of separating the respective influences of genetics from those of learning, since they are interactional.

Additional exam question

Discuss the functions of apparently selfish and altruistic behaviour in non-human species. **(25 marks)**
AEB (1988)

6.2 Ethology

Ethology is the study of the behaviour of animals in their natural environment.

Niko Tinbergen and **Konrad Lorenz** are generally regarded as the founders of modern ethology.

Ethologists study behaviour in an evolutionary context and are particularly interested in **instinctive** behaviour in animals and how this behaviour is adapted to the natural environment in which a species lives.

In Chapter 2 we saw how Skinner and the other behaviourists took a very experimental, laboratory-based approach to the study of animal behaviour and argued that learning was the means by which animals acquired their behaviour patterns. Ethology was introduced as a challenge to this approach, arguing that many behaviours were innate, not learned.

Comparing ethology and behaviourism

1. Ethology uses the method of systematic observation of animals in their **natural surroundings** with little restriction placed on their behaviour. Ethologists do conduct laboratory experiments, but only as a means of determining the critical variables which operate in the natural habitat.

   Behaviourists use controlled experiments in **laboratory conditions**. Animals are removed from their natural surroundings and are very restricted in the types of behaviour they can express.

2. Behaviourists are largely concerned with the investigation of the laws of **learning**; ethologists study instinctive, **unlearned** behaviour.

3. Behaviourists aim to discover **general laws** about behaviour, in particular laws of learning, which apply to **all** species. Thus, the particular species of animal they use is of little importance except convenience and they use **only a very few** species: mainly rats and pigeons.

   Ethologists believe that every species is different because their behaviour is uniquely adapted to their particular **ecological niche** and

they are concerned to explain the **function** that any piece of naturally-occurring behaviour has for the particular species in which it occurs. They therefore study an extremely **wide variety** of species.

Basic principles of ethology

Instinct

The major concern of ethology is the study of inherited behaviour of animals, that is, instinctive behaviour. To the ethologist, **instinct is an inherited behaviour pattern which is common to all members of a species**; it is innate, not learned, and tends to be **stereotyped**, that is, it is always the same.

The term 'instinct' has caused some problems since the word has been used to describe **motivation** as well as behaviour. Since ethologists prefer to study behaviour itself rather than the motivation for it, they concentrate on the readily identifiable units of behaviour and prefer to use the term **fixed action pattern** (FAP) rather than instinct.

Fixed action patterns (FAPs)

An example of a FAP analysed by Lorenz and Tinbergen (1939) is the egg-retrieval behaviour of the greylag goose. This bird builds its nest on the ground, and one of the constant problems that it faces is the tendency of an egg to roll out of the nest. When this happens the bird always retrieves it in the same way. It leans its head forward, puts its beak on the far side of the egg and gets the egg back into the nest using a scooping movement. This behaviour pattern never varies: the bird could use its feet or its wing but it never does. Yet this is not always the most efficient way of retrieving the egg since it often involves several attempts and sometimes fails completely (see Figure 6.1).

Fixed action patterns all show certain distinctive characteristics:

1. They are **stereotyped** behaviours: the behaviour always occurs in the same form and cannot be varied if conditions change. If a greylag goose is presented with a gigantic egg it still attempts to retrieve this egg using the same rigid method even though it is quite unsuccessful.

Figure 6.1 Egg retrieval in the greylag goose
Source: J. Radford and E. Govier (eds), A Textbook of Psychology (Sheldon Press, 1980), p. 195.

2. They are **species-specific**, that is, they occur in all members of a species.
3. They are triggered by specific stimuli called **sign stimuli** (see below).

Sign stimuli

A fixed action pattern is only triggered by certain, very specific stimuli. These highly selective stimuli which trigger a fixed action pattern are called sign stimuli.

Tinbergen investigated sign stimuli in male sticklebacks who, having built a nest, will attack other approaching males (including their own reflection in a mirror) but will court a female. The basic difference in appearance between males and females is that males have red underbellies, females have abdomens swollen with eggs. Tinbergen built a series of 'model' sticklebacks in which he varied the features that might be important in eliciting attacking behaviour. He found that shape was unimportant: only the red underbelly seemed to be the relevant feature (see Figure 6.2).

Sign stimuli are not necessarily visual; there are many examples of **auditory** and **chemical** sign stimuli. Experimental investigations using artificial stimuli have demonstrated that sometimes the most effective stimulus is not necessarily the one which is most like the natural stimulus. For example, herring-gulls will choose to roll an egg twice the size of a normal one in preference to a 'real' herring-gull egg. These artificial stimuli are known as **super-normal stimuli** (or super-releasers).

Innate releasing mechanisms

The aggressive response of the male stickleback is triggered by the red underbelly of another male. This suggested to early ethologists that there must be some built-in mechanism by which sign stimuli were recognised and in the 1930s Lorenz coined the term 'innate releasing mechanism' (IRM) to describe it. This term has, however, been criticised on several grounds:

1. The mechanism is assumed to be innate but we have already seen that the concept of innateness is problematic.
2. The sign stimulus does not always release behaviour; sometimes it simply orientates behaviour, or actually inhibits it. For example, young turkey chicks emit certain sounds which prevent the adult attacking and killing them. Thus the sound of the turkey chicks acts as an inhibitor not a releaser.
3. The term 'mechanism' implies that there exists, somewhere in the animal's nervous system, a single mechanism which filters stimuli so that only the important features are noted. However, there is no evidence that any such mechanism is singular or as simple as this term implies.

Environmental influences on behaviour

When investigating fixed action patterns, **isolation experiments** are often used to demonstrate that these behaviours are innate rather than learned. However, even with these seemingly rigid behaviours, environmental factors may influence behaviour.

Manning (1973) observed that infant rats who had been removed from their mother by Caesarian section died soon after birth due to rupturing of the bladder. Bladder emptying is a reflex and a reflex is the simplest form of fixed action pattern which it would be easy to assume is innate. In fact, this reflex has to be triggered from the environment, specifically, the mother giving a slight kick to the offspring at birth. Once this has occurred, bladder-emptying is entirely automatic.

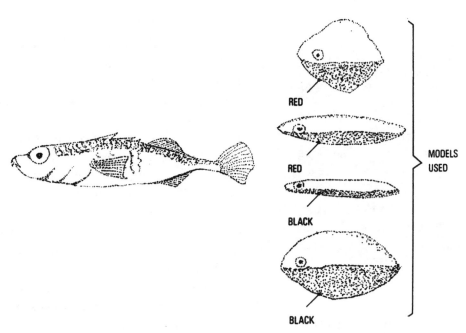

Figure 6.2 Models used to test for aggressive responses in the stickleback
Source: J. Radford and E. Govier (eds), A Textbook of Psychology (Sheldon Press, 1980), p. 198.

In view of these considerations, it is safer to talk of **inherited predispositions** rather than inherited behaviour.

Song patterns in birds

The development of song patterns of birds serves to demonstrate the complex interaction of innate and environmental factors. Marler and Tamura (1964) and Konishi (1965) have studied the American white-crowned sparrow. Each bird has a standard bird song with a distinct 'dialect' superimposed on the standard. Male birds start to sing at around eight months of age. By various experimental investigations the researchers showed the following:

1. If the birds are reared in total isolation they have the characteristic song but no dialect, even though they have never been exposed to the song. Thus, the basic song itself would appear to be in some way innately wired into the bird, whilst dialect must be learned by listening to adult birds and modifying the standard song accordingly.
2. If birds are isolated after four months, they still have a dialect when adult even though they have never sung before being isolated.
3. If birds are isolated from birth to four months and then mix, they do not produce the dialect when adult. There appears to be a **critical period** for

learning the dialect: some time in the first four months.

4. If birds are deafened after they have heard normal song during their critical period but before they themselves have sung, they cannot produce even standard versions of the song, just a series of disconnected notes quite unlike the song of isolated hearing birds. It appears that they need to hear their own voices in order to produce the song. Deafening birds after they have sung makes no difference; they still produce the song (Konishi 1965).

We can therefore conclude that it is not the capacity to produce the simple song which is inherited but some kind of **template** against which the bird matches the notes which it produces and adjusts them to fit. This, then, requires auditory feed-back which deafened birds cannot obtain. Furthermore, experiences in the environment during the critical period can modify the immediate laid-down template, so that a dialect is superimposed on it.

This study of birdsong in the white-crowned sparrow demonstrates how complex are the interactions between heredity and environment in the development of behaviours which appear at first sight to be completely instinctive.

Activity

In each of the following, say whether birds will learn a basic song only, a song with dialect or no song at all:

1. Normal bird, isolation after four months
2. Bird deafened immediately after hatching, total isolation
3. Isolated bird, deafened after four months
4. Normal bird, total isolation from hatching
5. Normal bird, total isolation from hatching to four months only.

Avoidance learning

Avoidance learning has an obvious biological usefulness. The animal's very survival may depend upon its ability to learn to stay away from **potentially dangerous stimuli**. In its natural habitat an animal that learned how to escape from predators by simply using trial and error would probably not survive long. Some animals appear to have a set of built-in defence responses that are modifiable by learning and that are especially useful in enhancing their chances of survival in harmful situations. These responses have been called **species-specific defence reactions** (SSDRs): fleeing and immobility are examples of SSDRs.

Garcia and Koelling (1966) demonstrated avoidance learning in the laboratory. They gave rats a distinctly flavoured water to drink and then made them sick about an hour later. The rats developed an aversion to the flavoured water, a taste aversion so strong that, even if thirsty, the rats would not drink the flavoured water. Now, for several reasons, this type of learning cannot be explained simply in terms of classical or operant conditioning.

1. If the stimulus is an electric shock rather than sickness then the rat does not avoid the flavoured water
2. Learning is full-strength on a single trial: classical conditioning usually takes several trials
3. It occurs with a very long time interval: normally, the UCS and the CS (remember Chapter 2) must be a few seconds apart, in this case the rats can be made sick up to 12 hours after drinking the flavoured water and they still learn to avoid it.

Biological preparedness

It would seem that an **association bias** is built into specific organisms so that poison avoidance is quickly learned. Such associative bias does not depend on past experience but is a **species-specific** characteristic of the organism. This emphasises the important role of heredity in the learning of certain associations. It is as if the rat has been **prepared** by its evolutionary history to associate immediately certain states, such as illness, with the taste of food. In its natural environment, should be rat receive sublethal doses of a distinctly flavoured poisoned food, it will recover from illness and afterwards avoid that food.

These findings constitute a serious challenge to the behaviourist view that all learning occurs by classical or operant conditioning and involves the same processes in all animals.

Imprinting

Lorenz (1937) noted the way in which young geese or ducks followed their parents around from very soon after hatching. (See Figure 6.3)

Lorenz called this process imprinting and defined it as **a rapid attachment which is formed as a result of following**.

After experimentation, he concluded that:

1. The tendency to become imprinted is **genetically determined** and **species-specific**
2. The fixed action pattern is **following**
3. The actual object on which the chick imprints is **learned**, in the wild, this will usually be the mother, but hand reared chicks will follow their human keeper in preference to a member of their own species.
4. This learning is very rapid indeed.

How does imprinting differ from other forms of learning?

Lorenz believed that imprinting has certain characteristics which make it different from other forms of learning:

1. It is **very rapid** and often requires only one exposure to a stimulus object

Figure 6.3 Imprinting: 'Imprinting in goslings'

2. It only occurs during a **critical period** early in the bird's life
3. Once it has occurred it is **irreversible**
4. It is associated with **no obvious reinforcement**
5. It influences patterns of behaviour which have **not yet developed** in the animal, for example, the choice of a sexual partner.

However, research has shown that these differences may be by no means clear-cut:

The 'critical period'

Lorenz (and Hess) showed that although the imprinting response could occur as early as one hour after hatching, the strongest response occurred between 12 and 17 hours after hatching and that after about 32 hours the response did not occur at all. They believed that imprintability is genetically 'switched on' during a time shortly after hatching and it was then 'switched off', and once switched off, imprinting could not occur at all. They called the period of imprintability the **critical period**.

However, many researchers have shown that if a young bird is kept in isolation it can be imprinted beyond the end of the critical period (Sluckin, 1961). Similarly, if kept in visually deprived or visually distorted environments (by being kept in darkness or wearing distorting goggles), imprinting may occur later. Sluckin (1965) coined the term **sensitive period** to replace that of the critical period. A sensitive period is one during which learning is **most likely** to happen and will happen most **easily** but it is not a question of once-and-for-all. (See the Core Study of this chapter.)

What is the difference between a **critical** period and a **sensitive** period?

How does this relate to Bowlby's work on attachment in human infants (Chapter 8)?

Reversibility and adult sexual preferences

The effects of imprinting on later sexual preference is called **sexual imprinting**. If a duck is imprinted on a hen it will act like a hen and try to mate with one when adult. This effect, according to Lorenz, was permanent and could not be reversed by later experiences. However several studies cast doubt on this conclusion.

Guiton (1966) reared some male chicks in isolation for 47 days and they imprinted on the yellow rubber gloves worn by an assistant who fed them. When released they tried to mate with the rubber gloves, that is, they were showing socially and sexually inappropriate behaviour, as predicted by Lorenz. However, when these chicks were introduced to female chicks, they preferred to mate with them and completely ignored the rubber gloves.

Nevertheless research since Lorenz's original work shows that imprinting can indeed profoundly affect later behaviour:

1. If individuals of one distinctly coloured breed are reared by parents of a different breed and colour, the offspring usually prefer to mate with birds of their **foster parents' colour** rather than their own (Warriner, 1963).
2. When cross-fostering studies are carried out with birds of a different species, the results again usually show a sexual attachment to the species of the **foster parent**.
3. Sexual preferences based upon imprinting often persist for a number of years. Immelmann (1972) cross-fostered Bengalese and zebra finches and then isolated them from their foster species for a number of years. Most of them bred successfully with members of their own species, but when they were eventually given a choice between their own and their foster species, they strongly preferred the **foster species**.

Functions of imprinting

Recognising parents

For many years it was thought that imprinting enabled an animal to recognise its own species. However, it is becoming apparent that imprinting enables the young to recognise one or both their parents **as individuals**. The species that are active and feathered at hatching must learn the characteristics quickly because the young must stay near the parent. If it approaches another adult of its own species it may be attacked or even killed. For this reason, as soon as the young animal is able to recognise its parents (or a substitute parent), it escapes from anything that is noticeably different.

Preventing separation

Imprinting facilitates reunion if offspring are separated. For example, shortly after giving birth, a mother goat labels her offspring by licking them and is sensitive to the smell of her kid for about an hour. During this period, a five minute contact with any kid is sufficient for it to be accepted as her own. If no such contact occurs, the kid will not be allowed to suckle.

Core Study

Imprinting and perceptual learning: W. Sluckin and E.A.

This paper is a review article summarising and evaluating many studies of imprinting by a large number of researchers. The main points of the review are as follows:

The original stimulus situation

A wide variety of both visual and auditory stimuli which are both brief and repetitive will cause chicks to approach and give contentment calls. Visual stimuli include moving objects, a rotating black and white disc and a flashing light. Auditory stimuli include short, repeated calls, knocking, tapping and rustling of paper.

The critical period

Many studies have shown that chicks will not follow a moving object if they are not exposed to it until they are 2 or 3 days old. This early period was called the 'critical' period by Lorenz and the 'sensitive' period by Sluckin (1965).

Guiton (1958) showed that if chicks are reared in total isolation they can be imprinted after 3 days and in some cases up to 6 days, whereas socially reared chicks cannot. Guiton suggest that this is because they are imprinted on each other. Guiton contends that the critical period comes to an end because, once imprinted, chicks become selective in their responsiveness; in this way, imprinting brings about its own end.

Hinde *et al.* (1956) and Hess (1957) propose an alternative explanation: that the end of the critical period is brought about by the development of a fear response which causes them to avoid strange objects.

Nevertheless, many studies have shown that if chicks are regularly exposed to an object to which they show extreme fear, they can eventually become imprinted on it. Salzen and Sluckin suggest

therefore that the evidence is against fear being the cause of the end of the sensitive period and that imprinting does indeed bring about its own end by making the chick more selective in its responses.

The effects of early experience and effort

Both experience and effort appear to affect the strength of the imprinting response.

i   Generally, the greater the **exposure** to a moving object, the stronger the imprinting response

ii   Hess (1958), by devising a runway in which chicks had to clamber over obstacles in order to follow, found that the greater the **effort**, the stronger the following response. However, other studies indicate that the effect of effort on imprinting is not yet clearly understood.

Imprinting and perceptual learning

In the introductory section, Sluckin and Salzen differentiate between two different types of study. In one type, chicks are required to discriminate between several objects by choosing to follow one rather than others. In the second type, chicks are repeatedly exposed to a single object and the extent of imprinting is measured by the strength of the following response.

Lorenz (1937) defined imprinting in terms of discriminating between the characteristics of one species as opposed to another species. This, then, uses the first type of study and Sluckin and Salzen point out that studies of the second type, measuring the degree of attachment to one object only, are not strictly studies of imprinting but rather studies of following responses. In their view, only studies which involve choosing between objects constitute imprinting studies.

Imprinting then, appears to be a form of **perceptual learning** involving learning to discriminate between different objects. Chicks first learn to discriminate between moving objects and static ones and then learn to discriminate further between different moving objects in terms of movement, colour, form and sound. This corresponds to Gibson's (1959) view of the development of general perceptual learning. Sluckin and Salzen conclude by stating that 'the imprinting process, then, could be regarded as part of a process of developing perception resulting from repeated stimulation'. Seen in these terms, it is not a special type of learning but part of the whole of the animal's perceptual development.

QUESTIONS

1. Define 'imprinting'. **(2 marks)**
2. Name *two* auditory stimuli which have been shown to elicit contentment calls in chicks **(2 marks)**
3. a In imprinting studies, how is the level of attachment in the bird measured? **(2 marks)**
   b What are the features that increase the level of attachment? **(2 marks)**

Oxford and Cambridge Specimen Paper

The acquisition of bird song

Imprinting-like processes also exist for the acquisition of bird song. Chaffinches learn their song only during the first 13 months of their lives. It is sufficient, however, that they are exposed to song at a time when they do not yet sing themselves.

Heinroth recorded the song of blackcaps in the same room as one-day old nightingales who were exposed to the blackcap song for only one week. The following Spring they sang the complete blackcap song rather than the nightingale one.

It therefore appears that **aural imprinting** is important in establishing correct song patterns, used in territory establishment and courtship rituals in later life.

Activity

1. What is meant by **aural** imprinting?
2. What kind of imprinting was Lorenz investigating with the geese and ducks?
3. What kind of imprinting does the text discuss with respect to goats?

Choice of mate

The work on sexual imprinting mentioned earlier indicates how sexual imprinting can result in inappropriate choice of mating partner when animals are imprinted on an inappropriate species.

Bateson (1979) suggests that sexual imprinting is important in order that offspring recognise their own family members, that is, their own kin. This enables the animal to choose a mate that appears slightly different, but not too different, from its parents and siblings. This would make it possible to strike a balance between the advantages of inbreeding and outbreeding.

Before you read further, make sure you know the ways in which Lorenz considered imprinting to be a special form of learning.

The nature of imprinting as a learned response

Lorenz believed that imprinting, as defined by him as an attachment formed by following, was a unique form of learning. For several reasons, this is no longer a popular view:

1. Imprinting is not learning to follow but learning

the characteristics of the parent(s), and the following response is a consequence of this learning. Research shows that following is not absolutely necessary for imprinting to occur.

2. Imprinting is not necessarily as rapid as Lorenz believed, and the longer the bird is exposed to the 'parent', the stronger the attachment to it.

3. Although imprinting was first described in ground nesting birds, and Lorenz believed it only existed in them, the type of imprinting shown in these animals is now seen as an extreme case of a far more general phenomenon. Something very like imprinting must occur in some insects and in mammals who learn to recognise their 'own group' by learning characteristics well during the sensitive period. The biological need to recognise close kin, both early in life and when adult, is a general one.

4. According to Immelmann and Suomi (1981), sensitive periods occur frequently in many species including fish, insects, sheep and human beings, and can apply to a much wider range of behaviour than just attachment. The existence of sensitive periods is considered to be of importance in human attachment, language development and gender identity.

Preparing for the exam

Key terms

association bias	innate releasing mechanism
aural imprinting	instinctive
avoidance learning	sensitive period
behaviourism	sexual imprinting
biological preparedness	sign stimuli
critical period	species-specific defence reaction
ecological niche	species-specific behaviour
ethology	stereotyped behaviour
fixed action patterns	super-normal stimuli
imprinting	template
inherited predisposition	

Types of exam question

1. The contribution of ethologists to the understanding of non-human and human behaviour.
2. Comparison of ethological and behaviourist approaches.
3. Whether imprinting is different from other types of learning.
4. The ways in which imprinting may be beneficial to animals.
5. The functions of imprinting.

Self-test questions

1. What is ethology? What methods do ethologists use to collect information?
2. Outline *three* differences between behaviourism and ethology.
3. What are the characteristics of a fixed action pattern (FAP)? Give an example of a fixed action pattern in non-human animals.

4. Describe *one* piece of research that suggests that fixed action patterns are influenced by the environment.
5. Explain why learning theory cannot explain avoidance learning. How can avoidance learning be explained?
6. What are the main characteristics of imprinting?
7. In what ways does Lorenz consider that imprinting is different from other forms of learning?
8. What are the effects of imprinting on adult sexual preferences?
9. Outline the functions of imprinting.

Exam question with guidance notes

1. **Critically consider the contribution that ethology has made to our understanding of behaviour (non-human and/or human).**

(25 marks)
AEB (1992)

First, ensure that you know what is relevant to a question on ethology: Pavlov and Skinner were *not* ethologists. The work on imprinting **is** relevant and you can, therefore, include any work from this section. Notice that the question asks you to 'critically consider' so a straightforward description of the work done by ethologists will gain few marks.

- Begin with a *definition* of ethology its main aims, including their criticisms of the behaviourist approach (its methods and conclusions).
- Consider the work on *FAPs*, *sign stimuli* and the *IRM*, including the *criticisms* of such concepts.
- Mention the ethologists' contribution to demonstrating how the environment and genetics interact, using examples such as bird song to illustrate the point.
- You can discuss imprinting, with the *modifications* made to Lorenz's original conclusions.
- You can make reference to biological *preparedness* and its usefulness in avoidance behaviour; you can also relate this to our increased understanding of the acquisition of *phobias* in humans. (In order to do this, use section 9.4 on Phobias.)
- Having introduced the criticisms of the behaviourist approach earlier, you can now discuss specific *criticisms* of this position, demonstrated by the work on imprinting (which is not learning by straightforward classical or operant conditioning) and on biological preparedness. You could also include other relevant criticisms mentioned in section 10.7 on Behaviourism.

Note
Questions on imprinting are straightforward, but pay attention to the question. They usually ask you to discuss whether or not imprinting is a distinct form of learning or to discuss functions of imprinting. Both of these are clearly covered in the text.

Additional exam questions

1. Use evidence to discuss what ethologists have found from their investigations of the nature and function of imprinting in non-human animals. **(25 marks)**
   AEB (1989)

2. **a** Describe the main features of imprinting. **(10 marks)**
   b Using evidence, discuss the view that imprinting is distinct from other forms of learning. **(15 marks)**
   AEB (1993)

3. How have ethologists contributed to our understanding of learning by studying non-human animals? **(25 marks)**
   AEB (1988)

6.3 Animal communication

Communication in the natural environment

There is a great deal of evidence that animals have evolved special structures and special behaviour patterns, the main function of which is to send information to another animal. Communication between animals, both among members of the same species and across different species, uses all the sensory modalities and serves many functions. We will consider each in turn.

The use of different senses for communication

1. **Tactile** communication is limited in its scope for transmitting information but is probably the most basic means of communication, since almost all animals respond to physical contact. In many invertebrates it is the main means of social interaction, as in the blind workers of some termite colonies which never leave their underground tunnels. Tactile communication is also important in many vertebrate species, especially those who live in social groups. It is not usually a means by which very specific information, like good feeding places or alarm signals, can be conveyed but is more usually a means by which more general information about **social relationships** between animals can be conveyed, as when one animal grooms another.

2. **Auditory** signals are usually much more specific than tactile ones. One of their main functions is to warn of impending predators by use of alarm calls. The alarm calls of several different species of birds living in the same location are often remarkably similar and have probably evolved towards each other so as to provide maximum protection.

   Fish and whales have an amazing range of sounds which can, in the case of some whales, travel as far as several hundred miles.

3. **Chemical** signals are particularly well developed in insects and mammals, but have the disadvantage that the signal cannot be terminated or changed quickly. Consequently, most chemical signals are used to pass a single, relatively stable message like territory marking by urination or the readiness of an animal to mate.

4. **Visual** signals can only be used over a relatively short range but can convey very detailed information. Colour vision is important in most animals except mammals. In higher-order animals, body postures and facial expressions convey a large amount of information.

Activity

Complete the following table:

Sense modality used	Example of communication	Main purpose
Visual	Bearing teeth	....
....	Bee dance	....
Chemical	....	Territory establishment
Visual	....	Courtship display
....	Bird song	....

Functions of communications

Anti-predator devices

These are devices intended to prevent an animal becoming the prey of another. When threatened by a predator, many animals adopt a posture designed to **intimidate** it, as in the case of porcupine raising its quills or a puffer-fish inflating itself to several times its original size.

Sometimes the display is pure **bluff**, as when certain species of moth suddenly expose eyelike spots on their hind wings if disturbed while resting. These eye spots are similar to those found in cuttlefish, toads and caterpillars and they serve to startle predatory birds, giving the moth a chance to escape.

Courtship

Many courtship rituals use elaborate visual displays, a very familiar one being that of the peacock. Some other courtship patterns, especially among insects, depend largely on **pheromones**. A pheromone is a chemical, or mixture of chemicals, that is released into the environment by an organism and causes a species reaction in a recipient member of the same species.

Finding food sources

Karl von Frisch (1955) documented that, on returning to the hive, worker bees perform two types of 'dance' which together provide information about food sources.

Territorial behaviour

Domestic cats have powerful scent glands on their face which leave an olfactory message which, together with other scents such as urine traces, mark out the boundaries of the cat's territory.

Other examples of the use of olfactory signals to establish territories is urination by dogs and defaecation by hippopotami.

Interpreting animal communication in terms of evolutionary theory

Many social behaviours do not evolve anew but develop from actions which originally served another purpose. Dawkins and Krebs (1978) argue that certain behaviours, originally designed to serve one purpose, have evolved through selection to influence the behaviour of others.

It is easy to explain how moths have evolved an eyelike spot on their wings, since this exploits an already existing avoidance behaviour in predatory birds. It is, however, more complicated to explain the evolution of other communication systems which cannot have taken advantage of already existing responses. Blest (1961) argues that, in many communication systems, any change in behaviour of the actor must be matched by a corresponding change in the responsiveness of the recipient, and not simply be dependent for a response on existing behaviour. The complex courtship display of a male bird, for example, could not have evolved unless, at the same time, the female evolved an appropriate response. Ethologists argue that the evolution of communication does not necessarily involve behaviour which originally served some other purpose, but that communication systems often involve a complex **coevolution** by actor and reactor. The exact evolutionary mechanisms by which communication systems have evolved is as yet still a matter of debate.

Teaching 'language' to primates

Is language unique to humans?

There is a major controversy within comparative psychology as to whether some non-human animals have the capacity to learn language, or whether it is the exclusive domain of human beings. **Noam Chomsky** believes that language ability is unique to humans; only humans are capable of language learning because they alone possess the necessary **innate linguistic mechanisms**. Before we consider this further, we need to consider what is meant by 'language'.

Characteristics of language

According to **Roger Brown**, a psycholinguist, there are **three** main properties which distinguish true language from the communications systems of animals. These are semanticity, productivity and displacement.

1. **Semanticity** (meaningfulness) refers to the fact that through language (whether signs or words) we can represent objects, events and abstract ideas in a **symbolic** way.

2. **Productivity** refers to the capacity to combine words (or signs) into new sentences, sentences that aren't simply imitations. In order to do this, it is necessary to have an understanding of **syntax**, that is, the structure of grammar.

3. **Displacement** refers to the capacity to communicate information about events and objects that are not present here and now; that are displaced in time and space. It also permits knowledge to be transmitted from one generation to another.

Studies conducted

Gardner and Gardner with Washoe (1969)

This is covered in detail in the Core Study of this chapter (p. 165). Important points to note are:

1. Washoe was taught **American Sign Language** (Ameslan) which is fully adequate for expressing everything that can be spoken.

2. By five years of age, she was able to use 133 signs, including 'you', 'please', 'cat', 'enough'.

3. She had learnt to spontaneously combine signs into strings of two to five words: for example, 'come open', 'hurry gimme toothbrush', thus demonstrating **productivity**.

4. She was also able to invent new combinations of signs for objects for which she didn't know the sign: for example, Alka Seltzer became 'hear water' and duck was a 'water-bird'. This means that she had achieved **semanticity** since she had to understand the meaning of the signs in order to use them in these novel combinations.

5. She generalised and overgeneralised just as young children do: for example, she learnt 'open' for a door and then applied it to opening boxes and even turning on a tap.

Fouts (1970)

Fouts put Washoe with two other non-signing chimps; he found that the chimps used signs among themselves, invented names, and learned signs from one another.

Premack with Sarah (1976)

Premack taught Sarah a language based on small plastic symbols. The chimp had to learn to associate each symbol with its meaning and then learn to arrange them in sequence to convey a message. Sarah could use **word order** to convey meaning and could carry out commands and answer questions using several symbols in combination.

Savage–Rumbaugh and Rumbaugh with Lana (1978)

They taught Lana to operate a computer keyboard and learn an artificial language called Yerkish which is dependent on precise word order. Lana could see what she had typed on a screen and she was able to correct her mistakes. Lana invented words, such as 'finger-bracelet' for ring and did seem to understand **syntax**: she could tell the difference between 'Lana groom Tim' and 'Tim groom Lana'.

Patterson with Koko (1979)

Koko, a gorilla, was taught Ameslan and after seven years she had approximately 400 signs, had developed syntax and a number of novel sentences. She had also invented her own combinations of signs for certain words e.g. 'white tiger' for zebra and 'quiet chase' for hide and seek. Koko understands spoken language, appears to remember and refer to things that have taken place at least six months earlier and can even use language to play tricks on her trainers.

Activity

a Provide an example of Washoe
  • demonstrating semanticity
  • demonstrating productivity
  • overgeneralising (if you are unsure of the meaning of this term, see Chapter 8).
b In what way did Lana and Koko both show a rudimentary understanding of syntax?
c How did Koko show displacement?

Terrace's criticisms

Terrace conducted a study with a chimp called Nim Chimpsky who was trained for five years in Ameslan; in 1979 Terrace published a paper concluding that although chimps can acquire a large vocabulary they are **not** capable of producing original sentences. Their ability to sign did not meet the criteria of productivity as put forward by Roger Brown.

The specific criticisms were:

1. Although both Washoe and Nim appeared to produce sentences, in fact they were being inadvertently cued by their trainers to produce words in a certain order and did not understand the importance of word order.
2. A large proportion of Nim's signs were simply imitations and the percentage of imitation increased as he got older. This is in contrast to the language of young children who, as they get older, use less imitation.
3. Although Nim's vocabulary increased as he got older, the communications did not get any more complex; the longer ones were simply a chain of words. This is again in contrast to children's language in which, as sentence length increases,

so does the amount of meaning conveyed.

Counterarguments to Terrace

1. The Gardners responded to Terrace's criticisms by pointing out that he had based them on only a few frames of their filmed evidence and had never looked at the remainder.
2. Other researchers point out the inadequacy of the training methods used on Nim. Apes, they argue, cannot be expected to learn language by training alone without reference to the remainder of their social environment. Nim was instructed in an extremely formal manner, rather than as part of the normal interactions involved in everyday life. He could therefore hardly be expected to acquire and use language in the same way as young children do.
3. Patterson pointed out that Koko, unlike Nim, uses very little imitation and often signs to herself, so signing is not simply done to gain a reward. This also applied to Washoe once she was put with previously non-signing chimps.
4. As to the argument regarding word order, Lana did understand the difference between 'Lana groom Tim' and 'Tim groom Lana'. Similarly, Sarah could use word order to convey meaning.

The debate as to whether language ability is unique to humans continues to this day.

We should not leave the subject of animal language without considering some of the **ethical issues** raised by this type of research. The animals used in this research are not volunteers and, although none of these apes have been removed from the wild to take part in this research, nevertheless they have not been reared in their natural environments. Researchers in this field believe that once apes have become accustomed to a rich human environment, it would be cruel to deprive them of it, and, with this in mind, these apes continue to receive human care and attention for the duration of their natural lives.

Core Study

Teaching sign language to a chimpanzee: R.A. Gardner and B.T. Gardner (1969)

This study was designed to help establish the extent to which another species, in this case a chimpanzee, might be able to use human language.

American Sign Language (Ameslan or ASL), a gestural language used by the deaf in North America, was chosen as the means of communication since use of the hands to make gestures is a spontaneous feature of chimp behaviour likely to be appropriate for instrumental (operant) conditioning of that species.

From the outset, the Gardners wanted Washoe not only to sign in order to obtain food, drink and so on, and not only to ask for objects, but to answer questions about them, that is, to develop behaviour which could be described as *conversation*. In order to do this, Washoe was treated much like a human child would be, with her providers being friends and playmates who introduced her to a great many games and activities which would involve a great deal of interaction. All her companions had had to learn ASL and used it extensively in her presence.

The training methods

Imitation

As part of her training many routine activities, such as feeding, dressing and bathing, became ritualised into games, accompanied by appropriate signs used as often as possible. By imitation she acquired a large vocabulary of signs.

Instrumental conditioning

The Gardners consider it unlikely that a human child acquires language simply by the use of instrumental conditioning alone but that, nevertheless, the so-called 'trick vocabulary' of early childhood is probably acquired in this way. Considering this, and the fact that a main objective of the project was to teach Washoe as many signs as possible, by whatever methods, instrumental conditioning was included in the training methods. The main reinforcer employed was tickling, used to shape behaviour until the signs were accurately expressed.

Results

Vocabulary

The criterion for a new sign having been acquired was at least one appropriate and spontaneous occurrence each day over a period of 15 consecutive days. 30 signs were acquired by the end of the 22nd month of the project.

Differentiation

As her vocabulary increased, Washoe was able to differentiate between signs. For example, she first used the 'flower' sign in several inappropriate contexts which all included smells (for example, the smell from a tobacco pouch) but gradually she learnt to differentiate between 'flower' and 'smell' although she continued to use 'flower' when 'smell' was in fact the correct word to use.

Transfer

Washoe was soon able to appropriately transfer signs which had originally been attached to a very specific referent. For example, she transferred the sign 'key', used originally to a particular padlock key, to all varieties of keys and locks.

Combinations

There were no deliberate attempts to encourage Washoe to use combinations of signs but these did appear spontaneously. She invented several combinations not used by her trainers, such as 'gimme tickle', 'open food drink' (for the fridge). Most combinations were Washoe's own inventions.

Concluding observations

The Gardners report that 'it is difficult to answer questions such as "Do you think that Washoe has language?" or "At what point will be \able to say that Washoe has language?" because they imply a distinction between one class of communicative behaviour that can be called language and another class that cannot. This in turn implies a well established theory that could provide the distinction. At present the Gardners do not believe that such a theory exists.

Until a considerably larger body of knowledge is acquired it would be unreasonable to suppose that language is the exclusive domain of humans.

QUESTIONS

1. What made American Sign Language (Ameslan) a suitable language to use with Washoe? **(2 marks)**
2. Washoe did not consistently sign words in the correct order. What is the significance of this observation? **(4 marks)**

Oxford and Cambridge Specimen Paper

(You may need to refer to the main body of notes in order to answer this question.)

Preparing for the exam

Key terms

Ameslan
auditory signals
chemical signals
coevolution
displacement
olfactory message
overgeneralise
pheromones
productivity

psycholinguist
semanticity
sensory modalities
syntax
tactile communication
territory marking
visual signals
Yerkish

Types of exam question

1. Description and discussion of systems of communication, including those using audition, olfaction and vision.
2. The evolutionary significance of non-human animal communication systems.
3. An evaluation of the effectiveness of attempts to teach primates to use language.

Note that the examiners' reports often complain about the anecdotal way in which questions on animal communication and the social behaviour of animals are answered. Beware of this: stick to the *psychological studies* and *theories* discussed in psychology textbooks and don't base your answers on observations of your own pets or on television programmes unless you are confident that the material is entirely relevant.

Self-test questions

1. What modes of communication are available to non-human animals? Give *one* example of each.
2. What are the functions of communication in non-human animals?
3. According to Roger Brown, what are the *three* properties which distinguish true language from the communication system of animals?
4. Describe *two* attempts to teach language to animals.
5. According to Terrace, how successful have these attempts been?

Exam questions with guidance notes

Describe and discuss how non-human animals communicate by using their visual, auditory and olfactory senses.   **(25 marks)**
                                                                    AEB (1991)

This is a fairly straightforward question but it was poorly answered, mainly for the reasons given in the note on examiners' reports above.

- For the 'describe' part, use at least *one* example from each of the senses, and do so in reasonable *detail*. Include examples which involve communication between members of the *same* species (as in courtship) and some which involve communication between members of *different* species (as in anti-predatory devices). By doing this, you will necessarily be including examples involving different *functions*.
- In the 'discuss' part, mention the *functions* of communication systems, using examples (which could include those you have already written about, so you just need to refer back to them). Mention as many different functions as possible.
- Then discuss the *evolution* of these communication systems – this is a little more difficult than the rest of the essay, but it is essential for a full answer. Discuss the concept of coevolution and why this is relatively easy to explain in some cases, as for certain anti-predatory devices, since they utilise existing behaviour patterns, but not so easy in others in which both animals have to evolve in synchrony rather than making use of existing behaviour patterns.

Use evidence to evaluate attempts which have been made to teach non-human animals to use language.   **(25 marks)**
                                                                    AEB (1990)

This is a straightforward question, but do not fall into the trap of simply listing studies. You have been asked to *evaluate* them.

- Introduce the essay with reference to the debate about whether language is *exclusive to humans*.

- You *must* include the properties which distinguish true language from other forms of communication (use Brown, or Hockett, if you prefer): you cannot possible evaluate without some *criteria* against which to make that evaluation.
- Use a *sample* of studies, paying special attention to examples which appear to demonstrate the acquisition of productivity, semanticity and displacement.
- Discuss *Terrace*'s criticisms in as much detail as possible as these constitute an essential part of the evaluation.
- Equally important are the *counterarguments* to Terrace.
- Conclude with reference to the ongoing nature of the debate with brief reference to *ethics*.

Additional exam questions

1. Describe and assess the effectiveness of attempts to teach primates to use language. **(25 marks)**
   AEB (1988)

2. a Explain what psychologists mean by the terms *language* and *communication* **(10 marks)**
   b Describe and evaluate any **one** comparative study of communication in non-human animals **(15 marks)**
   AEB AS (1994)

6.4 Social behaviour in animals: courtship, mating and parenting

The evolution of social behaviour: evolutionarily stable strategies

Earlier in this chapter, we looked at how, according to evolutionary theory, the behaviour of individual members of a species has evolved in such a way that an individual acts to **maximise the survival of its own genes**. The concept of evolutionarily stable strategies (ESS), developed by John Maynard Smith and others, explains how the behaviour of any one individual in a population has, in the course of evolution, been influenced by the behaviour of all other members of the population to produce the same end result: not survival of the species nor of the individual but of the individual's genes.

An ESS is a behaviour pattern that cannot be improved by an alternative strategy provided sufficient members of a population adopt it.

This means that an individual cannot successfully behave differently from the others in the population even if it may appear that there would be a short-term gain by doing so. For example, supposing a male belonging to a species in which both parents were required to raise the young in order for them to survive inherited a mutant gene which made it take no part in parenting but abandon the female immediately after mating in order to mate with another female, abandon her to mate with yet another and so on. The short-term gain, in terms of evolution, is that he has impregnated many females, producing, potentially, many offspring and therefore many copies of his own genes.

However, the success of his strategy depends on the behaviour of the female. In this case, she is incapable of raising the young alone and therefore none of them will survive. Thus, the male has not benefited from breaking away from the ESS and his mutant gene will not survive to change the behaviour of later generations. This is, of course, an extremely oversimplified example which makes exaggerated assumptions about the causal relation between genes and behaviour, but it serves to illustrate the general theory that the evolutionary success of one behaviour pattern depends on the behaviour of others.

Courtship

Courtship can be defined as those relatively fixed patterns of behaviour which occur as a preliminary to mating.

Functions of courtship

Proving suitability as a mate

In terms of evolution, the main aim of males is to compete successfully with other males to attract females. The main aim of females is to select sexual partners who will provide offspring with the greatest chances of survival and reproduction. The female must therefore try to ensure that she mates with males that are fully mature and sexually competent; this can be achieved by prolonging courtship so that unsuitable males can be rejected. In any sexual encounter it is usually the female who exercises the choice. Males need to demonstrate to females that they are a good choice of mate. In many species this is achieved by courtship feeding in which the male presents food or a food substitute to the female; courtship feeding is a good sign of how well the male will be able to provide for the young and is therefore a good indicator of a male's parental abilities.

Identifying an opposite sex member of one's own species

Hybrid mating is fruitless from an evolutionary perspective because any offspring produced are sterile. In captivity hybrid mating is not uncommon, yet in the wild it hardly ever occurs. This is because species have developed clear courtship signals which lead an animal to its correct species. In some lower orders, males get together during the mating season and deliver assembly calls which serve to attract females of their particular species. In cases where similar species live in close proximity the assembly calls must be distinctly different. By contrast, in closely related species which do not share the same

area, or in which the mating seasons are non-overlapping, then the assembly calls are similar.

Reducing aggressiveness

Many vertebrate males are extremely territorial and will fiercely attack any intruding males. Any potential mate must therefore differentiate herself clearly from a male intruder by use of a courtship ritual. It may be for this reason that many such rituals involve behaviour which implies subservience. Sometimes it is the male who needs to reduce aggressiveness in the potential mate. Certain male spiders must be extremely careful if they want to avoid becoming their mate's dinner!

Mating strategies

Just as there are many different patterns of courtship to suit the different ecological niche of different species, so there are many types of **mating behaviour**. There are many strategies used by males in order to try and ensure that they not only gain access to females but that they are the only male to fertilise the eggs. The male dungfly sits on top of the female after copulation and guards her until the eggs are laid. Some insects cement up the genital opening of the female after they have copulated. Non-dominant males use a variety of strategies to gain access to females. Young elephant seals behave like females in order to join the harem and then sneak copulation when the dominant male is preoccupied with a rival.

Other mating strategies are dealt with in the following discussion as they are inextricably linked with parenting behaviour.

Parental care

Evolutionarily stable strategies of parental care

The extent to which parents care for their young varies considerably from species to species. At one extreme, there is none whatsoever; at the other extreme, some infants are born totally helpless and parental care is provided for many years. Whatever the particular parental behaviour that has evolved, the optimal behaviour of one parent will depend upon the behaviour of the other parent, and these two behaviour patterns together will form an evolutionarily stable strategy. We therefore need to look at a **pair of strategies** in order to appreciate why they have evolved.

Maynard Smith (1978) summarises the main factors that determine whether or not parental care will take place and, if so, which parent will provide it. The **four** variables which he cites as being of particular importance are:

1. Whether parenting can effectively be carried out by one parent or requires both.
2. The extent to which a female can, on her own, guard against predators.
3. The chances that a male will be able to find a new mate if he leaves the first one. This depends to a large extent on the length of the breeding season: if this is short then the male will be unlikely to find another mate and his time and energy would be better spent in helping to rear existing offspring.
4. The extent to which the male can be certain that any offspring have been fathered by him. This depends partly on the mode of fertilisation and partly on how successful a male is at guarding his mate from rival males. If fertilisation is internal then the male has little guarantee that the offspring are his unless he can successfully defend his mate against other males. If fertilisation is external, as in the case of many fish, the male can be fairly certain that the brood is his.

Activity

Bearing the above considerations in mind, think about what type of parenting (none, mother only, father only, both parents) would be the most likely to evolve in fish, birds and mammals. Remember that you need to consider such factors as

- The amount of care needed by the offspring
- The mode of fertilisation
- The length of the breeding season.

Now check your ideas with those that follow.

The parenting strategies of particular species

In the light of these considerations, Maynard Smith has reviewed patterns of parenting in various species and explained them in terms of evolutionarily stable strategies.

In **fish**, there is usually no parental care at all and that which exists is usually provided by one parent only. This is because parenting consists mainly of simply protecting the eggs and fry from predators rather than providing food, and can therefore be done almost as well by one parent as by two. If fertilisation is internal, it is usually the female who provides any parenting since the male is unlikely to be around when the eggs are laid and even if he is, he has no guarantee that the brood is his. When fertilisation is external rather than internal, if any parenting occurs, it is likely to be done by the male, since he can be confident that the offspring are his and the female has often used up her reserves in the process of egg laying.

In **birds**, parental care is usually shared by both parents since it involves incubation, food finding and protection. If care were not shared, the eggs or newly hatched chicks would be quickly eaten while left unguarded.

In **mammals**, the females breastfeed the infants and it is therefore essential that they, at least, look after the young. Male mammals tend to mate with many females although some are monogamous. In some mammalian species the males obtain food for the young and protect them from predators.

The relationship between courtship, mating and parental behaviour

In general, there is a positive relationship between length of courtship and quality of parental behaviour in animals. Courtship may be perceived as a time in which animals assess each other's fitness as future sexual partners and as parents for their shared offspring. This is particularly important if the time that both parent animals spend in looking after their young is long. Where there is negligible parental care in a species courtship is minimal or non-existent.

The behaviour of any individual has been shaped by evolution to maximise the survival of its own genes, and courtship, mating and parental behaviour are no exception. Because animals have very different environments, it is necessary for different species to adopt very different mating strategies, but in every case the choice is directly related to behaving in ways that promote the genetic success of the next generation.

Social structure, territoriality and dominance hierarchies

Many animals live in groups. The variety of social organisation within these groups is enormous, ranging from those who simply gather together for a short time on a seasonal basis, and are therefore no more than a collection of individuals, to those who live a totally interdependent existence in complex social organisation with rigid division of labour, as in many insect colonies.

Living in a group confers both advantages and disadvantages, summarised in Table 6.1.

Territorial behaviour

A territory can be defined as an area of space which is held and defended by a single animal or a social group.

In some species territory holders are largely solitary, but the whole group of territories constitute a **social organisation**. This is common in birds and many species of fish. In other cases the social group defends a **communal territory**, as is the situation with, for example, primates and lions.

Territorial size and boundaries

Territory size varies enormously across species, with the larger species tending, not surprisingly, to occupy larger territories than the smaller ones. But territory size is also related to **function**: territories used only for courtship displays tend to be small whereas those used as a food resource and a place to rear young tend to be much larger.

Territories cannot exist without the necessity to deal with rival intruders. The boundaries of territories are not necessarily fixed. Manning (1973) suggests that territories resemble **elastic discs**: the centre is well defined and defended aggressively by the occupier, but further away from the centre the intruder is attacked far less aggressively. At the boundaries there is little or no actual aggression but instead, threat displays are used. These displays are a compromise when the two tendencies of attack and escape are finely balanced. Both animals will threaten until one retreats.

Dominance hierarchies

When territories are occupied by solitary animals, their owners have complete dominance in that area. Animals within a social group often have to compete for territory and within such groups there often exists a dominance hierarchy, sometimes referred to as a 'pecking order'.

Types of dominance hierarchies include:

1. A simple **linear relationship** between the group members, with one dominant member, a second-

Table 6.1 Advantages and disadvantages of living in a group

Advantages	Disadvantages
1. Better protection from predators (by spotting predators and providing warnings)	**1.** Large groups are more noticeable to predators
2. Easier to hunt and tackle large prey	**2.** Increased competition within the group for food, mates, nest sites and other limited resources
3. Improved defence of territory	**3.** Increased risk of infection by contagious diseases and parasites
4. Readily accessible mate	**4.** Increased risk of being tricked into caring for others' young
5. Improved care of young through communal feeding and protection	**5.** Increased risk of infants being killed by other group members

ranking animal who can dominate all except the top one, and so on down the group. This type of linear hierarchy is typical of many birds. The establishment of the hierarchy involves a good deal of fighting in the early stages but after a while the subordinates usually defer as soon as a more dominant bird approaches.

2. Several high-ranking animals **cooperating** to dominate the rest of the group; this is typical of many primate groups.
3. A **single dominant animal** with all others equally subordinate with little or no differentiation between them. This is often the case when mice or rats are kept in overcrowded conditions or if several male sticklebacks are put into a very small tank.

Interaction of dominance hierarchies and territory

The variety of ways in which dominance and territory interact are provided by the following examples.

1. Within some social species the more dominant animals hold larger territories, or hold them in the most preferred areas. The interaction of **territory and dominance** can be observed in the grouse. Grouse only use territories to attract females during the mating season. At the appropriate time of year all the males converge on a central area called a lek. The most dominant birds keep the best territories at the centre of the lek and the least dominant ones are confined to the outer areas, nicknamed 'poverty traps'.
2. The **ecology** of the area may also influence the social structure of the group. For example, in the rich savannah areas baboons live in troops comprising a number of males and females with several dominant males who have privileged access to food, water and females. Rich habitats tend to attract large predators and males cooperate in defence of the weaker members of the group and of their territory. In contrast, baboon troops in harsh environments are likely to be dominated by a single male rather than a number of cooperating dominant males.
3. Some species change social organisation and degree of territoriality on a **seasonal** basis. Many birds are territorial in the breeding season but form flocks in the winter, sometimes even joining with other species. During the winter months the advantages of moving and feeding as a group outweigh the advantages of territoriality.

The interaction of social organisation, territorial behaviour and dominance is a complex one, and it is impossible to consider any one of these factors in isolation. As always, evolutionary pressures have resulted in a huge variety of **behavioural organisations**, all designed to increase the inclusive fitness of the individuals within them.

Preparing for the exam

Key terms

courtship
dominance hierarchies
evolutionarily stable strategies (ESS)
hybrid mating

linear relationships
monogamous
territoriality

Types of exam question

1. Description and interrelation of courtship, reproduction and parenting.
2. Description of types of social organisation and advantages of each.

Self-test questions

1. What is an evolutionarily stable strategy?
2. What are the functions of courtship?
3. What are the variables determining whether parental care will take place and, if so, which parent will provide it?
4. Describe the parenting strategies in *two* separate species.
5. Outline the nature of the relationship between courtship, mating and parenting.
6. What are the advantages and disadvantages for non-human animals of living in a group?
7. What types of dominance hierarchies exist in groups of animals?
8. What are the advantages of territorial behaviour, and how does it relate to other behaviour patterns such as courtship and mating?

Exam question with guidance notes

Briefly describe patterns of courtship, reproduction and parental behaviour in non-human species. Discuss how these behaviours may be interrelated.
(25 marks)
AEB (1991)

Before we start, bear in mind the warning about *not being anecdotal*.
This is very clearly a two-part question.

Description

- This requires a straightforward account of *types* of courtship and so on. Courtship varies from none to that taking many months; it sometimes involves feeding. Females have preference and males compete. Examine the *functions* of courtship.
- *Sexual* reproduction confers considerable evolutionary advantage over *asexual* reproduction. (These advantages were discussed in section 6.1.) Fertilisation can be internal or external. If it is internal, the male cannot be certain that the offspring are his; mention the ways in which he can increase his chances of being the sole mate. If fertilisation is external then

he can be fairly certain that the offspring are his. The significance of this in terms of likely parenting should be left for the second part of the answer.

- *Parenting behaviour*, if it occurs at all, can be done by the female alone, the male alone or both. It can be non-existent or prolonged. The functions it serves are providing food, protection and opportunities for learning by imitation or conditioning.

Discussion

- You must start by discussing the concept of *evolutionarily stable strategies* (ESSs), which means that, in this instance, male behaviour patterns have evolved in relationship to female behaviour patterns and vice versa. Whatever pairs of strategies exist, they will have evolved to promote the perpetuation of the genes of individuals.
- In terms of the specific *interaction* of courtship, mating and parenting, the main points are:
  a There is a positive relationship between length of courtship and quality of parenting
  b Maynard Smith's work on the main factors that determine whether or not parenting will take place and, if so, which parent will provide it; use examples of fish, mammals and birds to illustrate the point.
- You can conclude by saying that different environments require different patterns of courtship, reproduction and parenting and they have been shaped to interact in such a way as to maximise the *survival of an individual's genes*, thus none of them can be considered in isolation.

Additional exam questions

1. How do dominance and territoriality influence the social behaviour of non-human animals?　　　　　　　　　　　　　　**(25 marks)**
   AEB (1989)

2. a Describe any *two* types of social organisation found in non-human animals.　　　　　　　　　　　　　　　　**(10 marks)**
   b Consider the selective advantage of these arrangements to the animals concerned.　　　　　　　　　　　　　　**(15 marks)**
   AEB (1993)

3. Discuss the role of dominance in the social behaviour of animals.
   　　　　　　　　　　　　　　　　　　　(25 marks)
   AEB (1994)

Bio-psychology

7

AEB	NEAB	O & C	Topic	Date attempted	Date completed	Self Assessment
✓	✓	✓	**The Nervous System**			
✓	✓	✓	**The Endocrine System**			
✓	✓	✓	**The Effect of Drugs**			
✓	✗	✓	**Consciousness**			
✓	✗	✓	**The Sleep Cycle**			
✓	✗	✓	**Dreaming**			
✓	✓	✓	**Emotion**			
✓	✓	✓	**Motivation**			
✓	✓	✓	**Stress**			

7.1 The nervous system

Bio-psychology is the study of the relationship between the body and behaviour.

The **nervous system** (NS) is the most important system for the production of behaviour and the experiences of mental events.

The nervous system is a complex communication network in which signals are constantly being received, integrated and transmitted.

The brain is at the centre of, and by far the most important part of, the nervous system. All human capacities – to gather information, learn and remember, act intelligently, feel emotions, relate to other people and many, many others – are managed within the brain.

Neurons

Neurons are the basic 'building blocks' of the nervous system, all of which, including the brain, is composed of billions of these highly specialised nerve cells woven into a complex tapestry of connections and interconnections. The nervous system also contains another kind of cell called **glia** (from the Greek for 'glue') which support the neurons but do not transmit information. There are about ten times as many glia as there are neurons.

A **neuron** is a cell specialised to receive, process and/or transmit information to other cells within the body. There is a great variety of neurons, but they all have the same basic structure (see Figure 7.1).

A neuron consists of **three** parts:

a   The **dendrites** are widely branching structures, and their basic job is to receive incoming messages from other neurons or sense receptors

b   The **cell body** contains the nucleus of the cell and cytoplasm that sustains its life

c   The **axon** is a single, thin fibre with branches near its tip; the axon conducts the information along its length, which may be several feet in the spinal cord or, in the brain, less than a millimetre.

Most axons are surrounded by a **myelin sheath** which is an insulator and prevents signals from adjacent cells from interfering with each other. As Figure 7.1 shows, the myelin sheath is divided into segments. Axons end in smaller branching structures called terminals. At the tips of the terminals are swellings, called **synaptic knobs**, through which the neuron is able to stimulate nearby glands, muscles or other neurons.

Types of neuron

There are **three** major types of neuron:

1. **Sensory neurons** (also called afferent neurons) carry messages from sense receptor cells in the sense organs to the spinal cord and brain.

2. **Motor neurons** (also called efferent neurons) carry messages from the brain and spinal cord towards the muscles and glands.

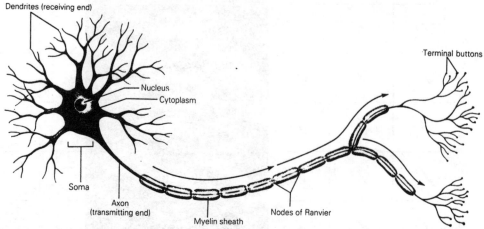

Figure 7.1 The major structures of the neuron
Source: P.G. Zimbardo, Psychology and Life (Harper Collins, 1992, 13th edn), p. 83.

3. **Interneurons** connect sensory and motor neurons since only very occasionally do motor and sensory neurons connect directly. Most of the billions of neurons in the brain are interneurons which relay messages from sensory neurons to other interneurons or to motor neurons.

A useful mnemonic if you get confused between efferents and afferents and think they sound the same, is <u>S</u>ensory = <u>A</u>fferent, <u>M</u>otor = <u>E</u>fferent, so they are, after all, the SAME.

Now check that you know the following:

a   What are the **three** main parts of a neuron?
b   What is the function of the myelin sheath?
c   What occurs at the synaptic knobs?

How neurons send their messages

Neurons carry messages in **one direction only**: from the dendrite or cell body, through the axon to the axon terminals and thence to other cells.

Neurons communicate with each other (and with muscles and glands) both electrically and chemically. When a stimulus is received, a wave of electrical voltage travels down the axon of the neuron. But electricity cannot jump across gaps, so when it reaches the tip of the axon (the synaptic knob), the impulse must now pass onto the next neuron (or other cells) by chemical rather than electrical means. Tiny chambers, called synaptic vesicles, in the axon's tip open and release a few thousand molecules of a chemical called a **neurotransmitter**. Once they have crossed the synapse, the molecules of the neurotransmitters fit into receptors on the receiving neuron and either trigger off an electrical impulse in that cell or inhibit an impulse from occurring (see Figure 7.2).

A single neuron may, at any one time, be receiving thousands of such messages, some inhibitory, some excitatory. Essentially, the neuron appears to respond by **averaging** all these messages, but as yet we don't really understand how this happens. What is clear is that any one neuron either sends an electrical impulse or does not, in other words, it either fires or it does not fire in an all-or-none fashion.

Neurotransmitters are chemical transmitters which travel the small distance across the synaptic space and excite or inhibit the next neuron. Neurotransmitters exist not only in the brain but also in the spinal cord, the peripheral nervous system and certain glands. They play an essential role in many psychological processes, such as **memory**, **mood** and **emotion**. It is now clear that abnormalities in the production of neurotransmitters can contribute to **mental disorders**.

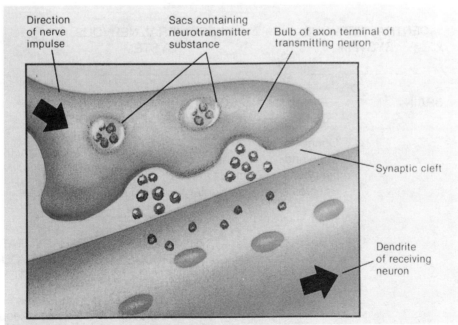

Figure 7.2 The synapse
Source: S.A. Rathus, Essentials of Psychology (Holt, Rinehart & Winston, 1991, 3rd edn), p. 45.

The 'nervous breakdown'

Figure 7.3 represents the structure of the nervous system.

As Figure 7.3 shows, the nervous system in humans is divided into **two** main parts:

1. The Central Nervous System (CNS), consisting of the brain and spinal cord.
2. The Peripheral Nervous System (PNS), consisting of the somatic and autonomic nervous system.

The brain

Although the brain weighs only about three pounds, it contains 90 per cent of the body's neurons: billions of cells that integrate information from inside and outside the body.

How psychologists study the functions of the brain

Brain injury

Accidental brain injury

Psychologists study the behavioural changes in people who have suffered brain damage caused by brain tumours, strokes, head injuries or other misfortunes. This has provided many major insights into the relationship between the brain and behaviour, especially in areas of **language** and **perception**, but it has obvious limitations: psychologists have no control over the location or extent of the injury or over any related complications, like trauma.

Lesioning

Information has also been obtained by deliberate and precise lesioning of the brains of otherwise healthy animals. Lesioning involves destroying a piece of the brain. These animals are then observed for any changes in their behaviour, for example, forgetting of previously learned material, changes in levels of aggression and so on.

Lesions are also carried out on humans as a form of medical treatment. A type of lesion used with some epileptics is severing of nerve fibres connecting the two halves of the brain. Such patients are known as 'split-brain' patients and are considered in detail in the Core Study of this chapter (p. 182).

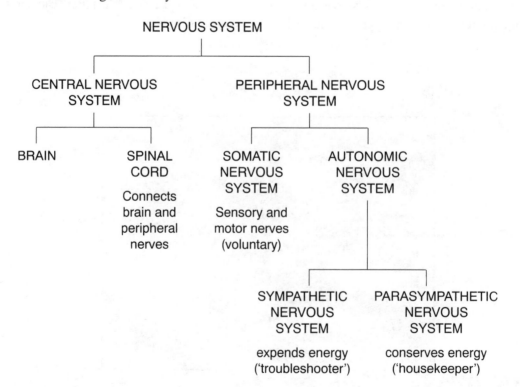

Figure 7.3 The structure of the nervous system

Electrical stimulation and recording

Recording

The **electroencephalogram (EEG)** can detect minute amounts of electrical activity in millions of neurons in particular regions of the brain. In order to do this, electrodes are attached to the surface of the scalp; a machine to which the electrodes are connected translates the electrical energy into line tracings commonly known as brain waves.

The EEG has been particularly useful in studying the stages of **sleep**; it has also been used to locate brain tumours and to diagnose a number of types of abnormal behaviour.

Stimulation

Penfield, a neurosurgeon, stimulated the brain surface of conscious patients about to undergo surgery. As a result of stimulation of various parts of the cortex, some patients reported strong emotional reactions, such as fear and elation, and vivid memories of past experiences.

Hess (1955) placed electrodes deep into the brain tissue of fully conscious cats and thereby stimulated various internal parts of the brain. He found that, depending on the particular brain area stimulated, he could produce such reactions as aggression, sleep, sexual arousal and terror. These responses disappeared as soon as stimulation ceased.

Computer-driven scanning devices

As their name suggests, these devices use computer technology to draw pictures of the **internal structure** or **activities** of the brain and they have revolutionised research on brain functioning.

Computer axial tomography (CAT or CT scan)

The CAT scanner projects X rays through the head at many angles and the computer then measures the amount of radiation at each angle and integrates these measurements into a three dimensional view of the brain. CAT scans have revealed many kinds of brain damage and other abnormalities of brain functioning. CAT scans can, however, only portray brain **structure**, not function.

Positron emission tomography (PET scan)

This scanning device utilises the fact that the more active any particular part of the brain is at any one time, the more glucose it will be using. People undergoing a PET scan are injected with harmless amounts of a radioactive compound mixed with glucose and, once inside the machinery, they are asked to engage in various cognitive and behavioural activities. The computer measures the amount of radioactive substance in various parts of the brain during these activities and generates a **dynamic picture** of the brain, showing which areas are the **most active** during each type of activity.

Magnetic resonance imaging

This is the most modern technique of all and involves the subject lying in a tunnel that generates a powerful magnetic field while being exposed to radio waves of certain frequencies. The magnetic fields and radio frequencies produce vibrations in the atoms of the brain cells and these vibrations are converted by computer into an integrated three dimensional image of the brain's anatomy, producing more precise and detailed images than does the CAT scanner. These images enable researchers to **detect abnormal functioning** in brain cells and to see which parts are **most active** during various physical and psychological activities.

Activity

Draw your own summary chart of the methods of investigating the brain, using headings such as **method; technique; uses; limitations**.

Structure and functions of the brain

The main structures of the brain are shown in Figure 7.4 and the functions of each part are shown in Table 7.1

Right brain/left brain

The cerebrum, the seat of complex thought, is divided

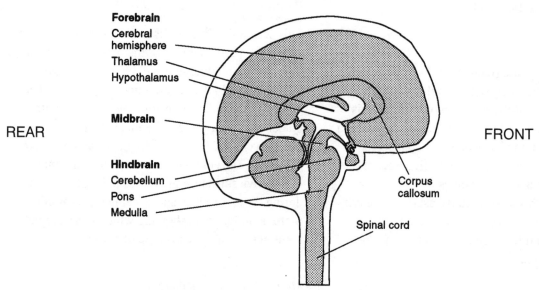

Figure 7.4 A cross-section of the brain, showing the hindbrain, midbrain and forebrain

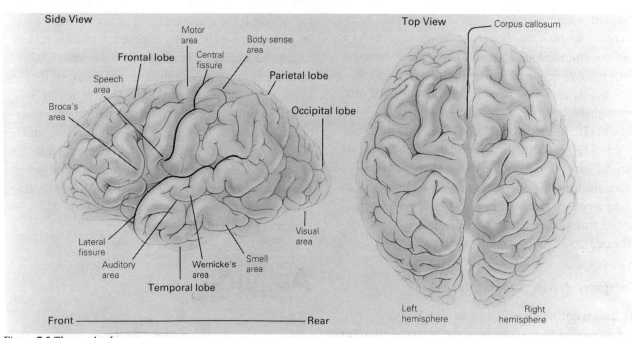

Figure 7.5 The cerebral cortex
Source: P.G. Zimbardo, Psychology and Life (Harper Collins, 1992, 13th edn), p. 63.

into two separate hemispheres: the left hemisphere and the right hemisphere (see Figure 7.5).

The two hemispheres have numerous interconnections, especially through the **corpus callosum**, a bundle of about 200 million nerve fibres that transfers information back and forth between the two hemispheres. Most of the nerve fibres connecting the brain to the various parts of the body cross from one side to the other. This means that the right side receives sensory messages and controls movement in the left side of the body, and vice versa.

Does each hemisphere have different functions?

The two hemispheres appear to make different contributions to the same functions: both hemispheres contribute to language and memory functions, to perceptual–cognitive functions and to emotional functions. However, although they both contribute to these functions, each hemisphere tends to **dominate the control**.

Table 7.1 Functions of the brain

Main sections	Subsections	Main functions	Other comments
HINDBRAIN – Vital Sections	MEDULLA	Vital functions not consciously willed, e.g. breathing, heart rate, blood pressure Also plays a role in sleep, sneezing and coughing	Since the medulla and pons control vital functions, almost any damage is fatal
	PONS ('bridge')	Involved in sleeping, dreaming and waking. Transmits information about body movements	
	CEREBELLUM ('little brain')	Maintains balance and controls motor behaviour, especially for complex, rapid motor skills such as playing the piano	Damage results in clumsy, uncoordinated movements, general loss of muscle tone and slurred speech One of the first areas to be impaired by alcohol
	RETICULAR ACTIVATING SYSTEM (also extends into mid-brain)	Controls sleep, attention and levels of arousal. Has connections with higher areas of the brain and screens incoming information, filtering out anything irrelevant, arousing the higher centres when their attention is demanded	Injury may result in permanent coma
MIDBRAIN		Functions include receiving information from the visual system and involvement in eye movements	
FOREBRAIN – higher functions	THALAMUS (the 'relay station')	As sensory messages enter the brain, it directs them to the relevant higher centres, e.g. a visual image would be directed to the visual centre. Also involved in sleep and attention in coordination with other brain structures	
	HYPOTHALAMUS	Involved in drives vital to survival (for example, hunger and thirst) Regulates the ANS Controls the pituitary gland	In conjunction with the limbic system, it seems to modify stereotypical behaviour so that humans are less likely, for example, to flee or attack when threatened but may choose an alternative strategy
	PITUITARY GLAND	Releases many hormones and regulates other endocrine glands	Although often referred to as the 'master gland', it is actually under the control of the hypothalamus
	LIMBIC SYSTEM (comprises the hippocampus amygdala and hypothalamus)	Involved in emotions shared by other animals, e.g. rage and fear. The hippocampus has been called the 'gateway to memory' because it appears to store information for future use	A person known as HM had his hippocampus destroyed and thereafter had no capacity to transfer events from short-term to long-term memory He would, for example re-read a newspaper repeatedly
	THE CEREBRUM the surface of which is called the CEREBRAL CORTEX	Divided into two hemispheres, called 'cerebral hemispheres': in general the left hemisphere controls the right side of the body and vice versa. The largest and most complex part of the human brain responsible for most complex mental activities including learning, remembering, thinking and consciousness	Contains almost 75% of all the cells of the human brain. 'Folded' to provide a massive surface area
		Divided into lobes: *Occipital lobes:* contain the visual cortex where visual signals are processed	Damage to occipital lobes can cause impaired visual recognition or blindness
		Parietal lobes: essential for body perception including perception of location and movement of body parts and orientation of the body in space	
		Temporal lobes: contain auditory cortex, the main processing area for hearing. Also involved in memory, perception, emotion, language comprehension and more complex aspects of vision	As this is involved in the more complex aspects of vision, damage does not result in blindness but impairs ability to recognise complex patterns such as faces or to identify in which direction an object is moving
		Frontal lobes: responsible for planning, creativity and taking initiative Contains primary motor cortex, responsible for fine motor movements Important for human language production	Prefrontal lobotomy is an operation involving damage to the prefrontal cortex Once used as a treatment for depression and schizophrenia Results in loss of emotion and initiative, a decrease in ability to concentrate and certain defects in memory These operations ceased in the mid-1950s

Core Study

Hemisphere deconnection and unity in conscious awareness: R.W. Sperry (1968)

This article is an account of studies of severe epileptic patients who, in an attempt to control the epilepsy, have had the corpus callosum completely severed, effectively disconnecting the left and right cerebral hemispheres from each other.

One of the most interesting features of these patients is that they behave in many ways as if they have two independent streams of conscious awareness, one in each hemisphere, each cut off from, and out of contact with, the mental experience of the other.

Most of the investigations of these patients use an apparatus in which the subject is asked to focus on a point in the middle of a screen onto which words or pictures are flashed so quickly that the eyes do not have time to move. Information going to each hemisphere is therefore completely separate.

These patients appear to have two separate visual inner worlds. If an object is shown in the right visual field and later in the left field, the subject responds as if he had never seen the object before.

Language is processed mainly in the left hemisphere. When words are flashed to these patients in the left visual field, so that they go to the right hemisphere, they appear not to recognise them at all. Yet, if asked to point with the left hand to a matching picture or object, they have no trouble. The non-lingual right hemisphere has seen the object but cannot name it or write about it.

When words are flashed partly in the left visual field and partly in the right, the letters on each side are responded to separately. In the 'key case' example shown in Figure 7.6 the subject might reach for a key with the left hand and spell out the word 'case'. When asked what kind of case he is thinking of, he does not relate anything associated with a key, but may suggest 'in case of fire', 'a case of beer'.

If two objects are placed simultaneously, one in each hand, and then removed and hidden in a pile of

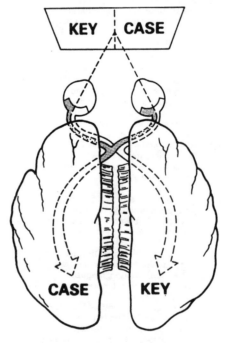

Figure 7.6 Right brain/left brain: things seen to the left of a central fixation point with either eye are projected to the right hemisphere and vice versa
Source: R.D. Gross, Key Studies in Psychology (Hodder & Stoughton, 1990, 1993), p. 202.

other objects, each hand will hunt the pile and selectively retrieve its own object, without knowledge of what the other hand is seeking.

The abilities of the right hemisphere

It is of great interest to researchers to gain insight into the abilities of the minor (right) hemisphere, but this is difficult without the capacity for language. Evidence indicates that the right hemisphere may be animal-like in that it cannot talk or write, but in other respects it shows mental capacities which are definitely human. For example, if asked to group or match objects, it will do so on the basis of function, not simply sensory outlines. A clock will be paired with a toy wristwatch, a hammer with a nail.

The right hemisphere can also perform simple arithmetic problems. Moreover, it can understand both written and spoken words to some extent, although it cannot express the understanding verbally. If a word like 'eraser' is flashed to the left visual field, the subject is able to search out an eraser from a collection of objects but cannot say what is being held. Nevertheless, the word must have been understood initially.

In conclusion, it would appear that the right hemisphere comprises a second conscious entity which is characteristically human and runs along in parallel with the more dominant stream of consciousness in the left hemisphere.

QUESTIONS

1. Sperry's **'split-brain'** patients had problems with the material presented to their left visual field.
   a Give *one* example of these problems.
      (2 marks)
   b What does this study tell us about the difference between the cerebral hemispheres?   **(2 marks)**
      Oxford and Cambridge (1994)
2. Why had the subjects of this study had their right and left hemispheres disconnected?
3. What do the findings tell us about the behaviour and experience of such people?

The left hemisphere

Language-related functions are dominated by the left hemisphere in most people. For this reason, the left hemisphere is usually larger and damage to it is likely to result in language disorders.

The two areas most involved in speech are:

Broca's area which lies in the frontal lobe near the motor cortex and appears to be responsible for controlling the muscles concerned with speech production. Damage to this area results in the tendency to use only short sentences, spoken slowly and laboriously.

Wernicke's area which lies in the temporal lobe near the auditory cortex. Damage does not affect speech production as such, but results in difficulty with 'finding the right words' and an impairment in the ability to understand what others are saying. Wernicke's area appears to be essential to understanding the relationship between words and their meaning.

Two brains in one skull

Further information about the differential functions of the two hemispheres come from studies of 'split-brain' patients. These are considered in the Core Study of this section (p 182).

The spinal cord

The **spinal cord** is an extension of the brain, running from the base of the brain down the centre of the back, protected by the vertebral column. The spinal cord connects the brain to the peripheral nervous system (PNS) and coordinates the activities of the left and right sides of the body. It is also capable of producing some behaviours on its own, independently of the brain. These behaviours are called **spinal reflexes**.

Spinal reflexes

Because these behaviours are not controlled by the brain, they are automatic, requiring no conscious effort at all.

For example, if you put your hand on something hot, you pull it away immediately without first thinking 'Oh, that's hot, I'd better pull my hand away' or less polite thoughts to that effect. It is only **after** the event that the brain gets to know what has happened.

In terms of the events occurring in the nervous system, the hot surface stimulates sensory nerves endings in the hand and a message travels along these sensory nerves to the spinal cord. The message is then transmitted to motor nerves which relay messages to the muscles in your arm to contract and pull your hand away. A message then passes up the spinal cord to the brain, informing it of what has occurred. (Figure 7.7 shows the neural circuitry involved, but to simplify matters it shows just one sensory and one motor nerve.)

The brain's influence on reflexes

Because of the connections between the brain and the spinal cord, it is possible for the brain to influence certain reflexes.

For example, urinating is a reflex action in response to a full bladder but we learn to control this reflex, thus involving the brain in a conscious decision about when to urinate. Many sexual responses are reflexive and people paralysed below the waist are capable of sexual responses in response to stimulation of the genitals. Nevertheless, many sexual responses involve the brain since there are a host of stimuli, other than direct genital stimulation, which trigger or inhibit sexual responses, stimuli such as erotic material or anxiety.

Activity

1. Think of stimuli other than erotic material and anxiety which influence sexual arousal.
2. To what extent to you think these are learned rather than innate?
3. Can you think of other reflex actions which are influenced by the brain?

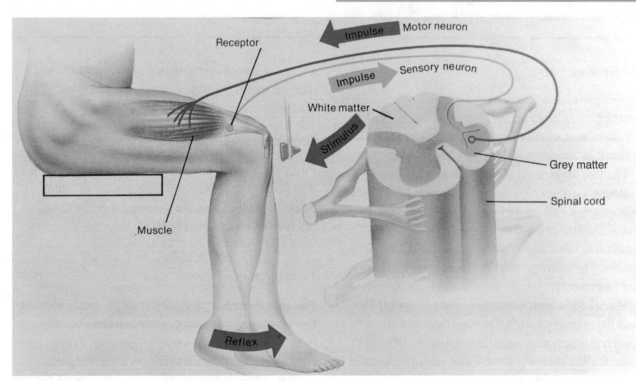

Figure 7.7 Spinal reflexes: the reflex arc
Source: S.A. Rathus, Essentials of Psychology (Holt, Rinehart & Winston, 1991, 3rd edn), p. 51.

The peripheral nervous system

Peripheral means 'outlying' and the peripheral nervous system (PNS) contains all portions of the nervous system outside the brain and spinal cord.

The CNS has no direct contact with the outside world and it is the PNS which provides the brain with information from the outside world and internal body organs. Without the PNS, the brain would receive no information at all.

a **Sensory nerves** in the PNS carry messages from special receptors in the skin, muscles and internal and external sense organs to the spinal cord and thence to the brain.

b **Motor nerves** carry messages from the CNS to muscles, glands and internal organs, enabling us to move and our glands to secrete chemicals including hormones.

The PNS is composed of two subdivisions:

1. The **somatic** nervous system
2. The **autonomic** nervous system (ANS).

1. The **somatic** (or skeletal) NS controls the skeletal muscles and permits voluntary action. When you get up and walk across a room, the somatic NS is in control. Even such a simple movement involves many messages to and from the sense organs, internal organs and muscles, precisely coordinating your movements. It also provides feed-back to the brain as to your exact position, thus enabling any adjustments that may be necessary: adjustments such as avoiding an object you see on the floor and want to avoid.

2. The **autonomic nervous system** sustains basic life processes of which we are not consciously aware, such as respiration, digestion and heart rate. It is responsible for survival both in terms of dealing with threats to the organism and in maintaining basic body functions. The ANS is subdivided into **two** sections:

    1. The **sympathetic** nervous system
    2. The **parasympathetic** nervous system.

Although it may sound strange, these two systems work together, in opposition, to adjust the body to changing circumstances.

The **sympathetic** NS deals with emergency situations by releasing large amounts of energy, mobilising the body and controlling behaviour with split-second timing.

The **parasympathetic** NS is responsible for restoring equilibrium once a threatening situation is past, and for the more everyday functioning of basic body processes.

If, when walking across the room, you had tripped, the sympathetic NS would immediately trigger the 'fight or flight' response: digestion would stop, heart rate would increase and blood would flow away from the internal organs to the muscles required to try and restore balance and grab onto something to 'save' yourself. You would be aware of this only **after** you had reacted: you would feel your heart pounding and generally be shaken. Once you were safe, the parasympathetic NS would return the body functions to normal: digestion would resume, heart rate would slow down and breathing would become more relaxed.

Put simply, the sympathetic system acts as an **accelerator**, mobilising you for action, while the parasympathetic system acts as a **decelerator**, helping to calm you down.

Biofeedback

The ANS is largely automatic, but not entirely so. Neal Miller (1978), using a technique called **biofeedback**, showed that people are capable of controlling such responses as blood pressure, blood flow, heart rate and skin temperature as well as many voluntary responses (see section 7.5 for more details of biofeedback).

Both the sympathetic and the parasympathetic nervous systems are involved in emotion and stress, as you will see later in this subsection.

The endocrine system

The endocrine system (see Figure 7.8) is a network of glands that manufacture and secrete chemical messengers called **hormones** into the bloodstream.

Although the endocrine system is not part of the nervous system, it is closely related to it, especially to the autonomic nervous system. Endocrine glands release hormones in response to the levels of

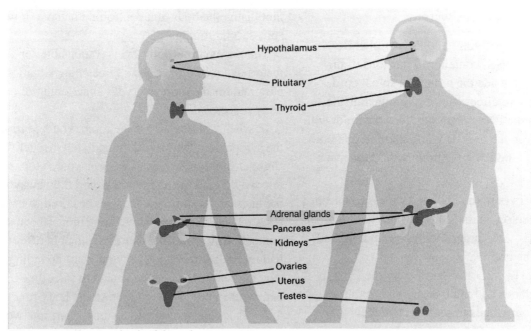

Figure 7.8 Location of major glands of the endocrine system
Source: S.A. Rathus, Essentials of Psychology (Holt, Rinehart & Winston, 1991, 3rd edn), p. 67.

chemicals in the bloodstream or because they are stimulated by other hormones or by nerve impulses from the brain. The hormones are secreted into the blood and travel to distant target cells with specific receptors.

Hormones control a wide variety of bodily functions and behaviours. Some of these are slow and continuous processes, such as maintenance of blood-sugar levels; others are extremely rapid and urgent such as the 'fight or flight' reaction. But the endocrine system is also responsible for the immediate 'fight or flight' reaction by releasing the hormone adrenalin into the bloodstream.

Hormones are controlled by the **hypothalamus** which sends hormonal instructions to the pituitary gland, either stimulating or inhibiting the release of other hormones.

As far as psychology is concerned, there are three groups of hormones which are particularly relevant (see Table 7.2)

The effect of drugs

Most drugs can be classified as **stimulants**, **depressants** or **hallucinogens**. These classifications are based on the psychological effects of drugs and do not refer to the chemical nature of the substances.

Depressants: examples are alcohol, barbiturates and tranquillisers such as valium. These reduce activity in the central nervous system. Also known as sedatives, they often make you calm or drowsy. They may reduce anxiety, guilt, tension and inhibitions. In large amounts, they usually produce insensitivity to pain.

Stimulants: examples are amphetamines and cocaine. These accelerate activity in the nervous system; they raise blood pressure, heart rate and respiration. In moderate amounts, they tend to produce feelings of excitement, confidence and euphoria but the after-effects are anxiety, depression and fatigue. In large amounts, they are likely to produce anxiety, jitteriness and sleep disturbances.

Hallucinogens: examples are LSD (lysergic acid diethylamide) and marijuana. These drugs produce a feeling of euphoria and increased sensory arousal. They also produce marked shifts in consciousness, changing thought processes and disrupting the normal perception of time and space.

The effects of some specific drugs are given in Table 7.3; we will now consider some of these in more detail.

Alcohol: although alcohol is a depressant, a small quantity has a subjectively stimulating effect, probably because it suppresses activity in parts of the brain that normally inhibit behaviour.

Table 7.2 The action of some principal hormones

Hormone	Produced by	Effect	
Insulin	Pancreas	Plays a crucial role in the body's use of sugar; affects appetite	
Cortisol	The adrenal cortex (The outer part of the adrenal gland)	Increases blood-sugar levels and enhances energy	
Adrenalin (also called epinephrine) Noradrenalin (also called norepinephrine)	The adrenal medulla (The inner part of the adrenal gland)	Together, these two hormones prepare the body for emergencies by increasing blood pressure, diverting blood from internal organs to voluntary muscles and increasing blood sugar levels	
Sex hormones: i androgens (for example testosterone)	The gonads (Testes in males: ovaries in females)	Produce secondary sexual characteristics in males Appear to influence sexual arousal in both sexes	Fluctuating sex hormones affect both mood and behaviour
ii oestrogens	All these hormones are produced by both men and women but in differing amounts	Responsible for secondary sexual development in females and influence the course of the menstrual cycle	
iii progesterone		Responsible for preparing the uterus for implantation of a fertilised egg	

Even moderate amounts of alcohol affect judgement, perception, coordination and balance.

After consuming large amounts of alcohol, it is not unusual for people to become aggressive. However, it appears to be a myth that alcohol 'releases' aggression in people who are not normally aggressive. The source of aggression is in the mind of the drinker: people do not become aggressive when they feel they will be held responsible for their actions (Critchlow, 1983).

When consumption of alcohol ceases after prolonged and heavy use, it may produce withdrawal symptoms of delirium tremens, a state of panic and confusion combined with nightmarish hallucinations.

LSD: LSD leads to alteration in consciousness which can lead to a highly irrational and disoriented behaviour and, occasionally, to a panic state in which the person feels she or he cannot control what the body is doing or thinking and may become paranoid.

PCP (phencyclidine): PCP, known as Angel Dust or Superacid, may cause hallucinations but it also makes the user feel dissociated or apart from the environment. In low doses it produces insensitivity to pain and an experience similar to a moderately drunken state. Unlike the person who experiences LSD, the PCP user is unable to observe his or her drug-induced state and frequently has no memory of it.

Marijuana: Marijuana produces much milder effects, including a perceived increase in the intensity of various stimuli and distortions in the sense of time. Regular users report a number of sensory and perceptual changes: a general euphoria and sense of well-being, some distortions of time and space, and a number of out-of-body experiences.

Factors influencing drug effects

The effects of a drug cannot be explained solely in terms of its chemical properties. They are also

Table 7.3 The effects of some commonly used drugs

Drug	Type of drug	Effect on mood and behaviour	Effect of overdose	Effect of withdrawal
Amphetamines	Stimulant	Alertness, insomnia, loss of appetite, elevated mood	Panic Convulsions Hallucinations	Apathy Depression
Cocaine	Stimulant	Euphoria, hyperactivity, irritability	Excitability Sleeplessness Paranoia Hallucinations	Irritibility Long spells of sleep Depression
Nicotine	Stimulant	Can cause calmness or alertness, depending on the setting	Heart disease High blood pressure Impaired circulation	Irritability
Alcohol	Depressant	Reduces inhibitions and anxiety. In larger quantities slows reaction time and impairs coordination	Blackouts, mental and neurological impairment Cirrhosis	'Delirium tremens' Disorientation Clouded consciousness Delusions
Cannabis (marijuana)	Mild psychedelic	Euphoria Relaxed inhibition Increased appetite Mild arousal	Hallucinations Loss of concentration Anxiety, paranoia	Insomnia Hyperactivity
Tranquillisers (e.g. Valium)	Depressant	Reduced anxiety and tension	Shallow breathing Weak and rapid pulse Death	Anxiety Insomnia Convulsions
Opium Heroine Morphine	Depressant	Euphoria, relief of pain, drowsiness and lethargy	Nausea Coma Possibly death	Agonising pain
LSD Mescaline Phencyclidine (PCP)	Hallucinogen	Hallucinations Exhilaration Insightful amnesia Anxiety Possible paranoid behaviour	Loss of contact with reality Seizures Death	None

influenced by many factors such as the prior experience with the drug, expectation as to its effects and the environmental setting.

1. **Prior experience** with a drug: often, the body develops a **tolerance** for the drug, meaning that greater and greater quantities are required to produce the desired effect. Most drugs produce tolerance, but some do so considerably more rapidly than do others.
2. **Expectations:** when people think that they are drinking alcohol, when in reality they are not, both sexes report increased sexual arousal and men behave more aggressively (Wilson, 1982).
3. **Environmental setting:** sometimes, if you are sitting quietly at home, a small amount of alcohol can make you fall asleep; larger quantities at a party can invigorate you and make you euphoric, but if you are already feeling a bit low, the same quantity can plunge you into a depression.

Drug dependence

The use of drugs is considered abnormal when users can no longer function normally without it. **Psychological dependence** is said to occur when the drug is no longer used as an occasional means of obtaining pleasure but when the user believes it to be essential in order to cope with everyday life. **Physical dependence**, or addiction, occurs when the body develops a tolerance for the drug and needs greater and greater quantities to obtain the desired effect. People may experience withdrawal symptoms when they stop taking the substance.

Activity

Make sure you understand the meaning of the words 'tolerance', 'dependency' and 'withdrawal symptoms' as related to drug use.

As this chapter has shown, biological factors such as hormone levels, neurotransmitter activity or brain injury all affect our behaviour. In turn, our social and physical environments affect our biological state. In stressful situations our adrenalin level rises; it is now well established that biological factors make some individuals vulnerable to certain forms of serious mental disorder, but it is also true that this vulnerability is triggered by stressful events.

Knowledge of the workings of the nervous and endocrine systems contribute greatly to our understanding of human behaviour. But we must be very careful not to reduce all complex behaviour to biology. The mysteries of human personality, happiness, despair, courage or compassion cannot be **reduced** merely to the chemistry and physics of the body.

Psychologists must look for explanations of behaviour at many different levels, and understanding the effects of biology on behaviour is only one part of the total picture.

Activity

In section 10.2 we discuss **physiological reductionism**: the attempt to explain all behaviour in terms only of neurochemical and biochemical processes. Consider this as you revise the whole of bio-psychology: what processes, other than biological ones, have an effect on behaviour?

Preparing for the exam

Key terms

afferent neuron	hormones
auditory cortex	hypothalamus
autonomic nervous system	interneurons
axon	lesion
Bio-psychology	magnetic resonance imaging
biofeedback	motor cortex
Broca's area	motor neuron
cell body	neurons
central nervous system	neurotransmitter
cerebrum	parasympathetic nervous system
computer axial tomography (CAT scan)	peripheral nervous system
	positron emission tomography (PET scan)
corpus callosum	
delirium tremens	sensory neuron
dendrites	somatic nervous system
depressants	spinal reflexes
efferent neuron	stimulants
electroencephalogram	synapse
endocrine system	synaptic knob
frontal lobe	temporal lobe
glia	Wernickes's area
hallucinogens	

Types of exam question

1. Consideration of the role played by neural processes in types of behaviour (sometimes only *one* type of behaviour is required).
2. The principles of synaptic transmission and its importance.

3. Interaction of the CNS, the ANS and the endocrine system.
4. The effect of drugs on behaviour.

Self-test questions

1. What are the *three* main types of neuron?
2. How do neurons communicate with each other?
3. Where would you find a neurotransmitter?
4. What is the function of a neurotransmitter?
5. How have psychologists been able to study the functioning of the brain?
6. What is a PET scan?
7. What is a CAT scan?
8. Summarise the main functions of the left hemisphere of the brain.
9. Summarise the main functions of the right hemisphere of the brain.
10. What is a spinal reflex? Give an example of *one*.
11. What are the *two* subdivisions of the PNS? Describe the function of each.
12. Describe the role of the sympathetic nervous system and the parasympathetic nervous system.
13. What *three* groups of hormones are psychologists particularly interested in?
14. Most drugs can be put into one of *three* categories. Name each category, and give an example of a drug from each of the three.
15. Briefly describe the effects of each of the drug groups named above.
16. What is meant by 'drug dependency'?
17. What else can effect the influence of drugs, other than their chemical properties?

Exam questions with guidance notes

1. **Critically consider the influence that drugs have been shown to have upon behaviour.**
   (25 marks)
   AEB (1993)

   Being a 'critically consider' question, it is *not* appropriate to simply list the effect of drugs, although this should certainly be your starting point. Then give details of the factors which influence the *effects* of drugs; factors such as prior experience, expectation and environmental setting. It is also appropriate to make brief reference to *drug dependence*.

2. a **Describe the structure of EITHER the Autonomic Nervous System OR the Endocrine System.** (10 marks)
   b **Discuss the effects that the system you have described has been shown to have on physiological and behavioural functions.**
   (15 marks)
   AEB (1994)

   We will consider both the alternatives in this question:

The ANS

a

- You need to put the ANS in the context of the *structure of the whole NS*; in other words, that it is part of the PNS (which you should briefly describe) and is divided into the sympathetic and parasympathetic divisions.
- You should also describe its building blocks, that is *neurons*.

b

For this, you will need to consult other sections of this chapter:

- Describe the main *functions* of the sympathetic and parasympathetic NS, using several examples.
- Discuss the *'fight or flight reaction'* in detail. This leads into the involvement of the ANS in stress (see Section 7.5). The parasympathetic and sympathetic nervous systems also have an important role in emotion (see section 7.3). Finally, you could discuss Miller and DeCara's work on biofeedback (see section 7.5).

The endocrine system

a

- Describe the main *endocrine glands* and their relationship to the NS and the bloodstream.
- Mention the role of the *hypothalamus* in the control of hormonal secretions.

b

- Select the main *hormones* (you could use only those in this text, or do a more detailed coverage).
- For each of the hormones you select, describe both the *physiological* and *behavioural* functions. So, for example, testosterone has the physiological effect of influencing secondary sexual development, the physiological and behavioural effects of influencing sexual arousal and the (hypothesised) behavioural effect of increasing aggressiveness.
- There is a considerable amount to be said about adrenalin/noradrenalin since they are involved in the 'fight or flight' reactions, stress and emotion (again, you need to refer to sections 7.3 and 7.5).

Conclude *both* essays with reference to the fact that human behaviour is always the result of complex interactions between physiological and psychological factors.

Additional exam questions

1. 'There is no question that the study of specialisation of function of the two cerebral hemispheres is one of the most important and productive lines of research in neuropsychology.'
   Discuss this statement in relation to split brain studies   **(25 marks)**
   AEB AS (1994)

2. Discuss the function of the endocrine system, and its interaction with the central and autonomic nervous systems.   **(25 marks)**
   AEB (1989)

---

3. a Outline the functions of the following:

   i Sensory and motor cortex **(4 marks)**

   ii Association areas of the cortex. **(6 marks)**

b Describe *two* methods used to investigate cortical functions and discuss problems associated with using such procedures with humans.

(10 marks)

JMB (1989)

7.2 Variations in consciousness

In essence, consciousness involves self-awareness: an awareness of our own thoughts, perceptions and feelings. This includes the awareness of our **self** as a unique person experiencing the world and an awareness of our own thoughts about these experiences.

A sense of self comes from watching ourselves from inside with, supposedly, greater knowledge than anyone else can have of us.

Structures of consciousness

Obviously our behaviour is controlled by conscious processes, but it is also controlled by **mental processes of which we are not aware**.

1. **Non-conscious processes** are all the mental processes that influence behaviour but of which we are totally unaware and of which we never will be aware.

   For example, we are unaware of hormonal secretions and many other body processes. We instantly and effortlessly perceive depth, but we are unaware of the organising processes which enable this to happen.

2. **The preconscious** contains all the storehouse of memories which only come into consciousness if something draws our attention to them.

   For example, knowledge of skills like swimming or playing tennis, which are performed effortlessly and unthinkingly. They only enter into the conscious mind if, for example, we want to teach them to someone else or something interferes with our usual performance.

3. **Subconscious awareness** involves processing information on which we are not focusing our attention but which can nevertheless influence our behaviour. A great deal of information to which we are not paying attention still gets registered and evaluated at some level below that of conscious awareness. This is considered in detail in section 3.3 on Attention.

4. **The unconscious** refers to mental processes which influence behaviour but of which we are not aware because, according to Freud, they are so unacceptable that they have been removed from consciousness by repression. They can only be revealed through such alterations in consciousness as hypnosis or dreaming.

Activity

Which structure of consciousness is likely to be involved in the following activities:

1. Driving along a familiar route?
2. Recalling some contents of a radio programme to which you were not really listening?
3. Forgetting a dental appointment?
4. The muscle movements you make when writing?

Consciousness and brain activity

As mentioned in section 7.1, brain waves can be detected by an instrument called an electroencephalogram (EEG). EEG activity is divided for convenience into four bands: beta, alpha, theta and delta. Different patterns of EEG activity are associated with different states of consciousness, as shown in Table 7.4.

Table 7.4 EEG patterns and states of consciousness

EEG pattern	Typical state of consciousness
Beta	Normal waking thought
	Alert problem solving
Alpha	Deep relaxation
	Blank mind
	Meditation
Theta	Light sleep
Delta	Deep, dreamless sleep

Changes in brain activity are correlated (although not perfectly) with variations in consciousness.

Normal states of consciousness: levels of awareness

As we go about our everyday business – sitting in a lesson, driving home, cooking dinner, reading this book – some of the time we will pay full attention to what we are doing and at other times we will 'drift off' and start thinking about something less immediate. Our conscious awareness changes all the time: we move effortlessly between paying careful attention and daydreaming and back again. There is no objective measure of changes of consciousness of this type, no changes in EEG. Consciousness is altered whenever there is a change from one state of mental functioning to a state that seems different to the person experiencing the change. **States of consciousness**, therefore, **are personal and subjective**.

Levels of awareness, from the most to the least alert, can be categorised as follows:

1. **Controlled processes:** one of the highest levels of awareness is alert wakefulness which involves focusing attention on specific things and events, filtering out what is irrelevant. Controlled processes require alert awareness and take all of our attention so that it is difficult to do anything else at the same time.
2. **Automatic processes:** a less alert form of awareness is the state of consciousness you experience when you're awake but doing something so familiar, easy or well-practised that you accomplish these actions 'without thinking'. Automatic processes require little attention and do not interfere much with other activities; you are hardly aware that you are doing them.
3. **Daydreaming:** this involves our attention wandering away from the immediate situation or task as we drift off into a world of fantasy. Although we are awake, our awareness of the world around us tends to be reduced. Virtually everyone daydreams frequently; research does indeed indicate that daydreams serve a variety of useful functions: they can help you relax, to endure frustration, to alleviate boredom or to rehearse how you're going to handle real-life challenges.
4. **Dreaming:** dreaming during sleep is a state of consciousness that everyone experiences every night and which we will be studying in detail later in this section.
5. **Lowest levels of awareness:** these are states of consciousness that people experience when in dreamless sleep or when under anaesthetic. Even in these situations, people continue to maintain a low level of awareness, shown by the fact that some stimuli can still penetrate awareness. We can discriminate between stimuli when asleep and people under anaesthesia occasionally hear comments made during surgery.

Activity

Which levels of awareness are likely to be involved in

1. A new mother who sleeps through a thunderstorm but wakes at the muffled sound of the baby crying?
2. Thinking about your latest romance whilst reading this book?
3. Learning to drive?
4. Driving after years of driving experience?

Sleep

Theories of sleep

Why do all humans and a great many species of animals sleep? There are two main theories: the restoration and repair theory and the evolutionary theory.

The restoration and repair theory

This states that sleep provides physical rest and recuperation and promotes physiological processes that **rejuvenate** the body each night. For example, during sleep neurotransmitters may be synthesised to compensate for quantities used in daily activities. This theory, therefore, implies that during our waking life the body is depleted of certain chemicals and that sleep is rather like resting and catching your breath after exercise.

Evaluation

a   The theory is supported by the fact that sleeplessness produces irritability, disturbances of perception, hallucinations and generally makes you feel drained, listless and miserable. In animals, forced sleeplessness may result in death.

b   Nevertheless, it cannot account for the fact that when we are deprived of sleep for some time, we do not need to make up for **all** the sleep we have missed; we are usually fully recovered after two or three hours more than our usual amount of sleep. Neither do we need sleep to rest our muscles or any other tissue except, perhaps, the brain, and after a day of extreme physical or mental activity we need very little more sleep than after a day of inactivity. Moreover, no-one has yet found a relationship between sleep and the restoration of specific chemical substances.

The evolutionary theory

This suggests that sleep periods have evolved because they have **survival value** in terms of conserving energy and reducing exposure to predators and other dangers. The timing of sleep has evolved to coincide with periods when the animal is least efficient at finding food and defending itself.

Evaluation

The evolutionary theory does not explain why it is necessary for us to lose consciousness during sleep since losing consciousness puts us at risk. Evans, a sleep researcher, commented that 'the behaviour patterns involved in sleep are glaringly, almost insanely, at odds with common sense'.

All that can be said at present is that each theory probably contains some truth, but as yet there is no completely satisfactory explanation of why we need to sleep. What we do know is that sleep is essential and that deprivation of sleep is an extremely unpleasant experience.

Activity

Summarise these two theories in a single sentence each. Consider the differences between them.

In terms of the evolutionary theory of sleep, which animals should sleep **most** (which are least in danger when asleep and could usefully preserve energy because food supplies are intermittent and unreliable); which should sleep least (because they need to remain alert)? Does this correspond to your experience of the animal world?

The sleep cycle

Rapid eye movement and non-rapid eye movement sleep

Sleep is by no means a continuous resting state. In all mammals, the sleep cycle consists of periods of **rapid eye movements (REM)** which alternate with periods of little eye movement, called **non-rapid eye movement (NREM)** sleep. Although there are significant individual differences in sleep behaviour, everyone goes through five stages while sleeping: stages 1–4 are periods of NREM sleep, while stage 5 is a period of REM sleep (see Figure 7.9).

Gradually, as we lose consciousness, we pass through the various stages of sleep.

Stage 1: brain waves slow down from the alpha rhythm and start becoming **theta waves** which have a frequency of about 6–8 cps. Heart rate slows and

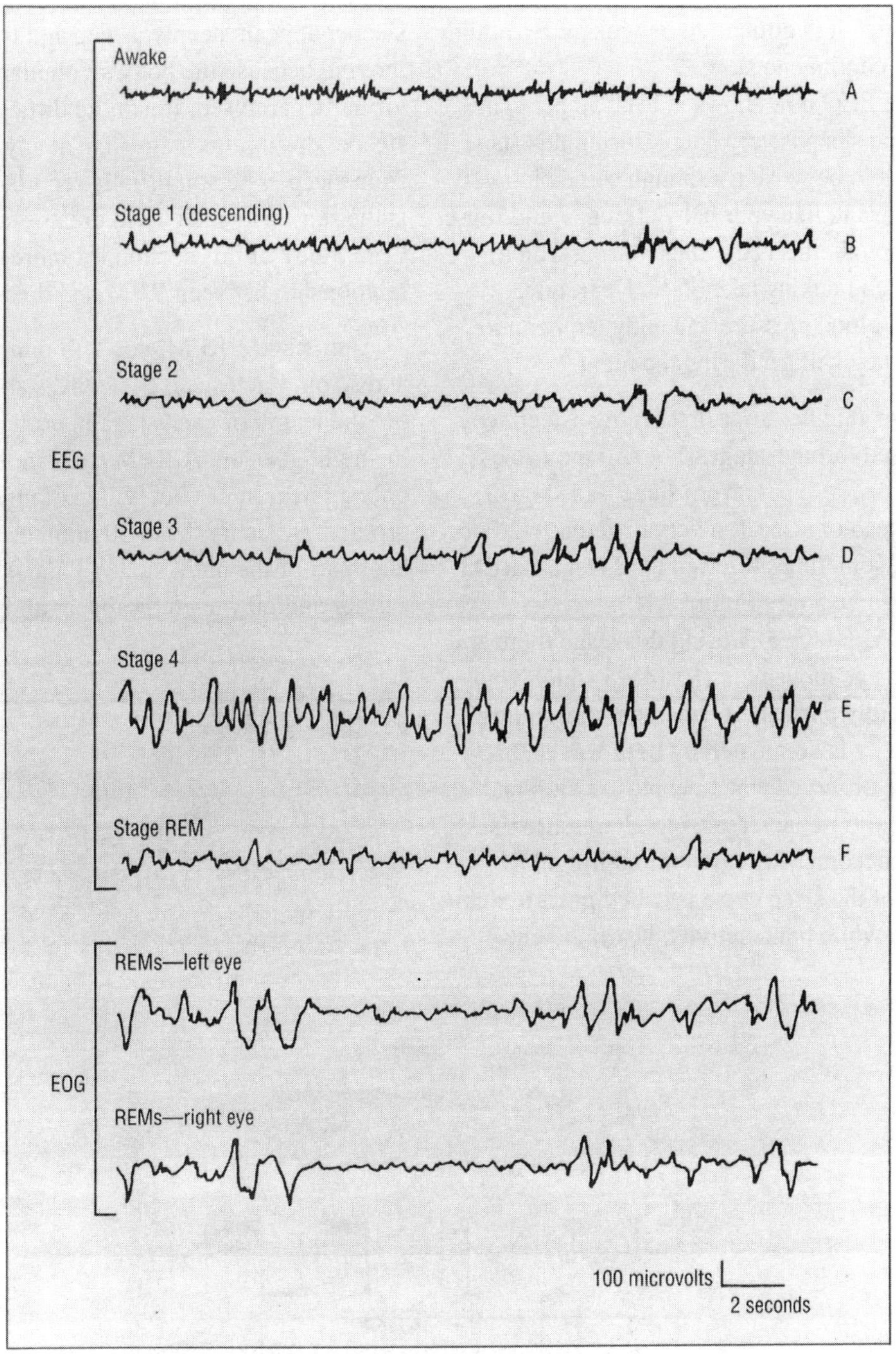

Figure 7.9 The stages of sleep: electroencephalograph (EEG) records A–F show brain wave activity during the five stages of sleep; the electrooculogram (EOG) records show eye movement during the REM stage
Source: R. Ornstein and L. Carstensen, Psychology: The Study of Human Experience (Harcourt, Brace & Jovanovich, 1991, 3rd edn),

muscles relax. If we are woken during this stage we may claim not to have been asleep at all. Common sensations during this stage are of floating or falling followed by a quick jolt back to consciousness.

Stage 2: brain waves now have a frequency of about 4–7 cps but these are punctuated by short bursts of rapid, high-peaking waves of 12–16 cps, called **sleep spindles**, each lasting about 25 seconds. Heart rate, blood pressure and body temperature continue to drop and eyes roll slowly from side to side. It is still not difficult to be woken from this stage, although minor noises probably won't disturb you.

Stage 3: the sleep spindles disappear and the brain occasionally emits very slow waves of about 1–3 cps.

These are **delta waves** and are an indication of deep sleep from which it is difficult to be woken. Breathing and heart rate continue to slow.

Stage 4: the EEG now shows at least 50 per cent delta waves and sleep is very deep. During this stage it is very difficult to be woken, although something very personally relevant, like your baby crying, could rouse you. Oddly enough, this is the stage during which sleep walking and talking take place. Heart rate, breathing rate, blood pressure and body temperature are as low as they will get during the night.

About 30–45 minutes after first falling asleep, you will have passed through stages 1–4 and the cycle goes into reverse. You pass from stage 4 to stage 3, then 2 but instead of stage 1, a very different kind of sleep appears, sometimes referred to as stage 1 REM, sometimes as stage 5 (see Figure 7.10).

Stage 1 REM (stage 5) During this stage there are bursts of rapid eye movement (REM) in which your eyes move rapidly back and forth under closed lids. The EEG activity is dominated by **beta waves** that resemble those observed when people are alert and awake. The heart rate increases, blood pressure rises and breathing becomes faster and more irregular.

This phase of the sleep cycle is called **paradoxical sleep** because, while brain activity, heart rate and blood pressure resemble waking consciousness, the sleeper appears deeply asleep and is incapable of moving because the body's voluntary muscles are virtually paralysed. It is more difficult to wake the sleeper during this stage than at any other. If woken from sleep, a person usually reports dreaming, for this is the stage in which vivid dreams take place (see the Core Study of this section for more details on the relationship between REM and dreaming).

After stage 1 REM, you will return to stage 2, 3, 4 and so on. Each sleep cycle takes about 90 minutes but the length of each stage in each cycle changes as the night goes on. A REM early in the night may last only a few minutes but will get longer as the night progresses, lasting from 30 minutes to an hour. In the later part of the night stages 3 and 4 get progressively shorter and may even disappear altogether.

Activity

Make your own table of the stages of sleep using the headings: **stage, brain wave pattern, body reactions, other comments**. 'Other comments' should include factors such as ease of waking.

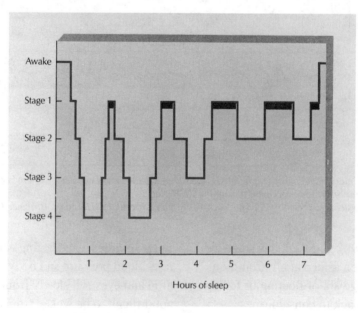

Figure 7.10 The changing rhythms of sleep: the pattern of a typical night's sleep for a young adult – time spent in REM sleep is shown by the heavy bars, REM periods tending to lengthen as the night goes on; in contrast, stages 3 and 4, which dominate non-REM sleep early in the night, tend to disappear as morning approaches
Source: C. Wade and C. Tavris, Psychology (Harper & Row, 1990, 2nd edn), p. 127.

Core Study

The relation of eye movements during sleep to dream activity: an objective method for the study of dreaming: W. Dement and N. Kleitman (1957)

In 1955 Aserinsky and Kleitman observed that if subjects were awakened in periods of rapid, connected eye movements during sleep, they reported a high incidence of dream recall, whereas subjects wakened at other times reported little dreaming. These periods of rapid eye movements (REMs) appear at regular intervals during sleep and correspond to changes in EEG patterns (Dement and Kleitman, 1955).

This paper presents the findings of further investigation of the relationship between REMs and dreaming. Three methods were used:

1. Subjects were awakened during REM and NREM (non-rapid eye movement) sleep. To help prevent bias, the experimenter to whom they reported their dreams (or lack of them) was not aware of the type of sleep from which they had been woken.
2. The subjects were asked to estimate how long they had been dreaming, and this was correlated with the length of REM they had experienced before being woken.
3. An investigation was made into whether the pattern of the eye movements was related to the actual content of the dream.

Method

The subjects for the experiment were seven adult men and two adult women. Five of these were studied in detail, the other four fairly minimally.

Subjects spent the night sleeping in a quiet, dark room of the laboratory. They had electrodes attached near the eyes to detect eye movements and attached to the scalp to record brain waves. At various times during the night, subjects were awakened to test their dream recall; subjects usually returned to sleep within 5 minutes.

Results

The occurrence of REM

All subjects showed periods of REM during sleep. These were characterised by a fast, low-voltage EEG pattern. In between REM periods the EEG patterns were either high-voltage, slow activity or spindles with a low-voltage background, both characteristic of deeper sleep. REMs never occurred at the beginning of the sleep cycle even though the EEG always passed through a stage similar to that shown in REM periods.

The mean duration time of REM sleep was 20 minutes, tending to increase later in the night. REM sleep occurred at regular intervals, the average period between REM phases being 92 minutes. For each individual the frequency of occurrence of each REM was fairly constant but different for different individuals.

Eye movement periods and dream recall

Different subjects were woken according to different schedules. Two were woken at random. One was woken three times in REM followed by three times in NREM and so on. One was woken randomly but told that he would only be woken during REM. Another was woken when the experimenter felt like doing so. Subjects were never told, after wakening, whether their eyes had been moving or not.

Results showed that reports of dreaming following REM awakenings was far more likely than after NREM awakenings. Nearly all dream recall in NREM occurred within 8 minutes of an REM, suggesting that the dream might have been remembered from the previous REM. When subjects failed to recall a dream during REM awakenings, this was usually early on in the night.

Specific eye movement patterns and visual imagery of the dream

The actual eye movements varied enormously during periods of REM sleep, even though brain wave patterns remained constant. Subjects were woken and asked to describe their dreams when one of four patterns of eye movements occurred:

i   mainly vertical
ii   mainly horizontal
iii   both vertical and horizontal
iv   very little or no movement.

In all, 35 such awakenings were made and dream content did appear to be related to specific eye movements. For example, one subject showing vertical eye movements was dreaming of throwing basketballs up at a net. Subjects showing little or no movement were typically gazing into the distance or staring fixedly at some object.

Conclusion

The results indicate that dreaming accompanied by REMs and a low-voltage EEG occurs periodically in discrete episodes during the course of a night's sleep and that dream activity does not occur at other times. It has therefore become possible objectively to measure dreaming by recording the number and length of REMs during sleep. It will then be possible to obtain an objective measure of the effect on dreaming of factors such as stress, drugs and environmental changes.

QUESTIONS

1.   **a**   When were subjects woken and what measures were taken to avoid bias?
     b   What are the major features of REM sleep?
                        (4 marks)
       Oxford and Cambridge Specimen Paper
2.   It is suggested that Rapid Eye Movements (REM) only occur during dreaming. Give *one* piece of evidence which supports this statement, and *one* piece of evidence which challenges it.
                        (4 marks)
            Oxford and Cambridge (1994)
3.   What were the main conclusions of the Dement and Kleitman study, and what further research into dreaming is suggested?

Dreaming

Dreams are mental experiences which occur during sleep and which often involve vivid imagery. Dreams are often illogical, irrational and disorganised but may well have coherent plots even if the content is fantastic.

Although most dreams occur in REM sleep, some dreaming of a rather different quality takes place during NREM periods. Dreaming during NREM is similar to the train of everyday thoughts, lacking the bizarre and dramatic qualities of REM dreams. But why do we dream?

Theories of dreaming

Freud's theory

Freud considered dreams to be a 'royal road to the unconscious'. He believed that all dreams represent primitive drives and wishes, often sexual in nature, which are censored in waking life since they are so unacceptable. Even in dreams these desires can rarely be directly expressed as that would arouse anxiety and wake up the dreamer, so they appear in disguised form. The actual content of the dream or **manifest content** is a symbolic representation of the underlying, true meaning, called the **latent content**. It is the task of the psychoanalyst to untangle the latent content from the manifest content in order to provide an insight into the dreamer's unconscious mind.

Freud believed that dreams provide a **safety valve** for the psyche. If we didn't dream, the energy invested in our unconscious desires would build up to such a level that our sanity would be seriously at risk.

Many psychologists disagree with the Freudian idea, believing that dreams are not an expression of deep-seated unconscious desires but represent a way of mulling over the concerns and excitement of everyday life such as work, sex, health or relationships.

The activation–synthesis theory

McCarley and Hobson (1977) propose that dreams reflect **biological** rather than psychological activity. They hypothesise that during REM sleep, random discharges from nerve cells occur. These outbursts begin in the pons (in the brainstem) and then stimulate the distant areas of the cortex, particularly those associated with vision, hearing and memory. These higher centres try to make sense of these random firings; they attempt to **synthesise** them by drawing on existing knowledge and memories to make a coherent story: hence a dream emerges. So, according to this theory, dreams are simply the brain's attempt to make sense of random electrical discharges in the brain. The actual content of the dream is likely to come from the current needs and concerns, past experiences and expectations of the particular individual dreamer. **Activation**, therefore, is the random discharge from the nerve cells. **Synthesis** is the attempt to make sense of them.

McCarley and Hobson further argue that REM sleep promotes the growth and development of the brain by providing an internal source of activation at a time when external stimulation is reduced.

At present, there is some physiological evidence to support the activation side of this theory, but even Hobson admits that there is as yet little to support the idea of synthesis. There is still much research to be done before we can establish the validity of the whole theory.

Dreaming to forget

Crick and Mithison (1983) propose yet another theory of the function of dreams. They suggest that REM sleep helps the brain to remove the day's accumulation of unwanted and useless material; in effect, we dream in order to forget. In this way dreams may serve to reduce fantasy and obsession.

The subjective nature of dreams makes it difficult to test these theories empirically. It may be for this reason that, at present, the function of dreaming is still rather a mystery.

Activity

Summarise these theories very briefly in terms of the **purpose** of dreaming, and consider any similarities and differences between them. Do they tend to contradict or complement each other?

More than one consciousness?

Janet (1889), a French psychiatrist, proposed that under certain conditions some thoughts and actions become split off, or **dissociated**, from the rest of consciousness and function outside of awareness.

Mild forms of dissociation include:

a   Our reaction when faced with a stressful situation: we may temporarily put it out of our minds in order to be able to function effectively

b   When bored, we may lapse into daydreams.

More extreme examples of dissociation are demonstrated by:

c   Split-brain patients – discussed earlier in section 7.1 and the Core Study

d   Persons with multiple personality; the Case Study of a person with multiple personalities is documented in the Core Study on p. 312

e   Hypnosis: it remains a matter of controversy as to whether this is a genuine split in consciousness.

The private nature of the consciousness makes it

difficult to investigate, but knowledge of this area has advanced in recent years:

To sum up

- Consciousness is the continually changing stream of mental activity
- Consciousness varies along a continuum of levels of awareness

- Controlled processes require heightened awareness, while automatic processes occur with little awareness
- There is some minimal awareness even during sleep
- Variations in consciousness are related to brain activity as measured by EEG.

Preparing for the exam

Key terms

alpha waves	non-rapid eye movement (NREM)
automatic processes	paradoxical sleep
beta waves	preconscious
consciousness	rapid eye movement (REM)
controlled processes	restoration and repair theory
daydreaming	sleep cycle
delta waves	sleep spindles
electroencephalogram	subconscious
evolutionary theory of sleep	symbolic representation
latent content	theta waves
manifest content	unconscious
non-conscious processes	

Types of exam question

1. The meaning of altered states of awareness and how they relate to physiological changes in the brain.
2. The nature and effects of body rhythms.
3. Discussion of theories of sleep, including functions of sleep.

Self-test questions

1. What is consciousness?
2. Briefly explain the following terms:
   a   non-conscious processes
   b   preconscious processes
   c   subconscious processes
   d   the unconscious.
3. What are the *five* categories of levels of awareness? Briefly describe each.
4. Outline *two* theories of why we sleep.
5. How many stages of sleep are there?
6. Which stage is known as paradoxical sleep, and why?
7. What is a sleep cycle, and how long does it last?
8. Very briefly outline *three* theories of why we dream.
9. Under what circumstance, other than sleep, may some thoughts become dissociated from our mainstream awareness?

Exam questions with guidance notes

1. 'Not simply the absence of waking, sleep is a special activity of the brain, controlled by elaborate and precise mechanisms. Not simply a state or rest, sleep has its own specific, positive functions' (Hobson, 1989). Discuss this view in the light of psychological research.

(25 marks)
AEB (1992)

   As ever, read the question carefully and do not simply write everything you know about sleep. You are being asked about *two* specific aspects of sleep:
   - *Brain activity* (and how it differs from that during wakefulness) and the *functions* of sleep.
   - Start by relating sleep to *brain wave patterns*. You can also mention the parts of the brain responsible for sleep (use section 3.1 on the brain for this). Go through each stage of sleep, giving details of brain wave patterns and other important characteristics.
   - Now deal with theories of the *function of sleep*: restoration and repair and the evolutionary theory are the main ones. Describe and evaluate each one.
   - Finally, since dreaming is an inevitable part of sleep, then it is important to mention briefly the theories of the functions of *dreaming*.

2. Use examples to show what psychologists mean by 'altered states of awareness'. Discuss how these altered states may relate to physiological changes that take place in the brain.

(25 marks)
AEB (1991)

   - Begin by going through each of the *levels of awareness*:
     a controlled processes
     b automatic processes
     c daydreams
     d dreaming
     e lowest levels of awareness
     and *describe* each one with the use of *examples*. There are examples in the text, including those in the form of questions, but it is preferable to use your own. For example, controlled processes involves any activity which requires your full attention and so on.
   - Now relate this to *EEG patterns*. Go through the beta, alpha, theta and delta patterns and describe the level of consciousness associated with each one, as given in Table 7.4 in this subsection.
   - Conclude by saying that there is no perfect correspondence between brain wave activities and levels of awareness and that, to a certain extent, some transitions – like moving from automatic processes to daydreaming – are *personal* and *subjective*.

Additional exam questions

1. How do psychologists study sleep? What have they discovered?

   (25 marks)
   AEB (1988)

   (Don't forget to use the Core Study.)

2. Compare and contrast any *two* theories of sleep. **(25 marks)**
   AEB (1994)

7.3 Emotion

The most straightforward definition of emotions is that they are states of feelings that range from being extremely pleasant to extremely unpleasant and that affect the way we behave.

Emotion in an evolutionary context

Charles Darwin believed that during the course of evolution, certain facial expressions of emotions had been biologically 'prewired' in to the nervous system of humans and that of some other animals. These facial expressions, he considered, were of survival value since they allowed rapid communication without learning or language. For example, an expression of fear could indicate that danger was approaching.

Support for this hypothesis comes from evidence that the facial expressions of different emotions are universal.

Ekman (1980) showed photos of faces showing six basic emotions, (anger, fear, disgust, happiness, sadness and surprise) to people all over the world, including some who had never had contact with Western culture. He found that there was generally universal agreement as to which emotions these facial expressions portrayed.

Identification and classification of emotions

Plutchik (1980, 1984), after detailed study of emotions, drew the following conclusions:

1. There are eight categories of **basic innate** emotions. They are: fear, surprise, sadness, disgust, anger, anticipation, joy and acceptance. These are the emotions which motivate adaptive behaviour.

2. Different emotions can **combine** to provide a wider range, for example, surprise and sadness together become disappointment.

3. All emotions can **vary in intensity**: mild anger is annoyance, extreme anger is rage. Thus, although there are only eight basic emotions, the range of total emotions is very broad indeed.

Activity

1. What evolutionary purpose is served by emotions?
2. What evidence is there that some emotions are innate?

The neurophysiology of emotion

The autonomic nervous system (ANS)

An emotional stimulus activates the autonomic nervous system, a part of the nervous system which consists of two branches, the sympathetic nervous system and the parasympathetic nervous system. (The working of the ANS was discussed in section 7.1.) Important points are:

1. A mild unpleasant stimulus arouses the sympathetic NS.

2. A mild pleasant stimulus activates the parasympathetic NS.

3. More intense emotions involve both systems and very strong emotions activate the 'fight or flight' response detailed in section 7.5 on Stress. Under

these circumstances, the sympathetic NS causes adrenalin and noradrenalin to be released, resulting in such responses as increased heart rate, raised pulse rate, increased sweating, and a decrease in the flow of saliva.

Activity

Think of situations which produce these physiological symptoms. Are the same emotions involved in each case?

Several studies have investigated whether different emotions are characterised by different patterns of physiological change. Results tend to show that there are few clear cut differences: **anger, fear and elation all have the same, or at least very similar, effects on the body**. The small differences which have been found are unlikely to be sufficient to enable a person to distinguish one emotion from another simply from their physiological reactions. This finding has implications for the theories of emotion, as we shall see later.

The brain

1. The principal parts of the brain which are responsive to emotional arousal appear to be the **hypothalamus** and the **limbic system**, both systems being among the first to evolve and responsible for the basics in life.
2. Lesioning or stimulation of these systems produces quite dramatic changes in emotional response. In many animals, stimulation of the hypothalamus results in fear and anger; brain damage in this area of the human brain can also produce irrational rage.
3. Attempts to link specific parts of the limbic system to specific emotions have been unsuccessful. The amygdala, which is part of the limbic system, appears to be responsible for attaching significance to any information which is received. If this part of the brain is damaged, patients show little response to situations and events that would usually evoke strong feelings.
4. Averill (1982) suggests that the more complex emotions in humans are influenced by the cortex, a higher brain centre responsible for intelligent

thought. These involve emotions to which we attach meanings and memories from past experience, such as fear of failing an exam, guilt at having lied to a friend.
5. Lewis *et al.* (1988) point out that certain emotions, such as guilt and shame, are likely to depend on the higher centres of the brain and are not experienced by animals or young babies, since they depend on a sense of self and the internalisation of the principles of right and wrong.
6. Research indicates that the left hemisphere of the cortex is the 'happy' side of the brain, responsible for positive emotions and that the right side is the 'misery', responsible for negative emotions. Damage to the left side results in a very pessimistic outlook on life, while people with right hemisphere damage seem to have a happy disposition.

Theories of emotion

The James–Lange theory

James and Lange independently suggested that certain events cause physiological changes in the body and that emotions are **caused** by those physical changes. To use James' example, when you come face to face with a grizzly bear (the event or stimulus), this causes various bodily changes such as raised heart rate, a flushed face and sweating. The emotion of fear is simply your awareness of these changes.

The James–Lange theory, then, argues against what might seem the common sense notion that crying is caused by sadness or trembling is caused by fear. On the contrary, it argues that we feel sorry **because** we cry and feel afraid **because** we tremble.

Although this may appear strange, there are occasions when we react so quickly that it is only afterwards that we are aware of any emotion. For example, if you trip on the stairs, you grab the bannisters and feel your heart pound and your stomach churn before you have a chance to feel fear.

Evaluation

If bodily changes alone **cause** specific emotions, then each emotion would need to involve different bodily changes. As already stated, there is little evidence that there are distinct bodily states for all our various emotions. In fact, some non-emotional states, like fever, produce the same physiological changes as do emotional states. Most physiological changes, like rapid heart rate, only tell us that an emotion is present and how **intense** it is, not the particular emotion we are experiencing.

The Cannon–Bard theory

This theory holds that emotions and bodily responses occur **simultaneously**, not one after the other. Cannon and Bard suggest that emotions are first experienced in the thalamus of the brain. (The thalamus is the 'relay station' that channels incoming information to the appropriate area of the cerebral cortex.) From here, nerve impulses are sent both to the body and to the cerebral cortex. Messages to the cortex give you the experience of emotion, messages to the body produce emotional behaviour such as a pounding heart and perhaps a raised fist.

Evaluation

1. This theory assumes that the experience of emotion (the cognitive aspects of emotion) is **independent of bodily responses**. This is only partly true. When people take tranquilisers they usually report that their experience of emotion is considerably less intense than before. It must, therefore, at least be partly due to bodily responses which have been suppressed by the tranquilisers.

2. There is not unequivocal evidence that bodily responses and emotions occur simultaneously, as the theory suggests. We may respond to a dangerous or a painful stimulus before we feel fear; the bodily response occurs before the emotional experience. There are also occasions when we have a narrow escape and only afterwards, when we have the time to consider how dire the consequences might have been, do we become shaky and aroused.

Figure 7.11 summarises the James–Lange and Cannon–Bard theories.

Schachter and Singer: the two factor theory

This theory, also known as the cognitive theory, suggests that our experience of emotion depends on **two** factors: a state of bodily arousal and clues from the situation as to what has caused this arousal. Thus, when we feel aroused, we use our cognitions to label these feelings. If we nearly drive into the car in front of us, we feel very shaken and sweaty and, hardly surprisingly, we interpret this as fear and dread. But what happens if we feel aroused and the immediate cause of this arousal is not obvious? To answer this question, you need now to read the Core Study of this section before reading further.

Evaluation of Schachter and Singer's cognitive theory

Both the study itself and the theory have attracted a variety of criticisms. Of course, these criticisms are

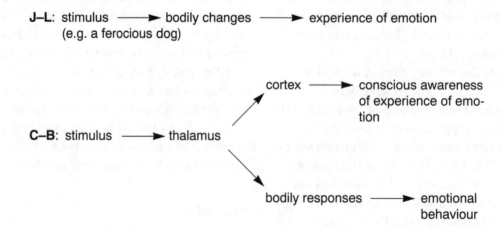

Figure 7.11 Summary of James–Lange and Cannon–Bard theories

linked because the theory is based on the research evidence of the Core Study.

1. Hilgard *et al.* (1979) point out that no assessment of the participants' mood was made prior to the injection. Participation in an experiment and anticipation of an injection could well have affected their mood.

2. Arousal produced by injection of adrenalin and under laboratory conditions may not be equivalent to the state of arousal experienced by emotional events in everyday life.

3. A considerable problem, mentioned by Schachter and Singer, is that the placebos, who were not aroused, did feel some euphoria and anger. Plutchik and Ax (1967) comment that all the results show is that people in a euphoria situation act in a happy manner while people in an angry situation act as if they are annoyed. The results are therefore hardly surprising and of no theoretical importance.

4. Several attempts at replication of the study have not supported the findings of Schachter and Singer.

In terms of the actual theory, the following criticisms have been made:

5. Zajonc argues that 'feelings come first'. We do not make an appraisal of the situation and then decide how we feel. A rabbit in the bushes doesn't consider what might be causing the rustle in the bushes before it runs away (Zajonc, 1980). For both humans and animals, some emotions are essential for survival; fear can save your life. According to Zajonc, cognition comes **after** emotion: whatever your immediate reaction to a situation, you invent ways to make this emotional reaction seem rational. Similarly, Tompkins (1962, 1981) points out that infants innately react to certain stimuli with an emotional response – no cognitive appraisal or prior learning is required.

There are then **three** main theories which seek to explain the relationship between physiological responses to emotional stimuli and the emotion which is experienced. These theories are all probably partially correct but none of them is fully satisfactory. Physiological responses and cognitive influences in emotion obviously interact in a very complex way. Either way, the experience and expression of emotion in humans depends on an interaction of innate bodily responses, perception of situational factors and cultural rules.

Core Study

Cognitive, social and physiological determinants of emotional state: S. Schachter and J.E. Singer (1962)

Schachter (1959) and others suggest that cognitive factors may be the major determinant of emotional states. Our body arousal is interpreted in terms of situational factors. The immediate situation determines whether the state of physiological arousal will be labelled 'anger', 'joy', 'fear' or another emotion.

How do physiological arousal and cognitive factors interact? In most situations, they are closely interrelated. Schachter and Singer use the example of a man walking alone down a dark alley when a figure with a gun suddenly appears. This initiates a state of physiological arousal; this arousal is interpreted in terms of knowledge about dark alleys and guns – the state of arousal is labelled 'fear'.

Physiological arousal induced by an injection of adrenalin is insufficient to experience an emotional state (Maranon, 1924), presumably because people know the cause of the arousal. Schachter (1959) suggests that, if people were aroused but not aware of the cause of arousal, they would need to understand and label their feelings and would do so in terms of available situational cues. If they were with a person whom they found sexually attractive, they might consider themselves to be experiencing the emotion of love. In any case, Schachter and Singer propose that emotional states are a function of the interaction of cognitive factors with a state of physiological arousal.

Procedure

Subjects were requested to have an injection of a vitamin supplement 'Suproxin' in order to study its effects on vision. They were given ample opportunity to refuse the injection; 184 of the 195 agreed.

Subjects were injected either with

a   Adrenalin – this causes increased arousal
b   Saline (salt) solution – a placebo that has no side-effects at all.

Manipulating an appropriate explanation

After receiving the injection, subjects were assigned to the following groups:

1. **Adrenalin informed** (Ad Inf): subjects were told the actual side-effects; they knew exactly what to expect and why
2. **Adrenalin ignorant** (Ad Ign): subjects were told nothing about the side-effects
3. **Adrenalin misinformed** (Ad Mis): subjects were told the side-effects would be numbness in the feet, some itching and a slight headache
4. **Control condition** (C): subjects were injected with a saline solution, thereafter treated the same as the adrenalin ignorant group.

Producing an emotion-inducing condition

It was decided to induce two very different emotions: euphoria and anger.

Euphoria: a stooge waited for 20 minutes with the subject before the 'vision test' and generally acted the fool and encouraged the subject to do the same. The act included playing a 'basketball' game by throwing paper in the bin, making and throwing paper aeroplanes and joking in a good humoured way. The routine was the same for all conditions and the stooge was unaware of the condition into which each subject had been placed.

Anger: in this condition the stooge and subject were asked to spend the 20 minutes filling in a questionnaire. The stooge commented that he thought being given an injection was unfair. The questionnaire started innocently enough but then grew increasingly personal and insulting. The stooge did his best to keep apace with the subject so that, at any one time, they were both answering the same question. In a standardised manner, the stooge made comments which showed increasing annoyance, culminating in him expressing considerable rage on reaching the question: 'How many times each week do you have sexual intercourse?' At this point he tore up the questionnaire and marched out of the room.

The adrenalin misinformed group did not have experience of the anger condition.

Measurement

Emotional state was measured in two ways:

1. Observation through a one-way mirror.
2. Self-reports on a number of scales (subjects were told that their mood, as well as the Suproxin, may affect the results of the vision test, so they were asked to give honest reports of how they felt).

After these measurements were taken, subjects were thoroughly debriefed and asked if they had any suspicions about the nature of the study. Eleven were so suspicious that their data was discarded.

Subjects

Male college students taking introductory psychology classes and given point credits towards their examinations for being part of a subject pool.

Results

As expected, subjects were more susceptible to the stooge's mood when they had no explanation of their own bodily states than when they did: both adrenalin ignorant and adrenalin misinformed felt considerably more euphoria or anger on behavioural measures as observed through the one-way mirror. The euphoria groups also showed their mood on the questionnaire. However, here the problems of sampling are revealed. The subjects were all psychology students who received points in the final exams for volunteering to be participants. Though they were willing to express anger when alone with the stooge, they were reluctant to do so on the self-rating and questionnaire which the experimenter might see. Only after debriefing were subjects willing to admit how annoyed they had been. Thus, only behavioural measures could be used in this condition.

The results, however, are not entirely as expected.

Although the misinformed and ignorant conditions showed greater anger or euphoria than the informed group, the placebo consistently fell between the ignorant and the informed. This makes it impossible to evaluate unambiguously the effects of the state of physiological arousal.

Discussion

Although this study does **not** rule out the possibility of physiological differences being responsible for different emotional states, it does show that manipulation of external factors can produce two very different emotional states when the arousal, being produced by an injection of adrenalin, is identical. It may, therefore, be the case that **cognitive factors are major determinants of the emotional labels we apply to feelings of arousal** of the sympathetic nervous system. Cognitive factors seem to be indispensable elements in any theory of emotion.

Summary

If emotional states depend on both a state of physiological arousal and a cognition appropriate to this state of arousal, then **three** propositions follow:

1. If a person is physiologically aroused without having an immediate explanation for this feeling, he or she will label this state according to the cognitive aspects of the situation
2. If a person is physiologically aroused and has an appropriate explanation for this arousal, he or she has no need to look for alternative explanations and is unlikely to label his or her feelings in terms of any other situational factors
3. People only react emotionally or describe their feelings as emotions when they are physiologically aroused.

QUESTIONS

1. a In the Schachter and Singer study, how did the experimenters measure the emotion of the subjects? **(2 marks)**

    b What are the problems with their chosen form of measurement? **(2 marks)**

    Oxford and Cambridge Specimen Paper

2. a What are the *two* factors in Schachter and Singer's two factor theory of emotion? **(2 marks)**

    b How was each factor manipulated in the study? **(2 marks)**

    Oxford and Cambridge (1994)

Preparing for the exam

Key terms

adrenalin
amygdala
autonomic nervous system
emotions
hypothalamus
lesion

limbic system
noradrenalin
parasympathetic nervous system
sympathetic nervous system
thalamus

Types of exam question

1. Compare and contrast theories of emotion.
2. Evaluate the Schachter and Singer study in terms of methodology and the theoretical conclusions drawn from it.

Self-test questions

1. What is the survival value of those facial expressions that express emotion?
2. According to Plutnik, what are the *eight* categories of basic innate emotion?
3. What parts of the brain are responsive to emotional arousal? What effect does a lesion to these parts have?
4. What do James and Lange suggest that emotions are caused by?
5. Outline *one* problem with James and Lange's theory.
6. Briefly outline the Cannon–Bard theory of emotion and present *one* problem with this theory.
7. Schachter and Singer suggest that emotions depend on *two* factors. What are they?

Exam question with guidance notes

Describe both physiological and alternative explanations of emotion. Discuss their relative contribution to our understanding of emotion.

(25 marks)
AEB (1991)

There are *two* ways in which this essay could be structured: you can either describe each theory and its contributions one after the other, or you can cover the descriptions first, followed by the contributions. We'll approach it from the second option.

- Introduce the essay with a *definition* of emotion and mention of the variety of *theories* which have been advanced.
- *Describe* each theory:
  a The James–Lange theory provides a physiological account of emotion
  b The Cannon–Bard theory assumes that the experience of emotion is independent of bodily responses.
  c Schachter and Singer's theory takes account of both physiological and cognitive factors.
- The contributions are based on the *evaluation* of each theory. Each of them has a contribution to make to our understanding of emotion but none of them is without its critics. At present, there is certainly no universal agreement as to which theory, if any, is correct. In fact, the evaluation of Schachter and Singer introduces points (by Zajonc and by Tompkins) which appear to favour the original James–Lange theory.

Additional exam question

Compare and contrast physiological explanations with other explanations of emotion. Use experimental evidence to illustrate your answer.   **(25 marks)**
AEB (1988)

7.4 Motivation

Motivation can be defined as an assumed process within an organism which impels or drives it to action. It is a hypothetical state because, as it cannot be measured directly, it must be inferred from behaviour. The psychology of motivation, then, is concerned with **why** organisms behave as they do.

Motives can be divided into **two** main groups:

1. **Biological motives** are based on physiological needs, those needs without which the organism or the species would not survive. Biological motives include hunger, thirst and sex

2. **Social motives** are based on psychological needs, including the need for affiliation, achievement and autonomy.

The distinction between biological needs and social needs is not clear-cut; even a heavily biological need such as hunger is shaped by social factors, as we shall see later. It is useful to outline some differences between the two sets of needs, since this is likely to influence the type of theory which best explains them.

Psychological needs differ from physiological needs in the following respects:

1. Psychological needs, unlike physiological needs, are not necessarily based on states of deprivation. The biological need for food is motivated by hunger, that is food deprivation, but achievement needs may follow years of success, not failure

2. Physiological needs are rooted in biology and are innate; psychological needs may be acquired through learning and experience.

3. There is a limited number of biological needs but a great many psychological (social) needs.

4. Since all humans (and members of any one particular species) have the same biological constitution, it is assumed that the physiological needs of all individuals within one species are the same (or, to be precise, that the needs of all males and all females are the same). On the other hand, as everyone's upbringing and experiences are different, individuals have greatly differing psychological needs.

Activity

Read through the above discussion once again and learn the differences between these two sets of needs. Then draw up your own summary table, headed **Psychological needs** and **Physiological needs**. Do this from memory, then go back and check your work.

Theories of motivation

Instinct theory

Instinct theory can be summarised as follows:

a All animals are born with certain behaviour patterns which are instinctive, preprogrammed and which, therefore, require **no learning**. They are essential for survival.

b These behaviour patterns are specific to a particular **species**. Thus, sticklebacks are born with one set of such behaviours, rabbits with a different set, and so on.

c Instincts motivate an organism to **behave** in a particular way. A hungry animal instinctively seeks food, a sexually receptive animal seeks copulation.

d William James (1890) and William McDougall (1908) suggest that people have various instincts that are necessary for **self-survival** and for **social behaviour**. James included pugnacity and sympathy in his list of instincts. McDougall listed 12 human instincts which he considered to be 'basic', including hunger, thirst and self-assertion.

Evaluation

a The overriding criticism of instinct theory is that it does not provide an **explanation** of behaviour. Simply hypothesising that if an organism does something, it must have an instinct to do it, is a circular argument that explains nothing. In fact, by the 1920s over 10,000 human instincts had been proposed (Bernard, 1924).

b Instincts by their very nature are the same in all members of the species and result in rigid, inflexible behaviour patterns. In humans, however, there is a vast individual difference in behaviour patterns and in the importance and variety of social motives. One person may have a great 'need for achievement', another may not be at all bothered by whether or not she achieves success. Most human behaviour, and a good deal of non-human behaviour, is not inflexible and rigid but is highly modifiable by **experience**.

c Particularly critical of instinct theory were the behaviourists who demonstrated that some important behaviours and emotions were **learned** rather than inborn.

d Many psychologists doubt that innate patterns play an important role in complex human behaviour. Nevertheless, some theorists, especially the sociobiologists, argue that they **do**.

Freud's theory

A rather different approach, but nevertheless one based on instinct, is that of Freud. Freud, you recall from Chapter 2, placed particular emphasis on the **life instinct** (including the need for sex) and **death instinct** (including an aggressive instinct). We are motivated to satisfy these instincts and, if they are not satisfied, tension builds up – tension which we are motivated to reduce. The means by which we do this depends to a certain extent on learning.

Evaluation

Freud's instinct theory, being an integral part of his overall theory, has its supporters and critics. Any evaluation depends on the evaluation of this general theory. For this, see Chapter 2.

Drive reduction theory

Drive reduction theory can be summarised as follows:

a   A major motivational force behind the behaviour of all animals is the reduction of needs and drives. Cannon (1932) observed that organisms seek to maintain **homeostasis**, a state of physiological stability or equilibrium. Thus, when, for example, the blood glucose level of an animal drops, it is motivated to seek food.

b   Clark Hull, a learning theorist, proposed that the need to maintain homeostasis results in a **drive**. A drive is an internal state of tension that motivates an organism to engage in behaviour that might reduce this tension. If an animal is hungry, tension builds up and the animal is driven to seek food. Food satisfies the hunger, thereby reducing tension by reducing the need to find food.

c   Hull proposed that all organisms had a set of **primary drives**, such as hunger, thirst and pain avoidance.

d   Through association, humans learn other drives, known as **acquired drives**. A common acquired drive is the desire for money: we are motivated to acquire money because we associate it with the satisfaction of primary drives or basic needs. According to Hull, the goal (or motive) is always reduction of tension.

Evaluation

a   Drive reduction theory can easily explain such biological motives as seeking food when hungry or seeking a sex partner when sexually aroused, since both involve tension reduction. However, it has definite limitations as a general theory of **motivation**. It cannot explain why humans, and even animals, sometimes deliberately heighten tension before satisfying a drive.

b   More importantly, this theory implies that in all animals the principal motivation is to reduce drives and thereby reduce the level of stimulation (or arousal). Yet humans and many other animals are motivated to **seek out stimulation** in the form of novel environments, to explore and to play. Many people actually seek to **increase** tension and arousal rather than reduce it.

c   Olds and Miller (1954) demonstrated a non-homeostatic drive when they showed that rats would not only press a bar to receive electrical self-stimulation of the brain, but that this 'drive' took precedence over eating, drinking and sex.

d   Finally, the theory ignores the role of external stimulation in motivating behaviour. We all know that hunger is not the only motive for seeking food – the smell of a delicious meal or the sight of a cream cake is quite enough to make many of us eat, regardless of whether or not we are hungry.

Activity

1.   Can you think of several ways in which people:
     a   Deliberately heighten tension in order to enjoy its reduction?
     b   Seek out stimulation and arousal rather than seek to reduce it?
2.   Above, you are given examples of stimuli other than hunger which motivate eating behaviour. Choose another biological motive and suggest **two** non-biological stimuli that may trigger the relevant behaviour.

Expectancy theory: a cognitive approach

The main points of this theory are as follows:

a   Expectancy theory differs from the instinct and drive theories by its emphasis on the influence of **external incentives** rather than internal states as a primary motivator. Many activities in life are motivated by **expectations**. You are probably reading this book because you expect this to increase your chance of getting a good grade in A level psychology, and it is this expectation which motivates you.

b   Our expectations about what we might gain from a behaviour depend on our past successes and failures. Rotter (1954) proposes that, as a result of early learning experiences, people differ on a dimension called **locus of control**. Some individuals have an **external** locus of control, a belief that they have little control over their own destinies because what happens to them depends largely on outside forces. In contrast, others, who have an **internal** locus of control, believe that outcomes depend on what they themselves do. This difference in approach provides individuals with very different motivational forces.

c Cognitive approaches concentrate mainly on human motivation, although some of their concepts do apply to non-human animals. One such is the concept of **learned helplessness** which was originally investigated using dogs (Seligman, 1971). People and animals who experience learned helplessness have little motivation to escape from unpleasant circumstances because of their expectation that such attempts will be futile. Expectancy theory suggests that our motivation to take part in an activity will only be high if we expect to succeed or to satisfy another need by so doing.

Activity

Bear this theory in mind if you intend to revise the cognitive model of abnormal behaviour, especially depression. How do concepts such as learned helplessness and external locus of control relate to lack of motivation and thence to depressive states?

There are other social-cognitive approaches to motivation, all of which, in the cognitive tradition, take account of expectations, options and alternatives as motivating forces behind human behaviour.

Evaluation

As already mentioned, the cognitive approach principally, though not exclusively, concentrates on human motivation. Its main advantage is that it considers motives which other approaches tend to ignore. It takes account of such factors as cognitive dissonance, self-efficacy beliefs, locus of control and learned helplessness; all concepts which are important in determining our motivational levels.

Humanistic theory of motivation: Maslow's hierarchy of needs

Maslow (1970) believed that humans are not only motivated by biological needs but by **growth motivation**, the need to be in a psychological state of well-being. Humans are motivated to realise their full potential, a state which Maslow calls **self-actualisation**.

Maslow proposes that our basic needs form a **needs hierarchy**, as illustrated in Figure 7.12.

At the bottom of this hierarchy are the basic **biological needs** which normally take priority over all other needs (a desperately hungry person will not spend time pondering the meaning of life). Until biological needs have been met, other needs are unlikely to influence our behaviour. Once these basic needs have been satisfied, our behaviour is motivated by **safety needs** such as avoidance of pain. When we are no longer concerned about safety we become motivated by **attachment** and so on up the hierarchy. At the apex of Maslow's hierarchy is the need for **self-actualisation**, the need to fulfil one's potential.

Evaluation

a Obviously Maslow's theory applies only to humans, it is not a theory which attempts to account for the reasons why other animals behave as they do. It takes full account of needs other than biological ones and recognises that humans have a need for beauty and order, to be creative, spontaneous and self-accepting.

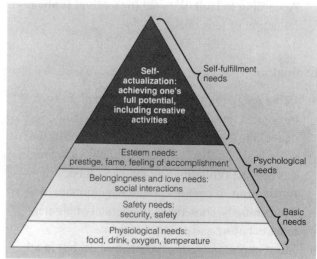

Figure 7.12 Maslow's hierarchy of needs

b   The emphasis on **positive** needs, as opposed to deprivation needs, was considered a welcome change by many psychologists.

c   The theory allows for the fact that all these motivations are **not equal**, that certain basic survival needs must be met before others can be considered.

d   Little research has been conducted on this theory, and what little has been done is not particularly supportive. The main criticism concerns the fact that, contrary to Maslow's idea, people are sometimes motivated by higher-level needs at the expense of lower ones. Mountain climbers brave extremes of discomfort and danger in order to reach the summit. Depending on the circumstances, almost all needs can take precedence over others, at least temporarily.

Activity

Can you think of other examples of people denying biological needs in order to satisfy needs higher up Maslow's hierarchy? Think in terms of, for example, low calorie dieters and martyrs.

Having considered general theories of motivation, we will take a more detailed look at one particular motive, that of hunger.

Hunger

Hunger is the most investigated of all drives, but our understanding of all the mechanisms involved in factors controlling eating is still incomplete.

The influence of brain mechanisms

There are **two** centres in the brain that control eating:

• The 'hunger centre' – the lateral hypothalamus (LH) is considered the hunger centre, since stimulation of this area causes an animal to eat. If this area is damaged or removed, an animal will stop eating all together.

• The satiation centre – the ventromedial hypothalamus (VMH) is known as the satiety centre since stimulation of this area causes an animal to stop eating. If this area is damaged, then animals, including humans, become obese.

Both these centres are situated in the hypothalamus and are controlled principally by the level of glucose in the bloodstream. At one time it was considered that the LH and VMH were the stop–start switches that control hunger; the LH was triggered when blood glucose levels fell, motivating the organism to eat and when blood glucose levels rose to a satisfactory level, the VMH was 'switched on' and eating stopped. While these two centres certainly play a role in the control of hunger, further research indicated that the on–off, stop–start formulation was oversimplified. This research showed that:

1.   Damage to the VMH has been found to cause obesity even when no extra food is consumed.

2.   Animals who have VMH lesions will not work to get extra food and are very finicky in their food preferences.

3.   Valenstein (1973) showed that LH stimulation does not specifically cause hunger but a general feeling of arousal which may be expressed in other activities if these are possible. (Valenstein said that LH stimulated animals eat because, being put in a small cage with a full food bowl, they have no other outlet for arousal, but, given the opportunity, they will do other things.)

4.   Other areas of the brain have an effect on hunger and satiety.

Researchers still believe that the LH and VMH are involved in the control of eating, but the precise nature of their role is still not clear.

The influence of learning

Learning has a profound influence over both what people eat and how much they eat.

Schachter and Rodin (1974) have investigated the influence of external cues such as time of day, the taste and appearance of food and its availability, on eating patterns in humans.

Schachter hypothesises that overweight people are more likely to use external rather than internal cues as a means of deciding when, and what, to eat. In other words, rather than being motivated mainly by hunger, they will eat if it happens to be the time at which they usually take a meal or snack. Similarly, if they pass a cake shop, they may well buy and eat a cake regardless of how hungry they happen to be.

However, Rodin (1978, 1981) considers this view to be too simple. She suggests that oversensitivity to external cues is only one factor among many determinants of obesity. She has shown that such external cues can actually produce internal changes in some people. The sight, smell and even the sound of food can result in increased insulin secretions that lead to increased hunger. Moreover, this happens to a greater extent in people who tend to respond to food-related cues by eating. Rodin also argues that Schachter has exaggerated the extent to which obese people respond to external food-related cues. Most overweight people do not, in fact, overeat to any great extent.

Set point theory

This theory states that every individual has a genetically determined point of optimal weight which the body strives to maintain. People may struggle against this set point, indeed millions of people in the Western world are obsessed with dieting, but it is difficult to maintain a weight which is very different from that determined by the set point. It is therefore as difficult for a lean person to put on weight as it is for a heavy person to lose weight.

It seems that eating is regulated by a complex interaction of biological and environmental factors. Animals, including humans, do not eat when they are fearful but many humans overeat when under stress. Cultural influences have a profound effect on food preferences and patterns of food consumption; generally speaking, we prefer to eat familiar food. These are but a few of the many factors which influence our eating behaviour. Hunger may be a basic motive, but it is not a simple one.

Preparing for the exam

Key terms

acquired drives	motivation
biological motives	physiological needs
drive reduction theory	primary drives
homeostasis	psychological needs
hypothalamus	self-actualisation
instinct theory	set point theory
locus of control	social motives

Types of exam question

Critical evaluation of theories of motivation, usually *one* physiological and *one* psychological.

Self-test questions

1. Give *two* examples of biological motives and *two* examples of social motives.
2. List *three* differences between psychological and physical needs.
3. Outline *two* criticisms of the theory that instincts motivate an organism to behave in a particular way.

4. What problem does Olds and Miller's research into self-stimulation pose for the drive reduction theorists?
5. Briefly outline the main points of expectancy theory.
6. Draw a diagram representing Maslow's hierarchy of needs.
7. What are the *two* centres in the hypothalamus that control eating?
8. What is the set point theory?

Exam question with guidance notes

1. **Describe and compare physiological and non-physiological explanations of motivation.**   **(25 marks)**

   AEB AS (1991)

   • Introduce the essay with a definition of *motivation*, mentioning that it is a hypothetical concept. Briefly show how complex the whole area is, especially in humans, by referring to the huge range of needs (some predominantly physiological, some predominantly psychological), requiring satisfaction and the complex *interaction* between them.

   • Both the instinct theory and the drive reduction theory are *physiological* explanations of motivation, the latter being based on the maintenance of homeostasis.

   • Expectancy theory (often referred to more generally as cognitive theory) and Maslow's theory are *psychological* explanations.

   • All are covered and evaluated in the text. When you compare them, consider the main cause of motivation advanced by each theory. Mention the extent to which each can be applied to *non-human animals*.

   • You could conclude by suggesting that, given the complex interaction of needs, as mentioned in your introduction, it is unlikely that a single theory can explain every single motivation in both humans and non-human animals.

Additional exam questions

1. a What do psychologists mean by 'motivation'?   **(3 marks)**

   b Describe *one* physiological and *one* non-physiological explanation of motivation.   **(10 marks)**

   c Critically consider the evidence for and against either *one* of these explanations.   **(12 marks)**

   AEB (1992)

7.5 Stress

In general terms, **stress** is the demand made on an organism to adapt, to cope or to adjust. In human terms, stress refers to our emotional and physiological reactions to situations in which we feel in conflict or threatened beyond our capacity to cope or endure.

Some stress is necessary to keep us alert and occupied, but stress that is too intense or prolonged can have harmful psychological and physical effects.

In everyday language, people often use the word 'stress' to refer to the circumstances which cause stress, but it is best to refer to these as **stressors**.

Stressors, then, are events or conditions that put a strain on the organism and make demands on it to adjust.

Sources of stress

Major life changes

Holmes and Rahe (1967) constructed the **Social Readjustment Rating Scale (SRRS)**, to measure the degree of adjustment required by the various major life changes, including events which we may consider enjoyable such as Christmas. They first identified 43 events which seemed particularly stressful and then, following research, assigned each a value of 'life change units' according to the degree of adjustment it took. Some values are as follows:

Marriage	50
Death of a spouse	100
Divorce	73
Going on holiday	13
Imprisonment	63
Buying a house	31

To use this scale, you simply tick each event that has happened to you in a certain period of time (usually a year) and add the scores to give a total of life change units.

Activity

Before we evaluate the usefulness of this scale, consider the following. Think of three people you know well, preferably three people of different ages and walks of life. Imagine that in the last year each of them has experienced Christmas, been on holiday abroad, had a change of job and experienced the death of a close friend. Consider each of these experiences in turn and think about whether the amount of stress experienced by each person would be similar, even roughly. If not, what does this tell us about the scale?

Evaluation

Contributions   Research shows that high scores on the SRRS are indeed associated with many types of physical and psychological problems.

Criticisms

1. Many items on the SRRS may be the **result** of psychological problems or illness, not their cause. For example, one item on the scale is a change in sleeping habits, but this is more likely to be the result of stress as you lie awake worrying about what might happen, rather than the cause of it.

2. Some events become more stressful once a person is **already** depressed or ill, so simply counting life change units is not an accurate measure of stress.

3. Recent research shows that some of the events on the scale, for example, children leaving home, don't cause stress in the majority of people. In addition, there is no evidence that positive events are related to an increase in illness.

4. Different events have different meanings for different individuals, and this may affect the amount of stress involved. Pregnancy for a 30 year old married woman may be quite a different matter than for an unmarried 15 year old schoolgirl.

5. Factors such as **personality** and the amount of **social support** available can make tremendous differences to the effect of life changes.

Everyday hassles

Hassles are everyday irritations and frustrations which prevent the smooth running of everyday routines. They are all too numerous and include bad weather, lost keys, running out of milk.

These may seem unimportant as compared to major disasters but research indicates that routine hassles better predict psychosomatic and physical symptoms than do major life events.

Continuing problems

Chronic conditions such as an unhappy marriage, constant money worries, experiencing daily discrimination because of one's race, are not really events as measured by the SRRS but they may, of course, be extremely stressful. Many researchers believe that we are better able to cope with **sudden acute stress** than with stress that is with us day in, day out and from which there is **little prospect of escape**.

Kiecolt-Glaser *et al.* (1987) studied 34 people who were caring for a relative in the advanced stages of Alzheimer's disease and found that these carers, compared to controls, had significantly lower numbers of lymphocyte cells, essential in providing an efficient immune system.

The environment

Catastrophes

Earthquakes, severe hurricanes and other disasters, natural or otherwise, cause severe stress. People who continued to live in the area after the explosion at Three Mile Island showed more physiological signs of stress and reported more depressions and anxiety than did control participants (Baum *et al.*, 1983).

Noise

Most of us find loud noises aversive especially when we have no choice but to listen to them. Studies show that noise contributes to heart problems, ulcers, irritability, fatigue and aggressiveness. There is evidence that high noise levels also impair learning and motivation.

Air pollution

Exhaust fumes from cars, smoking cigarettes, industrial smog and smoke from domestic and industrial chimneys all increase the amount of carbon monoxide in the air. Prolonged exposure to high concentrations of carbon monoxide can contribute to headaches, memory problems and fatigue. It may also impair the ability to attend to several things at once.

Crowding

People who live in overcrowded conditions are more prone to high blood pressure, psychiatric illness and a high mortality rate. Research suggests that it is not necessarily crowding *per se* which causes stress; indeed, crowds can be fun on the right occasion. Crowding becomes stressful when it reduces a person's sense of **freedom and control**.

Conflict within the individual

Conflict occurs when you have two or more incompatible impulses or motivations occurring at the same time. You have no choice but to choose, but making that choice is not always easy. Freud proposed that internal conflicts are a source of considerable psychological distress.

Emmons and King (1988), using a detailed questionnaire to assess the degree of internal conflict experienced by 88 individuals, found that higher levels of conflict were associated with higher levels of anxiety, depression and physical symptoms.

Activity

1. What type of environmental stressors are involved in the following (most involve more than one):
   a Trying to get served in a crowded pub
   b Revising in the college cafeteria
   c Shopping with three preschool children
   d Driving to work through a busy city.

2. One example of conflict within the individual may be deciding whether to go on to higher education or get a job. Think of other examples of conflict which may arise within an individual, thereby being a potential source of stress.

Responses to stress

The body's responses to stress

Fight or flight

When we first encounter a threat, our body responds with what is now popularly known as the 'fight or flight' response, a physiological reaction to threat in which the autonomic nervous system (ANS) mobilises the organism for attacking or fleeing.

The fight or flight response activates the sympathetic division of the ANS to produce the following bodily responses:

1. Increase in respiration rate
2. Increase in heart rate, allowing oxygen to be pumped more rapidly
3. Increase in blood pressure
4. Increased muscle tension
5. Movement of blood away from the skin
6. Inhibition of digestion
7. Dilation of pupils
8. Release of sugar from liver to provide more energy for the muscles.
9. Increase in blood coagulability
   (see Figure 7.13).

This fight or flight response had obvious advantages for our ancestors whose lives depended on fast reactions to extremely dangerous situations, like being faced by a sabre-toothed tiger. In those kind of circumstances bodily arousal would be short lived. But our ancestors did not carry 30 year mortgages or sit day after day in traffic jams, and what for them had a valuable adaptive purpose has become a mixed blessing for people living in a more modern culture.

General adaptation syndrome

Selye (1956, 1974) coined the term **general adaptation syndrome** (GAS) to describe the pattern of reaction to ongoing stress. GAS consists of **three** stages:

1. **Alarm:** this is the equivalent of the fight or flight reaction and occurs when the organism first recognises the threat. The body mobilises its resources: the adrenal glands become enlarged, produce more adrenalin and stored supplies of steroids are released.

   If stress is prolonged, the organism passes to the next stage.

2. **Resistance:** during this stage physiological changes gradually stabilise; the adrenal glands return to their normal size and begin to renew their supply of steroids. This is a period of adjustment during which the organism attempts to restore its lost energy and repair any damage which may have been sustained in the alarm stage. The arousal level is higher than usual but eventually levels off.

   If no more stress occurs, then the organism gradually returns to normal. But in the meantime it remains much more vulnerable than it was before. If a second source of stress is introduced at this stage then things go rapidly downhill. Humans are likely to become withdrawn and inactive, with little enthusiasm for life. Performance at work and elsewhere is likely to deteriorate.

3. **Exhaustion:** if the stress cannot be overcome then the adrenal glands become enlarged again, the body's resources become depleted, physiological arousal decreases and the organism will probably collapse, literally exhausted. Selye observed that the animals he studied died as a direct consequence of the physiological changes undergone in their own defence.

   In human terms, people reaching this stage are likely to suffer both physically and psychologically. They are likely to be depressed, irritable and unable to concentrate. They may turn to alcohol or drugs in an effort to cope. They may lose their appetite and feel tired and listless. Continued stress in the exhaustion stage may lead to what Selye called **'diseases of adaptation'**, which range from allergies to coronary heart disease and may lead eventually to death.

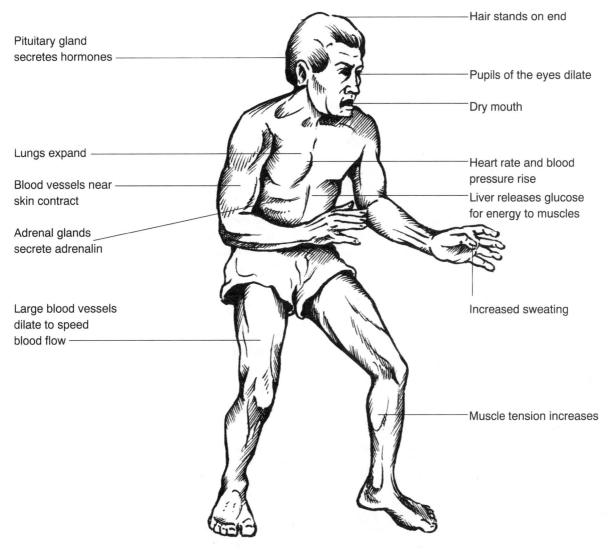

Hair stands on end

Pituitary gland secretes hormones

Pupils of the eyes dilate

Dry mouth

Lungs expand

Blood vessels near skin contract

Adrenal glands secrete adrenalin

Heart rate and blood pressure rise

Liver releases glucose for energy to muscles

Large blood vessels dilate to speed blood flow

Increased sweating

Muscle tension increases

Figure 7.13 'Fight or flight' reaction. Some physical reactions which occur in the body in response to activation of the emergency reaction

Endocrine activity during stress

As Figure 7.14 shows, the hypothalamus responds to stress in **two** different ways:

1. It excites the sympathetic division of the ANS (autonomic nervous system) which in turn stimulates the adrenal medulla (the central part of the adrenal gland) to release **adrenalin** and **noradrenalin** (together known as catecholamines) into the bloodstream. These produce the physiological responses associated with the fight or flight response.
2. It stimulates the pituitary gland to secrete the hormone ACTH which in turn stimulates the adrenal cortex (the outer part of the adrenal glands) to release **corticosteroids**. These cause

the liver to release stored glucose, thus increasing energy, and mobilises the chemicals that help inhibit tissue inflammation. They also stimulate the immune system to attack any invading antigens.

Activity

Before you go any further, learn the facts in Figure 7.14 very thoroughly – you will probably be put off by the unfamiliar names, but that is all the more reason to face up to learning it once and for all. It really isn't too difficult.

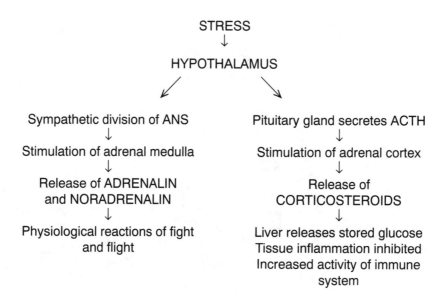

Figure 7.14 How the hypothalamus response to stress

Stress and illness

For many years stress has been implicated in the development of **psychosomatic illnesses**.

> Psychosomatic illnesses are genuine physical ailments which stem at least in part from mental and emotional causes.

These include bronchial asthma, tension headaches, ulcers, heart disease and hypertension.

Several studies indicate a link between illness and stress. Miller and Strunk (1979) found that children who died of an asthma attack were more likely to have lived in a stressful, unhappy family environment than children who survived equally life-threatening attacks.

Type A and Type B personality

Friedman and Rosenman (1974) proposed that a significant number of heart attack patients exhibit a cluster of behaviours which they called Type A behaviour:

Type A people are highly competitive, impatient, ambitious, hard-driving perfectionists who are often trying to do several things at once. They won't delegate and they take their worries home with them.

Type B people, in contrast, take a far more relaxed attitude to everything. They may work just as hard but are easygoing, patient, amiable and less hostile than Type A people.

Friedman and Roseman's research indicated that Type A people are six times more likely to develop heart problems than Type B people. However, these findings have not been replicated in other studies; indeed some research indicates that there is no link at all. Perhaps certain behaviours do increase the risk but only in those who would be prone to heart trouble anyway.

It is still by no means clear exactly **how** emotional states affect the body, or the extent to which they do. Much research is at present being conducted to test the hypothesis that certain behaviours and experiences interfere with the efficient functioning of our immune system but, as yet, the evidence is far from conclusive. Certainly the link between stress and illness seems to become more marked when a person can do nothing to **control** the source of stress.

It may be very easy to overestimate the psychological factors (such as attitude and behavioural style) and underestimate the economic and biological factors (such as poor diet, bad housing and genetics) which contribute to ill health. There is no doubt that stress has an effect on health, but there is considerable disagreement as to the extent of that effect, and even more over the extent to which a person's attitude can affect the progress of life-threatening conditions, including cancer.

Psychological manifestations of stress

Effects on task performance

The relationship between arousal and stress

Stress is closely related to arousal levels, as measured by physiological changes such as heart rate. Sudden, extreme stress is associated with high levels of arousal, especially in the immediate responses we make to a threat. If stress is very prolonged, however, arousal levels may become very low and the individual can become depressed.

According to the **Yerkes–Dodson law**, there is relationship between our levels of arousal and our ability to function effectively. This law states that:

1. As arousal increases, performance on a task of moderate difficulty first rises but eventually declines. This means that in order to function at our optimal level on a moderately difficult task, we need to be a little 'wound up' but not too much so.
2. But level of performance also depends on how difficult the task is. High levels of arousal allow us to perform better on simple behaviours whereas low levels of arousal facilitate performance on complex tasks (see Figure 7.15).

Put simply, we do better on simple tasks if we are highly aroused but to perform best on difficult tasks we need low levels of arousal.

This means that high levels of arousal are highly adaptive when the appropriate response is fighting or fleeing, but in order to work out solutions to some of the complex problems involved in stress situations, we need to be relatively calm.

Activity

If you have revised audience and coaction effects, think about how the Yerkes–Dodson law relates to this. Under what circumstances do we perform better when an audience is present and under what circumstances might an audience make us 'go to pieces'?

Stress and anxiety

The most prominent response to prolonged stress is **anxiety**, an uncomfortable feeling associated with the expectation that something disagreeable is about to happen. Anxiety is closely associated with fear, the main difference being that fear is a response to a specific stimulus (you know what you are afraid of)

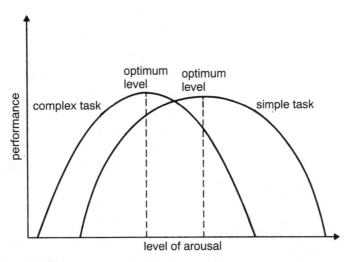

Figure 7.15 The Yerkes–Dodson law of arousal
Source: N. Hayes and S. Orrell, Psychology: An Introduction (Longman, 1993), p. 95.

but anxiety is usually free-floating, not focused on anything in particular, leaving you therefore with a constant underlying feeling of unpleasantness.

Some of the stressful situations most likely to cause anxiety are as follows:

a **Conflict of motives** within the individual, as mentioned earlier in the chapter. Making a decision one way or the other may bring new problems, but at least it tends to reduce anxiety.

b Acting in a way which is contrary to what we believe to be right. Festinger suggested that when our attitudes and behaviour do not correspond, we experience **dissonance**, a kind of psychological tension which is extremely troublesome, making us feel hypocritical and generally unhappy with ourselves. This concept is an integral part of Festinger's cognitive dissonance theory (see section 4.4).

c Being in an **unfamiliar situation** in which we are uncertain as to the 'correct' way to behave, for example, starting a new job.

d Being faced with situations in which the outcome is **unpredictable**, like taking your driving test.

e Facing the possibility of the **loss**, by death or other means, of someone to whom you are deeply attached.

In certain circumstances the stress is so extreme and the levels of anxiety it provokes so intense that the individual suffers from a condition called **post-traumatic stress disorder**. This condition had been recognised after wars throughout history as battle fatigue or shell shock. In peacetime the type of circumstances precipitating this condition would include the Hillsborough disaster, rape or a serious car accident. Individuals suffering from post-traumatic stress disorder feel prolonged anxiety and depression, have frequent nightmares, outbursts of anger, constant unhappiness and guilt.

Activity

Try to think of your own examples of circumstances which involve:

1. Acting in a way contrary to your beliefs (there are numerous examples of this in section 4.4 on Attitudes)

2. An unfamiliar situation in which you are not sure how to behave

3. A situation in which the outcome is unpredictable.

Stress and depression

Depression is an emotional disturbance in which the physical and psychological aspects of stress are closely interrelated. There is no doubt that some people are more prone to depression than others, perhaps because of their heredity. But even given differences in biological vulnerability, depression is usually precipitated by some stressful event, especially one which threatens an individual's sense of **identity or self-worth**. This would include events like divorce, loss of a parent or being dismissed from a job.

Coping with stress

Coping with stress involves making cognitive and behavioural efforts to reduce its effects. There is no single strategy that is effective for all kinds of people and all types of stress.

Biofeedback and relaxation

Biofeedback, a technique pioneered by DeCara and Miller, is particularly useful in controlling the physiological manifestations of stress and stress-related conditions such as hypertension, migraine headaches and asthma.

In biofeedback training, an individual is connected to a machine which provides him or her with information (feedback) about the working of a particular activity in the body (such as blood pressure) and instructions to try to control it. These instructions usually involve training in relaxation. In this way, the individual acquires voluntary control over biological processes which were once thought not to be under conscious control. Eventually these processes can be controlled without feedback.

Although biofeedback is a useful means of stress reduction, some researchers believe that simple relaxation is just as effective. Either way, relaxation is a useful and relatively inexpensive means of stress reduction that can reduce emotional turmoil and suppress physiological arousal.

Hardiness and optimism

Kobasa *et al.* (1982) studied a number of high-stress workers and examined the difference between those who suffered from high rates of stress-related illness and those with low rates of such illnesses. They found that the low-illness executives had in common a trait which they called **hardiness**. Hardiness has three components: **commitment**, **challenge** and **control**. People high in hardiness have a strong commitment to their work, family and to themselves. They see change as a challenge rather than a threat and they feel they can have an influence over most events and over other people; in short, they believe themselves to be in control.

Closely related to the trait of hardiness is that of **optimism**.

Optimism is the general tendency to expect things to turn out well. Scheier *et al.* (1986) found that people with an optimistic outlook coped with stress in ways different from the ways of pessimists. They were more likely to meet a challenge head-on and do their best to **change** the situation rather than surrender to it or deny it. They were also more willing to seek social support from others to help them cope with a stressful situation.

Social support

Much research indicates that being cared about and valued by other people is important in moderating our vulnerability to stress. Conversely, the lack of a social support system makes us more susceptible to disease and death.

Unfortunately, there are circumstances under which family and friends can actually increase stress. If they keep assuring us that everything will be all right and constantly minimise the seriousness of the problem, then they will not reduce our anxiety at all. Overall, however, having many social ties is related to a reduced incidence of stress-related illness and certainly makes us feel less lonely and more valued.

Activity

Of the three methods of coping with stress detailed above, one could be described as **social**, one **individual** and one **physiological**. Make sure you know which is which and can discuss each of these influences.

Coping with stressful situations, be they the everyday problems of work and family or major crises, is no easy matter. Successful coping may depend on finding the **strategy** best suited to a particular set of circumstances. We need to accept that no one strategy is always best for all people in all situations.

Preparing for the exam

Key terms

ACTH

adrenal cortex

adrenal medulla

adrenalin

anxiety

autonomic nervous system

biofeedback

corticosteroids

general adaptation syndrome

noradrenalin

post-traumatic stress disorder

psychosomatic

Social Readjustment Rating Scale

(SRRS)

stressors

stress

Type A personality

Type B personality

Yerkes–Dodson law

Types of exam question

1. Physiological responses to stress and ways in which psychological factors affect these responses.
2. Discussion of sources of stress (not alone but part of a longer question).
3. Practical implications of research on stress (again, likely to be part of a longer question).

Self-test questions

1. Define stress.
2. Give an example of a life event which is likely to be stressful. Suggest reasons why it is not likely to cause the same degree of stress to everyone who experiences it.
3. Give *three* examples of environmental stressors.
4. Describe the *three* stages in Selyes's general adaption syndrome.
5. What is a psychosomatic illness? Name *three*.
6. Describe the characteristics of a Type A and Type B personality. Which is more likely to develop heart problems?
7. According to the Yerkes–Dodson law, how does arousal effect performance?
8. What is anxiety, and what is likely to cause it?
9. Briefly describe how biofeedback can help an individual cope with stress.

Exam questions with guidance notes

1. **Consider potential causes of stress in people. Discuss the physiological and cognitive processes involved in coping with stress.**

   (25 marks)

   AEB (1989)

   Tempting though it may be, do not concentrate your answers solely on the stress involved in taking exams!

- Start by *defining* stress, mentioning that there are a host of potential sources of stress ranging from everyday irritations to major catastrophes and that stress is an inevitable (and not always negative) part of life.
- Use a *variety of stressors*, those of daily life, the environment and stress from within the individual including the work on stress and anxiety. (Freud's work is relevant here, but do not dwell on any one source for too long.) It is important to include some research (Holmes and Rahe, Kiecolt-Glaser *et al.*, Emmons and King are all mentioned in the text).
- Cognitive processes refer to factors *within* the individual such as attitude and expectation. Those involved with coping with stress include work on Type A and Type B personalities and on hardiness and optimism. Work on learned helplessness and locus of control could also be usefully mentioned here: they are not included in this section of the book but they are discussed in section 7.4 on Motivation. All of these factors have been researched, so name the researchers, outline the research and state the findings.
- Do please bear in mind, though, that the 'right attitude' is not a universal panacea which alleviates all stress overnight: there is always a complex interaction of physical and psychological factors.
- You could conclude, as the text does, by saying that no single method of coping is likely to suit all individuals and all situations equally well.

2. **Describe and discuss some physiological responses to states of stress.**

AEB (1988)

This is a very straightforward question, requiring you simply to detail the physical rather than psychological responses to stress and to discuss these.

- Give details of the 'fight or flight' response, emphasising that this is the response to *sudden* stress.
- Go on to describe *Selye's* work on the General Adaption Syndrome (GAS), detailing, if you are familiar with it, his work with rats but, more importantly, relating the research to humans.
- Provide detailed information on the *hormonal* (endocrinal) responses to stress, relating this to the 'fight or flight' response and to GAS.
- Since certain illnesses are believed to be at least partly caused by stress, mention the work on *psychosomatic illness* (some of which you will have already covered when discussing GAS); include the work on Type A and Type B personalities and other research related to stress and illness (such as that of Miller and Strunk).
- This leads neatly into a *conclusion* which states that physiological and psychological responses to stress are closely interlinked, and neither can be studied in isolation.

Additional exam questions

1. What is environmental stress? Explain how psychological and environmental factors may interact to cause stress responses. **(25 marks)**

AEB (1987)

2. a Discuss some of the major sources of psychological stress. **(13 marks)**
    b Evaluate, from a psychological viewpoint, some strategies which
       individuals use to cope with stress.   **(12 marks)**
                                                                AEB AS (1992)

8

Developmental Psychology

AEB	NEAB	O & C	Topic	Date attempted	Date completed	Self Assessment
✓	✓	✓	**Sociability and Attachment**			
✓	✓	✓	**Cognitive Development**			
✓	✓	✓	**Play**			
✓	✓	✗	**Language Acquisition**			
✓	✓	✗	**Moral Development**			
✓	✓	✓	**Gender Roles**			
✓	✓	✓	**Development of Self-Concept**			
✓	✓	✗	**Adolescence**			
✓	✓	✗	**Life events**			
✓	✓	✓	**Late Adulthood**			

8.1 Sociability and attachment

Sociability

Sociability refers to the ability to engage in social relationships.

1. **Sociability appears to be innate:** this is supported by the following studies:
    a   Condon and Sanders (1974) showed that babies as young as two days will respond to the sound of human speech by turning their head towards the speaker and moving their head and arms in time to the rhythm of the speech. They do not respond in this way to tapping or to someone making vowel sounds.
    b   Fantz (1961) demonstrated that infants of two weeks will spend longer looking at a diagram that represents a human face than they will at other stimuli (see section 3.2).
    c   Ahrens (1954) showed that babies of one month will respond with a smile to a picture of human eyes or even two dots on an oval shape even when the rest of the fact is blank. As they get older, children will only smile in response to a more complete and realistic representation of a face.
2. **There are individual differences in sociability:** evidence from a number of studies suggests that although sociability is universal, there are differences in the degree of sociability observable in very young babies, and that this may be inherited.
    Freedman and Keller (1963) found that identical twins were more alike than non-identical twins in terms of sociability, fear of strangers and smiling.

Learning to respond to specific faces

Carpenter demonstrated that babies of one to eight weeks of age recognise the face and voice of their own mother and expect the two to go together. When presented with their mother's face coupled with a stranger's voice, they became quite distressed. Carpenter also found that babies were more interested in a moving face than in a 'frozen' face.

The functions of sociability

1. **Drawing adults into an interaction:** the ability to respond to the adult face and voice has an obvious value in that it draws the adult into an interaction and makes him or her want to care for the child. When tiny infants cry and smile, these behaviours have social meaning to adults, who then respond in an appropriate manner. Infants enjoy the attention they receive in response to their own signals and will respond again in turn. This is the beginning of more complex interactions and 'conversations' that clearly occur between a baby and its carers.
2. **As a precursor to language development:** **Trevarthan and Richards (1974)** use the term **interactional synchrony** to describe the 'turn taking' which takes place between a carer and infant. In their study of babies up the age of six months, they found that the carer and infant take turns in cooing, talking, smiling and eye contact. Kaye points out that at first these interactions are initiated by the adult who responds to stimuli and interprets behaviour as having some social meaning when it may have none. Gradually, however, the infant takes a greater and more equal role and is soon initiating and directing increasingly sophisticated interactions. These early 'conversations' are very important as they involve the basics of 'turn taking' which is needed for subsequent social interactions.

Note that the study of Trevarthan and Richards (1974) may be useful in an essay on language acquisition.

Attachment

Attachment refers to the strong, emotional and enduring bond that is established between a young child and those who care for the child.

Schaffer (1977) describes three stages in the development of this attachment bond:

1. Babies are attracted to animate human faces and voices rather than to other stimuli. This develops at approximately six weeks of age.

2. Babies are able to distinguish strangers from non-strangers. This develops at approximately three months of age.

3. Babies show great distress when separated from the primary attachment figures and experience fear of strangers. This develops at around eight months of age.

Schaffer emphasises that attachment is a **two way process** involving a balanced and well tuned set of interactions between carer and child. He believes that the strength of the attachment is based on the sensitivity of the adult who cares for the child.

The quality of the attachment bond

Ainsworth (1971, 1978) devised the 'strange situation' in which mother and child pairs were brought into an unfamiliar room containing toys and then the child's reaction was observed as a stranger entered, as the mother left and, finally, as the mother returned.

On the basis of many such observations of babies around one year of age, Ainsworth identified **three** categories of attachment behaviour:

1. **Securely attached:** these infants explored the room quite happily whilst the mother was present and were able to use her as a **'secure base'** when the stranger entered. They were clearly distressed when the mother left the room and on her return they went to her immediately for comfort which she provided effectively.

2. **Insecurely attached:** these infants did not explore their new surroundings and the toys with confidence when the mother was present and had difficulty in using her as a safe base when the stranger entered. They were very unhappy at the mother's departure and were very clingy on her return, but also expressed anger by hitting her and crying.

3. **Detached:** these infants appeared to be unconcerned about who was with them in the room. They did not appear to mind when the mother left them with a stranger and showed little reaction on her return.

In a longitudinal study, Ainsworth found that:

1. The mothers of the securely attached infants were sensitive to their babies' signals and engaged in interaction more often than the mothers of the insecurely attached or detached babies.

2. The mothers of the insecurely attached infants were insensitive to their signals and generally quite poor at handling and caring for the child.

3. The mothers of the detached children were extremely neglectful and rejecting of them.

A series of follow up studies indicated that the security of the attachment was an accurate predictor of later social and emotional difficulties.

Activity

What method was used by Ainsworth in the 'strange situation' study? If in doubt, refer to section 11.1 on Methodology, where it is quoted as a useful example of this type of study.

Bowlby's theory of maternal deprivation

Bowlby is famous for his quote that 'Mother love in infancy and childhood is as important for mental health as are vitamins and proteins for physical health' (1953).

Bowlby's theory is based on the following beliefs:

1. Babies have a **biological need** for a warm, stable and continuous attachment with a mother or mother substitute.

2. The attachment bond is **monotropic**, that is, it is established between the infant and one person. Although other relationships are formed, they are qualitatively different from the one involving the infant and main carer and do not have the same impact on later emotional development.

3. The bond develops from around seven months of age. It is a **biologically adaptive mechanism** which is synchronised with the age at which a baby becomes mobile (starts to crawl) and serves to keep it close to the mother.

4. The child is biologically adapted to form the bond between the ages of seven months and three years (approximately). This is known as the **critical or sensitive period**. It is difficult, if not impossible, for the bond to form after this period.

5. If the child experiences **maternal deprivation**, that is, this bond is either not formed, or is broken by fairly frequent and prolonged periods of separation, then the child is at risk of suffering a number of short- and long-term consequences.

Breaking the bond

Short-term effects

The short-term consequences of breaking the attachment bond are illustrated by the work of **Robertson and Robertson** whose focus of interest was the distress suffered by children in enforced separations.

Robertson and Robertson describe **a syndrome of distress** involving **three** distinct stages:

1. **Protest:** the child demonstrates his or her anger and distress at being left by loud crying and attempts to follow the parent
2. **Despair:** the child is clearly pining and miserable but shows distress in a much more quiet and desperate manner, often by outbursts of deep sobbing
3. **Detachment:** the child appears to have 'settled' but is very unresponsive to anything and anybody in the environment.

If separation is prolonged, lasting several days, the detachment phase may continue for some time on reunion with the mother. The Robertsons believed that the child is left **emotionally vulnerable** by such an experience.

Long-term effects

Bowlby was particularly concerned about the possible long-term effects of maternal deprivation which, he believed, could include:

1. emotionally disturbed behaviour
2. growth retardation (developmental dwarfism)
3. depression
4. intellectual retardation
5. delinquency and affectionless psychopathy (an inability to form deep and meaningful relationships).

Bowlby's evidence

The main sources of Bowlby's evidence, other than that of Robertson and Robertson, described earlier, can be summarised thus:

Imprinting studies

The work on imprinting is discussed in detail in section 6.2. Bowlby believed that attachment in humans, like imprinting in chicks, has an important survival value since it ensures that the baby stays close to the mother where it is relatively safe. Bowlby also drew attention to Lorenz's finding that there is a 'critical period' for imprinting, and believed this to be the equivalent of the critical period for attachment formation in human infants.

Harlow's experiments on rhesus monkeys

Harlow (1958) conducted a series of experiments involving the isolation of baby monkeys. The monkeys were raised in a cage containing two 'surrogate mothers', a cloth mother and a wire mother (see Figure 8.1). One of the substitutes had a feeding bottle attached to it. Regardless of which surrogate provided the food, the baby monkeys spent most of their time clinging to the 'soft' substitute mother and used her as a safe base when they were frightened by a mechanical bear. This indicates that physical contact is important in the formation of attachments. When these isolated monkeys were eventually placed with other monkeys, they showed serious maladjustment, usually showing extreme fear and even self-mutilation, occasionally becoming very aggressive. Such female monkeys abused, rather than cared for, their own offspring.

Activity

What are the major problems of generalising from animals to humans? Check your answer with reference to section 10.6 on the use of animals in psychological research.

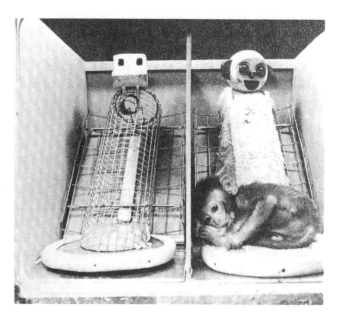

Figure 8.1 Attachment in infant monkeys
Source: S.A. Rathus, Essentials of Psychology (Holt, Rinehart & Winston, 1991, 3rd edn), p. 347.

Studies of institutionalised children

Goldfarb (1943) compared two groups of 15 children, one of whom had spent the first three years of their lives in an understaffed institution before being fostered, and the other of whom were fostered as soon as they left their natural mothers and who therefore never experienced life in an institution. Goldfarb conducted a longitudinal study, comparing these children at age three years, six years, eight years and twelve years and found that, compared to the early fostered group, the institutional children scored lower on intelligence tests and language ability and found it more difficult to make friends and form meaningful relationships. It was Goldfarb's conclusion that these differences were attributable to the lack of opportunity to form an attachment with anybody in the first three years of life.

Bowlby's study of juvenile delinquents

Bowlby (1946) compared 44 juvenile thieves from a clinic for disturbed adolescents with 44 youths who were emotionally disturbed but were not thieves (this latter group being a control group). He found that:

a   14 of the thieves displayed some of the characteristics of affectionless psychopathy and that nine of these youths had experienced a period of prolonged separation from their mothers in the first three years of their lives

b   Of the 30 thieves who did not show signs of affectionless psychopathy, only three had experienced such severe separation

c   None of the control group, only two of whom had experienced maternal separation, showed signs of affectionless psychopathy.

Criticisms of Bowlby's evidence

Much of the evidence cited has been criticised for the following reasons:

1.   With regard to the **imprinting** studies, the concept of a critical period has now been largely replaced by that of a more flexible **sensitive period**, indicating that the period for attachment is not as fixed as was first hypothesised.

   Many researchers also consider that it is inappropriate to generalise from animals to humans and that the imprinting process bears little relationship to attachment behaviour in primates.

2.   The monkeys in Harlow's studies experienced **social** as well as **maternal** deprivation. Moreover, Suomi and Harlow (1972) demonstrated that even when monkeys had been isolated for as long as one year, they could

recover if placed individually with a younger monkey.

3. As regards Goldfarb's study, there may have been an **initial difference** between the two groups of children, such that those who were more alert or less tetchy may have been more likely to be chosen for adoption.

   More generally, children in institutions at that period were deprived of more than a **primary attachment figure**. The intellectual retardation reported in a number of deprivation studies is probably due to lack of stimulation and necessary life experiences, including lack of one to one language, rather than a lack of a main attachment figure (Rutter, 1972).

4. Bowlby's own study of juvenile thieves has attracted a variety of criticisms. Bowlby selected his sample from a target population of juvenile thieves, resulting in a **biased sample**. It is quite possible that many people have experienced separation with no ill effects at all, but if the background of non-delinquent people is not investigated, then this cannot be established one way or the other.

   A further problem with this study is that it is **retrospective** (it looks backwards), relying on incomplete records and distorted memories to piece together the youths' histories.

In light of the criticisms and a large body of later research, considerable modification of Bowlby's theory has been offered by other researchers.

A reassessment of Bowlby's theory

Rutter (1972) makes a number of points which challenge Bowlby's conclusions:

1. Bowlby failed to make the distinction between maternal **deprivation**, in which a bond that has been made is broken, and maternal **privation**, which provides the child with no opportunity to make a bond. Rutter believes that privation is much more serious, as it leaves a child without ever having experienced a deep emotional attachment and could be the cause of affectionless psychopathy.

2. With respect to maternal deprivation, Rutter argues that the long-term effects of separation depend on a number of factors, including the reason for separation and the nature of the alternative care provided. In fact, Rutter contends that it is not separation as such which causes delinquency, but the amount of **discord** and **stress** present in the homes. Such discord can exist with or without separation.

3. Rutter argues that the chief attachment is not necessarily with the main carer and he stresses the importance of other relationships as demonstrated by the following study.

Schaffer and Emerson (1964) showed that babies between the ages of six and 18 months were able to make a number of attachments, all equally important, but each fulfilling a different function. For example, mothers may be used as a comfort source when the child is tired or frightened, whilst fathers may be used as the figure preferred for exploration and play.

The Core Study in this section (Hodges and Tizard) is a follow-up of a number of studies of the effects of maternal deprivation and provides a good overview of these effects.

Maternal deprivation: an overview

Bowlby's work has been at least partly responsible for the following social changes, some of which may be regarded as beneficial, others as detrimental:

1. Institutions now consider the emotional well-being of children in their care; provision for attachment formation is generally regarded as essential.

2. It is now commonplace for hospitals to permit parents virtually unlimited visiting rights and to provide 'foster parents' for children who cannot be visited often.

3. Research into the importance of attachment and 'mothering' skills has been established and there is, in general, a greater sensitivity to a child's emotional needs.

4. Many women suffered feelings of guilt about leaving their preschool youngster in the care of others, although, despite Bowlby's views, there is no evidence that good quality day care has any deleterious effects and may have some beneficial ones.

Core Study

Social and family relationships of ex-institutional adolescents: J. Hodges and B. Tizard (1989)

This research is a follow up of a number of studies carried out to examine the effects on a group of children of being raised in institutions and experiencing many changes of carer until at least the age of two years, and thereafter being brought up within a family environment.

Hodges and Tizard were interested in the extent to which the effects of early institutionalisation were felt at age 16 and they set about following up all the children who had been investigated at age eight (in a variety of studies carried out by Tizard and colleagues).

The sample

1. Out of 51 who were followed up at the age of eight, nine were unavailable at the age of 16.
2. A comparison group (with no experience of institutional care) was formed, matched on age, sex, number of parents, class and position in the family.

Method

The ex-institutional adolescents and their mother, father or care-worker were interviewed, as were the matched sample, together with a parent.

Each adolescent completed the Questionnaire on Social Difficulty (Lindsay and Lindsay, 1982). The parent or care worker filled in the 'A' Scale Questionnaire (Rutter *et al.*, 1970) on the behaviour of the adolescent.

The school, with permission from the parents and adolescents, was sent a 'B' Scale Questionnaire (Rutter *et al.*, 1970) and a questionnaire devised for the study, focusing on relationships with peers and teachers.

Results

1. At age 16 a high proportion of the comparison group and the adopted group were reported to be attached to their parents. However, only 50 per cent of those children who had been restored

to their natural parents were said to be attached.
2. The ex-institutional group, especially the restored group, had more problems getting along with siblings than did the comparison group.
3. There was no significant difference in affection between the comparison group and the adopted group but the restored group were significantly less affectionate.
4. The ex-institutional group had poorer peer relationships than the comparison groups. They were more likely to be friends with anybody who was friendly. Teachers rated them as more argumentative and less popular. From mothers' reports, it seemed they were less likely to have a best friend than were the comparison group.

Conclusion

Differences were found to exist between the ex-institutional adolescents and the comparison group, mainly outside the home and particularly in relationships with peers.

QUESTIONS

1. Outline some of the problems that Tizard and Hodges encountered when collecting data for their longitudinal study. **(4 marks)**
    (Oxford and Cambridge Specimen Paper)
2. What was the aim of the Tizard and Hodges study?
3. In what ways were the ex-institutional children different from those who had not experienced institutional care?

Preparing for the exam

Key terms

affectionless psychopathy
attachment
despair
detached
detachment
imprinting
insecure attachment

interactional synchrony
maternal deprivation
primary attachment figure
privation
protest
secure attachment
sociability

Types of exam questions

1. Consideration of the effects of early experiences on later development.
2. Evaluation of studies investigating separation and deprivation in childhood.
3. Consideration of factors affecting sociability and attachment.

Self-test questions

1. What evidence is there that babies are born with a certain amount of sociability?
2. How does sociability differ from attachment?
3. What is interactional synchrony?
4. According to Schaffer there are *three* stages in the development of the attachment bond. What are they?
5. What categories of attachment behaviour did Mary Ainsworth observe in her 'strange situation' study?
6. In a follow up study, Ainsworth investigated why children displayed different attachment behaviours. Briefly outline her findings.
7. In their study on the short-term effects of separation, the Robertsons identified *three* stages. What are they?
8. According to John Bowlby, what are the possible long-term effects of maternal deprivation?
9. What is the difference between privation and deprivation? Why is this an important distinction in understanding early experiences?

Exam question with guidance notes

Evaluate studies which have investigated the effects of separation and deprivation in childhood.   **(25 marks)**
                                                              AEB (1989)

There are two important points to note here: first, you are asked to *evaluate*, not simply describe, studies and, secondly, you need to ensure that the studies chosen actually do investigate the effects of *separation* and *deprivation*. Suitable studies would be Goldfarb, Bowlby, Robertson and Robertson, Rutter, Schaffer and Emerson and Hodges and Tizard (this last one is ideal as it is a follow up of a number of studies and is covered in detail in the text as a Core Study). You may be familiar with some case studies (Freud and Dann, Genie, the Koluchova twins and so on) but do not use *only* these since this gives a poor balance. Avoid the animal studies as far as possible; it could be argued that Harlow is relevant but there is no shortage of studies on humans.

- Begin by placing the studies in context by giving a *very* brief outline of attachment theory in order to provide the rationale for the studies. This should only be a short paragraph.
- Having selected your studies, keep description to a minimum.
- You should evaluate in terms of:
  a What the study has told us about the effects of such experiences
  b Whether the study has had any practical application (for example the Robertsons' work was instrumental in bringing about change for children in hospital)
  c Any methodological or conceptual weaknesses in the study. These are documented in the text as far as Bowlby, Goldfarb and Harlow are concerned. Point out the *limitations* of Case Studies (if you have used one), natural experiments (Hodges and Tizard), observation studies (Schaffer and Emerson) and so on.
- Choose a *range* of studies; not, for example, only those that support or only those that criticise Bowlby.

Additional exam questions

1. **a** Explain what psychologists understand by the terms 'attachment' in relation to the early socialisation of the child. **(5 marks)**

    b Using appropriate evidence, discuss whether problems in forming attachments in infancy have an influence on the child's later development **(20 marks)**
    AEB AS (1993)

2. Critically consider the psychological effects of factors which influence the development of sociability in the young child. **(25 marks)**
    AEB AS (1991)

3. Discuss, with reference to empirical work, the importance of caregiver–child interactions for the development of attachment in children. **(20 marks)**
    JMB (1991)

4. Discuss the findings of psychological research into the effects on children of enrichment and/or deprivation. **(25 marks)**
    AEB (1994)

8.2 Cognitive development

The term 'cognitive' refers to psychological processes connected with thinking and reasoning. Developmental psychologists are concerned with how thought and knowledge change and develop over time, particularly in the childhood years.

Piaget's theory

Piaget is the most prominent psychologist in the field of cognitive development. Piaget's main principles can be summarised as follows:

Adaptation

We are all biologically programmed to continually adapt to our environment. We are born with a few basic instincts, such as grasping and sucking, which are gradually expanded or **adapted** to give the young child an appropriate set of responses for dealing with the world.

Schemata

As a child interacts with the environment she gradually organises everything that she knows about a particular object or activity into a schema. A **schema** contains all the information, experience, ideas and memories an individual has about an object or sequence of events. It is by using schemata (the plural of schema) that she is able to organise information and make sense of the world.

Assimilation and accommodation

The adaptation of schemata takes place by means of **two** complementary processes: **assimilation** and **accommodation**:

Assimilation refers to the process whereby new experiences or information are incorporated into an existing schema without changing any other part of it or requiring a new schema to be formed.

Accommodation refers to the process whereby new experiences or information cannot be incorporated into an existing schema without either changing the schema in a fundamental way or creating a new schema.

Disequilibrium occurs if new information does not fit into an existing schema; the individual is then motivated to change the schema or form a new one to fit the information. Once this has been satisfactorily accomplished, a state of **equilibrium** is reached.

For example, young infants have a sucking reflex and whenever they are presented with a new object, the put it straight in the mouth. The action of sucking everything involves **assimilation**, since the existing sucking reflex already exists. But they cannot suck a new object in the same way that they previously sucked a nipple. They have to **accommodate** to the new object, perhaps by opening their mouth in a different manner. In this way the sucking schema has been changed to accommodate a new object.

An older child may have a schema of a squirrel as a small, furry animal which has a bushy tail, eats acorns and sleeps in the winter. If she discovers that squirrels can be grey or red, this extends the scheme but does not challenge any of her other previous ideas about squirrels. This, therefore, involves the process of assimilation. But suppose she then encounters a small animal that she assumes to be a squirrel but subsequently finds it does not have certain essential squirrel features – it does not have a bushy tail and lives in a cage, not a tree. This throws her into a state of **disequilibrium** because the structure by which she has made sense of the world is seen to be inadequate. She is told that it is a rabbit and, in order to make sense of the world of small animals, she creates a new schema for rabbit. This is the process of accommodation.

Assimilation and accommodation occur throughout life as we constantly shift from one to the other. Both processes are necessary, but it is mainly through the process of accommodation that important advances in knowledge and understanding are made.

Activity

There is a lot of unfamiliar vocabulary in this discussion. Before you go on, make sure you understand the meaning of: **schema**, **adaptation**, **assimilation**, **accommodation** and **disequilibrium**.

Suppose you like one of your teachers, Mr Jones.

You hear someone complaining that he was uncooperative when they asked for help. If your reaction is to think that the student is exaggerating in order to excuse poor work, you have not changed your schema. Is this assimilation of accommodation?

When you are later given similar treatment, you change your mind about Mr Jones. Is this assimilation or accommodation?

Piaget's stages of development

Piaget argued that intellectual development proceeds through four stages:

- The sensorimotor stage
- The preoperational stage
- The concrete operational stage
- The formal operational stage.

The sensorimotor stage (birth to two years)

Essential features of this stage are:

a Children interpret all the information they receive through the **senses** and understand and respond to the world through **actions**. Schemata are referred to as **action patterns** because the child does not have an internal set of thoughts about an object or event but merely a way of **responding** to them.

b Early in the sensorimotor stage, children are entirely **egocentric**, which, at this stage, means they are not able to distinguish themselves from the rest of the world. Everything is seen as an extension of self.

c Children are limited to thinking about the here and now: they do not dwell on the past or look forward to the future. This feature gradually disappears as the stage moves onwards. At approximately eight months of age, the child begins to develop the concept of **object permanence** and is able to understand that an object continues to exist when it is out of sight.

The preoperational stage (two to seven years)

a Sometime between the age of 18 and 24 months the child's thought moves to a new plane which is characterised by **symbolic thought**. This means that the child can now represent objects and events internally, in the form of language and thought. It is the ability to represent the world symbolically which differentiates the sensorimotor stage from the preoperational stage.

b The child is no longer limited to the here and now or to responding only to physical events. Despite this important change, the child's thought is still limited in a number of ways because a child's understanding is dominated by the way things **look**.

c It is the limitations of the stage that characterise it:

i The child remains egocentric. 'Egocentrism' now refers to the child's inability to see things from anything other than her own viewpoint. Piaget illustrated this, using the 'three mountains task' (see Figure 8.2). A child is presented with a model of three mountains and is asked to select, from a series of photographs, the view that would be seen by a doll sitting on another side of the model. During the preoperational stage, the child will simply select the view that she has of the mountains. This is due to the fact that preoperational children are unable to **decentre**, to step outside their own perspective and see things from another's point of view.

ii The child is a **moral realist**. She ignores the intention of a deed and judges the naughtiness of the act only by the consequences it brings. This is discussed in more detail in section 8.5 on Moral development.

iii The child is unable to **conserve**, she cannot appreciate that things remain the same even when their appearance changes. This is

Figure 8.2 Piaget's 'Three mountains' study
Source: N. Hayes, A First Course in Psychology (Nelson, 1988, 2nd edn), p. 122.

demonstrated by a series of experiments, a typical one of which is as follows: The child is presented with two identical, short, fat beakers of water, each filled to exactly the same level, and asked if they are both the same. The child acknowledges that they are, and the experimenter, in full view of the child, then pours the water from one of the fat beakers into a tall thin beaker, taking care not to spill any. The child is again asked if the beakers contain the same amount of water; she now believes that there is more water in the tall thin beaker.

Piaget devised similar tests to demonstrate conservation, or the lack of it, of number, length, substance, and area (see Figure 8.3).

The preoperational child has difficulty with such conservation tasks because she is guided by appearance rather than conceptual understanding and only pays attention to one aspect of a problem at one time. For example, by attending only to the **height** of the water, she ignores its **circumference**.

iv The child **cannot perform operations** (hence the name of the stage, preoperational). An operation is difficult to define but essentially it involves the ability to form a mental rule for manipulating objects or ideas into new forms and back to the original. Preoperational children are unable to do this: they suffer from **irreversibility**, an inability to work backwards mentally in order to solve a problem. In the conservation studies, they cannot mentally pour the liquid back into the original container and thereby recognise that it is the same.

The concrete operational stage (7 to 11 years)

This stage is characterised by the following features:

a The child is now able to perform operations which enable her to reverse concepts and understand things from a variety of angles and viewpoints. Egocentrism declines markedly. She is now able to conserve, though the concrete operational stage is well advanced before most children have grasped all types of conservation.

b The child is now able to classify objects, a task which requires a recognition of common features.

She is also able to rank objects in order of size.

c The main limitation of this stage is that the child cannot deal with abstract concepts or hypothetical tasks. In order to solve problems a child needs reference to **real objects**.

Formal operational stage (11/12 years upwards)

The child can now deal with hypothetical situations, and solve problems in a systematic, logical manner in which all possible combinations of factors are considered.

There is some doubt as to whether everybody actually reaches this final stage.

Activity

In order to learn these stages, you may find it helpful to

- Devise a mnemonic so that you learn the names of the stages in the correct order
- Draw a summary table of the main characteristics of each stage
- Learn the characteristics which mark the transition from one stage to another.

Methods used by Piaget

Naturalistic observation

Piaget conducted detailed studies of his own three children in their natural surroundings.

The clinical interview

Details of this method and that of naturalistic observation together with the advantages and limitations of each can be found in Chapter 11.

Cross-sectional studies

These involve the investigation of several groups of children, each of a different age. For example, separate groups of four year olds, six year olds and eight year olds may be compared on the same task to see how differently they perform.

1. Conservation of substance (6-7 years)

(a)

The experimenter presents two identical plasticene balls
The child admits that they have equal amounts of plasticene

(b)

One of the balls is rolled into a sausage shape
The child is asked whether they still contain equal amounts

2. Conservation of length (6-7 years)

(a)

Two sticks are aligned in front of the child
She admits their equality

(b)

One of the sticks is moved to the right
The child is asked whether they are still the same length

3. Conservation of number (6-7 years)

(a)

Two rows of counters are placed in one-to one correspondence
The child admits their equality

(b)

One of the rows is elongated (or contracted)
The child is asked whether each row still has the same number

4. Conservation of volume (6-7 years)

(a)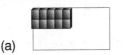

Two beakers are filled to the same level with water
The child sees that they are equal

(b)

The liquid of one container is poured into a tall tube (or a flat dish)
The child is asked whether each contains the same amount

5. Conservation of area (9-10 years)

(a)

The child and the experimenter each have identical sheets of cardboard
Wooden blocks are placed on these in identical positions
The child is asked whether each cardboard has the same amount of space remaining

(b)

The experimenter scatters the blocks on one of the cardboards
The child is asked the same question

Figure 8.3 Piaget's tests on conservation
Source: E. Hetherington and R. Parke, Child Psychology: A Contemporary Viewpoint (McGraw-Hill, 1975), p. 360 (slightly adapted).

Criticisms of Piaget

Methodology

a The clinical interview is considered by some to be too **subjective** and liable to lead the children in a certain direction.

b There is too much reliance on the observations he made of his **own three children**, who cannot be assumed to be representative of children generally.

c In questioning children, Piaget's researchers confused them and expected too much of their **memory and language skills**. This criticism has been made by a number of researchers and will be addressed in more detail later in the section.

Egocentricity in the preoperational child

The use of the three mountains task is seen by some researchers as too abstract. **Hughes (1975)** developed an alternative task which shows that a preoperational child can decentre. He presented children with a box divided into four quarters by cardboard walls and asked them to place a naughty boy doll in a place where a policeman doll could not see him (see Figure 8.4). Hughes found that the majority of preschool children could cope with this task, whereas few children under eight years of age could manage the three mountains task.

It is likely that the difference in results arose because with the policeman task, children found it easier to understand what they were supposed to do and why they were supposed to do it. In addition to this, and at least as importantly, they did not have to represent their solutions in terms of pictures but could demonstrate their answer directly by moving the naughty boy doll to the appropriate place.

Conservation and preoperational child

a **Rose and Blank (1974)** and **Samuel and Bryant (1984)** consider that in Piaget's original conversation experiments children were confused by being asked the **same question twice**. The children may have felt that a different answer was expected the second time and they obligingly provided it. Both sets of researchers showed that if, at the end of the procedure, the child was only asked once if the two substances were the same amount, they were much more likely to give the correct answer. Samuel and Bryant's research is documented in the Core Study in this section (p. 241).

b **McGarrigle and Dolandson (1974)** devised an alternative test of conservation of number. They showed that, if a glove puppet 'naughty teddy' was responsible for reorganising a row of counters, children were able to recognise that the number of counters remained the same despite the difference in appearance. They were not able to do this when the reorganisation was made by an experimenter. It seems that the children could relate to the antics of an interfering toy and were able to understand what had happened and why.

Stage theory

Some critics argue that Piaget's theory is not a true stage theory at all. Important changes occur within each stage and children move from one stage to another very gradually, probably being in two stages at once for periods of their development. A true stage theory would expound more clearly defined, non-overlapping stages.

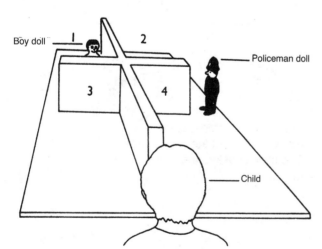

Figure 8.4 Hughes' 'Policeman doll' study
Source: N. Hayes, A First Course in Psychology (Nelson, 1988, 2nd edn), p. 125.

Core Study

Asking only one question in the conservation experiment: J. Samuel and P. Bryant (1984)

Samuel and Bryant's study is based on that carried out by Rose and Blank (1974), who reworked Piaget's conservation experiments but made **one** important change. Instead of asking the child twice if the two substances under comparison were the same, they asked them only once, at the end of the procedure. By doing this, they found that a significant number of children in the preoperational stage could conserve.

This present study repeats that of Rose and Blank but, instead of using only six year olds, as they did, uses a wider age range of children.

Subjects

252 boys and girls, divided into four age groups – approximately five, six, seven and eight year olds. Each age group was divided into three subgroups.

Design and procedure

The three subgroups within each age group were assigned to the following conditions.

a **Standard:** Piaget's original two question conservation task

b **One judgement:** the same conservation task but with only one question asked at the end of the procedure

c **Fixed-array control:** a task which required the children to make a judgement, but without having seen the transformation taking place.

Three different trials were conducted, using mass (playdough), number (counters) and volume (water in glasses). Each subject was given four trials with each of the materials, half with equal quantities and half where the quantities were uneven. The order of the trials was varied for each subject.

Results

Generally, the results are consistent with those of Rose and Blank in that all four age groups did better when they were asked once after watching the transformation rather than in the other conditions. Older age groups did better than the younger ages and all the children did better on the number task than on mass or volume.

Conclusions

These results indicate that children of this age range do understand the principle of invariance and, in the original Piagetian tasks, they make a mistake because the experimenter's repetition of the same question makes them think that they must change their answer the second time. This indicates that conservation experiments do not reveal whether or not children possess certain cognitive skills, but are tapping the different circumstances under which they will **use** them.

QUESTIONS

1. a In the study by Samuel and Bryant, how did they alter the method used by Piaget to investigate judgement in children?
        (2 marks)

    b What do their results tell us about why children make errors in the design used by Piaget? **(2 marks)**

Oxford and Cambridge Specimen Paper

2. In the study by Samuel and Bryant
   a what do the psychologists mean by the term 'conservation'? **(2 marks)**
   b Describe *one* of the ways in which the psychologists tested for conservation. **(2 marks)**
   Oxford and Cambridge (1994)

3. How does this study differ from that carried out by Rose and Blank?

Piaget's impact on education

Piaget has been responsible for a major change in the understanding of children's thinking and in the type of education provided for them. The main implications are as follows:

1. Children are seen as **active learners** who are motivated to experiment on their environment and discover things for themselves. This is reflected in the trend for student centred, discovery learning in schools, particularly in primary and early secondary education. Any return to traditional methods and content-laden syllabuses runs contrary to Piagetian principles.

2. Piaget believed that it was fruitless to expect children to grasp a concept for which they are **not cognitively ready**. The role of the teacher is to be aware of which stage a child has reached and provide the materials and activities which allow the child to move on at her own pace without having to make too big a jump. It is important to remember, especially when teaching mathematics and science, that children remain at the concrete operations stage for some considerable time. Abstract concepts such as molecular structure and the rules of geometry are best introduced by the use of three dimensional models and other appropriate 'concrete' stimuli.

3. It is important to provide the opportunity for **assimilation** (understanding new concepts and ideas with reference to what is already understood) and **accommodation** (having to change one's view and understanding of things in order to take on board something new). This may mean that every child will be moving at a different pace and discovering different things.

4. Piaget emphasised the importance of **social interaction** and **cooperation**, especially as a means of reducing egocentrism.

Bruner's theory of cognitive development

Bruner has been influenced by Piaget and there are significant similarities in their theories of cognitive development, the most important of which is that children learn through activity and discovery.

There are also important **differences** in the two approaches. One such difference is that Bruner does not explain cognitive development in terms of stages; instead, he describes it in terms of three main ways in which the child **internally represents the environment**. These modes of understanding and defining the world tend to emerge gradually as the child matures. The development of a new mode does not mean that previous modes are no longer used, a new mode is simply added to those already in existence. The three **modes of representation** are:

1. The **enactive** mode of representation is the only mode available to children in the first two years of life. In this mode the child understands the world entirely through action, never through imagery or words. In adulthood, we use this mode of representation to store information as to how to carry out motor activities such as swimming or riding a bike.

2. The **iconic** mode of representation begins to develop at about 18 months. This involves building up mental images of the environment. These images (which can be visual, auditory, tactile or olfactory) enable a child to construct a picture of the world, even if she cannot describe it in words. This mode allows the child to make plans about what she would like to do or where she would like to go, since she can now remember, for a while at least, what certain events are like. In adulthood the mode is used fairly extensively: for example, when writing a shopping list one may conjure up a mental image

of kitchen cupboard shelves to help organise thoughts about what is needed.

3. The **symbolic** mode of representation develops at approximately seven years of age. Bruner regarded this as a turning point in cognitive development because the child is now able to think in **language**. This frees her from the here and now and allows for more flexible, logical and abstract thought. Bruner believed that language is essential for logical thought and, in this, he differs from Piaget.

Language is the main symbolic system but not the only one. Number and music, for example, are represented symbolically in written form.

Which is the mode of representation principally used when you:

1. Write a letter?
2. Make a cup of coffee?
3. Follow a complicated recipe?
4. Give directions to the town centre?
5. Solve a murder?
6. Tie a shoelace?

The limitations of iconic thought

Bruner and Kenny (1966) devised an experiment that illustrates the child's dependence on language for logical and organised thought. Children were presented with a board containing nine glasses arranged in order of height and width (see Figure 8.5). The children were then asked to carry out two tasks:

- A **reproduction** task: all the glasses were removed and the children were asked to replace them in their original positions.
- A **transposition** task: all the glasses were removed and the one which had been in the bottom right hand square was replaced in the bottom left hand square. The children were then asked to replace the remaining glasses so the pattern was maintained, in other words they had to produce a mirror image of the original arrangement.

Children had no problem with the reproduction task but those who did not use the symbolic mode of representation (children under seven, on average) found the transposition task impossible. They could complete the reproduction task because this only required ionic representation, while the transposition task required symbolic thought. Older children, who could use language to guide them in their thought ('it gets fatter one way and taller the other way'), were able to complete the transposition task successfully.

Bruner's views on education

1. Bruner did not agree with the Piagetian view that teachers should wait for the child to be ready to learn, and he advocated a **more interventionist approach**. He believed that young children could gain an **intuitive understanding** of concepts if they were presented with them in an appropriate way.

2. He proposed the **'spiral curriculum'** by which he envisaged important issues and concepts being introduced to children at a young age and revisited at later stages at increasingly more sophisticated levels.

3. Bruner believed that the curriculum should be based around issues and values that are **important to society**, and believed that many subjects taught to young children served no useful purpose in adult life and merely cluttered the curriculum. He advocated that children should be encouraged to grasp the **structure of a discipline** rather than simply learn facts by rote.

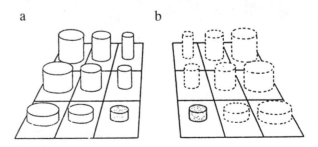

Figure 8.5 Bruner and Kenny's tests for the limitations of iconic thought
a Reproduction test
b Transposition test
Source: R.D. Gross, Psychology: The Science of Mind and Behaviour (Hodder & Stoughton, 1987), p. 497.

4. Bruner placed greater emphasis than did Piaget on the role of **language** in cognitive development, and argued that parents and teachers should encourage language skills through discussion and writing.

5. Like Piaget, Bruner believed that it is important to create classroom situations in which children can experiment and discover for themselves. The main area of difference between the two in terms of classroom practice was Bruner's greater emphasis on the need for **active intervention by the teacher**.

Preparing for the exam

Key terms

accommodation
adaptation
assimilation
clinical interview
concrete operational stage
conservation
decentre
egocentrism
enactive mode
equilibrium/disequilibrium
hypothetical tasks
iconic mode
irreversibility

moral realism
naturalistic observation
object permanence
operations
preoperational
reproduction task
schema/schemata
sensorimotor stage
spiral curriculum
symbolic mode
symbolic thought
transposition task

Types of exam question

1. Evaluation of theories of cognitive development with reference to research or educational practice.
2. Consideration of how cognitive development theories explain how children understand their environment.

Self-test questions

1. Describe what is meant by a 'schema' and how it is gradually adapted using assimilation and accommodation.
2. According to Piaget, what is the first stage of cognitive development? What ability marks its ending, and at approximately what age?
3. Briefly describe *three* characteristics of the second stage.
4. In Piagetian theory, what is an 'operation'?
5. Why is the last of Piaget's stages known as the formal operational stage?
6. How does a child learn in a Piagetian classroom?
7. What is the teacher's role in a Piagetian classroom?
8. Piaget and Bruner differ in their view on the role of language in cognitive development. Briefly explain how.
9. What are the *three* cognitive modes defined by Bruner?
10. What is the 'spiral curriculum'?

Exam question with guidance notes

a   Describe Piaget's ideas about the difference between preoperational
     and concrete operation thinking.   **(8 marks)**
b   Discuss one criticism of these ideas.   **(6 marks)**
c   Outline one way in which Piaget's work has been applied in the
     classroom situation with pre-operational children.   **(6 marks)**
                                                                          JMB (1991)

We shall examine each part in turn.

a

* Begin by defining the *nature* of operational thought, outlining the
  limitations of the preoperational thinker and showing how these limitations
  disappear as the child is able to perform operations provided material is
  presented in a concrete, familiar form.

* Bear in mind the number of marks for this question: it would be easy to
  write at great length about conservation experiments but don't fall into this
  trap: keep any evidence brief and concentrate on *theory*.

b

* The most obvious criticism made by some theorists is that children are not
  as limited in the preoperational stage as Piaget suggests. A number of
  studies show that children can conserve and decentre if they are asked in a
  manner to which they can relate: Rose and Blank, Samuel and Bryant (the
  Core Study), McGarrigle and Hughes have all conducted such studies.

c

* The application of Piaget's theory to classroom practice is covered well in
  the text. You could discuss the idea of learning through discovery, the use
  of suitably graded material, the role of the teacher, and so on.

Additional exam questions

1. Evaluate some theories of cognitive development in terms of their
   applications to education.   **(25 marks)**
                                                                          AEB (1988)

2. a Explain the main features of any **one** theory of cognitive development.
                                                                          (10 marks)

   b Discuss the extent to which this theory is supported by empirical
      research.   **(15 marks)**
                                                                          AEB AS (1992)

3. Critically evaluate Piaget's description of the cognitive abilities of the
   sensorimotor and preoperational stages of development.   **(20 marks)**
                                                                          JMB (1989)

4. Discuss how any *one* theory of cognitive development can be applied to
   education.   **(25 marks)**
                                                                          AEB (1994)

8.3 Play

Play is defined by Garvey (1977) as activities which:

1. Are regarded as **enjoyable** by the player.
2. Occur for their **own sake** – not in response to an outside objective.
3. Are **spontaneous** and **voluntary**.
4. Involve the player in an **active role**.
5. Can clearly be contrasted with 'non-play'. One child chasing another may be play in one case but not in another. It is through our knowledge and understanding of the **social context** in which the behaviour occurs that we are able to make the distinction.

Theories of the function of play

Development of intellectual skills

Bruner

Bruner saw play as a means of attaining cognitive and physical skills. In an unthreatening environment, the child is allowed to experiment with a number of different movements and skills which can later be combined to produce more complex activities.

Vygotsky

Vygotsky also stresses the cognitive value of play. He believes that, through play, children are able to construct make-believe circumstances which allow them to deal with situations and skills too complicated to cope with in real life. Thus children are able to attempt activities which are intellectually demanding and learn some of the important skills necessary for their successful mastery in later years. For example, a very small child may play at writing long before she or he is able to form letters or understand their meaning.

Piaget

Piaget believed that humans are constantly adapting to their environment and that adaptation takes place through the twin processes of accommodation and assimilation (these terms are explained in section 8.2 on Cognitive Development). During play, it is mainly assimilation which takes place as the child practises skills and bends reality to make it fit his or her particular view of life. When playtime ends, the child has to accommodate to reality.

Piaget defined **three** stages of play which correspond with the stages of intellectual development outlined in his theory of cognitive development:

Mastery play (corresponding to the sensorimotor stage, birth to 18 months): in this stage of play the child learns to manipulate and control objects and enjoys repetitive tasks

Symbolic or **make-believe play** (corresponding to the preoperational stage, two to seven years): the important feature of this stage is that the child uses one object to represent another, an essential feature of language which also begins at this time

Games with rules (corresponding to the concrete operational stage, seven years onwards): the child is now more logical and less egocentric, so better able to understand the concepts of cooperation, competition and fairness necessary for games incorporating rules.

Surplus energy theory

This theory is attributable to two philosophers, Herbert Spencer (1878) and before him Friedrich Von Schiller (18th century). The basic idea is that higher-order animals play because they do not use up all their energies in the mere process of survival and have 'surplus' energy that must find release. This would explain why children who have been kept inside for a long period tend to rush around on 'release'.

Nevertheless, it does not explain the very wide variety of play activities in which children engage, many of which involve little energy expenditure. Neither does it explain why children sometimes continue to play even when they are tired.

The practice of adult skills

Groos (1898, 1901) argued that, through play, important adult skills are practised and perfected. Kittens practise catching prey by stalking and pouncing on any convenient moving object, while human children observe and copy adult activities such as cooking, cleaning and child care. Groos believed that this was such an important function that it was the reason that humans have such a long childhood.

While there is a degree of **face validity** in this theory, in as much as children do observe and copy what they see around them, it does not account for the great variety of play in which children engage.

Activity

What is **face validity**? If you are not sure, refer to the section on validity of psychological tests in Chapter 11. This is an important concept which may be mentioned in a compulsory structured question.

Dealing with anxiety

In the **psychoanalytic** tradition play is seen as the natural medium of a child's self-expression and its main role is to provide a safe arena for dealing with anxieties and pent up emotions as well as an avenue for wish fulfilment. Play also provides a view of a child's unconscious mind, the equivalent of free association in adults.

Play therapy, a form of psychodynamic treatment for children, involves allowing the child a free choice of toys through which to 'play out' inner turmoil and anxiety in the presence of an accepting, non-directive adult therapist who can help the child discover the nature of his or her problems and work through them.

Development of social skills

It is through play that the young child learns how to be compatible with others, especially other children. The stages of social play listed in Table 8.1 have frequently been observed.

The child who is able to play cooperatively does not do so all the time but will often revert to parallel and solitary play. It is very important for children to have the experience of playing with other children because the ability to cooperate with others is a skill which is fundamental to the happiness and success of future life.

Table 8.1 The stages of play

Age	Play	Main features
0–2	Solitary	Child plays alone – little interaction
2–3	Parallel	Child plays alongside another without really cooperating or interacting
3+	Associative	Child's awareness of others increases as he or she begins to communicate with them
3+	Cooperative	Child begins to play games which require mutual cooperation.

Activity

Match each function with its corresponding theory in the following lists:

Function	Theory
A means of dealing with anxiety	Piaget
A means of learning to cooperate	Groos
A means of developing intellectual skills	Psychoanalytic theory
Practicing adult skills	Spencer and Schiller
Expending excess energy	Social skills development

Studies of play

Many theories of play have been proposed on an intuitive basis, with few, if any, empirical investigations to support them. Recently, more structured research has been undertaken into the nature and function of play.

Hutt (1966)

Hutt investigated exploratory play by giving three to five year olds a novel toy. They were presented with a red metal box on which a lever activated a number of interesting sounds and movements. The typical reaction to the box was one of curiosity and active experimentation. Having established what the box could do, the children started to incorporate it into their play. Hutt suggested that children proceed from **exploration** to **play**, and that these two behaviours are quite distinct.

Sylva, Roy and Painter (1980)

They carried out an observational study of preschool children in Oxfordshire in order to identify what kind of play activities had most value in terms of cognitive development. They identified 'complex' play, which has a high cognitive developmental yield and 'simple' play which does not. **Complex** play involves challenging activities which have clearly defined and achievable goals and includes such things as building, drawing and doing puzzles. **Simple** play includes such activities as unstructured social play and gross motor play. Between the two is play which produces some cognitive development but is not the best at achieving this end, activities such as pretend play, manipulating sand and play dough.

Connolly and Doyle (1984)

In a study of the social importance of play, they showed that the amount and sophistication of the fantasy play has a positive correlation with levels of **social competence**. Much sociodramatic play involves considerable negotiation about social roles, whilst rough and tumble play often involves considerable coordination skills.

In conclusion, the extensive research into the cognitive benefits of play has not conclusively demonstrated its advantages. Less research has been concerned with its social advantages, but the little which has been conducted indicates that these may be more extensive than the cognitive benefits. Few controlled studies have been conducted concerning the benefits of play as a means of emotional release. In all this theorising, let us not lose touch with the essence of play – that it is, besides all else, a valuable source of enjoyment for both adults and children.

Preparing for the exam

Key terms

associative play	play
complex play	simple play
cooperative play	solitary play
mastery play	Surplus energy theory
parallel play	symbolic play
play therapy	

Types of exam question

Most questions ask for a consideration of the nature and function of play.

Self-test questions

1. According to Garvey, what criteria does an activity need to meet in order to be regarded as play?
2. Name *three* theorists who recognise the intellectual function of play.
3. What are the *three* stages of play outlined by Piaget? To which stages of intellectual development do they correspond?
4. What are the stages of social play?
5. Whose theory:
   a Sees play as a means of getting rid of energy?

b Sees play as a means of practicing important adult skills?

c Sees play as a means of venting emotions and unconscious wishes?

6. According to Sylva *et al.* what is the difference between complex and simply play? Give an example of each.

Exam question with guidance notes

1. **Use psychological studies to discuss functions of play that may be related to social and cognitive development in children.** **(25 marks)**
AEB (1991)

Take careful note of the actual question: you need to use *actual studies* as a focus for discussing social and cognitive development.

- Introduce the essay with a *definition of play* and a brief statement to the effect that there are various theories concerning the *function* of play, two of which are that it helps develop intellectual and social skills.

- Sylva *et al.*'s study is a useful base for discussing theories concerned with *intellectual development*. You could usefully include Hutt's study as well and any others with which you are familiar (Piaget's studies, for example). Give an account of the studies and then move on to discuss the views of Bruner, Vygotsky and Piaget, all of whom emphasise the cognitive value of play.

- Similarly, Connolly and Doyle's study is a useful basis for discussing the *social value* of play. Include the social stages of play and comment on how each progressive stage requires greater and more complex negotiation between individuals.

- Conclude by mentioning that these two views of the function of play are in no way contradictory but are in fact *complementary*. Most research has focused on the cognitive value of play; little controlled research has been done on the social value of play but intuitively it seems likely that it is invaluable in encouraging cooperation and teaching negotiating skills. (Incidentally, there is some interesting research on gender differences in negotiation tactics in play, but that is beyond the scope of this book.)

Additional exam questions

1. Discuss *two* psychological explanations of the nature and function of play.
(25 marks)
AEB (1993)

(The examiners' report commented that some candidates wrote everything they knew about play, rather than focusing on *two* explanations.)

2. **a** Briefly outline *two* possible functions of play. **(6 marks)**

b Describe *one* empirical study in which play has been investigated.
(6 marks)

c Evaluate how this study contributes to our understanding of play in your children. **(8 marks)**
JMB (1992)

> **3.** **a** Name and briefly describe *three* functions of play for children.
> **(9 marks)**
>
> **b** Discuss, with reference to relevant studies, the importance of play for the development of social behaviour. **(11 marks)**
>
> **JMB (1989)**

8.4 Language acquisition

Language can be defined as an immensely complex system of communication which allows humans to share a wide range of sophisticated and abstract ideas.

The sequence of language development

The range of languages used by humans is wide but the **sequence** in which they develop is remarkably similar.

The pre-linguistic stage

a By six weeks the child begins **cooing** to express pleasure and thus engages the carer in conversation-like interaction.

Trevarthan and Snow (1974) studied babies up to six months of age and noted important 'pre-speech' behaviours which included speech-like movement of the mouth and tongue and low vowel sounds in response to adult speech directed at them.

b **Early babbling** is the first vocalising that sounds like human speech. Early babbling bears no relationship to what the infant hears; babies the world over babble in a similar way and deaf babies babble just as much as hearing babies.

c **Later babbling** does, however, depend on feedback. From around six months, deaf babies babble less while hearing babies babble more and begin to make sounds which are similar to the speech heard by the child.

Gradually, babbling begins to show signs of **intonation**, the rising and lowering of pitch which differentiates a question (you're going to bed?) from a statement or command (you're going to bed).

One-word stage

a At around a year, children begin to use recognisable words. These words tend to be those which are easy to pronounce and which refer to **familiar objects** or events (dada, byebye, doggie).

b During the next six to eight months, children build a large vocabulary of one-word 'sentences'. These single words are very often combined with gestures and convey a great deal of information which parents can usually glean from the context. When a single word is used to convey a whole sentence, then it is known as a **holophrase**. For example the word 'toy' may mean 'can I have that toy?' on one occasion or 'there's a toy in that shop window' on another occasion.

c Throughout the course of language development, comprehension (understanding) is more advanced than speech production.

Thompson and Chapman (1977), amongst others, have demonstrated that children can point to pictures of objects which they cannot name.

Sachs and Truswell (1978) demonstrated that although children in the one-word stage do not use grammatical constructions, they can understand simple verb–noun combinations such as 'tickle book', even though they are unlikely to have ever heard them before.

Activity

Think about how a single word such as 'mama' can, by intonation, become

- A question (is that you, mummy?)
- A plea for attention
- A plea not to be left
- A gleeful recognition of mother.

Early sentences

Stage 1 grammar (18 months to 30 months)

Children begin to put two words together ('daddy gone'; 'more sweets'). These early sentences are described by Brown (1970) as being **telegraphic** because the word order is similar to that used by adults but without any attempt at grammatical construction. So, for example, a child would say 'shoe foot' rather than 'put my shoe on my foot'. At this stage there are no plurals, tenses, conjunctives, articles or prepositions.

Stage 2 grammar

a By two years, sentences are longer and more complex. Children begin to use grammatical forms and to apply simple rules, such as adding -s to a noun to express a plural and -ed to verbs to express the past tense. The fact that they are applying rules rather than simply imitating is apparent when they make mistakes, for example, 'foots', 'sheeps', 'eated'. The tendency to make such grammatical errors is known as **overregularising**.

b One word may be used to refer to a whole class of objects or concepts, for example, 'daddy' used to refer to all men or 'moon' used to refer to everything round. This is known as **overgeneralisation** or **overextension**.

By the age of five years a child has learned many of the rules of language, has a vocabulary of around 2,500 words and makes sentences of six to eight words.

Theories of language development: the nature–nurture question

One of the longest ongoing debates concerning language acquisition is whether the ability to learn language is **innately** wired into our biology or whether we need to **learn** it.

Learning theory

Skinner believes that we learn language in the same way that we learn everything else, through the laws of **operant conditioning**: selective reinforcement,

shaping and imitation. He distinguishes **three** ways in which speech is reinforced:

1. The child uses **echoic responses**, imitations of what is heard.
2. The child produces a **mand**, a random sound like 'dede' to which adults attach meaning.
3. The child produces a **tact**, a correct sound in the presence of an object.

When children make a sound that resembles a real word, they often receive attention and smiles. Gradually, more and more accurate pronunciation is required before reinforcement is given; in this way, 'language behaviour' (Skinner's terminology) is **shaped** in a similar manner to other complex behaviours.

In recognition of the complexity of language, Skinner suggests that children do not learn specific and unique responses but a set of **response classes** that can be used in a range of circumstances. These response classes include the rules of grammar: a child does not learn every plural but the rule that an -s must be added.

Supportive evidence

1. Wulbert *et al.* (1975) compared children who were slow in developing speech with normal rate children. They found that mothers of slow developing children were less responsive verbally and emotionally.
2. Rheingold *et al.* (1959) found that the sounds made by infants as young as three months could be influenced by reinforcement.

Criticisms

1. Learning theory cannot account for
    a The speed and accuracy of language acquisition
    b The fact that children the world over go through the same sequence at approximately the same ages
    c How a child so easily applies complex grammatical rules
    d The frequency of new and creative utterances.
2. **Brown and Hanlon (1970)** observed that parents respond to factual accuracy and meaning but **not** to grammar. If they correct grammatical mistakes, it has little effect.

The nativist view

Chomsky (1968), a leading critic of the learning theory approach to language acquisition, offers the main alternative. Chomsky's view is that humans possess a brain mechanism for learning language which he calls the **Language Acquisition Device (LAD)**. This device enables children to understand the rules of grammar and apply them in their speech without being taught them.

Chomsky distinguishes between the **deep structure** and the **surface structure** of language:

- Deep structure refers to the **meaning of a sentence**
- Surface structure refers to the **grammatical form** the sentence takes.

For example the two sentences:

- The boy kicked the ball
- The ball was kicked by the boy

have the same meaning (deep structure) but different grammatical structure (surface structure).

Chomsky believes that the LAD is a prewiring of the nervous system that enables us to learn grammar by turning surface structure into deep structure. Chomsky believes that all languages share common characteristics at the deep level and differ only in their surface structure. It is the surface structure that children learn when exposed to language: the ability to transform what is said to what is meant and back again is innate.

Supportive evidence

1. Humans are **biologically equipped** for language. They have all the necessary vocal equipment and identified language areas in the brain. **Brain specialisation** indicates that humans are innately 'wired' for language acquisition. Furthermore, virtually all children, regardless of their intellectual ability, acquire language.

2. All over the world children acquire language in a **similar sequence**.
3. The fact that all languages share some common elements, known as **'linguistic universals'** (such as the use of verbs and nouns within a sentence) indicates an innate capacity for language in humans.

Criticisms

1. **Learning** must have a role in language acquisition as illustrated by studies showing the importance of supportive interaction (for example, Wulbert *et al.* 1975, cited earlier).
2. Recent evidence indicates that parents do provide **corrective feedback** about grammar (Bohannon and Stanowicz, 1988).
3. The assumption of a 'language acquisition device' is not an explanation. There is no account of what it **is**, how it **works** or of the **neural mechanisms** involved.

> Notice how the arguments in support of Chomsky tend to be the same as the criticisms of the learning theory approach.

The interactionist approach

Some theorists consider that, although Chomsky's approach is very valuable, it does not take sufficient account of the influence of **interaction**. Children need to speak to others on a one to one basis if they are to learn language; it is not sufficient for them simply to hear language being spoken around them. **Bruner** prefers the term **Language Acquisition Support System (LASS)**, acknowledging that there is a biological mechanism in the brain which enables language to be learned quickly and easily but which is not fully functional unless the child is given sufficient and appropriate **help** from adults.

Preparing for the exam

Key terms

babbling

cooing

deep structure

echoic responses

holophrase

intonation

Language Acquisition Device (LAD)

Language Acquisition Support System (LASS)

language

mand

overextension

overgeneralise

overregularise

prelinguistic stage

surface structure

tact

Types of exam question

Most exam questions require a discussion of theories of language development.

Self-test questions

1. Why is the prelinguistic stage important in the development of language?
2. What kind of words are likely to be a child's first?
3. What is meant by 'telegraphic speech'?
4. How does Skinner believe language is learned?
5. What does LAD stand for? To whose theory does it belong?
6. Distinguish between deep and surface structure of language. According to Chomsky, which is universal?
7. What evidence is there to support Chomsky's view of language?
8. What does LASS stand for and, according to Bruner, how does it operate?

Exam question with guidance notes

Critically evaluate theories of language acquisition in children. (25 marks)
AEB (1987)

This is obviously a very straightforward question but does *not* require you to write about the sequence of language development in children (as many candidates did).

- Introduce the essay with the *nature–nurture* question as it applies to language acquisition: is the ability to acquire language wired into the nervous system or is it learned in the same way that other abilities are?
- Give an account of *Skinner*'s theory with supporting evidence and arguments against it.
- Do likewise with *Chomsky*'s theory, including an explanation of exactly what LAD is hypothesised to do and the criticisms of this concept in terms of its vagueness and lack of explanatory power.

- Finally, present the *interactionist* view which can be seen as somewhat of a compromise between these two positions, although it leans more towards the Chomskian view.

Additional exam questions

1. Describe and evaluate **two** theories that attempt to explain the acquisition of language in humans. **(25 marks)**
   AEB AS (1994)

2. What do empirical studies tell us about factors that influence children's language development? **(20 marks)**
   JMB (1989)

8.5 Moral development

The study of moral development is concerned with the process by which children adopt and internalise the rules and expectations of society and develop a sense of right and wrong.

There are three main classes of theory concerned with how a child acquires this sense of morality:

1. Psychoanalytic theory: **Freud**.
2. Social learning theory: **Bandura**.
3. Cognitive theories: **Piaget** and **Kohlberg**.

Psychoanalytic theory

You need to refer to Freud's theory in Chapter 2. Important points as far as moral development is concerned are:

1. It is the **superego** that is the moral part, a kind of 'internal parent' which comments on all our behaviours and thoughts and passes judgements on them. It consists of two parts:

   The **conscience**, which is the part that tells us what we **should not** do and punishes wrong doings with feelings of anxiety and guilt. It represents the 'punishing parent'.

   The **ego ideal**, which is the part that tells us what we **should** do, what is right. It represents the 'rewarding parent'.

2. The superego emerges as a result of the resolution of the **Oedipus complex**, when the child identifies with the parent of the same sex. Freud argued that the fact that girls have a less powerful reason for identification than boys is reflected in the supposition that women are generally less moral than men.

Why do girls have a less powerful reason for identification than boys?
   Note that although Freud's theory of psychosexual development is a stage theory, his theory of moral development is **not** a stage theory, since the process occurs during only **one** of the psychosexual stages.

Evaluation

The evaluation in Chapter 2 is relevant here. Additional points are that:

1. Freud's theory implies that the superego emerges during the phallic stage; morality should then come upon a child very suddenly, somewhere around his or her fifth birthday. There is no evidence that this is the case; all the evidence suggests that morals are acquired **gradually**.

2. Freud based his theory, including the concept of the Oedipus complex, upon data obtained from the clinical case studies he made of his **adult patients** who were years removed from the experience. The only child Freud studied was 'Little Hans', and then only by correspondence.

3. There is no empirical evidence to support Freud's contention that men have stronger consciences than do women. Hoffman (1975) reviewed a number of studies in which children were tempted to disobey with apparently little chance of being detected. These studies revealed **no sex differences** overall, although one or two studies showed that girls were more likely to resist temptation than were boys.

4. Freud's theory is, of course, dependent on the universal existence of the Oedipus complex. Malinowski (1929) studied Trobriand Islanders in the South Pacific and found no evidence that the Oedipus complex was ever experienced by young boys.

Learning theory and social learning theory

Traditional learning theorists argue that morality is learned in much the same way as any other behaviour, through classical and operant conditioning, discussed in detail in Chapter 2.

1. Initially, children's behaviour is controlled through the use of punishments and reinforcements by parents and other key adults. Children experience a sense of anxiety when punishment is given and a sense of well-being when reinforced.

2. Eventually, through classical conditioning, they come to associate these feelings with the acts that produce the reinforcements or punishments rather than the reinforcements or punishments themselves. This means that they will experience anxiety for doing something for which they have previously been punished, even in the absence of an authority figure. Likewise, they will associate certain actions with a sense of well-being and self-worth.

3. In this way a sense of conscience becomes **internalised**, in that it becomes independent (though never completely) of outside influences.

Social learning theorists take account of the role taken by classical and operant conditioning, but also lay great emphasis on the role of **observation** and **identification** in the development of morality.

Children copy and identify with models observed from a variety of sources, from real-life models in their own environment to characters in books and television. They therefore learn their morality from the models around them.

Social learning theorists argue that the development of moral thinking in children is not a process which occurs in stages, but gradually. It becomes internalised and more sophisticated because of several changes in the child's experience and understanding:

1. As children develop, they are able to respond to more varied types of reinforcers and punishments.
2. They are better able to anticipate potential rewards and punishments, so they do not have to experience them in order to fear them or appreciate them.
3. They also begin to be able to provide themselves with rewards and punishments, both in the abstract by feelings of guilt or pride and in more concrete terms.

Evaluation

1. This theory is based on principles of learning which have been well established in other contexts and have some **predictive** value.
2. Probably the most serious shortcoming of social learning theory in the area of moral development is that it is based on controlled laboratory studies, often involving a single adult–child interaction. This lacks **ecological validity** since the child's socialisation process is infinitely more complex than this.

Activity

1. In what ways do individuals, including you, reward themselves?
2. How do they reprimand themselves?
3. What greater variety of rewards and punishments can be used on an older child which would not be effective with a younger child?
4. What is the main source of guilt according to (a) Freud and (b) Social learning theory?

The cognitive approach

Piaget's theory

Piaget regarded moral development as an important aspect of the totality of cognitive development. He investigated moral development by using the following procedures:

1. Asking children about the rules of the game of marbles – believing that their grasp of the rules of this game would be similar to their grasp of the rules of society.
2. Investigations of children's responses to various moral dilemma stories in which consequences and intentions had to be taken into account.
3. Asking children their views on punishment and justice.

Piaget proposed that children up to the age of about three years were **premoral**, unable to understand rules and therefore unable to make moral judgements. On the basis of his investigations, he distinguished **two** stages of moral development.

Heteronomous morality or moral realism

This stage applies from about three to six or seven years and is categorised by the following beliefs:

1. Rules are **absolute and sacred**, and should not, therefore, be changed.
2. Actions are either **totally right or totally wrong** with no allowance made for circumstances. Consequences are seen as being more important than the intention of a deed, thus a child who breaks ten cups whilst trying to be helpful is naughtier than the child who breaks one cup while being disobedient.
3. Naughtiness will always be punished, if not by parents or teachers, then by God. The belief that punishment is an inevitable consequence of wrong doing is known as **imminent justice**. Naughtiness must be severely punished.
4. **Obedience to authority** is seen as being of more importance than loyalty to friends.

Autonomous morality or moral relativism

This stage applies from around six or seven years onwards and the child now holds the following beliefs:

1. Rules are **flexible**, a product of agreement and for the benefit of all. They can therefore be changed if everyone is in agreement.
2. **Intentions** are seen as being more important than the consequences of a deed.
3. Punishments should **reflect the crime**, designed to make the offender reflect on their naughtiness. The belief in imminent justice declines.
4. **Loyalty** to friends is seen as being more important than obedience to authority.

The shift from heteronomous morality to autonomous morality has two principal causes:

1. Changes in cognitive development
2. Changes in the type and number of relationships in the child's life.

As the child moves from the preoperational stage of cognitive development to the operational stage (these stages are explained in section 8.2), thinking becomes more flexible and there is a dramatic decline in egocentricity. A child is obviously able to understand more about rules, the causes of naughty behaviour and the role of punishment.

The heteronomous stage involves a unilateral respect for authority, whereas the autonomous stage represents equality with peers. As children's level of understanding broadens, adults are able to reason with them and tend to become less authoritarian in the way they treat them. At the same time children establish more egalitarian relationships (friendships on an equal basis). This, combined with the decline in egocentrism, provides them with an understanding of how others feel, and the intentions behind others' actions. As they gain more experience of social interactions, children also begin to appreciate that rules serve everyone and should be a product of agreement rather than inflexible instructions imposed from outside.

Evaluation

1. Research supports Piaget's view that children up to about seven years are more influenced by

consequences than by intentions but on some occasions very young children can appreciate the importance of motive. Karniol (1978) has criticised the method of posing dilemmas and the actual stories used.

2. Despite these criticisms, children of nine or ten are far more likely to judge by intentions than are younger children, showing that the shift from consequences to intentions is an accurate portrayal of a child's moral development.

Kohlberg's theory

Kohlberg's theory of moral development overlaps that of Piaget and extends into consideration of the moral code of adolescents and young adults. He also used moral dilemma stories, the most famous of which is the following:

> In Europe, a woman was near death from a special kind of cancer. There was one drug that the doctor thought might save her. It was a form of radium that a druggist in the same town had recently discovered. The drug was expensive to make, but the druggist was charging ten times what the drug cost him to make. He paid 200 dollars for the radium and charged 2000 dollars for a small dose of the drug. The sick woman's husband, Heinz, went to everyone he knew to borrow the money, but could only get together about 1000 dollars which is half of what it cost. He told the druggist that his wife was dying, and asked him to sell it cheaper or let him pay later. But the druggist said 'No, I discovered the drug and I'm going to make money from it.' So Heinz got desperate and broke into the man's store to steal the drug for his wife.
>
> Should Heinz have done that? Why or why not?

From the responses he received to this and other dilemmas, Kohlberg devised a theory of moral development involving **three** levels of reasoning, as shown in Table 8.2.

Like Piaget, Kohlberg believes that moral development is limited by the stage of **cognitive development** a person has achieved.

A number of studies lend some support to Kohlberg's stage theory, most notably his own study (Kohlberg, 1969). Rest (1983) conducted a

Table 8.2 Kohlberg's theory of moral development: levels of reasoning

Stage	Characteristic
Preconventional	
Stage 1 Punishment and obedience orientation	The child decides what is wrong on the basis of what is punished
Stage 2 Instrumental relativist orientation	Good behaviour is that which is rewarded
Conventional	
Stage 3 Good boy/nice girl orientation	Good behaviour is that which pleases others and which is socially acceptable; 'being good' is important for its own sake
Stage 4 Law and order orientation	Being good or moral involves obeying the law and doing one's duty
Postconventional	
Stage 5 Social contract Legalistic orientation	Being good means respecting others' views and acting for the greater good; laws and rules should be upheld in order to preserve social order but they can be changed
Stage 6 Universal–ethical principles orientation	Being good now means following self-chosen ethical principles even if they clash with the law and the expectations of others; conscience dominates over the law

longitudinal study over twenty years and found that the stages do occur in the order suggested by Kohlberg, but that movement from stage to stage is very slow and many people do not reach the final stages. Kohlberg himself later admitted that his own more recent research (1978) showed there to be doubt as to whether the last stage exists at all apart from very rare cases.

Evaluation

1. The **scoring** of the responses to dilemmas has been criticised as unreliable and subjective. Kohlberg has now developed a new scoring system which has been shown to have greater reliability.

2. Moran and Joniak (1979) have shown that the level of morality is linked to the level of **sophistication** in language use. It is therefore possible that children apparently in the preconventional level of morality have a much more profound understanding of right and wrong than they are able to verbalise.

3. A number of critics argue that moral development is culturally relative and it is **ethnocentric** to argue that one level is higher than another. Snarey (1985), in a review of 17 cross-cultural studies, found that stages one to four were found in all societies at approximately the same ages. However, few studies found Stage 5 reasoning. Snarey and others argue that Kohlberg's Stage 5 is culturally biased, reflecting the individualistic, capitalistic orientation of Western middle class society.

4. The dilemmas used by Kohlberg have been criticised on the grounds that they involve situations which are **unfamiliar** and **irrelevant** to the lives of most people.

5. Carol Gilligan (1982) criticises the fact that all of Kohlberg's participants were **male**. The stages cannot, therefore, be assumed to apply to females.

Preparing for the exam

Key terms

autonomous morality	moral development
classical conditioning	moral realism
conscience	moral relativism
conventional morality	operant conditioning
ego ideal	postconventional morality
heteronomous morality	preconventional morality
identification	psychosexual development
imminent justice	superego

Types of exam question

Most exam questions require a discussion of the different theories of moral development, and the extent to which moral development occurs in stages.

Self-test questions

1. What is moral development?
2. Give a brief description of Freud's theory of moral development.
3. Explain how morality could be learned through classical conditioning.
4. According to Piaget what are the main features of the heteronomous stage of morality?
5. What is the next stage, and when do children move into it?
6. Outline *two* differences and *two* similarities between Piaget's and Kohlberg's theories of moral development.

7. What are the *three* levels of moral reasoning defined by Kohlberg?

Exam question with guidance notes

Critically discuss some of the theories of moral development. **(25 marks)**
AEB (1987)

Although this is a straightforward question, note that you are being asked to *critically discuss*, and so description should be kept to a minimum. It also asks for *some* theories, which obviously means more than one.

- You could discuss psychoanalytic theory, learning theory and *one* of the cognitive theories. This offers a good balance and gives plenty of scope for critical discussion.
- Psychoanalytic theory requires you to give an account of the Oedipus complex and the resulting identification with the same-sex parent. Discuss the problems which Freud suggests will arise from failure to resolve this complex and the purported differences between girls and boys in terms of morality. Evaluation of this theory is covered in the text. Freudian theory sees moral development as a relatively *sudden* process occurring during the phallic stage, morality being fully internalised by the age of six years or so.
- In contrast, learning theory (and social learning theory) see moral development as a *gradual* process, dependent on the internalisation of rewards and punishments, the association of anxiety, guilt and shame with certain acts and increased self-esteem with others. Studies in support of the theory are mainly laboratory-based and therefore may lack ecological validity and seriously underestimate the complexity of the socialisation process. These studies also tend to look at moral *behaviour* rather than moral attitudes. Nevertheless, the principles of learning are tried and tested and anxiety and guilt have been shown to be powerful determinants of behaviour.
- The cognitive theories are stage theories, in contrast to both of the above. They maintain that moral thinking is dependent on *cognitive development* as well as social factors. There is extensive evaluation in the text.

Additional exam questions

1. **a** Outline Kohlberg's theory of moral development. **(6 marks)**
  b Discuss *one* strength and *one* weakness of Kohlberg's theory.
  (6 marks)
  c Discuss *two* differences between the approaches of Freud and Kohlberg to moral development. **(8 marks)**
  NEAB (1993)

2. Discuss psychodynamic *and* social learning theories of moral development. **(25 marks)**
  AEB (1994)

8.6 Gender roles

Sex refers to the **biological differences** between males and females.

Gender is a psychological concept and refers to sex-related **behaviours** and **attitudes**.

Gender roles are patterns of behaviour considered appropriate for males and females in any society.

Gender identity refers to the individual's **awareness** of themselves as a member of a particular sex.

Not only are boys and girls physically different, they behave differently. For example, boys are physically and verbally more aggressive than girls and tend to do better in mathematics. Girls score higher than boys on tests of verbal ability (Maccoby and Jacklin, 1974).

The focus of attention for psychologists is the extent to which any behavioural and personality differences between males and females are due to

- Inherent, **biological** factors, or
- **Differential treatment** of the two sexes.

Activity

1. What is meant by 'differential treatment' of the two sexes?
2. In what ways, if any, are boys and girls treated differently by parents, teachers and their friends?
3. Think of an example of gender roles (patterns of behaviour which society encourages to be different for males and females) as they exist in your society.

The effect of biological factors

Sex hormones

1. Sex hormones are responsible for the formation of different sex organs and some researchers suggest that they may influence the developing brain in a way that predisposes individuals to behave in sex stereotyped ways (Diamond, 1977; Money, 1987). Research on brain differences is ongoing and the evidence still inconclusive.
2. Much of the research linking sex hormones to behaviour comes from the study of animals. Female rats who are prenatally exposed to male hormones are more aggressive and less likely than normal females to care for their young. Similar findings have been demonstrated in monkeys.

Activity

Why should we be very wary of generalising from animals to humans? If in doubt, look at section 10.6 on the use of animals in psychological research. You can use this to **evaluate** the view that biological differences affect behaviour *in humans*.

3. Money and Ehrhardt (1972) studied a group of girls who had been prenatally exposed to high levels of male hormones and found that they were more tomboyish and less likely to play with other girls than were a control group of girls of the same age. However, these girls did have a fairly masculine appearance and this may have influenced the way in which they were treated.

The effects of socialisation

Whatever the effect of biological factors, most psychologists agree that socialisation is a major determinant in gender role behaviour. There is a wealth of evidence that boys and girls are treated differently right from birth:

1. **Rubin *et al.*** (1974) found that when parents were asked to describe their newborn infants, sons were considered strong, active and well coordinated, girls as little, delicate, beautiful and weak. Since the researchers matched infants on size, weight and muscle tone, these descriptions must represent the differential **expectations** of the parents rather than any actual physical differences.
2. Fathers are more likely than mothers to describe their children in **sex-typed language** and to treat them differently. They are more concerned with

the cognitive development of their sons than of their daughters; girls are more encouraged to develop social skills than are their brothers (Block *et al.*, 1974).

3. Sears *et al.* (1957) found evidence that parents expect and encourage **aggression** in boys but not in girls. If provoked, girls often learn to feel anxious about the possibility of acting aggressively, boys learn that they are expected to retaliate (Frodi *et al.*, 1977).

4. Parents are not the only socialising agents; **peers** are a powerful influence in the development of gender differentiation. Boys are especially sensitive to such insults as being referred to as a 'cissy'. Children as young as three years will abandon a toy if other children criticise them for playing with it (Lamb, 1982).

5. Yet another powerful influence is the **media**. In an analysis of children's television favourites, Sternglanz and Serbin (1974) found that male characters were typically presented as being aggressive and constructive, whereas females were deferential and passive.

Theories of sex typing

Four theories attempt to account for the development of sex typing:

Freud's psychoanalytic theory

This holds that children identify with the same-sex parent in order to resolve the Oedipus complex (see Chapter 2). This theory implies that children assume sex appropriate behaviour to the extent that the same-sex parent exhibits it.

Social learning theory

This maintains that sex roles are learned through reinforcement, observation and modelling. Sex appropriate behaviour is reinforced by parents and others who also provide models of what type of behaviour is expected. The studies on the effects of socialisation (mentioned earlier) support this view.

Cognitive developmental theory

Kohlberg (1966) argues that children have to gain an understanding of **gender identity** before they begin to imitate same-sex models. Gender identity involves an awareness an individual has of themselves as a member of a certain sex. This occurs at around three years and thereafter children actively sex type themselves because they wish to be accepted into the group of which they are a member.

Whereas social learning theorists believe that reinforcement for sex appropriate behaviour stems from parents, peers and other outside influences, cognitive theorists maintain that simply belonging to, and being accepted by, one's own sex group is, in itself, strongly reinforcing.

Kohlberg's theory cannot, however, explain why children begin to display sex appropriate behaviour before they understand gender identity nor why many girls who have stable self-concepts value masculine activities.

Gender schema theory

Bem (1985) suggests that we are all cognitively programmed to organise information in terms of schemata and that, in many societies, gender is the most powerful organising schema of all. This means that being male or female is, according to society, of the utmost importance and leads to different expectations of the two sexes. Like social learning theory, this theory holds that sex typing is **learned** but in addition to this, society adds an extra dimension by deeming this particular schema to be of such importance.

The fact that males and females are expected to behave in certain ways is limiting to both sexes. It forces them into certain stereotyped roles and compels them to deny aspects of their personality which may not fit the expected form.

Core Study

The measurement of psychological androgyny: S.L. Bem (1974)

The idea that masculinity and feminity are bipolar ends of a single continuum is popular but denies two possibilities:

1. People might be androgynous, that is **both** masculine **and** feminine (for example, both assertive and yielding).
2. Strongly sex-typed people are seriously limited in the range of **behaviours** available to them.

Bem's research concerns the development of a sex role inventory that does not present masculinity/feminity at opposite ends of a continuum.

The Bem Sex Role Inventory (BSRI)

This differs from previous masculinity/feminity scales because:

1. It includes both a masculinity scale **and** a feminity scale
2. It includes characteristics which were selected as masculine or feminine on the basis of sex-typed social desirability
3. It characterises a person as masculine, feminine or androgynous on the basis of the difference between his or her approval of masculine and feminine personality characteristics
4. It includes a social desirability scale which is **neutral** with respect to sex and designed to ensure that the scale is not simply measuring social desirability.

Item selection

The final items were chosen on the basis of how desirable they were considered to be for each sex.

An eventual list of 20 characteristics each for masculinity, feminity and neutral items was chosen.

- **Masculine** items included: acts as a leader, aggressive, ambitious, analytical, assertive
- **Feminine** items included: affectionate, cheerful, childlike, compassionate, does not use harsh language
- **Neutral** items included: adaptable, concerted, conscientious, conventional, friendly.

Scoring

The BSRI asks a person to indicate on a seven-point scale how well each of the masculine, feminine and neutral personality characteristics describes him/herself. The scale ranges from 1 (almost never true) to 7 (always or almost always true).

Each person receives a masculinity score, a femininity score and, most important, an androgyny score; in addition, a social desirability score can be calculated. The androgyny score is a reflection of the relative amounts of masculinity/feminity included in the self-description.

If the score on masculinity/feminity differs greatly, then the individual is sex-typed; if they are similar they are androgynous.

Psychometric analysis

The BSRI was administered to 444 male and 279 female psychology students and 117 and 77 female paid volunteers at Foothill Junior College. Their data represents the normative data.

The score was proved to be internally consistent and test–retest reliability was high.

It was found that the BSRI did not correlate significantly with other sex-type measures, probably because it is measuring a different aspect of sex roles.

It was important to establish that the androgyny score was not simply tapping social desirability. Since correlations between androgyny scores and scores on social desirability were near zero, this confirmed that the androgyny score was not simply measuring social desirability.

Norms

A summary of the results is shown in Table 8.3 (summating both samples).

Table 8.3 Summary of BSRI results

	Females (%)	Males (%)
Feminine	37	7
Near feminine	14	7
Androgynous	32	39
Near masculine	9	18
Masculine	8	29

It can be seen from these results that androgyny is quite common.

Conclusion

It is time to question the traditional assumption that it is the sex-typed individual who represents mental health, and to begin to investigate the social consequences of a more flexible sex role self-concept: 'In a society where rigid sex-role differentiation has already outlived its utility, perhaps the androgynous person will come to define a more human standard of psychological health.'

QUESTIONS

1. Why does Bem challenge the idea that masculinity and feminity are bipolar ends of a single continuum?
2. How many items were selected for the Bem Sex Role Inventory (BSRI)? How were they chosen?
3. How is the BSRI scored?
4. How did Bem establish that the androgeny score was not just tapping social desirability?
5. Why does Bem consider androgyny to be psychologically healthy?

Preparing for the exam

Key terms

Cognitive development theory   gender
Gender schema theory   sex hormones
gender identity   sex
gender roles   socialisation

Types of exam question

Most exam questions require a discussion of theories of the construction of gender roles.

Self-test questions

1. What is meant by the following terms:
   a Sex?
   b Gender roles?
   c Gender identity?
2. What differences are consistently observed in the behaviour of girls and boys?
3. Briefly describe a study that indicates that sex hormones are responsible for sex differences.
4. Briefly describe a study that indicates that sex differences are due to differences in socialisation.
5. Describe how the following theorists account for sex differences:
   a Freud
   b Bem
   c Kohlberg.

Exam question with guidance notes

Critically consider the view that gender roles are socially constructed.

(25 marks)
AEB (1992)

This question is asking you to critically consider the extent to which gender roles are learnt as a consequence of socialisation. Since it is a 'critically consider' question you must present the arguments both *for* and *against*.

- Begin by defining the terms *gender* and *gender roles*. It may be helpful to provide a succinct example of gender roles (for example, in many societies, men are less likely than women to show emotional dependency).
- Point out that the *construction* of sex roles is an example of the nature–nurture debate and is difficult to investigate. (For reasons discussed in section 10.3 on the nature–nurture issue in Chapter 10).
- Social learning theory argues that gender roles are *socially constructed* and the studies considering the effects of socialisation support this view; you should make reference to a good range of these.
- Cognitive development theory and gender schema theory also agree that sex roles are socially constructed and should be discussed because they each offer a slightly different perspective.
- The main opposition to the view that sex roles are socially constructed is the view that they are *biologically determined*. The evidence that supports this view and an evaluation of this evidence should be presented.
- It would be reasonable to conclude that sex roles are socially constructed, at least in part. The extent to which *biology* is implicated in their construction is difficult to determine and remains a matter of controversy.

8.7 The development of self and self-esteem

The development of a sense of self is one of the most critical processes of the child's early life.

According to Murphy (1947) 'The self is the individual as known to the individual', and the study of the development of the self-concept is concerned with how the child forms a sense of who they are.

Stages in the development of a self-concept

Lewis (1990) considers that the development of self involves **two** main steps, the first involved an awareness of a sense of **separateness**, the second involves an increasing sense of **self-awareness**.

Stage 1: the existential self

During the second or third month of life the infant begins to realise that he and the rest of the world are not one entity. Maccoby suggests that the evidence by which the infant reaches this conclusion comes from **two** sources:

1. **Physical sensations:** the child becomes aware, for example, that if he falls over, it hurts but if someone else suffers the same fate, he himself feels no pain.
2. **An awareness of control:** he learns that his actions have certain consequences; if he touches a mobile, it moves.

Stage 2: the categorical self

For a full sense of self, the child must define himself in terms of his own qualities. This process is referred to as the 'categorical self' because it takes the form of placing oneself in an ever-increasing number of categories. Some of the first categories that the child identifies are **size**, **age** and **gender**. The self-concept changes as the child develops. Very young children think of themselves only in terms of **physical** characteristics; gradually they incorporate **moods** and **preferences**, and finally they include **interpersonal traits**, morals and life philosophies.

Studying self awareness

Lewis and Brooks (1978) used **the 'rouge' test** to try and determine just when a child has developed self-awareness. They secretly applied a dot of rouge to babies' noses and then placed them in front of a mirror. The test of self-recognition and, therefore, awareness of self, is whether they touch their own nose or the nose in the mirror. Babies between nine and twelve months never touched their noses but by 21 months, about 75 per cent of children did so. Self-recognition appears to begin about half way through a child's second year.

Lewis and Brooks-Gunn (1979) found that, when shown a picture of themselves, one year old children will refer to the picture as 'baby'. Shortly before they reach two, they will use their **own** name and by the age of three they can refer to themselves by use of appropriate pronouns, 'it's me'.

Factors involved in the development of the self-concept

Argyle distinguishes **four** factors which he believes have an important role to play in the development of the self-concept:

- The reactions of others
- Comparison with others
- Social roles
- Identification.

The reactions of others

We have already seen, in section 4.3 on the Social self, how Cooley, Mead and Goffman emphasise the importance of others in the development of a self-concept. Particularly important are those people who are very influential in our lives, persons such as parents and close friends.

The very young child has no frame of reference for evaluating the opinions of others and comes to accept as 'fact' these judgements. Children frequently hear such comments as 'You're so clumsy' or 'She's very shy'. Eventually, they **assimilate** these opinions into their self-concept and they then form part of their **self-attributions**, in that they then use these terms to describe themselves. Argyle uses the term **introjection** to describe the process by which we incorporate the opinions, attitudes and reactions of others into our self concept.

Guthrie (1938) provides a clear example of how the reactions of others are incorporated into our view of self. He describes how a group of male students decided to treat a dull, unattractive female student as if she were an extremely popular and attractive girl, taking it in turns to ask her out. Within a short period the girl had responded to this positive feedback by becoming more confident and fun-loving and therefore more attractive. Their trick worked as a **self fulfilling prophecy** and clearly changed the girl's self-image.

Comparison with others

Many aspects of the self-concept can only be seen **in relation to others**: the term 'intelligent' implies that one person is more intelligent than another. Similarly, one can only be considered 'tall' if most others are shorter in stature. Rosenburg (1965), in a study of adolescents, found higher self-esteem among those who, by their own comparison with others, did better at school and were leaders in their social groups.

Social roles

The social roles we play also affect our self-image. Young children make very little use of roles in the development of their self concept, using mainly physical characteristics as a means of self-description. As individuals get older, they incorporate more and more roles in their self-image partly because they gradually fulfil more roles and also because their ideas of self become less concentrated on physical factors and increasingly influenced by interpersonal factors. Throughout life roles change, and with them so does the self-concept. Many of these changes are gradual, as is the change from child to adult. Others are more sudden, like the change from worker to unemployed or retired.

Identification

Identification involves incorporating the characteristics of another person into the self-concept; a process which can occur consciously or unconsciously. We have already seen how Freud uses the concept of identification to describe the process by which children unconsciously take on the characteristics of the same-sex parent.

The development of self-esteem

Self-esteem is the **evaluative** part of the self concept and is the degree to which we value ourselves. Self-esteem is a particularly important aspect of self because it can strongly influence our thoughts, moods and behaviour:

- Those with **high self-esteem** meet their own standards, have a sense of their worth and are generally satisfied with themselves
- Those with **low self-esteem** see a discrepancy between what they would like to be and what they actually are.

It is difficult to pinpoint exactly how we come to place a value on ourselves; it is certainly not based on any objective measure and may be far removed from the value others place upon us.

The Coopersmith (1968) study of the development of self-esteem

Coopersmith conducted a longitudinal study of hundreds of boys, following their progress from age ten through to early adulthood. All were from middle class families and there were no significant differences between them in terms of intelligence and physical attractiveness. Based on a variety of measures of self-esteem the boys were categorised as being either high, medium or low in self-esteem:

- Boys high in self-esteem were confident, academically successful and popular
- Boys low in self-esteem were, according to Coopersmith, 'a sad little group', fearful, isolated, self-conscious, underachievers and very sensitive to criticism.

To a large extent these differences continued into adulthood.

Coopersmith found a difference in **parental attitudes** and rearing styles between the high and low esteem groups:

1. The parents of boys high in self-esteem similarly valued themselves highly, were firm but fair in their discipline techniques, and, above all, had a positive and accepting attitude towards their sons
2. The parents of the boys low in self-esteem were inconsistent in the treatment of their children, made little attempt to consult them and left them confused as to what was expected of them.

Coopersmith's data is only correlational and therefore we can draw no firm conclusions as to cause and effect, neither can we generalise his findings to girls or those in the lower socioeconomic classes, but his findings do provide the basis on which some hypotheses concerning the development of self-esteem could be formulated and tested.

Self-esteem as a multidimensional concept

Harter (1982) believes that we need to consider children's self-esteem not as a single concept but in terms of **three** areas of life:

- Intellectual achievement
- Physical skills
- Interpersonal relationships.

Harter found that children often rate themselves differently in these different domains; thus a child who feels that he is 'clever' may also consider himself to be clumsy and unpopular.

Research indicates that the level of self-esteem fluctuates during childhood. It falls sharply between the ages of 11 and 13 but rises steadily after this. Self-esteem, therefore, is not fixed, but does appear to be a fairly stable personality characteristic after the age of about seven or eight (Harter, 1990).

Since low levels of self-esteem can be a major contributor towards unhappiness, depression and serious mental disturbance, this is an area which warrants serious research.

Preparing for the exam

Key terms

assimilate

categorical self

existential self

identification

introjection

self-attributions

self-awareness

self-concept

self-esteem

self-fulfilling prophecy

self

social roles

Types of exam question

1. Consideration of how a child develops a sense of self.
2. Discussion of the role of socialisation in the development of self.

Self-test questions

1. What is:
   a the existential self?
   b the categorical self?
2. Argyle identifies *four* ways in which a child develops a sense of self. What are they?
3. Describe how the reaction of others can shape our view of self.
4. Briefly describe the illustration provided by Guthrie (1938) of how this can occur.
5. In Coopersmith's study of self-esteem, describe the difference between high and low self-esteemers.
6. Coopersmith found a difference in parental attitudes and treatment between high- and low-esteem boys. Briefly describe his findings.
7. Why can we not assume that styles of parenting **caused** the boys to have high or low esteem?

Exam question with guidance notes

Critically consider the view that the self develops as a result of socialisation processes.

(25 marks)

AEB (1993)

- Begin by stating that socialisation is the process by which a person comes to behave in ways that society *expects* and *requires*. Briefly relate the *two* stages of development of self-awareness, with emphasis on the categorical self since categories depend to a large extent on socialisation. (Even the early basic categories like size or gender are products of socialisation since they are a product of feedback by parents and other significant people in the child's life.)
- Socialisation is very much concerned with the *feedback* we are given by others, and the people and roles we observe and with whom we identify.

All of these are covered in *Argyle*'s four factors, so discuss all of these, using the correct psychological terminology such as assimilation, introjection, identification.

- *Self-esteem* is an essential part of the self concept, so *Coopersmith*'s research and its implications can very usefully be included.
- Research into *sex roles* indicates that girls and boys are socialised differently and this clearly affects their sense of self. (This is not essential material but it is relevant. You will need to refer to the section on gender in this chapter and *very briefly* refer to research on how differential treatment of males and females leads to different self concepts.)
- As you are asked to *critically discuss* it is advisable to include a view that argues that the self is formed in some other way. Bem's self-perception theory could be used (see section 4.3 on the Social self).
- An appropriate conclusion would be that socialisation is clearly very important in the development of self and self-esteem and that child rearing practices, amongst other things, make a crucial difference to how we see ourselves and the extent to which we value ourselves.

Additional exam question

How does a child develop a sense of self-esteem and self-image.   **(25 marks)**
AEB (1988)

8.8 Adolescence

Adolescence is the stage of life that begins at the onset of puberty, the age at which a young person starts to become sexually mature. The end point of adolescence is not easy to pinpoint, as there is no convenient physical marker; it tends to be determined by **psychosocial factors** such as the assumption of adult roles and, therefore, varies greatly from culture to culture.

Adolescence as a time of 'storm and stress': myth or reality?

G. Stanley Hall (1904) considered adolescence to be a period of storm and stress, characterised by extreme mood swings and unpredictable, difficult behaviour. Hall attributed this inner turmoil to the rapid biological changes experienced during this time and the resulting confusion about self-image.

This has become the traditional view of adolescence, but more recently many researchers have consistently shown that adolescence involves no more turmoil than do other periods of life. Certainly important physical and emotional changes do occur and adolescence is a challenging time, especially in the area of identity formation, but most young people get through it without too much trauma.

Adolescence as a culturally determined phenomenon

Anthropologists Margaret Mead (1928) and Ruth Benedict (1938) found cross-cultural evidence that the problems of adolescence reflected cultural influences and expectations and were not, as G. Stanley Hall suggested, the result of biological changes. Both Mead and Benedict conclude that the stress and conflict that has been traditionally associated with adolescence is not a feature of the period itself but is a product of the demands placed on the young person by **society**.

Coleman's focal theory of adolescence

Coleman (1978, 1980) challenges the traditional view of adolescence as a time of great turmoil. Drawing on research involving 14,000 British children, he concludes that in the vast majority of cases, problems are coped with, adjustments are made and maturity increases without undue pressure.

Coleman and Hendry (1990) investigated self-image, friendships and parental relationships in 800 teenagers. They found that, although each of these areas was often a cause for concern, problems tended to occur at separate times and did not have to be faced all together.

Coleman's focal theory suggests that problems are dealt with one at a time, and in this way adolescence is not significantly different from any other time, except that there are more problems to be dealt with in a relatively short space of time.

Physical development and early and late maturation

The onset of puberty is marked by the beginning of menstruation in girls and by the production of sperm in boys. These are the first of many physical changes as secondary sexual characteristics develop. Hormone levels fluctuate and may contribute to the mood swings some adolescents experience. The psychological effects of these changes appear to be greatest among early and late maturers.

Jones and Bayley (1950) found that boys who mature early were more popular, successful and likely to be leaders than were late maturing boys. The latter lacked self-confidence and self-esteem and this difference continued into adult life.

The position is somewhat less straightforward for girls. Magnusson *et al.* (1985) found that early maturing Swedish girls were more likely than their peers to be involved in drinking, smoking and early sexual activity.

Livson and Peskin (1980) found early maturing girls to be less confident and sociable than their late maturing peers, although these differences soon disappeared when their peers also reached maturity.

Interpersonal relationships

As adolescents become increasingly more independent of their parents, they spend less time with them and more with their own age group. Increasingly they look to their peers for social and emotional support. Females seem particularly concerned about popularity and acceptance.

The amount of conflict between adolescents and their parents has been greatly exaggerated. **Rutter** *et al.*, (1976) interviewed adolescents and found that most conflict between themselves and their parents was caused by criticism of their choice of friends, too much interference in their social life and too little financial support.

Despite these areas of tension, their fundamental values tend to remain similar to those of their parents, and it is their mother and father they are likely to consult over educational and career plans (Congor, 1991).

The search for identity

Erik Erikson, a psychoanalyst, saw adolescence as the most important period in the development of adult personality. According to Erikson, adolescents experienced a **crisis of identity and role confusion**. Their main task is to solve this crisis and emerge with a clear sense of adult identity. Their old childish identity is no longer appropriate and they have to forge a new one. The lack of an occupational identity is, according to Erikson, very disturbing and makes adolescents extremely clannish and intolerant of anyone who is even slightly different. The group to which the young people belong offers much-needed security while they struggle to form an integrated identity.

Marcia (1966, 1980) contends that adolescents deal with identity formation in a variety of ways. On the basis of detailed interviews with adolescents, Marcia concludes that identity status can take one of **four** forms. An individual may use only one of these statuses or go through several at various times. These are not stages but **orientations** that may occur at a particular time:

1. **Identity diffusion** is a state in which the young person has not thought seriously about the issue

and has no commitment. Although this condition serves to evade the responsibilities of adult life, it means that the individual has no real purpose in life and hence, no satisfactory identity.

2. **Foreclosure** is a commitment to values and roles prescribed by parents, without the consideration of any alternatives. This means that there is no real struggle for identity, but it can lead to problems later on in life if the individual then starts to question these values.

3. **Moratorium** involves a delay in decision making while seriously considering all possible alternatives.

4. **Achievement status** involves the achievement of a commitment after serious consideration of all alternatives.

Waterman (1982), in a review of several studies, reported that diffusion and foreclosure statuses were most frequent in the teenage years (11–17) and Meilman (1979) found that only just over half of men had reached identity achievement by the age of 24. It seems that identity experimentation is more gradual and less of a crisis than Erikson suggests, and that identity achievement goes on well into adulthood.

Erikson, Marcia and many other theorists believe that adequate identity formation is the foundation for coping successfully with adulthood.

Preparing for the exam

Key terms

achievement status	identity diffusion
adolescence	maturation
focal theory	moratorium status
foreclosure status	puberty
identity crisis	role confusion

Types of exam question

1. Consideration of individual and social factors affecting development.
2. Discussion of the view that adolescence is a time of stress and crisis.

Self-test questions

1. How can adolescence be defined?
2. Why is adolescence traditionally viewed as a time of storm and stress?
3. What did Erikson consider to be the crisis of adolescence?
4. Marcia identified *four* identity statuses. What are they?
5. Describe what a young person in moratorium status with regard to their career may be experiencing.
6. Briefly outline Coleman's focal theory of adolescence.

Exam question with guidance notes

a **What is meant by the term adolescence?** (4 marks)

b **Discuss *one* psychological study concerned with adolescence.** (7 marks)

c **Critically consider whether adolescence must inevitably be a period of 'storm and stress'.** (14 marks)

AEB (1993)

a

- This is straightforward, but bear in mind the number of marks available and keep it *brief*. Remember to include factors which denote the start *and* end of adolescence; many students forget to include the latter.

b

The examiners' report complained that many students wrote about *theories* rather than *studies*.

- *Marcia*'s study is covered well in the text. It should be described and discussed with reference to the theory it supports. You may also question the method used (interview – the advantages and disadvantages of which are covered in Chapter 11) and the conclusions drawn.
- Alternatively, you could discuss *Jones and Bayley* (1950) (noting the date of this in your evaluation) or *Rutter* et al. (1976) but you will require more detail than that included in this text.

c

- Begin by presenting the view, originally presented by Stanley Hall, that adolescence is a time of *stress*.
- You can describe briefly the factors which can make it *stressful*, and Erikson's theory of identity crisis.
- Mention that *Marcia*'s research gives some support to this view, but this support is limited (do not describe Marcia again, simply refer to it: you cannot be credited twice for the same material).
- Now present the *alternative* views. *Mead* and *Benedict* suggest that if adolescence is a particularly stressful time it is because of the demands made by society and not a feature of the period itself.
- *Coleman*'s focal theory also challenges the 'storm and stress' concept by suggesting that different problems are dealt with at different times.

8.9 Life events

Life events refer to circumstances that oblige individuals to change their life pattern in some way.

Marriage

According to **Erikson** the crisis of young adulthood is **'intimacy versus isolation'**. Erikson saw the establishment and maintenance of an intimate relationship with another person as the major task of this period of life. For many people this means marriage or cohabitation.

Types of marriage

Duberman (1973) distinguishes **three** types of married couple:

1. The **traditional marriage**, in which the husband makes decisions and is authoritative and the domain of the wife is the home and children
2. The **companionship marriage**, in which there is very little difference between male and female roles; equality and companionship are emphasised
3. The **colleague marriage**, in which role differences are accepted but not necessarily traditional; each does what they are best at.

The latter two categories are increasingly popular among young middle class couples but in truth few relationships fit neatly into these, or any other, categories. Certainly, if slowly, attitudes to marital roles are changing with a greater emphasis on **shared** roles and a breaking down of traditional boundaries. This is especially so in households where women go out to work. Bahr (1973) found that the husbands of women that work were much more involved in housework than those whose wives did not work. However, working women still do more housework than their husbands and retain overall responsibility for the running of the home.

Adjustments and satisfaction in marriage

1. When a couple start to live together, inside or outside marriage, considerable adjustments have to be made; routines and activities have to be coordinated and compromises made.
2. Couples report the highest level of satisfaction in their marriage in early, prechildren stage. Satisfaction takes a dip when children are young and returns to higher levels as the children get older (Cole, 1984).
3. Married people report greater happiness and satisfaction with their lives than do single people (Campbell, 1981). Evidence suggests that marriage demands more difficult adjustment from women, and that it is more beneficial to men. Bernard (1972) found that married women are more likely than either married men or single women to experience psychological problems. Married men, on the other hand, are more psychologically stable, healthier and happier than single men.

Parenting

According to **Erikson**, parenting solves the crisis of **generativity versus self-absorbtion** since it offers the opportunity to nurture and guide the next generation. Erikson regards the raising of children as the most important achievement of most adults.

Adjustments

1. The upheaval that the birth of a first child brings is enormous and most people are unprepared for the stresses involved. For most people it means
   - A reorganisation of working life
   - A great curtailment of social life
   - Serious disturbance in sleep patterns.
2. This is a time of considerable strain in a couple's relationship as they struggle to find a routine and way of sharing the many new domestic tasks that parenthood requires. Belsky and Pensky (1988) report that, following the birth of the first child, couples have more arguments and feel less satisfied with marriage.
3. Despite the stress and work involved in child rearing, few people express regret at having undertaken it.

The timing of parenting

Women are biologically best suited to motherhood in their twenties. Increasingly women in the middle classes are not beginning a family until they are in their thirties because they wish to get established in a career before they disrupt it for children. However Daniels and Weingarten (1982) found that many women who do have children later report feeling worried about the large age gap between themselves and their children.

The empty nest syndrome

At one time it was commonly believed that parents, especially mothers, experience a profound sense of loss when their youngest child leaves home. However, empirical evidence does not support this concept. Serlin (1980) found that middle aged women whose children had left home became more assertive, independent and motivated to achieve. Similar findings are reported by Andrews (1994) who conducted a 7-year longitudinal study of 102 working class women. Women also report feeling more relaxed, confident and satisfied with their marriages (Reinke *et al.*, 1985) after children leave home. In fact, research suggests that a considerable cause of stress to parents is the failure of young adults to leave home (Wilen, 1979).

Bereavement

> **Bereavement** refers to the loss of someone who has been close to us. **Grief** is the emotional response to loss; **mourning** is the way that grief is expressed.

Stages in the expression of grief

Parkes (1972) studied the grief reactions of widows, and he described **four** stages:

1. Numbness, disbelief and shock. The bereaved person often feels angry and may even deny the fact that their loved one has died.
2. 'Pining', a strong sense that the loved one is still present and a need to feel close to them by going to familiar places.
3. Depression and listlessness. The person realises that the loved one is really gone and will not reappear. Grief is experienced in waves and gradually the time between each wave gets longer.
4. A period of recovery and reorganisation in which grief is less intense and individuals start to reorganise and re-evaluate their lives.

The grieving rituals and procedures that are a feature of all cultures and religions, in varying forms, provide the bereaved person with some order and purpose at a time of great stress. People who have suffered such a loss may never forget the deceased person but most of them eventually come to terms with the loss and may grow in compassion as a result of it.

Preparing for the exam

Key terms

bereavement

colleague marriage

companionship marriage

generativity

self-absorbtion

traditional marriage

'empty nest syndrome'

Types of exam question

Most questions require a consideration of the impact of critical life events. Sometimes the questions involve a consideration of both life events in middle age and those of late adulthood (which, of course, involves life events such as retirement). This is the subject of section 8.10.

Self-test questions

1. What is meant by a life event? Give *three* examples.
2. Who is likely to gain most satisfaction from marriage – men or women?
3. When are married couples likely to be most satisfied with one another?
4. Describe some of the changes experienced by new parents.
5. To what extent do parents experience the 'empty nest syndrome'?
6. Briefly describe the *four* stages of grief as defined by Parkes.

Exam question with guidance notes

Discuss what psychologists have learned about the impact of critical life events during adulthood.

(25 marks)

AEB (1989)

Make sure that you focus on the *impact* of life events. The examiners' report complained that many candidates tended to produce a list of horrors, concentrating almost exclusively on negative events, with little reference to impact. Throughout the essay, *refer to the work of psychological research, naming the researchers* rather than lapsing into anecdotal accounts of possible effects.

- You can select just those life events detailed in the text but obviously there are other relevant ones such as divorce or unemployment, although these are inevitably more negative events. Do not try to cover too many or your discussion will be superficial in the time allowed. *Three* events, properly covered, are sufficient.
- As far as *marriage* is concerned, discuss the adjustments required, the alterations in levels of satisfaction throughout the course of the marriage, the differential satisfaction of both sexes and the different types of married or cohabiting relationships.
- Similarly for *parenting*. There is research not only on the effects of parenthood in the early stages but the longer-term effects on parents,

especially mothers, of children leaving home (Serlin, 1980) and the myth of the 'empty nest syndrome'.

- *Bereavement* has a major impact on most people's lives. Discuss this in terms of Parkes' stages of expression of grief; (bear in mind that this research was conducted on widows only); even this event does not end on an entirely negative note.

Additional exam question

1. Describe and evaluate psychological evidence of the impact of any *two* critical events.

(25 marks)
AEB (1992)

8.10 Late adulthood

Senescence is the term given to the onset of the physical decline associated with growing old. The age at which senescence begins varies a great deal depending on physical health, mental agility and outlook and genetic inheritance.

Ageing is a part of human development that has traditionally been viewed as a time of degeneration and general decline in physical and mental abilities. Many people feel that it is time for a more positive outlook, especially now that the number of people reaching the age of 65 and well beyond is ever increasing.

Physical and cognitive changes

1. Older people experience include a **loss of acuity** in seeing and hearing and a slowing in reaction time.
2. The **immune system** functions less well, making the elderly more vulnerable to disease.
3. **Intelligence** is usually thought to decline in old age, but this depends on what definition of 'intelligence' is used.
   a Cattell distinguishes between **fluid** and **crystallised** intelligence. Fluid intelligence refers to mental agility and quickness and the ability to solve problems. Crystallised intelligence refers to knowledge and skills acquired through life experiences. Crystallised intelligence goes on improving until the early eighties whereas fluid intelligence tends to decline after reaching a peak in the thirties.
   b Older people tend to perform less well on intelligence test items that rely on memory but may do better than their younger counterparts on items requiring general knowledge and verbal ability. In his later years, Skinner remarked that this supposed decline was more a function of the 'ageing environment' than of the ageing person.
   c The effects of ageing on intellectual functioning varies widely from individual to individual. Schulz *et al.* (1980) found that the elderly who continue to be mentally active decline less swiftly than those who do not. Denney (1979) found that intellectual performance can be increased through training and educational programmes.
4. **Short-term memory** is also affected by age. Poon (1985) found that, in a test of digit span, people in their sixties and seventies typically perform less well than younger adults. However, a measure of digit span bears little relationship to everyday life and such studies have been criticised for contributing to a negative view of ageing whilst failing to put the findings in context. There is, for example, evidence to indicate that many elderly persons function effectively by using appropriate strategies to compensate for any memory loss. For example, if they are likely to forget what they need from the shop, they take a list with them.

Older people have little difficulty in recalling material they use regularly, but have problems recalling material that is rarely required. The idea that the elderly can remember the events of their childhood with greater clarity than the events of yesterday does have some support, but memory is selective and those childhood events recalled so vividly probably represent the most exciting, interesting or amusing times.

Social changes

Retirement is regarded by many people as one of the positive features of ageing. **Argyle** (1989) identified some of the factors likely to lead to satisfaction with retired life, none of which provide any great surprises: they include being in good health, having sufficient money, being an educated member of the middle classes and having strong interests and leisure pursuits.

Even for people with a highly positive attitude to retirement, **adjustment** is necessary. Retirement involves loss of social contact, reduced income and a drastic change in a routine which may have lasted many years.

Theories of ageing

Theories of ageing are concerned with attempts to understand the factors which result in happiness and contentment during the later years of life.

Erikson's theory

In his theory of lifespan development, Erikson describes the crisis of old age as one of **ego-integrity versus despair**. A successful resolution of this conflict requires the individual to have taken stock of his or her life and come to terms with the course it has taken. Having done this, even in the face of death, life can be perceived as meaningful and worthwhile.

Disengagement theory

Cumming and Henry (1961) suggest that old people gradually withdraw from society and that society, in turn, slowly closes the door on them as it removes many responsibilities. This withdrawal, according to the theory, is desirable: being able to shed social and emotional responsibilities in the later years is the route to satisfaction and happiness.

There is no doubt that many older persons gradually become less involved in society, but it is questionable whether this is voluntary and mutually beneficial or simply a reflection of society's negative attitude to those who no longer make a financial contribution. There is little evidence to suggest that the disengaged individual is more contented than one who remains active in the community.

Activity theory

In contrast to disengagement theory, activity theory advocates that successful ageing involves staying active and participating in as many social activities as possible (Havinghurst *et al.*, 1968). There is some evidence to support this view. Langer and Rodin (1976) showed that elderly people show better health and psychological well-being when they exert control over their own lives. Their study only considered the issue of control rather than the extent of wider social involvement, but it is likely that there is a close relationship between activity, responsibility and control.

Possibly, neither the activity nor the disengagement theory applies to everyone. Unfortunately, withdrawal from society is often not a matter of choice but of circumstances. But when choice is available, how people live their lives in their later years may differ greatly. Throughout life, some people prefer solitude while others love to be socially active.

A positive growth model of ageing

Until recently, much that was written about the ageing process was a fairly depressing account of degeneration and decline. But there are positive aspects to growing old, as Kalish (1979, 1982) points out. Many elderly people find joy through grandchildren and great-grandchildren. Responsibilities decrease, relationships are more relaxed, there is time for leisure interests. Beauty in all its forms becomes more precious, life more orderly and outlook more philosophical.

Preparing for the exam

Key terms

Activity theory
chrystallised intelligence
Disengagement theory
ego-integrity

fluid intelligence
senescence
short term memory

Types of exam question

1. Consideration of how social and cultural factors affect the experience of senescence (growing old).
2. Discussion of psychological changes experienced in late adulthood.

Self-test questions

1. What is senescence?
2. List the physical changes that occur in late adulthood.
3. Not all aspects of intelligence decline in old age. Using Cattell's model of intelligence, identify the aspect that declines and the aspect that continues to improve.
4. How is memory affected by ageing?
5. What social changes are likely in old age, and why?
6. According to Erikson, what is the crisis of old age? How can it be resolved successfully?
7. What are the positive aspects of ageing?

Exam question with guidance notes

'For people in middle age and onwards there are many opportunities for positive psychological development.' Use psychological studies to discuss this claim.

(25 marks)
AEB (1991)

The examiners' report indicates that this question was not well answered, largely because of the inability of candidates to recognise anything positive about ageing, other than taking up a new hobby, such as macrame! In these guidance notes, we have concentrated on late adulthood, but you could usefully include some data from section 8.9 on Life events. For example, evidence shows that, contrary to the 'empty nest syndrome', parents find new interests and satisfaction after children leave home.

- Begin by acknowledging that the study of ageing often focuses on negative aspects such as decline in physical health and greater dependency but that there are *positive* aspects to this period of life.
- Throughout the text there are examples of *positive* development:
  a Some aspects of intelligence increase as we get older (Cattell); especially if we keep active (Schulz)

    b Retirement offers opportunity for a renewed satisfaction with life (Argyle)

    c Erikson argues that it is possible to achieve 'ego-integrity' and face death feeling that our life has been meaningful; if such an acceptance of death and contentment with life is possible, this represents a very positive aspect of age

    d Disengagement and activity theory both show the way to 'successful ageing' (though they suggest different routes), implying that the experience can be a positive one.

- Conclude by listing those aspects of life which are very enjoyable during the later years: pleasure through grandchildren, less responsibility and so on.

Additional exam questions

1. 'One of the many myths of old age is that work is central to an individual's self-concept and that retirement is a sign of declining self-worth' (Schaie and Willis, 1986)
Discuss this statement in relation to psychological research into the process of adjusting to retirement. **(25 marks)**
AEB AS (1992)

2. Discuss how social and cultural factors affect development in adulthood and senescence. **(25 marks)**
AEB (1990)

3. **a** Explain what is meant by the term 'senescence'. **(3 marks)**
    b Outline *one* social and *one* individual factor which have been shown to influence development in senescence. **(6 marks)**
    c Discuss the findings of psychological research into how people *adjust* to ageing. **(16 marks)**
AEB (1994)

4. **a** Outline and comment on *one* study investigating an aspect of *either* senescence *or* the impact of unemployment.
    b Imagine that a person about to retire from employment has written to you, as a psychologist, for advice on how to adjust to the transition. What advice would you give? Justify your advice by reference to theory and research. **(14 marks)**
NEAB (1993)

Individual Differences

9

AEB	NEAB	O & C	Topic	Date attempted	Date completed	Self Assessment
✓	✓	✓	**Intelligence**			
✓	✓	✓	**Intelligence Tests**			
✓	✓	✓	**Personality**			
✓	✓	✓	**Personality Tests**			
✓	✓	✓	**Abnormal Psychology**			

9.1 Intelligence

We all use the adjective 'intelligent', yet neither the general public nor the psychologists have found a universally accepted definition of the word.

Wechsler (1975) defines intelligence as 'the capacity to understand the world and the resourcefulness to cope with its challenges'. **Heim** (1970) suggests that 'intelligent activity consists of grasping the essentials in a situation and responding appropriately to them'.

Theories of intelligence

Theories concerning the nature of intelligence can be grouped into two broad categories:

1. **Factor theories** which view intelligence as consisting of one or more mental abilities.
2. **Cognitive theories**, also known as information processing models, which are concerned with the **steps** or **processes** people go through in solving problems.

Factor theories

Spearman's two factor theory: g and s factors

Spearman investigated the nature of intelligence by using a statistical technique called **factor analysis**. This involves the analysis of an individual's scores on various categories of intelligence test to measure the extent to which they correlate. The assumption is that if scores are highly correlated then the tests are measuring a general intellectual ability, but if there is little or no correlation between different scores, then we can assume that each test is measuring separate, unrelated abilities. Spearman found that the scores of an individual on a variety of tests were correlated, not highly, but sufficiently to conclude that all the tests were tapping a common, general intellectual ability. Spearman called this general ability the **g** factor. **g** represents broad reasoning and problem solving abilities and is, according to Spearman, responsible for the differences in intelligence between people.

However, he did accept that most individuals were better at some kinds of intelligence test items than at others, and he suggested that specific, or **s**, factors account for particular areas of competence.

Thurstone's primary mental abilities

Thurstone (1938) found low correlations between scores on tests of specific ability, and therefore little evidence for the **g** factor. Believing that Spearman's model of intelligence was too simplistic, he offered an alternative model identifying seven separate, unrelated factors or **primary mental abilities**:

1. **S** – spatial ability
2. **P** – perceptual speed
3. **N** – numerical ability
4. **V** – verbal reasoning
5. **M** – memory
6. **W** – word fluency
7. **I** – inductive reasoning.

Thurstone regarded **g** as merely the sum of all the separate scores and essentially meaningless, since it told you nothing about an individual's **strengths** and **weaknesses**.

A number of researchers are critical of Thurstone's findings and conclusions, pointing out that there is some correlation between different test scores. Thurstone himself re-examined his initial data and admitted that there seemed to be some **g** involved, but he still considered it to be of secondary importance.

Evaluation of factor theories

Factor theories, all of which are based on factor analysis, vary a great deal. This throws doubt on the technique as a useful means of analysing the nature of intelligence. The results obtained from factor analysis and the conclusions drawn seem to depend on how the data is **analysed**, who the **participants** are, and who **interprets** the data. The technique and the resulting theories are very much concerned with intelligence as measured by intelligence tests.

Further evaluation is considered in the following subsection.

Activity

In your experience, were individuals at school who were good at one subject also good at others?

1. If so, which theory is supported?
2. If not, which theory is supported?
3. How could you conduct a proper study of this?
4. Why is using 'school subjects' in such an investigation rather limited?

Cognitive theories

Sternberg's triarchic theory

Sternberg believes that intelligence involves a much broader variety of skills than those considered by the factor theories, and that we need to take a much greater account of the **real world** in our attempts to understand intelligence.

Sternberg (1985) suggests that there are **three** distinct types of intelligence (hence the **triarchic** theory):

1. **Contextual intelligence** is the practical ability to manage day-to-day life; it involves being 'street wise' or possessing 'business acumen' or just plain common sense
2. **Experiential intelligence** is concerned with creativity, the ability to cope with new situations and to represent the commonplace in unique and interesting ways
4. **Componential intelligence** concerns the ability to think critically and analytically and to do well on IQ tests.

Sternberg points out that it is only componential intelligence that is tested in conventional tests of intelligence, and that this is a serious limitation in any attempt to assess intelligence.

Evaluation

Sternberg's theory is complicated because he breaks componential intelligence down into many processes, but it does present a view of intelligence which encompasses a wide variety of skills, many of which help us cope effectively in real life situations.

Gardner's theory of multiple intelligences

Gardner defines intelligence as the ability to do something that other people **value** within one's culture. He believes that people have **multiple abilities** including language abilities, logical and mathematical reasoning, spatial ability, musical ability, body movement skills and social sensitivity. Gardner points out that these abilities may be **unrelated**, so that people who excel in one type of intelligence may perform only moderately in others.

Gardner believes that one type of intelligence is as important as another, but the extent to which each is valued is culturally determined. In the West, linguistic ability and logical and mathematical ability are the most valued, but in other cultures, where it is more necessary to navigate using the stars or to hunt and fight, spatial and kinaesthetic ability would be more greatly esteemed.

A true test of all these types of intelligence demands more than the traditional intelligence test, which is strongly geared to linguistic, logical, mathematical and spatial intelligences. It would require observations and tests of an individual in all kinds of situations and activities.

Measuring intelligence

The Simon–Binet test

Binet and Simon, the first psychologists to devise intelligence tests, aimed to devise test items that children with no special training could answer, items that measured the ability to **handle intellectual tasks rather than specific knowledge acquired in school**.

Mental age

A revised version of the Simon–Binet test, intended for use with all children, was published in 1908. In order to provide objective test measurement, children of various ages were tested and the average score for children at each age was computed. Each child's performance was then compared to the average of other children of the same age. This measure was known as **the mental age**.

The Simon–Binet Test is still used. Up until 1986, all items were scored together to give a single overall

IQ score. Since 1986, four categories have been used:

- Verbal reasoning
- Abstract/visual reasoning
- Quantitative reasoning
- Short-term memory.

This gives a better overall view of the relative strengths and weaknesses of an individual.

The concept of IQ

Before a mental age can have any significance, it must be compared with **chronological** (actual) **age**. Stern (1912) produced the concept of IQ which was calculated using the following formula:

$$\frac{\text{Mental age}}{\text{Chronological age}} \times 100 = IQ$$

Mental age ceases to have any significance after the age of 18, and therefore adult IQ is calculated in a different way. A set of questions is developed that will produce a **normal distribution** in a large sample of people representative of the population. On an IQ test the mean score is 100 and the standard deviation is 15. The concept of IQ is purely statistical and an individual's IQ will vary depending on the test and on the sample on which the test was standardised.

Activity

Using the graph in Figure 11.1 (p. 363) and bearing in mind that mean IQ is 100 with standard deviation of 15, work out the approximate percentage of people who have IQs within the following ranges:

a Below 70
b Between 85 and 115
c Above 115
d Above 85
e Between 100 and 130

Answers: a 2.4 **b** 68 **c** 16 **d** 84 **e** 47.5

The Stanford–Binet test

Terman adapted the test questions in the Simon–Binet test to suit US schoolchildren and, by testing thousands of children, established age norms. This new test, published in 1916, is called the **Stanford–Binet Intelligence Scale**, and provides a measure in terms of IQ. Terman, unlike Binet, believed that intelligence was largely **inherited**, and implicit in this belief is the assumption that the IQ test measures an underlying, unchanging ability.

Wechsler tests

Wechsler was dissatisfied with the Simon–Binet test because he felt it relied too much on language ability. He devised a series of scales for use with adults and children: the **Wechsler Adult Intelligence Scale (WAIS)** and the **Wechsler Intelligence Scale for Children** (WISC). The scales each have two parts, a

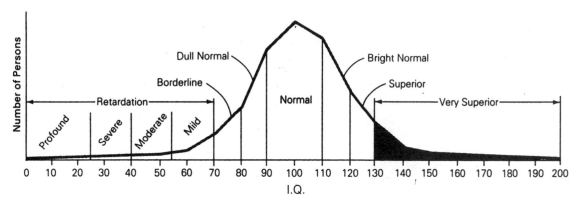

Figure 9.1 Distribution of IQ scores among a large sample
Source: P.G. Zimbardo, Psychology and Life (HarperCollins, 1992, 13th edn), p. 551.

verbal and a performance scale, and each of these scales is further subdivided so that the test provides a clear picture of an individual's strengths and weaknesses as well as giving an overall measure of IQ.

Group tests

Intelligence tests were originally administered to children individually. To a certain extent, this permitted testers to observe factors that could affect test performance, for example, to see if the child was nervous, had poor vision or did not understand what was expected.

Group tests were introduced during the Second World War by Yerkes. They were designed so that they could be scored quickly and were then used to

test huge numbers of recruits in order to assign them to appropriate positions. They have since been used for a wide variety of purposes, some of which are very dubious. This use is discussed in the Core Study (p. 285).

Culture free testing

Psychologists have attempted to devise tests which are not biased in favour of English-speaking people who are part of the same culture as the test originators. An example of a 'culture free' test is the **Raven's Progressive Matrices Test**. The test is devised to test abstract reasoning and requires no verbal ability or specific information (see Figure 9.2 for examples of the matrices used).

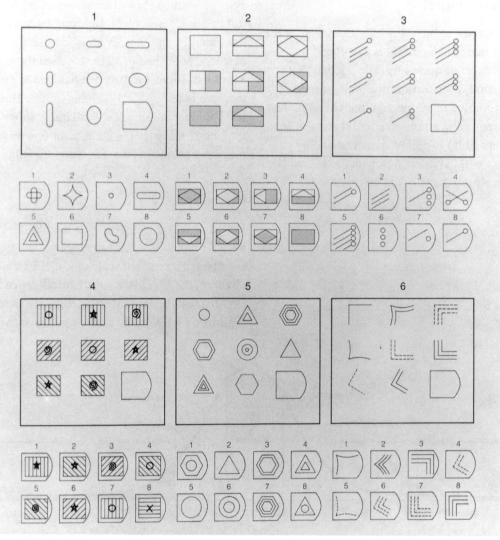

Figure 9.2 Raven's Progressive Matrices Test
Source: J.W. Kalat, Introduction to Psychology (Brooks/Cole, 1993, 3rd edn), p. 423.

Core Study

A nation of morons: S.J. Gould (1982)

Robert **Yerkes** seized the opportunity of the First World War to promote the use and status of mental testing and with it the status of psychology as a serious science. He persuaded the US Government to have all army recruits tested for intelligence – some 1.75 million in all.

In 1917, Yerkes and other noted hereditarians of the day (Terman and Goddard) devised a series of mental tests to use for the purpose. The tests included:

1. Army Alpha – for literate men.
2. Army Beta – for men who failed the Alpha. This test used pictorial items (though it still required the ability to recognise and write numbers).
3. Individual examinations for men who failed the Beta.

Each recruit was to be graded from **A+** to **E−** and suggestions as to suitable army placements were to be made. Men scoring below grade **C** were not thought to be suitable officer material.

Each test took less than an hour to complete and could be given to a large group. Many of the items included in Alpha have become familiar features of modern tests.

Yerkes claimed that the tests would measure 'native intellectual ability', though some items clearly did not, for example:

Crisco is a: patent medicine, disinfectant, toothpaste, food product

Conditions in which tests were taken were unsatisfactory. The time allowed was insufficient and an air of panic surrounded the whole procedure. To men unused to the written word or number, the event must have been extremely bewildering.

After the war, Boring put together data based on the scores of 160,000 men and stunned America with the resultant statistics:

1. The average mental age of the White American Male was 13 years – just above the 'moronity' level
2. The mean mental age for most immigrants was much lower: Russians = 11.34, Italians = 11.01

and Poles = 10.74
3. The lowest mean score, 10.4 years, was attributed to Black Americans.

America was indeed a nation of morons – or seemingly so. The political impact was greatest relating to the statistics on racial and national intelligence. A book written by a follower of Yerkes, Carl Brigham, called *A Study of American Intelligence* was instrumental in converting the statistics into social action.

Both the army data and Brigham's book influenced the debates on immigration – a major political issue of the time. The Immigration Restriction Acts followed. The first, in 1921, imposed a quota of 3 per cent of immigrants from any one nation then resident in the US. The 1924 Act was far more severe and meant that many immigrants were refused entry to the country. In the 1930s many of the potential immigrants turned away were Jewish refugees. Some found refuge elsewhere, but many had no other choice but to return to Europe and take their chances in the Nazi regime.

Gould concludes his article with the chilling remark, 'The paths to destruction are often indirect, but ideas can be agents as sure as guns and bombs'.

QUESTIONS

1. In the IQ test described by Gould, suggest *four* features that would obtain a culturally biased response. **(4 marks)**
   Oxford and Cambridge Specimen Paper
2. Why were *three* different tests devised to test Army recruits?
3. In what ways were the tests not fair to all recruits?
4. For what political ends were statistics from the Army tests used?

Activity

Make sure you read section 11.4 on Psychological testing in Chapter 11 and that, in relation to IQ tests, you know:

1. The characteristics which make a test scientific (characteristics of a 'good' test).
2. The meaning of 'reliability' and 'validity'.
3. Ways of establishing validity and reliability of IQ tests.

Criticisms of intelligence tests

1. Psychologists have failed to agree as to the exact nature of intelligence, and therefore it cannot be assumed that intelligence tests are actually **valid**.
2. IQ tests are based on the assumption that intelligence is a **fixed characteristic**. This is far from agreed, and is an area of major scientific and ideological debate.
3. An IQ score gives a false impression of **objectivity**. It is presented as a statistic of intellectual ability, like height or weight, but it is very different from these kinds of statistics. IQ is only meaningful as a comparison with others, whereas height is an absolute measure which remains unaffected by the nature of the sample with which it is measured.
4. Many researchers consider that intelligence tests are **biased** against ethnic minority groups and lower socioeconomic classes. Critics claim that IQ tests measure knowledge and skills which are the focus of middle class, white education, and that therefore people who do not belong to this group are likely to achieve lower IQs than those who do. See the Core Study for more detail.
5. Intelligence tests measure a very **narrow range** of intelligence. They fail to measure creativity, interpersonal skills, physical skills, the ability to make sensible decisions in a crisis and many other of the skills necessary to cope effectively with everyday life.

Uses of intelligence tests

Some tests, such as the Wechsler scales, identify a child's strengths and weaknesses in specific areas.

This information can be used in planning individualised instruction programmes if this is considered appropriate.

The self-fulfilling prophecy

Many people assume that IQ tests reveal some permanent, inherited trait underlying all intelligent behaviour. Intelligence tests are sometimes used to predict school performance and they do this fairly well. This may be because intelligence does not change greatly over the course of several years, or even over a lifetime. However, these findings can be interpreted in a completely different way: it may be that this predictive ability of intelligence testing is caused by the **self-fulfilling effect**.

Rosenthal and Jacobson (1968) demonstrated the effect of the self-fulfilling prophecy. These researchers, using an imaginary test score, informed a group of primary school teachers that certain of their young students were 'bloomers' who would show considerable improvement during the course of the following year. Despite the fact that these children had been chosen at random, they did indeed do better than their classmates. This study provided no direct evidence as to why this happened, but there is ample evidence to show that when teachers expect children to do well, they respond to their efforts more warmly, provide greater encouragement, teach more material and give these children increased opportunities to ask and answer questions.

Determinants of intelligence: the nature–nurture issue

Investigating heritability

Details of the precise methods by which psychologists attempt to estimate the extent to which characteristics are inherited is covered in the nature–nurture section of chapter 10.

You need to know this!

Heredity: the nature side

If intelligence is largely an inherited characteristic, then we would expect people sharing common genes to have a more similar level of intelligence than those who have no genetic similarity.

A review of IQ correlations carried out by Bouchard and McGue (1981) (not including Cyril Burt's now discredited data) provides the following correlations:

MZ twins reared together	0.86*
MZ twins reared apart	0.72
DZ twins reared together	0.60*
Siblings reared together	0.47
Child and Natural Parent	0.50
Child and Adoptive Parent	0.19

*See below for the definition of MZ and DZ.

These results appear to strongly support the hereditarian view. But before we draw any conclusions, a number of considerations need to be taken into account:

1. All methods of investigation use scores from conventional intelligence tests to measure IQ. As we have already discussed, these tests measure only a very limited type of intellectual activity.
2. Non-identical (DZ) twins are no more genetically similar than are siblings (brothers and sisters), yet their IQs are more highly correlated. This greater similarity cannot be due to heredity, so a reasonable explanation is that twins experience a more similar environment than do other brothers and sisters. If environment accounts for the difference in correlations between siblings and DZ twins, it may also account (at least in part) for the finding that IQ measures of identical (MZ) twins are more highly correlated than IQ scores of DZ twins. It is quite probable that identical twins are treated more similarly, and therefore share a more similar environment, than are non-identical twins.
3. Identical twins who have been separated at birth are such a rarity that comparatively few such pairs have been studied.
4. In some cases, identical twins who had supposedly been reared apart had shared very similar environments. Some had even been raised by branches of the same family, and had had frequent contact with each other. Even when separation is more complete, environments may not be dissimilar. Adoption agencies usually match the families with which each twin is placed.

The environment: the nurture side

There are innumerable studies which emphasise the influence that **environmental** factors have on intelligence. We will consider just a small sample of these.

1. The **prenatal environment** can affect intelligence. Harrell *et al.* (1955) compared two groups of economically deprived pregnant women, one group of whom were given a dietary supplement while the other group were given only a placebo. When given intelligence tests between the ages of three and four, the children of the mothers who had taken the supplement scored significantly higher than the other children.
2. If intelligence is genetically determined, then attempts to boost it by **environmental enrichment programmes** should have little effect. One of the largest such programmes, known as Operation Headstart, was targeted at disadvantaged preschool children in the USA. It proved to have considerable long-term advantages. By the age of 15 years, Headstart participants scored higher on the WISC or the Stanford–Binet than a matched group who had not participated; they were also more socially competent and self-confident.
3. Zajonc and Markus (1975), after reviewing extensive research concerning the relationship between IQ, family size and birth order, concluded that intelligence test scores declined with **birth order** and with **family size**. This can hardly be due to genetic factors.
4. Children raised in deprived orphanages often show serious intellectual deficits and make marked intellectual progress if removed to a **more stimulating environment** (Goldfarb, 1944; Skeels, 1966).

Environment, heredity and intelligence: summing up

It seems reasonable to assume that both heredity and environment contribute to human intelligence, so neither should be ignored. The real debate centres around the relative importance of each and is an extremely complex one. Indeed, many would argue that any attempt to establish a universally applicable percentage of intelligence which is inherited is misdirected.

Preparing for the exam

Key terms

cognitive theories

componential intelligence

contextual intelligence

culture free tests

dizygotic (DZ) twins

experiential intelligence

factor analysis

factor theories

Gardner's multiple intelligences

g factor

group tests

heritability

Intelligence Quotient

intelligence

mental age

monozygoitc (MZ) twins

Operation Headstart

primary mental abilities

s factors

Simon–Binet test

Sternberg's triarchic theories

Two factor theory

Wechsler tests

Types of exam question

1. Discussion of theories of intelligence.
2. Appreciation of how theories relate to testing.
3. Consideration of the pros and cons of intelligence testing.
4. Discussion of the nature – nurture debate.

Self-test questions

1. Briefly distinguish between factor theories and cognitive theories of intelligence.
2. Describe the factors in Spearman's Two factor theory.
3. Briefly describe the *three* types of intelligence suggested by Sternberg.
4. Who were the first people to devise an intelligence test? What form does the most recent update of their test take?
5. What is the formula for IQ?
6. Briefly describe the tests devised by Wechsler.
7. Outline *four* criticisms of IQ tests.
8. What methods have been used to investigate the nature–nurture debate in intelligence?
9. Outline *one* study which indicates that there is a genetic component to intelligence and *one* study which indicates that it is affected by environmental factors.

Exam question with guidance notes

If ... the impression takes root that [IQ] tests really measure intelligence, that they constitute a sort of last judgement on the child's capacity, that they reveal scientifically his/her predestined ability, then it would be a thousand times better if all the intelligence testers and their questionnaires were sunk without warning' (Lippmann, 1922).

> Discuss the above view in the light of controversy surrounding the use of IQ tests.
>
> **(25 marks)**
>
> **AEB (1992)**

With questions on any topic, try not to be put off by a long, and perhaps complex, quotation, such questions really are *not* as difficult as they might appear. Read the quote carefully and you will see that what it concerns is:

- Whether IQ tests really measure intelligence
- Whether this measurement is innate and fixed for life
- Whether IQ tests are scientific.
- Start with the *validity* of intelligence tests. Are they measuring what they are claiming to measure? Both Sternberg and Gardner, in their theories, argue that intelligence is far more broad based than this. Other points are made in the subsection on Criticism of intelligence tests. Of particular relevance here is the *cultural bias* in testing, that IQ tests do not measure intelligence but knowledge and skills imparted to white, Western, middle class children. Make use of parts of the Core Study here to illustrate this bias. If IQ tests are not valid, they cannot possibly be scientific.
- Neither is there evidence that IQ tests are entirely *reliable*. Evidence indicates that there are large practice effects, indicating that the ability to do tests depends at least partly on learning.
- In order to be scientific, tests not only need to be reliable and valid, but properly standardised on a large and *representative* sample of the population. However, representative samples are very difficult to obtain have often not been used; for example, the Stanford–Binet 1960 revision was tested only on white children.
- Many psychologists, including some who have devised IQ tests (for example Terman), do consider IQ is a fixed characteristic and therefore a predictor of future performance. But there is plenty of evidence that it is neither innate nor fixed. Provide examples of the evidence that shows the effect of environmental influences, with special emphasis on studies which show the degree to which IQ measures *can change*, such as Goldfarb (1944) and Skeels (1966).
- Even in cases where IQ does not appear to change, this may be due to the *self-fulfilling effect*. Discuss this, using the Rosenthal and Jacobson study to illustrate the point.
- You can now discuss the uses to which IQ tests have been put:
  - **a** Segregation of children into different schools or streams within schools with consequent lack of opportunity.
  - **b** Demonstration of supposed racial inferiority and consequent justification of racial segregation.
  - **c** The eugenics movement.

  Again, the Core Study is useful here.
- In conclusion, it is probably true to say that if Lippmann, writing in 1922, had been able to see into the future, he would almost certainly have been in favour of tests and their users being sunk without trace. Since this has not happened, we need to be extremely cautious in the uses to which we put such tests.

Additional exam questions

1. Discuss ways in which psychologists have investigated environmental and genetic influences on intelligence. What conclusions have been reached as a result of these studies? **(25 marks)**
AEB (1988)

2. Discuss the functions of intelligence tests and the controversies that relate to their current usage. **(25 marks)**
AEB (1990)

3. a Describe briefly the structure and content of *one* intelligence test.
(4 marks)

   b Discuss *two* problems in defining intelligence. **(8 marks)**

   c Discuss the strengths and weaknesses of using twin studies in assessing the inheritance of intelligence. **(8 marks)**
(Total **20 marks**)
NEAB (1993)

9.2 Personality

Mischel (1986) describes personality as 'reasonably stable patterns of behaviour, including thought and emotions, that distinguish people from one another'.

To a greater or lesser extent all personality theories attempt to explain how people come to develop different patterns of behaviour and ways of responding to life's events. They also seek to identify the ways in which people are similar in their behaviours and responses.

However, although theorists share a common purpose, they differ greatly in the explanations they offer and in the way in which they study personality.

The **idiographic** approach emphasises the uniqueness of the individual and its main tool is the Case Study. On the other hand, the **nomothetic** approach attempts to identify ways in which individuals are similar. Correlational techniques (see section 11.1) are used to establish traits which are likely to go together.

Theories of personality

Freud's psychodynamic theory

This theory of personality is discussed in Chapter 2.

Activity

The use of the idiographic and nomothetic approach is discussed in detail in section 10.4.

1. Is Freud's approach nomothetic or idiographic?
2. What are the relative strengths and weaknesses of the two approaches?

Humanistic theories

The self theory of Carl Rogers

Humanistic psychology emerged in the 1950s and 1960s and offers an alternative view to behaviourism and the psychodynamic approach, a 'third force' in psychology, to quote Maslow. Both behaviourism and the psychodynamic approach are heavily deterministic in different directions; humanistic psychologists emphasise freewill and personal growth and they strongly believe that the individual should be seen and understood as a whole entity.

Humanistic psychology is considered to be **phenomenological**, stressing the importance of how the individual **perceives reality** as being crucial to understanding their behaviour. Each person has a different view of the reality of the world in which they live, and of the reality of themselves. It is the view of humanistic psychology that all individuals are innately good and worthwhile.

One of the best known humanistic psychologists is Carl Rogers. Rogers believes that all human beings are motivated toward **self-actualisation**, which involves the ultimate fulfilment of potential. The drive for self-actualisation is the basic drive behind the development of personality.

From childhood we evaluate ourselves and our actions and have an intuitive understanding of what things can be evaluated positively and what cannot be. If parents or other significant others show **unconditional positive regard**, a complete unqualified acceptance of the person, it is possible for children to feel positive about all aspects of themselves and have high self-esteem.

However, if children experience conditional positive regard, that is, love is only shown when they behave in the way in which others demand, they are likely to deny important aspects of themselves and have a mismatch between self-concept and ideal self.

If we can recognise, accept and positively evaluate our own feelings, we can experience a feeling of psychological wholeness, a harmony between our self-concept, thoughts, feelings and behaviour, which Rogers called **congruence**. Once we have experienced this, the path to self-actualisation is open.

Maslow's hierarchy of needs

Maslow also emphasises the need in humans to strive toward self-actualisation. However, before we can attend to this high-order need, we must make sure that lower-order needs have been satisfied. This theory, together with a diagram demonstrating Maslow's 'hierarchy of needs' is covered in section 7.4.

According to Maslow, self-actualising people have satisfied their needs for aesthetic pleasures, they accept themselves and others, they are creative and

humorous and able to enjoy life. In many respects they represent the epitome of mental health.

Humanistic theories are optimistic about the human condition; viewing people as integrated wholes with insight into their own actions and thoughts and the freedom to make choices about the direction of their lives.

Evaluation of humanistic theories

1. Humanistic theories do not lend themselves to experimentation and therefore cannot be proved or disproved. How do you tell if someone has achieved self-actualisation? The only way is to rely on **self-reports** which depend on the honesty of the person involved and in their understanding of self-actualisation.
2. They do not take into full account the influence of **past experiences** or developmental aspects of personality.
3. They **reduce the complexity** of personality by focusing only on the self-actualising tendency.
4. They make no attempt to predict how people will **behave** in any situation.

Trait and type theories

Trait theorists seek to identify relatively permanent personality characteristics that go together within an individual, for example, 'talkative', 'sociable' and 'lively'. Some trait theorists see traits as **predispositions** that cause certain categories of behaviour, others use traits only as descriptions of behaviour.

Traits exist on a **continuous dimension**. For example, the trait 'talkative' can range from 'garrulous' (very talkative) to 'quiet' (not at all talkative).

This is one of the main differences between traits and type theories: **types** tend to describe **discontinuous, discrete categories**.

Allport's trait approach (1937, 1961 and 1966)

Allport considered traits to be the **basic units of personality** and believed that they could be divided into **two** main categories:

1. Common traits to be found in all members of a particular culture or society.
2. Individual traits which are unique to an individual and can only be discovered by studying the individual in detail; individual traits can be subdivided in the following way:

   a **Cardinal traits:** these traits are central to all others and dictate the way that life is lived; an example of a cardinal trait could be the desire to help others. They are not necessarily possessed by everybody.

   b **Central traits:** these represent the major characteristics of an individual; for example, kindness and honesty.

   c **Secondary traits:** these refer to less consistent and more peripheral characteristics such as taste in clothes or music.

Allport believed that these three kinds of traits form the **structure of personality**. He also maintained that personality traits were more important than environmental conditions in determining behaviour.

Cattell's trait theory

Cattell measured a wide range of personality traits in a very large sample of people and identified **two** types of traits:

- **Surface traits** refer to those aspects of a person which can be readily observed in what a person does and says: for example, assertive, ambitious, courageous.
- **Source traits** are those which lie behind the surface traits – they are more central and all-pervading: the source trait underlying the surface traits of assertive, ambitious and courageous, for example, might be dominant.

Cattell used factor analysis (a statistical technique which involves seeing which personality characteristics correlate with which) to identify 16 source traits, each representing one end of a continuum. For example, one source trait he identified is 'outgoing' which represents one end of a continuum – the other end being 'reserved'. He also developed a test to identify where on each of the personality continuums an individual is placed. The test, known as the **16PF** (16 Personality Factor

Questionnaire), results in an **individual personality profile** (see Figure 9.3).

The big five

McCrae and Costa (1985, 1987) used factor analysis to arrive at just **five** basic traits which underlie all others:

1. Extroversion versus introversion
2. Agreeable versus disagreeable
3. Conscientious versus irresponsible
4. Emotional stability versus emotional instability
5. Open to experience versus closed to experience.

Agreement on these five dimensions is not universal but it is considerable. They have been found in a number of different samples. Since almost any trait can be related to one of the dimensions included in the five, they offer a degree of flexibility and are not attached to a particular theory.

Hans Eysenck's type theory

Eysenck's model of personality combines traits and types, linking them together in a **hierarchical system**.

At level one of the hierarchy are single responses made in specific situations; level two comprises habitual or typical responses; level three describes personality traits and the highest level is that of types.

Activity

Consider someone who belongs to the type 'extrovert'. Think of examples of:

1. Two personality traits (level three)
2. Two typical responses (level two)
3. A response to two specific situations such as an invitation to a party (level one).

Eysenck's types fall into **three** bipolar dimensions:

1. Extroversion version introversion (**E**)
2. Neuroticism versus stability (**N**)
3. Psychoticism versus normality (**P**).

However, unlike other type theories, Eysenck does not see these types as discrete categories but as extreme ends of a **continuum** on which everybody can be placed (see Figure 9.4).

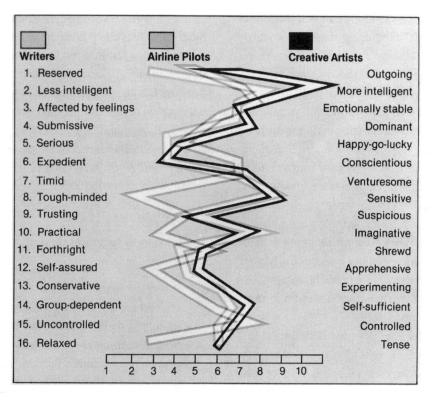

Figure 9.3 Cattell's personality factors: three personality profiles
Source: S.A. Rathus, Essentials of Psychology (Holt, Rinehart & Winston, 1991, 3rd edn), p. 393.

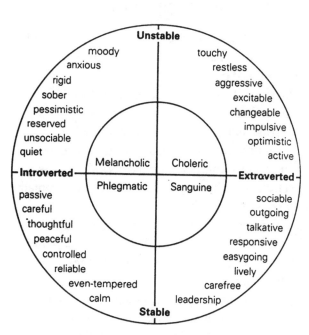

Figure 9.4 Eysenck's personality circle: the four quadrants
Source: P.G. Zimbardo, Psychology and Life (Harper Collins, 1992, 13th edn), p. 514.

Eysenck believes that personality is biologically determined and depends on the nature of the individual's nervous system, so:

1. **E** is based on the nature of the reticular activating system (RAS), the part of the brain stem responsible for determining arousal levels. In extroverts, the RAS strongly inhibits incoming sensations, resulting in the need to seek stimulation. In introverts, the RAS amplifies sensory input, hence they seek less stimulation.

2. **N** is controlled by the level of the reactivity of the autonomic nervous system (ANS) (see section 7.1). People with high **N** scores have an ANS which reacts with greater speed and strength than low **N** scorers.

3. Eysenck is less clear about the origin of a high **P** score (which refers to the tendency to be solitary, uncaring and troublesome), but he suggested that it might be connected with hormone levels, particularly androgen levels.

Evaluation

1. There is some evidence to support Eysenck's claims about the **biological** basis of personality.

Harkins and Green (1975) found that introverts were better at tasks requiring long periods of concentration.

2. Claridge and Herrington (1963) showed that introverted neurotics were more difficult to **sedate** than extroverted neurotics; Eysenck would claim that this is because introverts are more highly aroused.

3. Eysenck also claims that because introverts are more highly aroused and therefore sensitive to incoming stimuli, they are easier to condition than extroverts. He extended this view to his theory of **criminality** – criminals being unstable extroverts who have not been successfully conditioned to behave in a socially acceptable way. However, evidence does not seem to support his view (Cochrane, 1974).

4. Eysenck's model does not provide a thorough analysis of exactly how biological factors **govern** personality; it is very vague in this respect. There is, for example, little evidence that the RAS simply operates as a 'volume control' for arousal.

Activity

Note that Freud's theory can also be considered a type theory, although one that is in total contrast to Eysenck's and far more of a 'pigeon-hole' theory than one based on extremes on a continuum.

What 'types' of personality are contained in Freud's theory? (Think in terms of the psychosexual stages of development.)

The learning theory approach

The radical behaviourism of Watson and Skinner states that **environmental variables** are almost exclusively responsible for individual preferences and behaviour. From birth onwards, we develop habits based on regular reinforcement of certain behaviour. Personality is viewed as a collection of habitual responses.

Social learning theorists stress the role of learning through observation and the role of cognitive processes. They believe that not only does the environment influence the individual but that the individual influences the environment. People are thus able to construct and manipulate the environment to meet their own ends. Bandura calls such interactions between personalities and their environment **reciprocal determinism**. A person may be prone to be aggressive, but whether he is aggressive in any particular situation depends on many factors, including expectations of what will happen if he responds aggressively. According to Bandura, human personality develops out of this continuous interaction of personal standards (learnt by observation and reinforcement), situations and behavioural consequences.

Evaluation of learning theory

1. Many theorists believe that radical behaviourism is limited in its attempt to describe and understand personality because it ignores thoughts, feelings and other **inner experiences**.

2. Social learning theorists, however, do take account of cognitive factors. They have retained the scientific approach and most of their claims are supported by empirical findings. Social learning theory represents a compromise between behaviourism and some other approaches and it has offered useful explanations for the **inconsistencies** of human behaviour.

The consistency of personality and the situationist approach

The trait and type approaches considered are based on the assumption that personality is relatively permanent and consistent.

Block (1971), reported a longitudinal study in which 100 men and women were assessed over a 25 year period and it was found that qualities such as dependability, emotionality, and aestheticism remained fairly constant over the period. Olweus (1981), showed that aggression levels tend to remain fairly constant over time.

There is less evidence to support situational consistency. A number of studies carried out in the 1920s demonstrated that behaviour changes according to circumstances.

Hartshorne and May (1928) found that when school children were given the opportunity to lie, cheat and steal in a variety of settings, dishonesty in one setting did not correlate highly with dishonesty in other situations.

Social learning theorists argue that a similar lack of consistency can be found with a wide range of characteristics, and they argue that the situation represents an important influence on behaviour.

A compromise between the trait approach and the situationist approach is an **interactionist approach**, which stresses the influence of the enduring personality characteristics of an individual and the situation in which they find themselves.

Personality tests

Personality tests can be divided into two broad categories: self-report personality inventories and projective tests.

Self-report personality inventories

Self-report tests involve asking individuals to answer a series of questions about their characteristic behaviour, based on the notion that we know ourselves well and can therefore provide all the required information. The questionnaires often present a limited range of responses from which to choose and administration and scoring of the tests follow simple and objective rules. One such personality inventory is the EPI.

The Eysenck Personality Inventory (EPI)

The EPI claims to measure personality using **two** bipolar dimensions (extroversion/introversion and neuroticism/stability), which Eysenck claims underlie all personalities. Respondents are required to give a 'yes' or 'no' answer to questions such as:

- Are you an irritable person?
- Do you often long for excitement?
- Do you like playing pranks on others?

Answers will indicate a neuroticism and an extroversion score. A lie scale is included to detect respondents who try to choose socially acceptable answers or deliberately lie.

Evaluation of self-report inventories

1. The purpose of many items is easily identifiable and thus it is possible for respondents to **fake** personality characteristics. Lie scale items are included but are not difficult for respondents to detect.

2. There is a tendency in some respondents to answer in a particular way to all items without reference to the **content** of the item (this is known as 'response set'). Response set can usually be avoided by constructing questions so that someone with a particular personality trait sometimes has to tick 'yes' and sometimes 'no'.

3. Respondents are given a choice of a small number of **fixed answers** to each question, none of which may reflect their view.

4. Most self-report tests involve **objective** administration and scoring procedures and therefore scores will not be greatly influenced by the bias of the examiners.

Projective tests

Projective tests involve presenting respondents with ambiguous stimuli and asking them to describe what they see. The underlying rationale is that the respondent will **project** their personality into their answer.

The Rorschach test

This test consists of ten cards each showing a different ink blot pattern (see Figure 9.5). The respondent is asked to say what they think each one looks like and responses are interpreted by a trained person. The test is thought to provide insight into such characteristics as intelligence, interests, cultural experiences, extroversion, and anxiety.

The thematic apperception test (TAT)

Respondents are shown a series of pictures depicting scenes which can be interpreted in a number of ways, and are asked to construct a story about each picture. The content and structure of the stories are analysed in order to learn something about the respondent's preoccupations, concerns, anxieties, fantasies and personality characteristics. McClelland *et al.* (1953) claims that the test is, among other things, a useful measure of achievement motivation. Respondents with a high achievement motive tended to produce

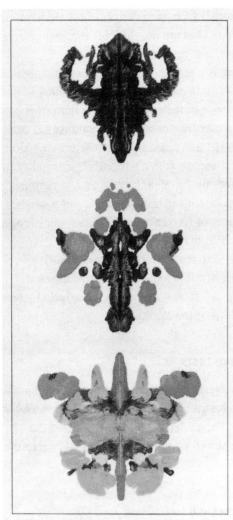

Figure 9.5 Ink blot patterns in the Rorschach projective test
Source: C.G. Morris, Psychology: An Introduction (Prentice-Hall, 1988, 6th edn), p. 489.

stories with strong themes of ambition and strivings for success.

Evaluation of projective tests

1. Interpretation is highly **subjective** and requires considerable training and experience, making reliability and validity difficult to establish.
2. Compared to self-report inventories:
   a Respondents are far less likely to engage in **intentional deception**.
   b Respondents are not limited by fixed choice questions, thus responses are more likely to reflect the **personality** of the person answering than about the person who devised the questions.
   c They are much more sensitive to **unconscious** and non-obvious features of personality.
3. Some clinicians claim that they are a useful tool, allowing them to probe areas untouched by the more objective tests.

Preparing for the exam

Key terms

16 PF	personality
congruence	projective tests
EPI	psychoticism
extrovert	reciprocal determinism
factor analysis	Rorschach Test
ideal self	self-actualisation
idiographic	self-report personality inventories
introvert	Thematic Apperception Test
Maslow's hierarchy of needs	trait theories
neuroticism	type theories
nomothetic	unconditional positive regard

Types of exam question

1. Discussion of personality theories. Often trait versus type or situational versus individual.
2. Evaluation of theories in terms of assessment and practical use.

Self-test questions

1. What is meant by the terms 'idiographic' and 'nomothetic' with reference to the study of personality?
2. According to Rogers, what is 'congruence', and how do we achieve it?
3. What is self-actualisation?
4. Outline *one* positive and *one* negative evaluation of humanistic theories of personality.
5. What is the difference between trait and type theories of personality?
6. Briefly outline one of each.
7. What is a self-report inventory? Briefly outline an example of *one*.
8. What are the main limitations and problems with self-report inventories?
9. What is a projective test? Briefly outline an example of *one*.
10. What are the main limitations and problems with projective tests?

Exam question with guidance notes

Describe *one* theory of personality and critically evaluate this theory in terms of its method of assessment and its practical use (25 marks)
AEB (1992)

How you go about answering this question obviously depends upon which theory you choose. We will use Eysenck's theory but these comments are still a useful guide were you to choose a different theory, for example Freud's theory and the use of projective tests.

- The question requires you to start with a *description* of the theory. Keep this fairly brief; do not be tempted to spend too long on this at the expense of the second part.

- The question asks for evaluation *in terms of its method of assessment and practical use*, so keep your discussion focused on these points. This theory assesses personality by means of a self-report test, the EPI, which can be *criticised* on the following grounds:
  a Response set.
  b Some fairly transparent questions used which could make it possible to fake personality characteristics (in fairness to Eysenck, he does include a lie scale).
  c Only 'yes'/'no' fixed choice answers are permitted; such limitations are frustrating for the respondent and must also reduce the validity of the final profile. In this sense, it is a fairly crude and inflexible tool. (There is a useful evaluation of fixed choice questionnaires in general in Chapter 11.)
- Now consider the *uses*:
  a *Research*, for example looking at personality patterns in criminals; gender differences; the relationship between personality and biology and so on.
  b As a means of *clinical assessment*. It is worth adding that, given the limitations of the questionnaire this is somewhat disturbing: if it is used alongside other methods of assessment it is more acceptable.
  c As a means of *personnel selection*. The same argument applies.
- *Conclude* by saying that all personality tests are limited in their ability to measure personality and the findings of these tests should be treated with caution. The safest approach is to use as many methods of assessment as possible: tests together with interviews, references, case histories, observations and so on.

Additional exam questions

1. Critically discuss trait *and* type approaches to personality.   **(25 marks)**
   AEB (1989)

2. Critically discuss individual and situational approaches to personality.
   (25 marks)
   AEB (1990)

9.3 Abnormal psychology: 1 – definitions, models and classification

Defining abnormality

There is no single, universally acceptable definition of abnormal behaviour. The difficulty is that there is no absolute boundary which separates normal from abnormal behaviour and they are best viewed as different positions on a continuum of psychological adjustment.

Rosenhan and Seligman (1989) suggest that behaviour can be judged on the basis of **six** criteria, any combination of which may indicate the presence of a psychological disorder. These criteria are as follows:

1. **Personal Distress:** experiencing unpleasant emotional experiences such as guilt, anxiety and depression to an excessive degree
2. **Maladaptiveness:** behaviour which interferes with the ability to meet everyday responsibilities and cope with everyday demands of family, work and social life
3. **Irrationality:** behaviour which has no rational basis and is unconnected to reality, for example, holding beliefs such as 'I am Napoleon'
4. **Unpredictability:** behaviour which is impulsive and seemingly uncontrollable, especially when this behaviour disrupts the lives of others or deprives them of their rights
5. **Unconventionality and statistical rarity:** abnormal behaviour is shown by a minority and is therefore statistically rare, *but rarity is only regarded as abnormal if it is considered undesirable by the particular society in which it occurs.* After all, genius is rare but is not considered abnormal.
6. **Observer discomfort:** breaking the unwritten and unspoken rules by which most people abide and the violation of which is considered abnormal: for example, talking to oneself in public.

The more of the above elements there are and the more clearly each one is present, the more likely it is that the behaviour will be considered to be abnormal. To an extent this will be based on the **personal judgement** of the person observing the behaviour.

The concept of normality

'Normality' is as difficult to define as 'abnormality'. It can be defined in terms of those personality traits that enable an individual to adjust to their environment, in terms of making satisfactory relationships and finding a place in society.

Atkinson, Atkinson and Hilgard (1983) suggest the use of the following personality traits which, they emphasise, the normal person possesses to a **greater degree** than the individual who is diagnosed as abnormal.

1. **Efficient perception of reality:** a fairly realistic appraisal of oneself and others, such that the individual has a rational perception of their own and others' motives and personality, and does not greatly overestimate or underestimate their own and other people's abilities
2. **Self-knowledge:** a reasonable insight into one's own motives and feelings
3. **Ability to exercise voluntary control over behaviour:** the capacity not to be too impulsive or lacking in restraint, nor too inflexible
4. **Self-esteem and acceptance:** a feeling of self-worth and confidence to express opinions; the ability to feel fairly comfortable in social situations
5. **An ability to form affectionate relationships:** the capacity to enjoy the company of others, to empathise and sympathise, to give and receive support; and the capacity to love and be loved without making excessive demands on others
6. **Productivity:** an ability to have some enthusiasm for life and to channel energies into some purposeful activity.

Problems of diagnosis

Judgements of normality and abnormality reflect prevailing cultural values, social trends and political forces as well as scientific knowledge. Behaviour that is considered deviant or maladaptive in one society may be quite acceptable in another. Cultural norms regarding acceptable behaviour may change over time.

Researchers point to the need to distinguish between mental disorders that appear to be **universal** and those that are **specific** to certain cultures. Schizophrenia and depression occur in all societies (Kleinmann, 1988) but children's hyperactivity is unlikely to be considered abnormal in every culture.

There are many problems, both ethical and practical, associated with diagnosing behaviour as abnormal and these are considered in more detail later in the chapter.

Activity

We have stated that judgements of normality and abnormality reflect prevailing cultural and social values.

1. Can you think of at least **one** behaviour which would be considered normal in one culture but not in another (besides the example given in the text)?
2. Can you think of at least **one** behaviour which, in your culture, was thought abnormal 50–100 years ago but is no longer considered to be so (or vice versa), reflecting social trends.

It may be helpful to use these examples to illustrate an appropriate essay.

Models of abnormality

The medical model

This model views abnormal behaviour as an expression of some underlying disease or biological abnormality.

Biochemical factors

Neurotransmitters are chemicals that are responsible for communication between nerve cells. A few of the many known neurotransmitters are believed to be associated with abnormal behaviour.

Neurological factors

Damage to the nervous system, especially the **brain**, is likely to lead to disruption of normal functioning. Clinicians have discovered definite connections between a number of mental disorders and specific problems in the brain.

Genetics

Some conditions such as depression, schizophrenia and alcoholism are believed to be caused in part by genetic factors. Meehl (1962) and Rosenthal (1970) have developed the **diathesis–stress theory** which holds that it is not a particular abnormality that is inherited but a **predisposition** to develop the illness (diathesis). Certain stressors in the environment may activate the predisposition, resulting in a disorder. It is therefore possible for some genetically vulnerable individuals who remain in a supportive and benign environment to remain psychologically healthy.

Although the main emphasis of the medical model is on physical factors, it does not necessarily rule out the contribution of other non-biological variables.

Evaluation

Limitations and problems

1. **Szasz** argues that so-called mental illnesses are not diseases of biological origin but are 'problems in living' caused by **psychological** and **social** factors. He believes that people whose abnormal behaviour is due to a genuine brain disease should be referred to as neurologically impaired. Labelling **all** abnormal behaviour as mental illness implies that **all** abnormal behaviour has a biological cause when, he argues, society has invented the concept of mental illness in order to control and change people whose behaviour is considered a threat to social order.
2. Other critics argue that even if it is accepted that there is a biological component in the cause of abnormal behaviour, this can only be a partial contributor to the problem. **Social** and **interpersonal** causes must be taken into account.
3. Many studies used to support the theoretical view of the medical model have been done on **animals**, and there is no evidence that animals experience the human disorders under investigation.

4. Studies designed to detect a genetic link are open to other interpretations, since genetically related individuals are usually reared in **similar environments**.

5. The model cannot adequately account for some of the more complex forms of abnormal behaviour for which **no organic cause** can be found.

Contributions and virtues

1. This model has led to the recognition that some conditions are mainly **biological** in origin even when their manifestation is mainly psychological

2. Biological treatments often afford significant help and relief after other methods have failed.

The psychodynamic model

This model is based on Freud's theory which is covered in detail in Chapter 2.

Freud argued that the forces responsible for behaviour occur mostly at the unconscious level. Behavioural disorders are symbolic expressions of unconscious conflicts between the id, ego and superego. When this conflict is excessive, defence mechanisms become overused, seriously distorting reality and leading to self-defeating behaviour. Before people can effectively resolve their problems, they need to become aware that the source of these problems lie in **childhood**. This is the purpose of psychoanalysis.

Evaluation

Limitations and problems

Refer to the criticisms of Freud in Chapter 2.

Additional points are:

1. There is little satisfactory evidence that Freud's patients were 'cured' by the use of psychoanalysis

2. There are no clear guidelines for predicting whether someone may eventually show abnormal behaviour. A good theory should be **predictive**.

Contributions and virtues

1. Freud helped us to appreciate that psychological conflict is a universal experience and only leads to abnormal functioning when conflict becomes excessive

2. Freud did a great deal to remove the idea that abnormal functioning is due to demonic possession

3. He argued for a respectful attitude toward, and humane treatment of, people who were considered to be mentally disturbed.

The behavioural model

The behavioural model is based on the principles of the learning theories which were covered in detail in Chapter 2.

According to this model, abnormal behaviour is acquired in the same way as all other behaviour, by classical and operant conditioning. The symptoms of psychological disorders arise because an individual has **learned self-defeating or ineffective** ways of behaving.

For example, people who complain of feeling depressed may receive positive reinforcement for their complaints if their friends and family express sympathy and pay more attention to them. Punishment for early childhood sexual activity may result in adult anxieties over sexuality.

Since all behaviour is learned, maladaptive behaviour can be **unlearned** using the same principles, those of classical and operant conditioning.

Evaluation

Limitations and problems

1. The fact that clinical symptoms can be simulated under laboratory conditions does not prove that they are ordinarily acquired in this way in everyday life

2. The model provides a very mechanistic view of people as puppets controlled by the strings of the environment. It makes no allowance for the role of personality, consciousness or free will in behaviour.

Contributions and virtues

1. This model is based on a theory which is precise and testable. A number of clinical syndromes have been created in the controlled conditions of a laboratory using the principles of conditioning, thereby suggesting that mental disorders could develop in this way
2. The use of these same principles has been effective in treating certain specific disorders.

Activity

In Chapter 2 there are two very different case studies of phobias, one of 'Little Albert' and the other of 'Little Hans'. Make sure you are familiar with the studies and can summarise them very briefly. You can then use them to illustrate an answer on models of abnormality or in an essay concerning the origins of phobias.

The cognitive–behavioural model

This model seeks to include the role of cognitive factors, such as thoughts, feelings and beliefs, on behaviour. According to this model, the individual is an active processor of information, and it is the way we perceive, anticipate and evaluate events rather than the events themselves which has the greatest impact on our behaviour.

Social learning theory holds that many maladaptive behaviours, such as fear and excessive aggression, can be acquired by observational learning.

Evaluation

Limitations and problems

1. Some theorists, especially those of a psychoanalytic persuasion, argue that this approach still neglects the influence of the unconscious in abnormal functioning and therefore still tends to treat the **symptoms** rather than the underlying causes
2. The model exaggerates the role of **cognitive** factors while underestimating the influence of emotional factors. Emotional reactions such as

intense fear are not caused simply by cognitive factors
3. The model is **narrow** in scope, only taking account of specific cognitions rather than looking at an individual as a whole person
4. It is possible that cognitive processes could be the **consequence** rather than a cause of difficulties; once there are problems, people lose confidence in themselves and their ability to cope, resulting in low self-efficacy.

Contributions and virtues

1. The model focuses on an essential element of being human, our thinking processes, as the main contributor to both normal and abnormal behaviour
2. It lends itself to **testing**. There is a considerable body of evidence showing that people often do exhibit the assumptions and specific thoughts that supposedly contribute to abnormal functioning.

Activity

Revise the section on social learning theory in Chapter 2. This provides the basis for one cognitive–behavioural model. What **cognitive** aspects of a situation does Bandura emphasise as being important?

The theory states that we are more likely to imitate some models than others. Which models are we most likely to copy and what are the (fairly obvious) implications for abnormality?

Towards a more eclectic approach

Although these models have been presented separately, many researchers take the view that no single model can possibly account for all the diverse types of abnormal behaviour. Many psychologists take an eclectic approach and look to more than one model to help them explain and treat psychological disorders.

Classification of abnormal behaviour

A classification system is simply a comprehensive list of categories, including detailed descriptions of the symptoms characteristic of each.

Classification is useful for the following reasons:

1. It provides a basis on which the clinician can **organise the symptoms** exhibited by the patient. Once data is organised, these symptoms are easier to analyse
2. It is an aid to **communication** between clinicians and researchers; the names of categories provide a precise summary of symptoms and disorders in an agreed-upon and meaningful way
3. It enables researchers to gather a **representative sample** of people with similar symptoms and to investigate their problems; this helps to develop a body of knowledge about the causes of various patterns of abnormal functioning
4. It enables adequate **statistical counts** to be made of the incidence of various disorders; this is useful in itself, and is also of value in comparing the incidence of various disorders in different cultures, subcultures, socioeconomic groups and so on.

Emil Kraeplin developed the first influential classification system for abnormal behaviour in 1883. This has provided the foundation for the psychological part of the classification system now used by the World Health Organisation, called the International Classification of Diseases. This system is currently in its tenth revision, known as **ICD-10**.

Very similar to ICD-10 is the classification system developed by the American Psychiatric Association and used widely in the USA, the Diagnostic and Statistical Manual of Mental Disorders. This system is also regularly revised: the current edition, **DSM-III-R** (the third edition with minor revisions) was published in 1987 and **DSM-IV** is due to be published in 1994. The primary aim of each edition is descriptive and it makes few assumptions about causes.

Reliability and validity of classification

In order to be a valuable tool, a classification system must be **reliable** and **valid**.

Activity

Before going on, read the section on reliability and validity in Chapter 11.

1. Make sure you understand what is meant by 'reliability' and 'validity'. Now try to think of these concepts in more general terms, rather than simply their meaning in the context of psychological tests.
2. Be aware of the ways in which reliability can be **tested**.

Reliability in this context means that different diagnosticians agree that a given pattern of behaviour should be assigned to a particular diagnostic category. If they cannot agree, then the classification is not reliable. This may mean that the criteria on which the classification is based is not sufficiently **precise** to determine whether the disorder is present or absent.

DSM-I was widely criticised for being unreliable. DMS-III-R is considerably more reliable but does contain some very vague and imprecisely defined categories, such as 'depressive disorder not otherwise specified'.

Validity, as applied to classification of mental disorders, refers to the extent to which the categories say something basic about the disorder, enabling a clear **distinction** to be made between patients in one category and those in another.

Given the complexity of human behaviour, perhaps we should not be surprised that both reliability and validity have proved extraordinarily difficult to achieve in the classification of abnormal behaviour.

Difficulties of diagnosis

There are many factors that can adversely affect attempts to make an appropriate diagnosis.

1. Assessment is inevitably influenced by a clinician's assumptions, preconceptions and theoretical orientation.
2. Clinicians may overemphasise personality traits as the cause of people's problems, while not paying sufficient attention to stressors and other environmental factors in the individual's life.

3. Clinicians may make the assumptions that if an individual presents for diagnosis, then he or she must have a disorder. Phares (1979) refers to this as the 'reading in syndrome'.

4. Once a diagnosis has been made, all other behaviour is treated as though it were a symptom, blinding the diagnostician to any errors that may have been made. (Points **3** and **4** are both demonstrated in the Rosenhan Core Study in this section, p. 305.)

5. Some clinicians bring misconceptions to the assessment procedure. Chapman and Chapman (1967) found that some researchers insist that when clients see anal images and feminine clothing in the Rorschach stimuli, this means that they have homosexual tendencies, yet there is no evidence for this contention. (The Rorschach test is a projective test of personality, discussed in section 9.2.)

Dangers and ethics of diagnosis and labels

Once a diagnosis has been made, a **label** is attached to an individual and although this is intended to aid treatment, it can have some unfortunate and unintended consequences:

1. Because of society's stereotypes and misconceptions about the mentally disturbed, once someone is labelled in this way they are likely to be viewed as dangerous, unstable and unpredictable, unable to function normally within society.

2. It may cause people so labelled to have a very **negative self-image**.

3. A diagnostic label may become a **self-fulfilling prophecy**. Once people are viewed as mentally ill, they are more likely to be treated as if they are incapable or inferior and this may lead those who are treated in this way to believe that they do possess the characteristics assigned to them and to behave accordingly, thus confirming the diagnosis even when it is incorrect.

4. A label can cause people to interpret all activities of the affected individual as though they were symptoms of the condition and therefore pathological.

5. Labelling can blind observers to changes in behaviour.

Despite these limitations, diagnosis and classification still have an essential role. Akiskal (1989) and others argue that it is the best way to work towards improving knowledge and can reveal information which may well promote greater understanding and better treatment of people in distress. If no diagnosis is made, then these individuals may be deprived of help for which they may be desperate and without which both themselves and others may be in danger.

Core Study

On being sane in insane places: D.L. Rosenhan (1973)

The basic question asked by Rosenhan is 'Does the concept of abnormality lie in the individual person or is it in the mind of the observer?' DSM represents the belief that patients present symptoms which can then be categorised. Laing (1960), Szasz (1963) and many others argue that psychiatric diagnoses are in the minds of the **observers** rather than being based on an objective assessment of an individual's behaviour.

If, by faking a single symptom of mental disorder, sane people could be admitted to a psychiatric ward and then be diagnosed as sane, it would mean that sanity can be distinguished even in an insane context. If, on the other hand, the pseudopatients were not detected, despite behaving perfectly normally once admitted, then it would strongly suggest that a diagnosis of mental disorder made in that context is unreliable.

Eight pseudopatients, three women and five men, were admitted to different hospitals after complaining of hearing voices which were unclear but appeared to be saying 'empty', 'hollow' and 'thud'. The symptom and the name and occupation of the pseudopatient were the only falsehoods. Since none of the pseudopatients had any history of pathology, none was mentioned during interviews with the clinicians.

As soon as they were admitted onto the wards, all pseudopatients behaved normally. Some showed a certain degree of nervousness at first, as would be expected of anyone entering a strange residential place for the first time. When asked by staff how they were feeling, they reported themselves fine and free of all symptoms. All but one pseudopatient was anxious to be discharged so they were highly motivated to behave as normally as possible.

Not one of the pseudopatients was detected. All but one was diagnosed as schizophrenic and, when discharged, as schizophrenic in remission. Length of hospitalisation ranged from seven to 52 days, 19 days on average. Despite none of the clinicians recognising the pseudopatients as sane, many of the patients declared them to be frauds and made comments such as 'You're not crazy. You're a journalist, or a professor'.

After diagnosis, many normal, everyday behaviours were interpreted as manifestations of schizophrenia; one example was 'excessive note taking'. **Once people are labelled abnormal, all of their behaviours and characteristics are coloured by that label.**

Although public attitudes have improved from the days when the mentally ill were seen as witches or possessed by demons, people so labelled are still stigmatised. 'Mental illness' is not akin to physical illness and is viewed very negatively even by professionals. When a relevant request, such as 'When am I likely to be discharged?' was made in a polite and non-threatening manner to a member of staff, the pseudopatients were given little eye-contact and were treated in an extremely offhand manner, often given an irrelevant or vague response if, indeed, any response was given at all. This reflects avoidance and **depersonalisation**. In these circumstances people feel profoundly powerless. Powerlessness is pervasive in a psychiatric hospital: patients have reduced legal rights, their freedom of movement is restricted, their personal histories are available, there are not even any doors on the toilets.

Rosenhan concludes that we cannot distinguish the sane from the insane in psychiatric hospitals. The behaviour of anyone classed as a patient is judged in a distorted manner. Patients suffer powerlessness and depersonalisation. This was not a deliberate policy of the staff in these hospitals who were caring and intelligent. What they failed to do was take account of the extent to which the environment and labelling can affect attribution of cause to a person's behaviour.

QUESTIONS

1. **a** In Rosenhan's study, what diagnostic criteria were used to label the pseudopatients as 'schizophrenic'?   **(2 marks)**

    b In what ways do these criteria differ from the generally agreed symptoms of schizophrenia?   **(2 marks)**

    Oxford and Cambridge Specimen Paper

2. **a** What are the basic findings of the Rosenhan study?   **(8 marks)**

    b What do these findings tell us about the behaviour and experience of people?   **(8 marks)**

    c What have been some of the practical or theoretical consequences of this work?   **(6 marks)**

    d How have these studies contributed in a positive way to our understanding of people?   **(8 marks)**

    Based on Oxford and Cambridge Specimen Paper

Preparing for the exam

Key terms

abnormal behaviour
behavioural model
biochemical
cognitive–behavioural model
depression
diathesis–stress theory
DSM-III-R
eclectic
ICD-10
irrationality
maladaptiveness

medical model
neurological
normality
observer discomfort
productivity
psychodynamic model
Rorschach stimuli
schizophrenia
self-fulfilling prophecy
unconventionality
unpredictability

Types of exam question

1. Description and evaluation of ways of defining abnormality.
2. Practical and ethical problems of defining and diagnosing abnormality and normality.
3. Evaluation of the models, often just a single model and especially the medical model.

Note

Although the AEB guarantee a question on this section of the abnormal syllabus, you must be prepared to take evidence and arguments from other areas, not consider sections in isolation. You will see how this has been done in the Exam question with guidance notes below.

Self-test questions

1. What *six* criteria do Rosenhan and Seligman suggest as a means of judging whether behaviour is abnormal?
2. What *six* personality traits do Atkinson, Atkinson and Hilgard suggest that normal people possess to a greater degree than abnormal people?
3. Why are abnormality and normality difficult to define?
4. According to the Medical model, what is the cause of mental illness?
5. What is the diathesis–stress model?
6. Outline Szasz's objection to the Medical model.
7. What other limitations are there with the Medical model?
8. How does Freud account for mental illness?
9. How does the Behavioural model account for mental illness?
10. What are the limitations of the Behavioural model?
11. How does the Cognitive–behavioural model differ from the straightforward Behavioural model?
12. Why is the classification of abnormal behaviour attempted?
13. What are the ICD-10 and the DSM-III-R?

14. Why is it important that a classification system be reliable and valid?

15. Why is diagnosis of mental illness difficult?

16. What ethical problems are there in diagnosing an individual's behaviour as abnormal?

Exam question with guidance notes

Discuss *assumptions* of the medical model to the concepts of normal and abnormal behaviour. (25 marks)

AEB (1990)

- Introduce the essay with the main assumption of the model, that mental illness is caused by *biological factors*.

- Make reference to the *evidence* in support of this model. You could include brief reference to the hypothesised biological causes of schizophrenia, detailed in section 9.4 or to any other disorder you have studied.

- Consider the *contributions* of the model, including the usefulness of **somatic treatments**, covered in section 9.5. Ensure that you give credit for the usefulness of these therapies, including drug treatment, while acknowledging that they are unlikely to be a 'cure-all'. (The examiners' report commented that some candidates criticised this model out of hand without consideration of any of the benefits it might have conferred, such as drug treatment.)

- Now move on to the *criticisms*: there are several in the text. Mention the main critic, Szasz; you could also consider Laing (his work is covered under schizophrenia).

- You could conclude with a statement to summarise the limitations and contributions towards understanding of abnormal behaviour and the diathesis–stress model as a useful *interactive* approach.

Additional exam questions

1. **a** Describe any **one** system of classification used in the diagnosis of abnormal behaviour. (10 marks)

   b From a psychological viewpoint, discuss some of the problems involved in classifying abnormal behaviour. (15 marks)

AEB AS (1994)

2. Discuss the concepts of abnormality and normality in terms of their ethical and practical considerations. (25 marks)

AEB (1989)

9.4 Abnormal psychology: 2 – examples of disorders

Phobic disorders

The American Psychiatric Association (1987) states that phobic disorders are characterised by an intense fear of an object, activity or situation and a powerful urge to avoid feared stimuli.

DSM-III-R places phobic disorders within the larger category of anxiety disorders; it distinguishes **three** categories of phobic disorders: agoraphobia, social phobias and simple phobias.

1. **Agoraphobia** is an intense fear of being in places or situations from which escape would be difficult or in which immediate help would be unavailable if the individual suffered a panic attack or other debilitating reaction.
2. **Social phobias** involve irrational, severe and persistent fear of situations in which an individual may be scrutinised and evaluated. This fear is often associated with a specific event like public speaking, eating in public or using a public toilet.
3. **Simple phobias** involve a persistent fear of an object or situation other than being in public places or in a socially humiliating situation. These phobias include animal phobias, fear of injury or disease, fear of heights, fear of enclosed spaces.

Explanations of phobic disorders

Psychoanalytic

According to Freud, phobias are symptomatic of unconscious sexual or aggressive conflicts that are displaced from their original source. The classic case of 'Little Hans', the Core Study in Chapter 2, illustrates the theory. Hans had displaced the fear of the father onto the fear of horses. In a similar way, the Freudian view of agoraphobia is that it is caused by the fear that you might act out unacceptable sexual drives in public.

Evaluation

See Chapter 2 for evaluation of the theory. Additional points are raised by Rachman and Wilson.

Rachman and Wilson (1980), among others, propose that if a phobia is only a symptom of a more deep-seated problem, then treatment of the symptom should either be ineffective or lead to new symptoms, or produce overwhelming anxiety in the individual. In fact, there is no evidence at all to support this contention, since many behavioural treatments are extremely effective and produce no secondary symptoms.

Behavioural

Behaviourists view phobias as the result of maladaptive learning by **classical conditioning**, maintained by operant conditioning. Social learning theorists propose that phobias can also be acquired as a result of modelling.

Activity

Make sure you can use the study of 'Little Albert' recounted in Chapter 2 to illustrate this theory.
What was Albert conditioned to be phobic towards? To what other objects did this phobia generalise?

Operant conditioning serves to maintain the avoidance behaviour that results from phobia. Avoidance is strongly negatively reinforced by the reduction in anxiety that occurs each time the fearful situation is avoided.

Modelling may also contribute to the development of phobic responses. Bandura and Rosenthal (1966) have demonstrated that observing fear in others can result in fear of the same object by vicarious conditioning.

Evaluation

Virtues

1. It has been demonstrated (in some very ethically dubious studies) that classical conditioning can be

used to teach laboratory animals to fear certain objects.

2. Likewise, the demonstration on Little Albert shows that intense fear can be classically conditioned in humans.

3. Bandura and Rosenthal (1966) provides evidence that fear responses can be produced by modelling.

Criticisms

1. The fact that phobias can be produced in such a manner under laboratory conditions does not necessarily prove that this is the means by which they are ordinarily acquired.

2. Several studies have been singularly unsuccessful at classically conditioning fear reactions under laboratory conditions (English, 1929; Bregman, 1934; Bancroft, 1971).

3. A substantial proportion of phobics fail to recall any traumatic or unpleasant event occurring prior to the development of the disorder.

4. The theory does not explain why some phobias are more common than others. After all, if the feared stimulus had at one time been associated with pain, then car phobia and phobia of electrical appliances should be far more common than snake phobia, but are virtually unknown.

The next theory provides a model to explain this phenomenon.

Behavioural–biological: preparedness theory

Some phobias are far more common than others; people are rarely afraid of meat, houses or pyjamas but they are of spiders, mice and darkness. **Seligman** (1971) and Marks (1977) propose that human beings have evolved a **predisposition** (preparedness) to fear certain stimuli, such as snakes and darkness, because such fears had survival value for pretechnological humanity in their natural environment.

Evaluation

This theory provides a very plausible account of the development of some phobias, but it is difficult to see how it can explain some simple phobias and most social phobias, like fear of public toilets.

Treatments of phobic disorders

To obtain a full account of available treatments, see the later section on therapies. With particular reference to phobias note that:

1. There is little evidence that psychoanalysis (therapy based on Freudian theory) is effective with phobic disorders (Beck and Efran, 1983). Indeed, Freud himself said that psychodynamic techniques alone may be insufficient to cure phobic disorders (Freud, 1919).

2. Behavioural therapies include systematic desensitisation, flooding and modelling. All these techniques have a high rate of success with simple phobias. Such treatment for social phobias is fairly recent and, so far, the success rate is also high.

The anti-social personality disorder

Cleckley (1976) lists **five** characteristics shared by most psychopaths:

1. Superficial charm and good intelligence
2. Shallow emotions and lack of empathy, guilt or remorse
3. Impulsive, unmotivated behaviours
4. Failure to learn from experience and absence of anxiety
5. Unreliability, insincerity and untruthfulness.

Activity

Before reading on, go over the section on ways of investigating the nature–nurture debate in Chapter 10, paying particular attention to comparison of genetically related and unrelated individuals. You need to know:

1. What is meant by MZ and DZ twins, and why they are useful sources of data
2. The problems of interpreting the findings of these studies.

Explanations of the anti-social personality disorder

Biological factors

Genetic factors

Generally, adopted children whose biological parents have psychopathic tendencies have a higher rate of psychopathy than adoptees whose biological parents showed no psychopathic behaviour (Cadoret and Cain, 1981). Most studies comparing MZ and DZ twins do show a tendency for MZ twins to have a higher concordance rate than DZ twins for psychopathy, delinquency and criminality (Mednick and Christeansen, 1977).

Many studies, however, do not distinguish between criminality and psychopathy and they draw their samples only from criminal populations. Truly representative samples of psychopaths are rarely used.

Disorders of the nervous system

There is physiological evidence to suggest that psychopaths show a deficiency in emotional arousal and a reduced level of fear and anxiety. The combination of low levels of arousal and the lack of response to painful stimuli may result in a desperate need by psychopaths to seek thrills and stimulation (Hare, 1968).

However, Vaillant (1975) argues that this emotional underarousal could be learned. He believes that psychopaths show no less anxiety than normals but they have learned to handle anxiety differently, by concealment and escape.

Family relationships

McCord and McCord (1964) carried out an extensive review of the literature and concluded that the primary cause of the anti-social personality is a lack of parental affection and severe parental rejection, resulting in a **lack of empathy**.

A higher than average percentage of psychopaths have psychopathic fathers who may serve as a powerful model for anti-social behaviour.

Sociocultural factors

There is a much greater frequency of anti-social behaviour in the lower socioeconomic groups. It has been suggested that urban ghettos are a breeding ground for anti-social behaviour, since youngsters, especially males, become alienated from and hostile towards a broader society which provides them with evidence of affluence and no means of attaining it. They reject the **social norms** of the wider society and this results in inadequate conscience development and a lack of concern for others.

Conclusion

Reid (1981) and others argue that the anti-social personality is a complex interaction of environmental and biological factors.

Treatment of the anti-social personality disorder

Treatment programmes for psychopaths have not met with any great success. Vaillant (1975) argues that outpatient treatment is doomed to failure and that treatment is only effective if the setting is one in which the psychopath can be controlled. Intense group therapy which provides the opportunity to learn to care for others and a place to be accepted by peers offers the most promising course of treatment. Nevertheless, to date any improvements achieved through therapy appear to be short-lived unless the families and peers work hard to maintain appropriate behaviours.

Schizophrenia

Schizophrenia is a severely disabling disorder which involves the disintegration of the whole personality and represents what, to the lay person, is the real meaning of the word 'madness'.

Schizophrenia means literally 'split mind', and was intended to convey a splitting of mental functions, especially between emotion and reality. It was **not** intended to suggest a split into two or more personalities, as in the study documented overleaf, although it is often misinterpreted in this way.

Many clinicians consider schizophrenia to be a **group of disorders** rather than a unitary concept. Carpenter *et al.* (1988) consider schizophrenia to be a group of many distinct disorders that share common features. Schizophrenia exists world-wide with an overall rate of 1 per cent; males and females are equally likely to be affected. Onset of the disease is before the age of 45 years.

Core Study

A case of multiple personality: C.H. Thigpen and H. Cleckley (1954)

The idea of two or more people inhabiting the same body is a fascinating one. For this reason it has been popularised in literature but appears so rarely in everyday life that many people, including some psychiatrists, are sceptical as to whether it actually exists. Is there really such a thing as 'multiple personality'?

This study documents the case study of one Eve White who clearly showed the symptoms of multiple personality.

When Eve White, a seemingly unremarkable woman, was first seen by a doctor (one of the psychiatrists who authored this paper), her only symptom was severe and blinding headaches. However, it soon became apparent that she also suffered 'blackouts', periods of amnesia during which whole hours, sometimes even days, would pass without her remembering what had occurred during that time. Nevertheless, nothing indicated the existence of any serious mental confusion.

The first signs of anything unusual in this case was the receipt by the doctor of a letter, most of which had been written by Eve White, but with a concluding sentence in a different, childish, hand. Eve White remembered starting the letter but not having completed or posted it. In an interview soon after this incident, she hesitantly admitted to hearing the occasional voice, a fact which greatly surprised the doctor, since she had no schizoid symptoms whatsoever. While discussing this symptom, one which caused Eve White great emotional distress, she suddenly changed all her body movements, attitude and voice and introduced herself extrovertly and cheekily as Eve Black. The transformation was so remarkable that it was difficult to grasp or document. Eve White was a gentle, frightened, conventional, quietly spoken middle-class woman. Eve Black was a flirtatious, extrovert, fun-loving person with a very independent attitude. Eve White had no idea of the existence of Eve Black who seemed to be able to 'take over' the body only

occasionally and then used it to have great fun, shopping for clothes and going 'out on the town'. Eve Black knew of the existence of Eve White whom she found tedious and boring. She was tolerant of Eve White's four year old daughter, but had no affection for her. She despised Eve White's husband, but rather as a tedious bore than with any real venom. Eve Black's outlook on life was essentially immature and hedonistic; she seemed incapable of deep feelings and emotions, whether positive or negative; her aim was simply to have a good time, to seek out excitement and pleasure without responsibility.

Eve Black's presence had, in fact, been kept a secret not only from Eve White but from everyone around her. When Eve Black was 'out', she largely avoided anyone who Eve White knew and, on the occasions that she did spend time with them, she skilfully passed herself off as Eve White, imitating her tone of voice, gestures and attitudes.

Psychometric and projective tests carried out on the two Eves revealed the following:

- Both were of above average intelligence.
- The Rorschach ('inkblot') test showed that Eve Black was actually more healthy than Eve White. Eve Black had an hysterical tendency, while Eve White showed anxiety, obsessive–compulsive traits, rigidity and an inability to deal with her hostility.

The problem appears to have started very early in childhood. Eve experienced strong feelings of maternal rejection, especially after the birth of her twin sisters. She feels great hostility to her roles of wife and mother, hostility she cannot accept and from which she flees by becoming Miss Black. By this means, she can regain her premarital freedom and escape the conflicts brought about by her roles of wife and mother.

After about eight months of treatment, a third personality, 'Jane', emerged. Jane appeared to be more mature than either of the Eves. She eventually took over some of Eve White's responsibilities at work and appeared capable of compassion and, probably, of genuine love.

The authors conclude by admitting that they may have been hoodwinked, but this is very doubtful. There is no doubt, however, as to the necessity for further detailed investigation into the whole concept of 'multiple personality'.

Postcript:

It later emerged that Chris Sizemore, the real name of the patient, had at least 22 personalities, at least nine of which existed before Eve Black. Together with her cousin, Elen Pittillo, she has written the book, *I'm Eve* (Sizemore and Pittillo, 1977), a fascinating account of her life.

QUESTIONS

1. Multiple personality and schizophrenia are two conditions which are often confused with one another but which are fundamentally different. Name *two* important differences between multiple personality and schizophrenia. (You may find it helpful to think in terms of major symptoms, hypothesised causes and possible treatments.) **(8 marks)**

Symptoms of schizophrenia

Schizophrenia involves many specific symptoms that vary greatly from one individual to another: the following list represents the most common symptoms:

1. **Disturbances in content of thought:** delusions, ideas that have no basis in fact and are often absurd
2. **Disturbances in the form of thought:** loose associations in thinking, making incoherent statements, shifting from topic to topic with no logical or meaningful connections between them
3. **Distortion of perception and attention:** auditory hallucinations (hearing voices) are frequently experienced
4. **Disturbance of emotion (affect):** an extreme lack of correspondence between the situation and the emotion displayed
5. **Disrupted volition:** a lack of interest in anything and no will to get involved in any activities at all
6. **Detached relationships with the external world:** preoccupation with their own thoughts and beliefs to the almost total exclusion of everyone around
7. **Confused sense of self:** schizophrenics may be perplexed about who they are and whether or not they actually exist
8. **Disturbed psychomotor behaviour:** there are two extremes of disturbed psychomotor behaviour: an excited sort of hyperactivity and minimal activity.

Diagnosing schizophrenia

Schizophrenia is a notoriously difficult condition to diagnose. There is no single symptom that provides a definitive diagnosis, and to complicate matters further, there are different types of schizophrenia, each characterised by different symptoms.

Subtypes of schizophrenia

DSM-III-R lists **five** subtypes of schizophrenia:

1. **Disorganised** schizophrenia involves severe disintegration of the personality, starting at an earlier age than any other type and showing very immature and regressed behaviour
2. **Catatonic** schizophrenia involves either extremely excited or extremely withdrawn behaviour
2. **Paranoid** schizophrenia is a condition characterised by persistent and systemised delusions often of a very complex nature; the most common delusions are of persecution, but delusions of grandeur and of jealousy are also fairly typical

4. **Undifferentiated** schizophrenia is a term reserved for individuals who show symptoms of schizophrenia but whose symptoms do not fit into the pattern shown by the three major categories listed above.

5. **Residual** schizophrenia is a category used for people who have had one schizophrenic episode in the last six months and who still show some mild symptoms but not strongly enough to warrant classification in the major categories.

Causes of schizophrenia

Biological causes

Heredity

1. **Twin studies:** Kendler (1983) reports a concordance rate of 50 per cent between identical (MZ) twins and 15 per cent between fraternal (DZ) twins. This indicates both a genetic and an environmental element.

2. **Adoption studies:** Kety *et al.* (1988), in an extensive study of adopted children, found that those children whose biological parents were schizophrenic were ten times more likely than average to develop the disorder.

3. **An abnormal gene:** Gurling *et al.* (1988) have produced evidence that an abnormal gene or cluster of genes on chromosome five may be related to some cases of schizophrenia, although other researchers challenge this evidence (Kidd *et al.*, 1988).

The dopamine hypothesis

This states that schizophrenia results from excess dopamine activity in certain parts of the brain. Evidence for this comes from several sources:

1. If normal individuals take large doses of amphetamines, drugs which increase dopamine levels, then they exhibit symptoms very similar to paranoid schizophrenia

2. Phenothiazines, drugs which are effective in treating some schizophrenics, are known to reduce the action of dopamine receptors

3. Brain scans indicate that there is a greater density of dopamine receptors in the brains of untreated

schizophrenics compared to non-schizophrenics (Wong *et al.*, 1986).

It should be noted that there is no evidence of a large excess of dopamine itself in the brains of schizophrenics, but there is a greater density of dopamine receptors on cells in various parts of the brain.

Goldstein (1986) points out that the evidence is only circumstantial and that there is no explanation of exactly how dopamine levels may be related to the specific symptoms of schizophrenia.

Abnormal brain structure

There is evidence that between 25 and 50 per cent of schizophrenics have enlarged ventricles, particularly on the left side of the brain, suggesting some deterioration in brain function.

Psychosocial factors

The family

R.D. Laing hypothesises that schizophrenia is the result of an individual's desperate attempt to deal with the confusion and unhappiness caused by their social and family environment and if left alone to explore their inner selves they would emerge stronger and less confused. According to Laing, any attempts to 'cure' the individual simply makes the situation worse.

Social class

Several studies indicate that the rate of schizophrenia is highest amongst the lower socioeconomic classes, especially those living in densely populated inner city areas. There are several possible interpretations of this data:

1. The **stresses** associated with poverty are likely to trigger schizophrenia in those who are already genetically vulnerable

2. The **downward drift hypothesis**: that people suffering from the condition are likely to end up living in deprived areas, unable to obtain responsible employment, if any

3. Schizophrenics in the upper classes are less likely to come to the attention of the authorities since they are **sheltered** by their families.

An integrated view

The most promising avenue of research is probably the **diathesis–stress** model which, when applied to schizophrenia, suggests that the condition is the result of a combination of genetic vulnerability and environmental stress.

> The diasthesis–stress model is discussed in section 9.3 under the Medical model.

Treatments and outcomes

Drug therapy

1. The phenothiazines, a class of anti-psychotic drugs, work by reducing the brain's dopamine activity. However, at least 10 per cent of schizophrenics receive no benefit from the phenothiazines. They also have some very serious side-effects such as muscle tremors and spasms of involuntary jerky movements. An irreversible condition known as **tardive dyskinesia** affects 25 per cent of all patients who have taken anti-psychotic drugs for seven years or more; this is a movement disorder involving involuntary facial movements commonly known as 'flycatching'.
2. Clozapine, a relatively new drug, does not have these side-effects, but in a very small number of patients it has caused a fatal blood disorder. It is possibly too soon to assess the long-term effects of clozapine.

Behaviour therapy

This has little influence on the primary symptoms of schizophrenia but is effective in developing specific abilities such as improved communication, good personal hygiene and self-help skills.

Family therapy

This concentrates on altering communication patterns within families and on the development of appropriate social skills, including the appropriate ways of expressing emotion. Its aim is to reduce the rate of relapse rather than effect a cure and in this it has been reasonably successful.

Milieu therapy

This is a residential treatment programme aimed primarily at enabling the patient to cope with life outside the institution but also at providing a better quality of life while he or she remains hospitalised. Patients are given a wide range of responsibilities, are encouraged to make their own decisions and to take an active part in hospital life rather than the passive role traditionally associated with institutional living.

Effectiveness of treatment

Nowadays, around 90 per cent of patients will be released within a year of their first admission to hospital but many will be rehospitalised within two years.

Schizophrenia is still a very difficult disorder to treat but today's therapies, combining drugs with good quality psychological and social therapies, offer some hope for the future.

Preparing for the exam

Key terms

agoraphobia

anti-social personality disorder

behaviour therapy

catatonic schizophrenia

clozapine

delusions

disorganised schizophrenia

dopamine receptors

emotional arousal

family therapy

milieu therapy

paranoid schizophrenia

phenothiazines

phobic disorders

Preparedness theory

psychopath

residual schizophrenia

schizophrenia

simple phobias

social phobias

systematic desensitisation

tardive dyskinesia

the dopamine hypothesis

undifferentiated schizophrenia

vicarious conditioning

Types of exam question

1. The symptoms and possible causes of schizophrenia (NEAB).
2. Discussion of how genetic, neurochemical and environmental factors contribute to problems of effective diagnosis.
3. Consideration of problems associated with diagnosis of psychosis as a mental disorder.

Self-test questions

1. What are the *three* types of phobic disorders distinguished in DSM-III-R? Outline the main characteristics of each.
2. Briefly describe the phobia of horses experienced by 'Little Hans'. How did Freud explain the cause of the phobia? How would behaviourists suggest that the phobia may have arisen?
3. Outline how Watson and Rayner used classical conditioning to induce a fear of white rats in 'Little Albert'.
4. Outline *three* weaknesses in the behavioural account of phobias.
5. What is the preparedness theory of phobias?
6. What is a psychopath?
7. According to Cleckly, what are the *five* characteristics of a psychopath?
8. What evidence is there that the anti-social personality disorder is due to biological causes?
9. List and briefly describe the *five* subtypes of schizophrenia.
10. Briefly outline *four* theories of the cause of schizophrenia.
11. What is the most commonly used treatment for schizophrenic patients?
12. What drawbacks does this treatment involve?
13. What alternative treatments are available and how successful are they?

Exam question with guidance notes

a   **Distinguish between neuroses and psychoses.**   (4 marks)
b   **Discuss some of the difficulties in diagnosing mental disorders.**
(10 marks)

c   **Discuss the influence of** *either* **genetic** *or* **neurochemical** *or*
environmental factors on mental illness.   (11 marks)
AEB (1993)

a

- This distinction is now rarely used in modern classification systems. The main distinguishing feature between these conditions is contact with reality. A neurosis does not involve loss of contact with reality; the sufferer recognises the symptom as irrational but is unable to modify it. A psychosis, on the other hand, does involve such loss of contact with reality and the sufferer has little or no insight into his or her condition. (Schizophrenia is a psychosis, phobias are neuroses.)

b

- The answer to this question comes mainly from section 9.3 on abnormality, under Difficulties of diagnosis and includes problems of subjectivity on behalf of the diagnostician, the tendency to attribute behaviour to personality rather than situations (the fundamental attribution error) and so on. Use the Rosenhan Core Study to illustrate these points.

c

- Be careful to obey the *rubric* of this particular part: you only have to discuss *one* influence. The examiners' report commented that the environmental option was answered consistently less well than the genetic or neurochemical and that evaluation was not strong in any of the options. Whichever you choose, you need to point out that, since there are many types of mental illness, then these factors are obviously not going to be equally influential in every type of condition.
- If you choose *environmental* factors
  a   Start with the *behavioural* model (reinforcement, modelling and so on as causes), and its limitations;
  b   include *family* influences,
  c   cover other *social* influences such as social class.
     Use any or all three of the *specific examples* covered (schizophrenia, the anti-social personality disorder, phobias) to discuss these influences in more detail. For example, there are social class differences in rates of schizophrenia and the anti-social personality disorder: discuss the possible implications of these findings.
- Now *evaluate*: consider the problems of separating environmental from genetic or neurochemical influences. Don't forget that environmental causation implies that behavioural treatments will be more effective than biological ones: to what extent is this true?
- If you choose either of the other two options, the same applies. For either of these, the theoretical base is the *medical model*; describe and evaluate it.

- Use the examples of specific disorders to discuss the influence of *genetic* or *neurological* factors in more detail.
- Don't forget that evaluation in the case of neurochemical factors should include the effectiveness and disadvantages of *drug treatment*.
- Whichever of the three options you choose, you should consider evidence for a more *interactive* interpretation and the fact, mentioned earlier, that the strength of influence of each of these factors depends on the specific disorder.

Additional exam questions

1. a Describe the main symptoms of schizophrenia.   **(4 marks)**
    b Outline *two* possible causes of schizophrenia.   **(6 marks)**
    c Critically evaluate any *one* psychological treatment programme for schizophrenia. Refer to empirical studies in your answer.   **(10 marks)**
                                                             NEAB (1993)

2. Consider the relative contributions of biological and environmental factors to any *one* psychopathological condition.   **(25 marks)**
                                                             AEB AS (1992)

9.5 Abnormal psychology: 3 – treatments and therapies

Biologically-based (somatic) therapies

Biologically-based therapies use physical and chemical means to change the biological disturbance presumed to be at the root of the psychological problem. There are **three** main types of somatic therapy: electroconvulsive therapy, psychosurgery and drugs.

Electroconvulsive therapy (ECT)

An electric current strong enough to produce a strong convulsion is passed from one side of the head to the other. The patient loses consciousness and upon awakening is often confused and suffers memory loss for events immediately prior to the treatment. Patients typically receive about eight sessions of ECT, two to three days apart.

There are several reasons why ECT remains a controversial technique:

a It still retains an unwelcome legacy from the time when it was indeed frightening and dangerous

b The idea of deliberately producing convulsions is an anathema to many people, compounded by the fact that no one knows why it works

c The side-effects of memory impairment can remain for months or even years.

These days, ECT tends to be a treatment of last resort, reserved for severely depressed or suicidal patients who do not respond to other forms of treatment.

Psychosurgery

Prefrontal lobotomy, introduced by Moniz in 1935, is brain surgery which involves severing the nerve pathways between the prefrontal lobes and the lower centres of the brain. The crude procedures originally used involved the additional destruction of much brain tissue and the irreversible effects were devastating.

This is now very rarely used, and then only as a last resort for those suffering from severe disorders that have continued for a prolonged period and have resisted all other treatments. When it is used, only minute areas of the brain are selectively destroyed and side-effects are far less debilitating.

Drugs

Nowadays, drug therapy is by far the most common biological therapy. **Four** main classes of drugs are used: ·

a **Anti-psychotic drugs** are used for the treatment of the schizophrenias rather than for any other condition, and have been already covered in section 9.4.

b **Anti-depressants** tend to alleviate the physical aspects of depression by making patients more active and less prone to sleep and eating disorders. On their own they cannot address the problems of living faced by many depressed people, but they do make them more receptive to psychotherapy which should be used in conjunction with these drugs.

c **Anti-anxiety drugs** work by depressing the activity of the sympathetic nervous system, reducing anxiety and tension. Their regular use can produce physical dependency if taken in large doses over a long period of time and patients may also develop a tolerance. For this reason they are probably best used on a short-term basis to help the individual cope with any immediate crisis and prepare him or her for psychotherapy.

> Section 7.1 covers the effects of anti-depressants and anti-anxiety drugs in more detail, and also explains the meaning of 'dependency' and 'tolerance'.

d **Anti-manic drugs**, the principal one of which is **lithium**, appear to work by moderating the level of noradrenalin. This moderates or even prevents the cycles of mania and depression. It is basically a preventative treatment which needs to be taken indefinitely and has transformed the lives of many manic depressives. It can, however, produce some unpleasant side-effects including kidney damage and impaired memory and motor speed.

Evaluation

1. The use of drugs, especially the anti-psychotic and anti-manic ones, has been a great source of relief for many people suffering from severe psychiatric disorders

2. Their main limitation is their lack of effectiveness in a certain percentage of people and the side-effects which they produce

3. ECT has been effective in reducing depression when drugs fail

4. Drugs alone do not cure disorders; they cannot solve social and interpersonal problems, but they can help individuals to feel fit to start facing these problems, or to seek psychological forms of therapy to do so.

Activity

You may find it helpful to draw and complete a table using the following subheadings; one line is done for you:

Class of drug	Example	Condition for which it is prescribed	Problems
Anti-anxiety	Librium	Anxiety conditions e.g. intense agoraphobia	Tolerance

Behavioural therapies

The principles underlining the behavioural approaches were discussed in section 9.3 above.

Behaviour therapy, also called behaviour modification, is an umbrella term for treatments that are based on the application of learning principles in order to replace maladaptive behaviour with more effective responses.

Systematic desensitisation

This treatment for phobias was developed by Joseph Wolpe (1958). The procedure consists of **three** phases:

a Relaxation training

b Construction of a fear hierarchy

c Counter-conditioning by pairing the feared object with a relaxation response.

The patient is first trained in deep muscle relaxation. In the meantime, he or she constructs a list of feared stimuli and ranks them from the least to the most disturbing. The patient is then required to use the learned relaxation technique when presented with the feared stimulus, starting with the stimulus which causes the least anxiety and working gradually up the ladder of fears. The relaxation response is physiologically incompatible with the fear response, which is thus replaced. The stimulus may be physically present or the patient may be asked to imagine it.

Flooding

During this treatment, the patient directly confronts the object or situation that provokes the fear. For example, a claustrophobic person may be placed in a closet for four hours. Implosion therapy is a similar technique but involves the phobic person imagining a long exposure to the terrifying stimulus.

The theoretical basis for this technique is that the patient will stop fearing things when he or she is made to face the fact that they are actually quite harmless. In this way, extinction of the conditioned response is able to occur.

Although this treatment is effective, some therapists are reluctant to use it because of the intensity of the anxiety experienced by the patient in the early sessions.

Aversion therapy

This attempts to eliminate undesirable behaviour by pairing it with an extremely unpleasant stimulus, such as nausea or an electric shock.

Aversion therapy has been used to treat alcoholics, heavy smokers, drug addicts, gamblers and people with sexual disorders. It has also been used to prevent or reduce self-mutilation in autistic children. Aversion therapy has several problems associated with it:

a The drop-out rate is high
b The suppression of undesirable behaviour may only last as long as the therapy
c Clients may become anxious and hostile

d Some therapists believe strongly that therapy should not involve punishment.

In its defence, aversion therapy is only used as an absolute last resort for people who are already suffering, for example to reduce self-mutilation in children whose mutilation is painful and harmful and who have remained resistant to all other treatments.

Token economy

This aims to modify patient behaviour by the use of secondary reinforcers, namely tokens, which can be exchanged later for desirable items such as watching television, luxury food or additional recreational time.

It is especially effective with problem school children, juvenile delinquents, the developmentally disabled and psychotic patients.

Behaviour shaping

The principles of behaviour shaping are discussed in Chapter 2. Shaping has proved useful in teaching speech and other skills to developmentally disabled children, for improving the sexual performance of individuals and for promoting social and interpersonal skills in severely withdrawn individuals.

Modelling

This involves learning appropriate responses by observing and imitating another person, often the therapist, performing the behaviour. It has been used successfully in treatment of phobias and, in combination with other methods, is very effective in teaching appropriate social skills and assertiveness to very shy and withdrawn individuals.

Evaluation

Criticisms

1. Psychodynamic therapists consider behaviour therapy to be a **superficial** treatment which does not get down to the root of the problem and is therefore ineffective in the long run.
2. Not all improvements extend beyond the laboratory situation into real life and not all are **maintained** without further treatment (Jacobson 1989).

Advantages

1. It usually achieves discernible results in a relatively short period of time because it targets **specific symptoms**, thereby providing rapid relief of an individual's distress.
2. It is used in the treatment of a wide variety of disorders and is especially effective with disorders in which **anxiety** is a major symptom. It will never be a cure-all, nor indeed would most therapists claim it to be, but it is an extremely useful method of therapy for certain conditions.

Psychodynamic therapy

Psychoanalysis is a very long-term procedure which uses **four** techniques to uncover the repressed memories, fears and conflicts.

Free association

The patient relaxes comfortably and says literally anything that comes to mind, no matter how personal or embarrassing. Interpretation of this material by the analyst provides insight into the unconscious and, eventually, the type of defence mechanisms being used.

Dream analysis

Analysts uncover the disguised meanings of the dream and thereby provide the patient with insight into the motives and feelings which are causing anxiety.

Freud's theory of dreams is covered in more detail in Chapter 7. You may find it helpful to read this.

1. What did Freud believe that all dreams were?
2. How do dreams provide insight into the unconscious mind?

Analysis of resistance

The patient's unconscious mind attempts to block being uncovered; unacceptable motives are painful to acknowledge even to oneself. Once resistance is shown, by, for example, the client objecting to the analyst's interpretation or by 'going blank' during free association, the analyst uses this as a means of revealing vital unconscious conflicts.

Transference

As therapy progresses the clients redirect the feelings they had for the parents onto the analyst, thereby re-enacting early conflicts. In a sense, what is happening is that the patient is recreating an earlier neurosis which, in a therapeutic environment, can be resolved.

Evaluation

Criticisms

See Chapter 2 for criticisms of the underlying theory.

1. As the therapy does not lend itself to scientific testing there is **inadequate proof** of the effectiveness of the therapy.
2. There is no objective means of judging whether the **insight** provided by the therapy truly **reflects unconscious conflicts**, or whether the patient has simply succumbed to the persuasive powers of the analyst.
3. Psychoanalysis has been accused of neglecting the client's immediate and pressing problems while searching for unconscious conflicts in the **remote past**.
4. Traditional psychoanalysis is only available to a highly **selective** clientele, namely those who can afford it, are verbally articulate and intelligent. This excludes large numbers of people, including most children and those suffering from severe psychopathological conditions such as the schizophrenias.

Advantages

Clients have reported a reduction in anxiety and maladaptive behaviour following therapy and, in its modified form at least, it remains a popular form of treatment for those who are seeking extensive **insight into their own personalities**.

Cognitive–behavioural therapies

There is no single cognitive–behavioural therapy but all the approaches are based on the premise that certain attitudes, assumptions and beliefs create and compound psychological disturbances. It is therefore necessary for clients to undergo a process of **cognitive restructuring**, changing these irrational and self-defeating thoughts and attitudes for more accurate and adaptive ones.

We will consider one such approach, that of Albert Ellis.

Albert Ellis's Rational Emotive Therapy (RET)

This is a **confrontational therapy**, bluntly spelling out to clients how irrational and damaging their belief systems are and how much these beliefs control their emotional responses to themselves and others, often making them feel worthless failures.

Ellis has produced a list of **ten** commonly held irrational beliefs, such as 'you must be loved and approved by everyone, all of the time'. The therapist first helps the client to seek out his or her irrational beliefs, which are not always easy to pinpoint, and then uses persuasion, argument, reasoning, even humorous sarcasm to try and change them. Clients are given homework assignments which require them to see how their beliefs operate in everyday life. The emphasis is on less misery, less self-criticism and more positive action.

This type of cognitive restructuring helps clients to gain a more positive sense of self-worth and a more emotionally satisfying and fulfilling life.

Evaluation

Criticisms

1. Psychodynamically orientated analysts say that it ignores the unconscious and the profound effects of childhood experiences.
2. Zajonc (1980) maintains that emotions are not simply the result of cognitive processes and therefore that changing these beliefs will not automatically lead to a more emotionally satisfying existence.
3. Arnkoff and Glass (1982) maintain that

maladaptive thought processes are not simply the product of irrational beliefs but a reflection of a more fundamental **personality structure** which is 'close-minded' and is therefore unlikely to be changed simply by a process of cognitive restructuring.

Advantages

These therapies have been successful, especially in the treatment of depression.

Humanistic therapy

Activity

Before reading on, go over Carl Rogers' theory in section 9.2 on Personality.

What did Rogers believe was the ultimate state of fulfilment which could be reached? Why was this stage never reached by most people?

Client-centred therapy: Carl Rogers

According to Rogers, problems stem from the fact that people receive **conditional** rather than unconditional love and, in trying to seek the approval of others, they lose touch with their own genuine feelings, resulting in impaired personal relationships and forms of maladjustment.

Therapists aim to provide a warm and close atmosphere in which the client can move towards greater self-acceptance and self-esteem so that they are able to fulfil their potential and become self-actualised. An important aspect of the therapy is that it is **non-directive**: the therapist does not advise or interpret, but listens attentively and acceptingly. In this way, the therapist helps the client to clarify the feelings and ideas that he or she is exploring. Once in touch with their true inner feelings and needs, people have the capacity to lead themselves to improved psychological health.

Evaluation

1. Humanistic therapy has been accused of being based on vague, unscientific and untestable concepts.
2. Some humanist therapists do not consider that experimental methods are appropriate for testing the effectiveness of their therapeutic methods and, therefore, almost no controlled research has been conducted.
3. Rogers has shown that during the course of client-centred therapy, people become less negative in their attitudes and gradually show increased hope and self-acceptance with a greater interest and confidence in future plans.

Effectiveness of therapies

The critical question as far as all therapies are concerned is 'Do they **work**?' More precisely, do they help people cope with or overcome psychological problems? Unfortunately, this is an extremely difficult question to answer. The problems involved in assessing the effectiveness of treatment include the following:

1. There is no agreed definition of 'cure' or 'improvement'. Should a treatment programme for a schizophrenic be considered a success if the client has been symptom-free for six months or only if they have returned to the level of functioning they attained before becoming schizophrenic?
2. Even if we can **define** them, how do we **measure** improvement or success? The most common assessment methods involve one or more of the following measures.
   a The therapist's impression of the client's mental state prior to and after treatment
   b The client's own view of his or her state of mind
   c Reports from family and friends
   d Pretreatment and posttreatment personality test scores
   e Measures of change in certain specific behaviours.
      There are problems involved with all these measures.
   • The first three are unlikely to be completely unbiased

   • Personality tests are not necessarily a valid means of predicting whether or not behaviour in real-life situations has become more adaptive
   • Although behaviour therapies may lend themselves well to measuring changes in specific behaviours, it is a great deal more difficult to measure changes in **attitudes and beliefs**, which is what the cognitive–behavioural therapists are trying to change.
3. It is virtually impossible to conduct fully controlled experiments in order to measure the effectiveness of treatments, mainly because such research designs require matched subject groups, one of which is an untreated control.
4. On a more philosophical level, psychodynamic and humanistic–existential therapists maintain that the scientific method is inappropriate for judging the effectiveness of their treatments, and they themselves must be the judges. This results in obvious problems of bias.

Studies of the effectiveness of treatments

Eysenck (1952)

Eysenck published a paper claiming that some forms of therapy actually **retard** improvement. Eysenck analysed 24 studies in which people were either given psychoanalysis or an eclectic form of psychotherapy. He concluded that those who received no treatment were more likely to show improvement than were the treated individuals.

Eysenck's paper attracted much criticism, including the fact that he had used much more stringent criteria for improvement in the treated than in the untreated groups; many researchers did not accept his conclusions.

Smith et al. (1980)

In a very extensive review, Smith *et al.* (1980) looked at 375 controlled studies involving almost 25,000 clients and, using a statistical technique called meta-analysis, found that the 'average' person who received treatment was more improved than were 75 per cent of the untreated control subjects.

Luborsky *et al.* (1975)

They reviewed a series of controlled studies and found that no single type of therapy was consistently better than another. Smith *et al.* (1980) also found that overall behaviour therapy, psychodynamic and humanistic–existential therapies were equally effective but that the last two fostered greater self-awareness.

Kazdin (1986)

Kazdin stated that some therapies do appear to be more effective than others for treating specific disorders:

a Behaviour therapy is the most effective treatment of all for phobias.

b Drug treatment is most successful with schizophrenic disorders and cognitive–behavioural therapies have the best results with sexual problems.

c Cognitive and drug therapies are both equally successful for depression, but the best results for this disorder are obtained by combining these two therapies.

d Shapiro and Shapiro (1982) found that cognitive therapies were better than psychodynamic or humanistic–existential therapies for anxiety and depression.

> There are very many **ethical issues** that are raised by the intervention of therapists in people's lives, and these must not, of course, be ignored. Make sure you read section 10.5 on Ethics and relate the guidelines to this area.

Most therapists do not stick rigidly to one particular therapy but take an **eclectic** approach which takes account of the uniqueness of each individual client and their situation.

Preparing for the exam

Key terms

analysis of resistance	electroconvulsive therapy (ECT)
anti-anxiety drugs	flooding
anti-depressants	free association
anti-manic drugs	humanistic therapy
anti-psychotic drugs	modelling
aversion therapy	prefrontal lobotomy
behaviour shaping	psychodynamic therapy
behaviour therapy	psychosurgery
client-centred therapy	rational emotive therapy
cognitive restructuring	somatic therapies
cognitive–behavioural therapies	systematic desensitisation
counter-conditioning	token economy
dream analysis	transference

Types of exam question

1. Description and evaluation of any type of treatment – often only a single, specified one.
2. Evaluation of effectiveness of various treatment programmes.
3. The problems associated with assessing effectiveness of treatments.

Self-test questions

Self-test questions

1. What are somatic therapies? Briefly describe the *three* main ones and say when they are likely to be used.
2. What are the *four* main types of drugs used for treating mental illness? Briefly describe the effects of each and say when they are likely to be used.
3. Describe *two* types of behaviour therapy.
4. With what type of condition is behaviour therapy particularly effective?
5. What techniques are used by psychoanalytic therapists?
5. Briefly describe rational emotive therapy. What criticisms have been made about such therapy?
7. Describe the principles of Rogers' client-centred therapy.
8. In determining the effectiveness of therapies, what difficulties are encountered?
9. Which type of therapy do studies indicate are most effective with the following problems:
   a schizophrenia
   b psychopathy
   c sexual problems
   d agoraphobia
   e depression?

Exam questions with guidance notes

1. **Compare and contrast the psychoanalytic and somatic approaches used in the treatment of abnormal behaviour.** **(25 marks)**
   AEB (1990

   The first thing you need to ensure is that you know that somatic treatments are *biological* treatments.

   • Start with a description of the different treatment methods but be *brief*.
   • Contrast the *underlying assumptions* on which they are based: the psychoanalytic model as opposed to the medical model. Briefly evaluate each model (don't forget to use information in Chapter 2 to evaluate the Freudian approach).
   • Now provide a more detailed *evaluation* of the effectiveness of each type of treatment, including drug therapy, ECT and psychosurgery for the somatic approaches.
   • Briefly discuss any *ethical implications* of these treatment programmes.

2. **Describe and evaluate behavioural approaches used in the therapeutic treatment of abnormal behaviour.** **(25 marks)**
   AEB (1989)

   Introduce the essay by outlining the rationale underlying behavioural therapies. They are based on the principles of classical and operant conditioning: this approach views maladaptive behaviours which are not biological in origin as caused by either failure to learn appropriate coping techniques or learning of maladaptive behaviour maintained by reinforcement, or both.

Describe each of the main behavioural treatments: systematic desensitisation, flooding (including implosion therapy), aversion therapy, token economies, behaviour shaping and modeling.

You can also include biofeedback (see page 222) since this is a behavioural treatment for stress, based on the principle of positive reinforcement.

Evaluation includes the following points:

- Compared with psychoanalysis and most other psychotherapies, behaviour therapy targets specific behaviours, the methods used are very precisely formulated and any changes in behaviour can be measured, thus providing an accurate assessment of effectiveness.
- Since these therapies are based on the theories of learning, established by carefully controlled experimental methods, they are scientifically valid.
- In terms of time and cost these therapies are relatively economical, especially compared to years of psychoanalysis. In some cases relief from distressing symptoms is achieved quickly. This is, of course, especially valuable when these symptoms (for example, of disabling phobias) have previously prevented the individual from leading a productive and self fulfilling life, as occurs if they feel unable to leave their own home.
- Behaviour therapy is more effective with some conditions than with others. Kazdin (1986) reports that it is the most effective treatment overall for phobias. On the other hand, behaviour therapies are not particularly effective for conditions which are very pervasive and thus affect many aspects of behaviour or for conditions in which symptoms are vague rather than specific such as generalised anxiety disorder in which feelings of anxiety are not associated with specific objects or events as they are in phobic disorders. This means that such therapies are rarely used with personality disorders but are often used with sexual dysfunctions.
- Humanistic therapists maintain that, by treating specific symptoms, behaviour therapists do not give sufficient regard to, or show sufficient respect for the whole person. Psychoanalysts believe that behaviour therapies, by treating symptoms rather than underlying causes, are bound to be ineffective in the long term.

3. a   Describe *one* type of therapy or treatment for mental illness or behavioural disorder.   (10 marks)
    b   Discuss the difficulties of evaluating this type of therapy or treatment.   (15 marks)

                                                                        AEB (1992)

Since the guidance notes for the previous question are concerned with behavioural therapies, we will not choose this alternative but much of what was written in the answer to the last question could be used to answer this one if behaviour therapies were your chosen option. Having said that, remember never to use prepared answers – all answers must be appropriate to the particular question asked.

We will consider this question from the psychodynamic perspective.

Part (a): Very briefly describe the rationale underlying the psychodynamic approach to therapy – that it seeks to uncover repressed (unconscious) desires, thoughts and conflicts resulting from early childhood experiences in order to help the individual come to terms with them from an adult perspective. Describe the techniques involved: free association, dream analysis, analysis of resistance and transference. Mention that psychoanalysis, as developed by Freud, is an extremely long term and intensive therapy but that some more recent psychodynamic therapies are much more short term, some limited to a mere 12 weeks, and tend to concentrate on relief of specific symptoms.

Part (b): To an extent, the difficulties of evaluating any therapy have factors in common. Start with these common problems:

- a lack of agreement on a *definition* of 'cure'. Psychoanalysts maintain that simply removing symptoms is not a cure since it does not remove the underlying unconscious conflict. Behaviour therapists, in contrast, believe that the symptoms are the disorder and their removal constitutes a cure.
- the problems of *measuring* improvement.

For more details of the above, see the text.

Now we need problems specific to psychodynamic therapies:

- Analysts (people who use psychodynamic treatments) do not believe that the scientific method (the use of experimental procedures) to test the effectiveness of the therapy is appropriate, thus little if any evidence of effectiveness exists.
- Psychoanalysis aims to help the individual gain insight and achieve major personality change: this means that assessment of effectiveness is extremely difficult. Not only does it entail comparison over a long period of time, since psychoanalysis is so long term, but the main source of information is the analyst who cannot be consider unbiased. The concepts of gaining insight or changing personality are difficult if not impossible concepts to objectively assess.
- Psychoanalysts argue that effectiveness is not quantifiable. Psychoanalysis is a treatment which, by making fundamental changes to people and their relationship with others, changes those people for the better by providing increased self awareness. These are not outcomes which can, or, some would argue, should, be assessed.

Additional exam question

1. Describe how different types of therapy may be applied to *one* type of problem behaviour. How might their effectiveness be determined?

   (25 marks)

   AEB AS (1989)

10

Perspectives in Psychology

AEB	NEAB	O & C	Topic	Date attempted	Date completed	Self Assessment
✓	✓	✓	**Freedom v. Determinism**			
✓	✓	✓	**Reductionism**			
✓	✓	✓	**The Nature–Nurture issue**			
✓	✓	✓	**Idiographic/Nomothetic Approaches**			
✓	✓	✓	**Ethics**			
✓	✓	✓	**Ethics of Social Control**			
✓	✓	✓	**The Use of Animals in Psychological Research**			
✓	✓	✓	**Behaviourism**			

The Perspectives section of the AEB syllabus consists largely of an overview of topics considered in previous sections. It is a compulsory section, so you need to revise it well. When writing essays on perspectives, bear the following in mind:

1. Use **examples** from the syllabus, drawing them from as **many areas as possible**. Do not simply list studies in a jumbled and disorganised fashion: make a point and illustrate it with reference to studies in topic areas, as appropriate. Suggestions as to how this can be done are made throughout the text. You will need to refer back to previous sections to find these studies: this is good for revision!
2. It is inappropriate to go into any studies in detail; the purpose of this section is not to provide detailed information but to draw together **philosophical strands** which pervade the whole of psychology.
3. There is a great deal of overlap in these sections so, although it is easier to study them as separate sections rather than all together, bear this in mind when considering the issues.

10.1 Freedom versus determinism

One of the most difficult philosophical questions in psychology is the extent to which we are in control of our own actions. **The free will view** regards people as the cause of their own actions; **determinism** holds that actions come from forces over which we have no control. Our intuitive, private impression is that we decide what we want to do, we make free choices. At the same time, we recognise that this freedom only exists within certain limits.

Free will

Logically, if freedom is taken to be the opposite of determinism, this would imply that behaviour is random, entirely unpredictable and has no cause. This is an untenable argument and psychologists use the concept of free will to express the idea that people actively respond to forces rather being passive in the face of them. Behaviour does have a cause, and that cause lies within the individual. The term **soft determinism** is used to express the fact that we do have choice, but our behaviour is always subject to some **environmental** and **biological** constraints.

Determinism

In a sense, every psychological investigation is looking at the causes of behaviour, and is therefore a test of determinism. An investigator tries to measure how a factor (a variable) influences and, therefore, determines behaviour. Nevertheless, this does not remove the strong, private impression that we are free to make choices. The determinist position has very important implications: if behaviour if entirely determined then this removes **responsibility** from the individual. Praise for altruistic actions or blame for anti-social ones become meaningless. Punishment and reward still serve a purpose, but simply as a means of changing future behaviour rather than as a source of congratulation or retribution. The extreme determinist view also implies that behaviour is both predicable and controllable.

The most important arguments **against** determinism are:

1. Current behaviour is not determined solely by past experiences, it depends on **future goals**
2. Since humans have self-awareness, they can behave deliberately and therefore are not entirely controlled by the determinist laws
3. Determinism implies that behaviour is predictable, yet even in the physical sciences there is some uncertainty in outcome. In human behaviour, the uncertainty is far greater.

Activity

Different psychological approaches have different views on this issue: before reading further, think about the views taken by

- learning theory
- social leaning theory
- cognitive theory
- the humanistic approach
- the psychodynamic approach.

The psychodynamic approach is deterministic: behaviour is caused by unconscious forces over which we have little, if any, control and, indeed, of which we are largely unaware. (In an essay, expand on this, mentioning Eros and Thanatos.) This is a form of **biological determinism**.

The radical behaviourist (learning theory) approach represents the extreme in **environmental determinism**: our behaviour is entirely shaped by earlier reinforcement. In this case, external rather than internal conditions control our behaviour.

Skinner takes a very uncompromising stand on this issue. He argues that behavioural freedom is an illusion; we are not free. Skinner advocates that we should abandon our belief in behavioural freedom and design an environment in which behaviour will be directed towards socially desirable ends almost exclusively through the use of positive reinforcement.

The social learning approach advocates a position which Bandura refers as to **reciprocal determinism**, the notion that not only does the environment determine behaviour, but **behaviour determines the environment**. (A simple example is that different individuals seek out different experiences.) In addition to this, mental factors, such as expectations and beliefs, influence and are influenced by both behaviour and the environment. In short, internal mental events, external environments and behaviour all influence one another. When a person uses reason and judgement to decide how to deal with an environment, they are exercising **choice**. According to Bandura, we neither entirely determine our own fate nor are we completely at the mercy of factors beyond our control.

The humanistic approach holds that people are free to choose their own destinies. It is the very decisions made by individuals that create the unique individuals that result. Rogers' client-centred therapy is based on the belief that we are in charge of our lives and responsible for our own personal growth. He does, however, acknowledge that we choose our actions within a 'framework' of those which are likely to have positive consequences.

The biological perspective points to the biological limitations on our freedom of choice. To an extent, all the approaches acknowledge some biological limitation; the biological approach pays particular attention to them and to the interaction of **physiology and the environment**. The argument is that the effect of the environment is limited by genetic, biochemical and constitutional factors which, in turn, have been shaped by evolutionary forces. This is a form of biological and environmental determinism. Nevertheless, certain research, especially in the area of stress, has shown that we do have some influence over our bodily responses: this remains a controversial issue.

Stevens (1984) says that humans are both autonomous and determined that this paradox lies at the heart of our existence: we are influenced by factors outside our control, yet capable, to some degree, of **transcending** these influences.

10.2 Reductionism

Reductionism is the attempt to explain complex phenomena by reducing them to combinations of simpler components. It contrasts with the holistic approach which focuses on the whole living organism. As applied to psychology, reductionism takes several forms:

Physiological reductionism

This is the attempt to explain all behaviour in terms **only** of neurochemical and biochemical processes. The argument is not concerned with whether these biological processes exist, but with whether they **alone** can provide insight into our higher mental processes. Many would argue that our hopes, plans, feelings and desires cannot simply be explained in terms of biological processes. Piaget argued that, when considering the higher forms of conduct, including self-awareness, it is necessary to formulate abstract theories which propose **psychological** laws of cause and effect.

Biological/genetic reductionism

This is an attempt to reduce all behaviour to the action of genes. It views such concepts as intelligence and personality as mainly determined by inherited factors. **Sociobiology** is a reductionist approach to the study of social behaviour, in which all such behaviour is explained in terms of 'units of natural selection'. The motive for all behaviour is assumed to be the perpetuation of one's own genes. Thus, for example, all altruistic behaviour is explained in terms of the action of a 'selfish gene' (see section 6.1 for a fuller discussion). This approach has serious weaknesses as pointed out by Hayes (1986):

a   It reduces everything to a **single simple cause** (gene perpetuation) and ignores the complexity of human experience

b   It is also extremely **selective** in the examples of behaviour which it considers, ignoring numerous examples of both animal and human behaviour which do not fit the theory

c   It has little **scientific evidence** to support its arguments; it proposes genes for various pieces of behaviour (such as altruism) but there is no physiological evidence on which to base these assumptions.

Behaviourism

This approach maintains that the basic units of behaviour are **S–R** (stimulus–response) links and that complex behaviour is simply a series of S–R chains. A detailed criticism of this approach is covered in section 10.7 on Behaviourism: for an essay on this section of the syllabus, select one or two pertinent criticisms.

Machine reductionism

This attempts to explain such activities as problem solving and perception by means of computer analogies. This approach has produced some complex and impressive computer simulations of various processes, particularly problem solving, but it does have one major problem: the reproduction of the unique qualities of humans. We, unlike computers, are affected by boredom and tiredness, we have a sense of humour, ambitions and dreams and we are influenced by anger and love. In short, humans are affected by all kinds of **emotions**, computers are not.

The reductionist approach is strongly challenged by other schools of psychology. **Gestaltists** (whose approach is considered in section 3.2 on theories of perception) argue that when studying any aspect of human functioning, from perception to personality, it is essential to look at events as a whole. Likewise,

humanistic psychologists believe that personality can be understood only as a whole: they believe that values and beliefs cannot possibly be reduced to laws of conditioning or biochemical processes in the brain. According to the humanists, any attempt to analyse personality in terms of simple responses to stimuli (as is done by, for example, Hans Eysenck) is not only futile but is a 'display of disrespect for the unique quality of the human spirit' (Matson, 1971).

Rose (1976) reasons that there are many levels on which behaviour can be explained, from holistic to reductionist, and that no single level is alone sufficient to provide a complete explanation of human behaviour. The levels are, in fact, **complementary**; each one is valid in its own right.

Schizophrenia is a good example. We need to consider the suggested **physiological causes** (that it is a brain disorder) but we also need to take account of other **social factors** both within the patient's immediate social group and within society as a whole. It is only by taking account of all these factors that we can provide adequate therapy: drugs, behaviour therapy, milieu therapy, family therapy and a social policy for providing schizophrenics with supportive environments within the community.

Activity

Consider other examples you could use: personality (contrast Eysenck's biological determinism with the humanist approach); intelligence (relate it to the nature–nurture debate); gender (can differences be accounted for solely on the basis of biology?).

The topic of reductionism is very closely related to that of determinism, since reductionism implies determinism: after all, we have little control over our biology or over the S–R connections which have already been established.

10.3 The nature–nurture issue

One of the central issues in psychology is to analyse the extent to which behaviour is determined by heredity (**nature**) and the extent to which it is determined by experience and the environment (**nurture**). Because of its profound implications, this is possibly the most contentious and divisive issue in psychology, and one which we have encountered frequently throughout this book.

Many psychologists argue that it makes no sense to pose the controversy in terms of an either/or question. All behaviour is **both** genetically **and** environmentally determined because people could not develop at all unless they had both heredity and environment.

Nature and nurture **do not simply add together** to give a certain percentage contribution. They **interact** throughout life in a complex manner, one constantly affecting the other.

Ways of investigating the nature–nurture debate

Untangling the effects of nature from those of nurture is a major problem for psychologists. Many aspects of behaviour cannot be measured at birth; besides which, humans, having spent nine months in the uterus prior to birth, are influenced by the environment long before they are born.

Methods of study vary, depending on the topic under investigation, but include the following:

1. Study of **human neonates**.
2. Studies of **animals**, both neonates and mature. This sometimes takes the form of manipulation (for example, injecting female monkeys with testosterone; depriving cats of a normal perceptual environment).
3. **Cross-cultural studies:** the underlying rationale is that characteristics which are common across cultures are likely to be biological in origin; those which greatly differ are likely to have been influenced by the environment.
4. **Comparison of genetically related and unrelated individuals**, using correlation: the underlying rationale is that if it is true that the more closely two people are genetically related, the higher the positive correlation in the behavioural variable being measured, then a genetic component can be assumed to exist. Various relationships can be explored: identical (MZ) twins; fraternal (DZ) twins; siblings; parents and children. There are various problems

with this type of research, principally that people reared together are likely to share the same environment (look at section 9.1 on Intelligence for greater detail). This problem is partly, though by no means wholly, addressed by investigating twins reared apart and using adoption studies.

The different approaches and the nature–nurture debate

- **Behaviourists** emphasise nurture (learning)
- **Freud** emphasised nature (the id) but acknowledged the secondary influence of the environment in terms of different experiences as the child passes through the psychosexual stages
- **Cognitive psychologists** are interactionist in their approach
- **Humanists** believe that both nature and nurture set the boundaries within which we are free to develop

Activity

In an exam question on this topic, explore two or three areas. Topics could include: aggression, intelligence, perception, schizophrenia, language acquisition, sex and gender differences.

The **implications** of this debate are profound, and these should be explored. Using other sections of this book, think about the implications in each of these areas, for example:

- **Intelligence:** is it worth investing in enrichment programmes? Should children be streamed at some point, as they were in the days of the 11+ exam? What about the even more contentious issues of race and IQ?
- **Schizophrenia:** if it has a biological cause, this has implications for therapy. If it is environmental (especially family) then this also has implications of 'blame' as well as for prevention and treatment.
- **Aggression:** look at this section with special reference to control of aggression, a matter of profound importance to any society. Because the

Freudian and social learning theorists offer radically different views on nature–nurture and aggression, they have profoundly different views on control.

- **Sex and gender:** another area of great contention and profound implications. Are we defying biology if we challenge the status quo or placing both men and women in straitjackets if we don't?

In conclusion, there can be no doubt that both nature and nurture influence behaviour and that they **interact**. Rather than pursuing sterile questions such as which one has the greater influence, perhaps we need to consider the way in which what happens with one affects what happens with the other. This is an extremely complex issue and there is no easy answer to the question of how exactly the environment and genetics influence behaviour.

10.4 The idiographic and nomothetic approaches

There are **two** basic ways in which psychologists can gather data on which to base hypotheses and further research:

1. The **idiographic** approach involves the detailed study of the lives of **particular individuals**. This might be in the form of Case Studies, sometimes of people who are considered representative of the population, sometimes of special cases. (The term 'idiographic' derives from the Greek *idios*, meaning private and personal.)

2. The **nomothetic** approach involves studying a relatively large number of people and **comparing their responses**. The nomothetic approach is a scientific one: most psychological experiments or correlational procedures are nomothetic in type. It seeks to provide **general laws** of behaviour which are generally applicable to all. (The term 'nomothetic' derives from the Greek word for law.)

The debate as to which of these approaches is more appropriate in psychology may seem small and limited but it is arguably one of the most fundamental issues in psychology because of its implications for how psychologists should carry our research and how it affects psychology's standing as a scientific discipline.

Using the two approaches in conjunction

From idiographic to nomothetic

Because these two approaches provide very different types of data, it is very often productive to use both methods in conjunction. We can see how this operates in the following ways: The idiographic approach does not allow us to generalise beyond the single case, though it may suggest hypotheses that can be tested in other people. Consider Piaget's research: he spent a great deal of time making an extensive and intensive study of his own children and then used that as a basis for formulating hypotheses which were tested out on a large number of children, using the nomothetic approach.

From nomothetic to idiographic

The nomothetic approach enables us, within the limits of the representativeness of the sample, to generalise about people and to predict group results, but it does not help us with predictions of the behaviour of any particular individual. In clinical psychology, many individuals who have similar symptoms may be studied in order to draw up a diagnostic category, including prognosis and treatment (the nomothetic approach). But if practitioners are to help particular individuals overcome their problems, they must have the fullest possible understanding of the person. When dealing with particular individuals, the idiographic approach is invaluable in order to provide an accurate assessment of the individual and provide an individual treatment programme.

The approaches of the different schools

The different schools of psychology differ in their use of the two approaches: learning theory and social learning theory predominantly use the nomothetic approach; the psychodynamic and humanistic schools use the idiographic approach.

When answering an examination question, you can also consider the following:

1. The uses of these two approaches when applied to research into **personality** (see Chapter 9).

Eysenck and Cattell are nomothetic, Freud and the humanists are idiographic. Allport is unusual because he uses the idiographic approach in order to develop a trait theory. Allport insisted that no two individuals ever possessed exactly the same trait: although there may be similarities in traits, everyone is unique in the way any particular trait operates within them. The study of common traits can therefore only be helpful as long as we are not blinded to the uniqueness of the individual.

2. Since the idiographic approach depends primarily on the **Case Study** method, consider the uses and limitations of this method. Use examples of studies which use Case Studies, hence the idiographic approach: Washoe, (section 6.3) Chris Sizemore ('Eve') (section 9.4), K.C. (section 3.1) and so on.

3. Consider the argument raised by the humanists and others that the use of the nomothetic approach runs the risk of **'losing the individual'**.

Many would suggest that the argument over which method is more fruitful is not productive because both approaches are needed:

- The idiographic approach is useful in **new areas of research**.
- The nomothetic approach is useful when more **precise definitions** and **generalisations** are required.

10.5 Ethics

The fundamental ethical question in psychological research is **'Does the end justify the means?'**: a balance must be struck between the interest of the participants and the value of the research. Guidelines have been issued in order to provide any person engaged in psychological research with an ethical framework within which to work.

In 1990, the British Psychological Society (BPS) issued revised ethical guidelines for research with **human** subjects. These can be summarised as follows:

Consent: participants should give their informed consent; in studies involving children, informed parental consent should be given. Payment should not be used to induce risk taking behaviour.

Deception: participants should not be deceived unless there is no viable alternative, in which case the approval of other psychologists should be sought before the study goes ahead.

Debriefing: participants should be fully debriefed and any stress caused should be removed.

Withdrawal from the investigation: participants should be made fully aware that they are free to withdraw from the study whenever they wish to do so without incurring any penalty or scorn.

Confidentiality: the source of all information provided by participants should remain confidential.

Protection of participants: investigators should protect participants from physical and mental harm during the investigation.

Observational research: unless participants have given their consent to being observed, investigators must only conduct observation in circumstances where people could normally expect to be observed by strangers.

Giving advice: psychological research must only he given if the psychologist is qualified to give advice in that particular area.

Colleagues: psychologists have a duty to take action if they have cause to believe that these guidelines are being violated by a colleague.

As far as **animals** are concerned, the main guidelines provided by the BPS (1985) are as follows:

Number of animals: the minimum number of animals should be used.

Type of research: animals should not be used for trivial and meaningless research.

Species used: no endangered species should ever be used.

Discomfort and pain: these should be minimal and take account of the species used. Caging of monkeys causes more distress than caging of cockroaches.

Method of study: naturalistic studies are preferable to laboratory ones, but animals in their natural habitats should be disturbed as little as possible.

Laws controlling animal research: psychologists should be fully aware of the law regulating the use of animals for the purposes of research, and should at all times abide by these laws.

The ethics of psychological studies

Consider some psychological studies which have **not** adhered to these guidelines: examples you can consider are:

1. Watson and Rayner with 'Little Albert' (Chapter 2): the mother did not give informed consent, stress and fear during the procedure, long-term psychological harm
2. Konishi's deafening of birds (Chapter 6): permanent mutilation, long-term consequences in terms of mating
3. Sherif's boys camp studies (Chapter 4): inducing prejudice and consequent aggression and other unpleasant effects
4. Asch's conformity studies (Chapter 5): stress, embarrassment, feeling extremely foolish
5. Milgram's obedience studies (Chapter 5): deception, continuous pressure not to withdraw, extreme stress, possible long-term psychological effects
6. Zimbardo's prison study (Chapter 5): extreme stress during the study, possible long-term psychological damage (but note, no deception and no prior knowledge or inkling that the behaviours elicited would be so extreme)
7. Blakemore and Cooper's deprivation studies in cats (Chapter 3): possible immediate stress while in the restricted environment, long-term perceptual damage
8. Harlow's monkey studies (Chapter 8): severe stress and misery over a very long period of time; permanent, extreme emotional damage.

The ethics of different methods

Take note of the fact that no one **method** of research has the monopoly on ethics. Some experiments are completely ethical, some case studies and observations are unethical. Methodology is irrelevant – **all studies, whichever design they use, should follow the ethical guidelines**.

The principles considered so far offer a framework for the conduct of research but they do not address the issue of the **uses** to which this research should be put. The BPS, in their 1978 document on ethical principles for research, state that 'psychologists can and should promote the public understanding of psychological knowledge in such a way as to prevent its misuse or render misuse ineffective'.

There are no easy answers on the question of ethics. Some studies, whether ethical or not, provide information that is so trivial or obvious that you wonder why they were conducted. On the other hand, some of the more ethically dubious, including the work of Milgram and Hofling, have certainly provided some startling and disturbing findings which should make us sit up and think about their implications.

The ethics of social control

When psychology is proposed as a means of social control, in that psychologists attempt to exert control over people's lives, then the ethical issues of such **manipulation** must be considered. Most scientific research has potential for good or bad and investigators have no right to abdicate responsibility for the use to which their research is put. They have a duty to consider whether such use will be to the benefit or detriment of society. The main problem involves deciding what is beneficial and what is harmful, and who should take responsibility for making such decisions.

Skinner, in his book *Beyond Freedom and Dignity* advocated the control and manipulation of the whole of society. Whereas most people have few qualms about behaviour therapy and other techniques being used on individuals to alleviate distress, they may be quite horrified at the idea of such totalitarian control. Skinner advocated that **behavioural engineering** should be used to prevent problems such as overpopulation and pollution, and that it was unethical not to do so.

Behavioural control does involve someone else planning what an individual or a whole society should do and, as such, threatens their freedom. In every society people's right to choose is limited for the good of others. The extent to which behavioural control is put into practice will depend on the ethics in the existing society.

10.6 The use of animals in psychological research

The practical reasons for using animals

1. There is an **evolutionary continuity** between humans and other animals; it is considered worthwhile to study simpler species in order to help understand the more complex ones.

2. The environment of animals can be manipulated in a way in which human environments cannot. This provides cause–effect data which could not be obtained from human studies. Such studies include **deprivation** and **enrichment**.

3. Many **generations** of certain animals can be studied over a relatively short time span. This is especially useful in studying genetic processes and the effects of early experiences on adult behaviour.

4. It is legally possible to treat animals in ways which are neither desirable nor practical in humans (and which, some people would argue, should not be permitted in animals). Since their environments can be strictly controlled and manipulated, animals can be subjected to **more rigorous experimental procedures** than can humans.

Activity

In an essay, go through these points and provide examples (very briefly, no details required). For example:

1. Pavlov, Skinner, Hubel and Wiesel
2. Harlow, Blakemore and Cooper

and so on.

Contributions that animal research has made to psychological knowledge

1. Knowledge of the processes of **learning** through operant and classical conditioning has been useful in many respects, for example, as the basis for the treatment of phobias and other anxiety conditions.

2. Research on animals has led to the development of some anti-anxiety drugs, new methods of treating pain and depression and insight into how drugs may affect the developing foetus.

3. Data on the factors producing learned helplessness have provided a model for the causes of certain types of **depression**. This has formed the basis for prevention and treatment of a common problem which causes intense suffering in humans.

4. Animal research is responsible for much of which we know about the **brain**, about how drugs affect behaviour and about sensory systems.

5. Animals can provide useful **hypotheses** for subsequent testing on humans.

The case against animal research

This can be considered as two different but closely related problems: the **limitations** of the research (what animal research cannot tell us about humans) and the **dangers of extrapolating** from animal behaviour.

Limitations

1. The ethologists have demonstrated that each species is adapted to its own **ecological niche** (environment) and adapted differently according to lifespan and other important features. Therefore generalising from one species to another, especially when they are greatly distanced on the phylogenetic scale, is not appropriate. (An example of this generalisation is Bowlby's comparison of imprinting and human attachment.)

2. The ethologists have also shown that much complex behaviour, such as maintenance of territories and courtship patterns, is largely **instinctive** in animals. This behaviour is so varied in humans that there is little evidence that it is instinctive.

3. The behaviour of animals reared in laboratory conditions bears little resemblance to that of animals in their **natural settings**, never mind a resemblance to human behaviour.

4. **Language** has a profound influence on human behaviour, including the transmission of

information from one generation to another. There is very little evidence of cultural transmission in animals, and what little there is applies only to a few higher-order species. (Cultural transmission is discussed in section 6.1)

Dangers of extrapolation

We must be very cautious in generalising from animals to humans. Several unwarranted assumptions may be made:

The use of analogy

An **analogy** is an argument based on the assumption that behaviours which **look** the same in animals and humans have the same **cause** or **motivation**. Thus, Bowlby compares imprinting in chickens with bonding in humans. Some sociobiologists equate behaviour which benefits other animals with altruism in humans and assume they have the same motive. This, bees dying to defend the hive are equated with humans risking their lives, or dying, to save or protect others.

Anthropomorphism

This is the assumption that human motives and emotions exist in animals. To talk of lemmings committing suicide implies that they consciously decide to end their own lives.

One of the greatest dangers of extrapolation is the assumption by theorists that, since these behaviours are often innate in animals, then they are innate in humans. This applies to such areas as sex differences, aggression and altruism.

The ethics of animal studies

See section 10.5 on Ethics. This is very important.
The use of animals in psychological research is extremely contentious. Many people feel that psychologists needlessly subject animals to extreme cruelty, often in order to carry out research which is trivial and pointless. Others argue that animal research can make a valuable contribution to our knowledge of human behaviour, especially in the area of relieving human suffering, and is therefore justifiable.

Note:
the use of animals is one of the most emotive issues in psychology. Be careful not to put a completely one-sided argument or dwell too long on ethics if the questions is of a more general nature.

10.7 Behaviourism

The school of behaviourism was founded by **John Watson**, who argued that psychology should adopt a scientific approach. It should reject introspection as a method and abandon terms like 'mental state', 'mind' and 'emotion', since they have no explanatory value. Behaviourism insists that the only subject matter for psychology should be **behaviours** that can be **observed** and **measured**.

Behaviourists argue that all behaviour is shaped by the environment. Each stimulus gives rise to a response; learning consists of a change in the connections between stimuli and responses. For this reason, behaviourism is referred to as stimulus–response, or S–R, psychology. Behaviour, being determined by the laws of conditioning, can therefore be controlled and altered.

Criticisms and limitations

An underestimation of the complexity of human beings

Behaviourists, in trying to reduce all behaviour to S–R connections, have failed to appreciate the **complex nature** of human thinking. Human intelligent behaviour is amazingly complex and no matter how many clever tricks Skinner taught to animals, there is simply no comparison in terms of complexity with that of even very young humans.

A failure to take account of mental experiences

Behaviourism concentrates solely on **observable behaviour** and ignores feelings, desires, hopes and ambitions. Many people would argue that it is these aspects of humans, the pleasures, pains and deeply felt emotions, which are the very essence of humanity and a much more worthy subject for study than simple behaviour patterns.

The restricted range of behaviour studies

Behaviourists studied animals rather than humans; they argued that they must first study the simple units of behaviour in order to understand complex behaviour. In the event, behaviourists only generalised their findings to very **limited aspects** of human behaviour, leaving many aspects unexplained in terms of the laws of conditioning. Aspects of perception, cognition and development were often not studied at all.

Lack of explanatory power

Related to the last point is the fact that there are vast areas of human understanding and behaviour which **cannot be explained** in terms of S–R connections and the laws of conditioning. A few examples will suffice:

a **Tolman (1932)** demonstrated that rats can form internal cognitive representations (a 'map in the head') of a complex maze. This learning is not necessarily shown immediately but may appear later when, for example, the rat is reinforced for running the maze. For this reason it is called **latent learning**. The important point is that reinforcement did not occur at the time of learning, and therefore defies the laws of conditioning.

b **Kohler (1925)** demonstrated that apes may make a sudden realisation of the solution to a problem, a phenomenon known as **insight learning**. Again, this does not obey the laws of conditioning.

c Despite Skinner's attempt to explain language acquisition in terms of operant conditioning, many psychologists do not accept that the laws of conditioning can possible cope with the **complex nature** and **speed** of language acquisition.

Contributions

The scientific method

It has been argued that the introduction of the scientific method to the study of human behaviour is the single most important contribution that behaviourism has given to psychology. Before the advent of this approach, no systematic attempt was made to establish cause and effect by manipulation of variables and strict control of conditions.

Behaviour therapy

This is discussed in section 9.5 and has made a valuable contribution to the treatment of abnormal behaviour, especially phobias.

Biofeedback

This is discussed in section 7.5 on stress. It has contributed to control of blood pressure and other dangerous conditions (though some would question its effectiveness).

Treatment of some childhood problems

The laws of operant conditioning, carefully and systematically applied, have been effective in the treatment of some behavioural problems in children, often those associated with aggression, temper tantrums and defiance of authority.

In conclusion, many psychologists appreciate that behaviourism has made some important contributions to the understanding of behaviour, but few would agree with the principles of radical behaviourism. They would maintain that such phenomena as cognition, consciousness, emotion and self-awareness must be given due consideration in the study of behaviour.

Preparing for the exam

Key terms

anthropomorphism

behavioural engineering

biological determinism

biological/genetic determinism

determinism

environmental determinism

extrapolation

free will

Gestalt

idiographic

introspection

machine reductionism

nomothetic

physiological reductionism

reductionism

social control

soft determinism

Types of exam question

Read the discussion at the beginning of the chapter, bearing in mind that essays in the perspectives section must be an overview of different areas. Essays are of *three* main types:

1. The contributions of the different schools or approaches: the psychoanalytic, behaviourist, cognitive, social learning approach and so on.
2. An evaluation and comparison of the different methods: these questions are covered in Chapter 11 on Methodology.
3. Philosophical issues such as the nature–nurture debate, freewill versus determinism and so on.

Self-test questions

1. What is meant by the term 'soft determinism'?
2. Outline *two* implications of the determinist position.
3. Outline *two* objections to the deterministic position.
4. Which of the following approaches are determinist:
   - Psychoanalysis
   - Humanistic
   - Behaviourism
   - Biological approach
   - Social learning theory?
5. What is meant by the term 'reductionism'?
6. What objection do Gestaltist and humanists have towards reductionism?
7. What is the nature–nurture debate in psychology? List areas in which it is an issue.
8. List the ways in which the nature–nurture debate has been investigated.
9. What is the idiographic approach?
10. What is the nomothetic approach?
11. Outline an advantage and a disadvantage of each.
12. Briefly outline the main ethical principles that the British Psychological

Society (BPS) recommend should be taken into account for research:

a on humans

b on animals

13. Name *three* studies which do not meet these ethical guidelines and say why.

14. Why are animals used in psychological research?

15. What are the basic premises of behaviourism?

16. Outline *three* criticisms of behaviourism.

17. What have been the main contributions of behaviourism?

Exam questions with guidance notes

1. **Use evidence to discuss ethical problems involved in psychological research.** (25 marks)

AEB(1988)

Beware of simply listing studies in a disorganised way.

• The guidelines provide a basis for discussing problems: we suggest you go through them *one by one*, mentioning studies which might be considered to breach these guidelines. Examples of such studies are listed in the text, and you should be able to provide additional or alternative ones if you so wish.

Additional points to bear in mind are:

• *Deception* is a particular problem, especially in social psychology, because many studies would be invalid if participants were fully informed. Some forms of deception are more justifiable than others. For example, the deception involved in the Clark and Word (1972) study of helping (section 5.5), in which participants believed that the purpose of the study was to fill out a questionnaire whereas the study was actually designed to investigate the conditions under which a person might go to another's aid, seems reasonably easy to justify.

• It's not always possible to anticipate the level of *stress*; this was pointed out by both Milgram and Zimbardo.

• By all means use Milgram but do *not* make his research the only study you consider. Neither should you concentrate entirely on research using animals. As always, when answering questions in the perspectives section, draw from a variety of areas in psychology, and consider a number of issues.

• Whatever method of study is used, ethics must be a prime consideration.

2. **Discuss the use of animals in psychological research and consider the ethical issues raised by such research.** (25 marks)

AEB (1992)

Read the question! The first part says 'discuss the use of animals in psychological research!' It is *not* therefore simply concerned with ethics, although this is obviously an important part of the answer.

• You need to include *all* the material given in the text on the section on the use of animals:

a practical reasons for using animals

b the contributions of animal research

c the limitations of animal research

d the ethical guidelines to be followed when animal research is conducted

e examples of studies which cause distress, physical and psychological suffering to animals and/or permanent disability.

Use as many references as possible. The examiners' report commented that many candidates seemed unable to do justice to *both* requirements of the question. They further remarked that 'evaluation was often emotive rather than informed'.

Additional exam questions

1. Discuss the issue of freedom versus determinism in a psychological contest. **(25 marks)**
   AEB (1990)

2. 'Reductionism will eventually reveal the answers to all problems of explaining behaviour.'
   To what extent do you agree? **(25 marks)**
   AEB (1988)

3. Discuss the nature–nurture issue in psychology, using appropriate evidence to support your answer. **(25 marks)**
   AEB (1989)

4. Compare and contrast idiographic with nomothetic explanations of psychological issues. **(25 marks)**
   AEB (1987)

5. Evaluate the contribution of the behaviourists to psychology **(25 marks)**
   AEB (1990)

6. Describe and evaluate the *contributions* of EITHER the psychoanalytic approach OR the behaviourist approach to an understanding of human behaviour. **(25 marks)**
   AEB (1993)

   (Guidance notes are provided for this question from the psychoanalytic view in Chapter 2.)

7. A number of Core Studies were conducted on animals, for example Sluckin and Sluckin (imprinting), Gardner and Gardner (Washoe), and Rawlins (rhesus monkey research). Some psychologists believe that the study of animals can tell us a lot about human behaviour and experience. Other psychologists, however, believe that we can learn very little about people from the study of animals.
   Evaluate the advantages and disadvantages of using animals in psychology, using the above studies to illustrate your answer. **(30 marks)**
   (Hint: you might consider ethical and practical issues with the use of animals and also the implications for theory.)
   Oxford and Cambridge (1994)

8. In psychology the nature–nuture issue is concerned with the extent to which behaviour is determined by nature (heredity) and the extent to which it is determined by experience and the environment (nurture).

The following core studies provide some insight into the relative contributions of nature and nurture to our understanding of behaviour:

1. Deregowski: pictorial perception and culture.
2. Bandura, Ross and Ross: transmission of aggression.
3. Sluckin and Salzen: imprinting and perceptual learning.
4. Gould: a nation of morons.

For each of these studies:
    i   Briefly outline the main findings of the study.   **(12 marks)**
    ii   Evaluate the studies in the light of what they tell us about the relative contributions of nature and nuture to the particular behaviours with which they are concerned: perception; aggression; imprinting; intelligence.   **(18 marks)**

9. In the *Guidelines for Ethical Principles in Psychological Research* published by the British Psychological Society (1990), it is suggested that research workers should take account of the following issues:

Consent: have the subjects of the study made an informed consent to take part? Have the parents of child subjects given informed consent to the research procedures? Have payments been used to induce risk taking behaviour?

Deception: have the subjects been deceived? Was there any other way to carry out the study other than by using deception? Have the procedures been approved by other psychologists?

Debriefing: have the subjects been effectively debriefed? Has any stress caused by the procedures been removed?

Withdrawal from the investigation: are the subjects clear that they can withdraw from the study at any time without penalty or scorn?

Protection of the participants: investigators must protect participants from physical and mental harm during the investigation.

Take any *two* of the following studies and consider each in the light of the following questions.

a   Piliavin
b   Schachter and Singer
c   Milgram
d   Festinger and Carlsmith
e   Bandura.
(Write down the names of the two you have chosen.)
    i   What type of method was used in these studies (design, choice of subjects, where it was carried out, use of controls, etc.)? **(8 marks)**
    ii   In what ways do these studies conflict with the ethical guidelines?
        (6 marks)
    iii   Evaluate whether the studies should have been performed.
        (4 marks)

iv How could the studies have been altered to conform to the ethical guidelines? **(8 marks)**

v How would these changes have affected the results? **(4 marks)**

Oxford and Cambridge Specimen Paper

11

Methodology and Statistics

Topic

AEB	NEAB	O & C		Date attempted	Date completed	Self Assessment
✓	✓	✓	**Methods in Psychology**			
✓	✓	✓	**Writing Hypotheses**			
✓	✓	✓	**Sampling**			
✓	✓	✓	**Psychological Tests**			
✓	✓	✓	**Descriptive Statistics**			
✓	✓	✓	**Inferential Statistics**			

11.1 Methods

No single method can be applied to all the activities that are of interest to psychologists; for practical and ethical reasons, a variety of methods must be used.

Non-experimental methods

Observations

In order to test a hypothesis, it is sometimes sufficient to observe behaviour in either a natural or structured environment. Observations are often used prior to a more controlled study in order to provide more specific hypotheses concerning cause and effect. The main problems are the lack of control over extraneous variables and that of observer bias.

Observer bias

Bias is particularly difficult to avoid in observational studies because every individual is likely to pay attention to different aspects of behaviour and make different interpretations of what they see. Psychologists try to control bias by

- Having a clear idea of exactly **what** they are observing
- Using a system for **categorising** and **recording** information
- Using **more than one observer**.

Inter-rater reliability (or inter-observer reliability) is a measure of how much agreement there is between two or more observers. If each observer produces similar data then inter-rater reliability is high and it can be assumed that they have objectively recorded the behaviour in question.

Types of observations

1. **Naturalistic observation** involves observing the behaviour of people or animals in their **natural surroundings**.

Uses and advantages

- It has high **ecological validity**, especially if the participant is unaware that he or she is being

observed. ecological validity is the extent to which the behaviour corresponds to its equivalent in an everyday, real-life setting.

- It can be used in situations in which manipulation would be **impractical** or **unethical**.
- It is particularly useful when working with young children or animals.

Problems and disadvantages

- There is **lack of control** over variables.
- The method cannot be used to infer **cause** and **effect**.
- **Observer bias**, discussed above.
- Observing people without their knowledge and consent raises **ethical** issues, whereas observing people with their knowledge tends to produce behaviour which is self-conscious and stage-managed. One way of reducing this effect is for the researcher to become a familiar and accepted part of the environment so that participants forget that they are being observed. Alternatively, discretely placed video cameras can be used to record behaviour, which has the added advantage of allowing detailed analysis later.
- Studies cannot be **replicated**.

2. **Controlled observation** is that which take place in a **controlled environment** which has been manipulated by the researcher.

Uses and advantages

- There is more **control** over the situation as compared to naturalistic observation
- More **specific** behaviour can be studied, as this is elicited by the situation
- It is easier to use cameras and other recording equipment than in naturalistic observations.

Problems and disadvantages

- The more controlled situation **reduces ecological validity**
- It may involve **ethical problems** (though not necessarily the same as those in naturalistic studies), such as causing discomfort, deception and invasion of privacy
- **Demand characteristics** are more likely to be a problem (see 'The Experimental Method' for a definition of demand characteristics).

3. **Participant observation** involves the observer taking an active part in the situation he or she is observing.

Uses and advantages

- It allows an **indepth understanding** of a situation that non-participant observations simply cannot provide.
- It has **high ecological validity**.

Problems and disadvantages

- It is **time consuming**.
- It is **ethically questionable**, as participants are usually unaware of being observed and their privacy is likely to be invaded to a greater extent than when observed from the outside. Participants may confide personal feelings to the observers which might have remained confidential if they had been aware they were part of a study.
- It may lead to increasingly **subjective perceptions**, as the researcher becomes more involved in the situation.
- It can be quite **dangerous**.

Activity

1. What are the ethical guidelines for observing people without their consent? Check your answer by referring to section 10.5 on Ethics, and include it in an essay on the observation method.
2. There are examples of all these types of observation studies in this book, for example:
   - **Naturalistic observation:** Schaffer and Emerson (attachment)
   - **Controlled observation:** Ainsworth (attachment)
   - **Participant observation:** Rosenhan (Core Study, section 9.3).

   In each case, ensure you can describe these *very* briefly, using them to illustrate the uses and problems involved in different types of observational methods, including specific ethical problems.

Survey

A survey involves asking a lot of people for information, often relating to beliefs or opinions, or asking people for information about some aspect of their behaviour which would be difficult to study in any other way. Questions can be posed **verbally** or, more commonly, in the form of a **written questionnaire**. Surveys often involve a very large sample and attempt to generalise findings to the whole population.

Uses and advantages

- It samples **large numbers of people** at relatively little cost
- It provides information (on attitudes and opinions and so on) which **cannot be obtained by direct observation**.

Problems and disadvantages

- It is difficult to obtain an **unbiased sample**. It is likely that many people selected as part of a random sample will refuse to participate.
- People **may not tell the truth**. There is a tendency for people to portray themselves in a positive light, the so-called **social desirability bias**, and also to give the answers that they think the researchers would like.

Questionnaire

A questionnaire is a set of written questions that can be answered easily. It has to be constructed with great care so that it can be easily understood and accurately answered. Questions can be fixed choice or open-ended.

Fixed choice questions are those in which respondents have to choose an answer from a certain number of alternatives.

Uses and advantages

- Such questions are relatively **quick and easy** to answer so respondents are more likely to complete the questionnaire

- It allows **comparisons** to be made between participants
- It enables statistics to be **compiled** and **analysed**.

Problems and disadvantages

- It does not allow respondents to express opinions different from those offered in the fixed choice answers
- It reduces spontaneity of expression.

Open-ended questions are those in which respondents are **not restricted** in their choice of answer.

Uses and advantages

- It allows respondents to answer more fully and in their **own terms**, thus providing answers which reflect participants' views more fully and accurately.

Problems and disadvantages

- It is difficult to **code** and **quantify**
- It cannot be **statistically analysed**.

Interviews

The interview technique is used a good deal in psychology and the style varies depending on the purpose of the research and the treatment of results.

Types of interview

1. **An informal interview** avoids predetermined lists of questions; the researcher has a focus of interest and may use some **unstructured and open questions** to guide the interviewee who is encouraged to talk freely and in their own terms.

Uses and advantages

- This is a particularly useful tool in **case studies**, especially when interviewing people who have psychological problems or have had unusual experiences
- It is likely to produce a variety of responses, including some very **rich** and **insightful** material.

Problems and disadvantages

- It is very difficult to **quantify**.
- It is almost impossible to **analyse** objectively.

2. **A structured interview** involves a list of questions that require the respondent to choose from a selection of possible answers. In many respects such an interview technique is merely a **verbal questionnaire**.

Uses and advantages

- It is **quantifiable** and can be **analysed** easily
- It allows **comparisons** to be made between respondents
- Compared to paper and pencil questionnaires, it is more **friendly** and allows interviewers to check answers which may appear contradictory.

Problems and disadvantages

- It is **inflexible**
- It produces **shallow** and possible **inaccurate** data
- Since answers must be verbally expressed to another person, it increases the tendency to give **socially desirable** answers rather than true ones.

3. **A semi-structured interview** falls somewhere between the extremes of the informal and structured interview. An example would be a **structured interview using open-ended questions**. The researcher has a predetermined set of questions, and requires responses to all of them, but allows the participant to answer in his or her own terms.

Uses and advantages

- The interviewer is able to **follow up** any particularly interesting and revealing answers
- It allows a degree of **flexibility** which enables participants to provide the information they want to give, and researchers to gain greater insight.
- Data can be **quantified** (though not as easily as the structured approach).

Problems and disadvantages

- It is difficult to **replicate**

- Compared to the structured interview, interviewers may be more inclined to **influence** the respondents' answers.

4. **A clinical interview** is an unstructured interview used in a particular way. It is often quite long and its purpose is to gain an insight into an individual's **thought processes**. The interviewer often begins with the same question for all interviewees, but subsequent questions are tailored to the particular responses given.

Uses and advantages

- It is very useful in providing insightful information on a very **specific** topic.
- It is useful in interviewing **children** when a structured approach may result in valuable information being missed.

Problems and disadvantages

- It is unlikely that any two interviews will be **comparable**
- Interviewers using this technique need to be **well trained** because they have to keep the overall purpose of the interview in mind, and pose questions carefully in order to provide responses which focus on the area of interest but do not 'lead' the participant too much into a particular train of thought.

Activity

Which famous developmental psychologist used clinical interviews (see section 8.2, on Cognitive development). Use this as an example in an appropriate essay question.

Case Study

A Case Study is a detailed investigation of an individual or group of similar individuals. It may include information gained from records, interviews and psychological tests.

Uses and advantages

- It is invaluable in studying individuals who have had an unusual experience or a rare condition, such as severe deprivation, brain damage or an unusual ability. Clinical psychologists often build up case histories of their patients in order to identify possible **roots** of psychological problems.
- It provides **detailed information** about people which could not be obtained by other methods.

Problems and disadvantages

- **Generalisations** cannot be made from the information
- Many case studies are **retrospective** and involve incomplete records and memories which are likely to be distorted and inaccurate
- They are very **time consuming**.

Activity

1. It would be useful to compile a list of Case Studies which you can use in essay questions to demonstrate its use. Try to obtain a selection from the following (depending which areas of the syllabus you are studying).
- A study of brain damage, perhaps involving problems with perception or memory
- A study involving the effects of restored sight
- A study of severe deprivation
- A study of primate language acquisition
- A study used by Freud
- A study demonstrating unusual sexual/gender development.
2. How does the problem of incomplete and probably distorted data relate to Bowlby's study of juvenile thieves covered in section 8.1 on Sociability and attachment?
3. Why was Freud criticised for using Case Studies as the basis of theories which supposedly apply to everyone?

Correlational study

A correlational study seeks to establish the extent to which two variables are **related**. For example, suppose we measure the number of hours of sunshine and the number of ice creams sold. It is possible that:

a   As one increases, so does the other
b   As one increases, the other decreases
c   There is no relationship.

Positive correlations involve a relationship in which, as one variable **increases**, the other **increases**.

Negative correlations involve a relationship in which, as one variable **increases** the other **decreases**.

In the case of ice creams and sunshine there is likely to be a positive correlation. Between sale of ice creams and sale of umbrellas there is likely to be a negative correlation.

This method does not involve the manipulation of one variable, as in the experimental method. It simply involves the measurement of two variables in order to see if a relationship exists between them. **It does not tell us anything about the reasons why the relationship exists.**

Uses and advantages

- **Predictions** to be made from the data; if there is a correlation between two variables, then knowledge about one allows us to predict what may happen to the other
- **Inter-rater reliability** and **validity and reliability of tests** can be established (see section 11.4 on psychological testing)
- It provides data that can then be used for more detailed analysis of cause and effect.

Problems and disadvantages

- It does not demonstrate cause and effect, simply a **relationship**
- A correlation coefficient only expresses a **linear relationship** (as one variable increases, the other decreases or increases), it does not allow for more complex relationships such as that between arousal and performance (the Yerkes–Dodson law, mentioned in section 7.5).

Activity

1. Why do we need to be cautious about the interpretation of studies showing a positive correlation between watching violent television and aggressive behaviour, as discussed in section 5.6?
2. Correlational studies can be particularly useful in the study of intelligence when we wish to see if there is a relationship between different types of abilities.
    a   If a positive correlation exists between different abilities, which theory is supported?
    b   If little or no such relationship exists, which theory is supported?

The experimental method

The essential feature of an experiment is that it involves the deliberate **manipulation** of one variable, while trying to keep all other variables **constant**.

The experimenter starts with a **hypothesis**: an informed guess which states that one variable is likely to have an effect on another. An example is that noise level affects performance.

Variables involved

Independent and dependent variables

The variable which it is believed will affect another (in this case, the noise level) is called the **independent variable (IV)**. The variable which is likely to be affected (in this case, the performance) is called the **dependent variable (DV)**, because, if the hypothesis is correct, it depends on the independent variable. In other words, in our example, performance **depends** on noise level.

Activity

Identify the **independent** and the **dependent** variable in the following:

1. An experiment to investigate the effect of fatigue on reaction time.
2. An experiment to see if men drive faster than women.
3. An experiment to see if vitamin tablets can boost IQ.

   Answers: 1. IV = fatigue level, DV = reaction time; **2.** IV = sex, DV = driving speed; **3.** IV = the taking of vitamin tablets or not, DV = IQ gains

Operationalising variables

The experimenter decides on an accurate way of **operationalising** the two variables, that is, putting them into a form that can be accurately **manipulated** and **measured**. Performance may be measured on a variety of tasks and tests. Decisions need to be made about the type of noise and the various levels which will be used.

Extraneous variables

These are all the factors other than the IV which might have an affect on the DV and therefore give a false set of results.

Some of these variables may have a **constant** effect and result in **constant errors**, others may be **random** in their effect and lead to **random errors**. In our example, the experimenter must ensure that all participants do exactly the same tasks and tests under the same conditions except the noise level, that there is no extra uncontrolled noise, that all participants are tested at the same time of day and so on.

Constant error variables may include how stuffy the room is and what type of lighting is used; these are constant for everyone.

Random error variables might be how individual participants are feeling, what their opinion of the noise is, their ability to hear it and so on.

Any variables which are uncontrolled and mask the effect of the independent variable are known as **confounding variables**.

Demand characteristics and experimenter bias

These are both potential sources of error. In an experimental situation, both experimenters and participants have expectations about the study.

Demand characteristics are those features of an experimental setting that encourage the participants to make a particular interpretation of the study and behave accordingly, perhaps in the way they think the experimenter would want or expect.

Experimenter bias may occur if experimenters, albeit unconsciously, convey to the participants how they are expected to behave.

Reducing extraneous variables

There are several ways in which this can be done. *Matching groups* A very important control in an experiment is to ensure that, if separate groups of participants are used in each condition of the study, they are **matched**. In the example used, the experimenter may use two groups of participants, one at a high noise level and the other at a low level. It is essential that there are no initial differences between these two groups in terms of their ability to do the tasks and tests. For various practical reasons, it is often not possible to test the participants before the proper study is conducted, so the experimenter matches the two groups on any factors which might affect performance (in general terms, the factors that might affect the dependent variable): age, general intelligence, sex and so on.

Activity

Many students, when asked how participants should be matched, make the automatic response of age and sex. Often these are important variables on which to match, but don't assume that they are always important or that they are the only variables on which matching should be done. The general rule is: match on anything which is likely to affect the **dependent variable**. This is important, as exam questions often ask how participants should be matched.

If, for example, you were comparing the effect

of two teaching methods on students' ability in chemistry, you would match them first on ability in chemistry (or science), not simply on general intelligence, as this is too vague. You would then need to match on age and sex as well.

Using standardised procedures   Every step of the experiment is described beforehand, so that the experience of all the participants is identical, or as nearly identical as possible. This ensures that the experimenter does not unconsciously influence the results by varying the experiment slightly.

Using standardised instructions   Instructions for every participant should be identical. These are decided beforehand, thereby ensuring that all the participants are given exactly the same information.

Using a single blind design   In this, participants do not know in which condition they are being tested.

Using a double blind design   In this, neither the experimenter nor the participants know under what conditions the participants are being tested.

Design of experiments

The independent groups design

Also known as independent samples design, this involves using **completely different individuals** in each condition of the study. For example, if we are testing the effects of a drug, we would use two separate groups, one of whom was administered the drug and one who was not.

One of the most common ways of using an independent groups design is by dividing participants into two groups, the **experimental group** and the **control group**, and then introducing a change for the experimental group and not the control group. The control condition gives us a **baseline** against which to judge our results. A control group, then, is a group for whom the experimenter does **not** change the IV.

The repeated measures design

This involves using the same individuals and testing them under **two or more different conditions**. Suppose, for example, we want to find out if people react more quickly to an auditory stimulus (like a bell) or to a visual stimulus (like a light). We can use the same participants and test them with both types of stimulus. On the other hand, we may wish to discover if reaction time depends on time of day. In this case, we would again use the same people but test them once at one time of day (say, at 9.00 hours) and again at another time (say, at 21.00 hours).

Order effects
A repeated measures design however, introduces other confounding variables which we must be careful to control, namely **practice effects** or **fatigue** and/or **boredom**, together known as **order effects**. We can use a technique known as **counterbalancing** in order to try and control for order effects. Counterbalancing involves systematically varying the order of presentation of the trials.

If we return to our example of research times:

*   When investigating the effects of time of day, we would test half the participants at 9.00 hours, then at 21.00 hours and then reverse this for the other half, testing them at 21.00 hours, then at 9.00 hours.
*   When investigating the effects of the type of stimulus, we would carry out the whole experiment at one time but randomise the order of the trials, so lights would flash and buzzers sound for all the participants in a different order for each one.

Comparing the two designs

The independent groups design

Uses and advantages

*   It can be used in cases where a repeated measures design cannot be used, such as looking at **sex differences**
*   There are **no order effects** to confound the results
*   Participants do not disappear between one condition and another.

Problems and disadvantages

- There may be important differences between the two groups before the study begins and these differences, rather than the IV, may be responsible for differences in the DV. There are various ways we can try to overcome this:
  By **random allocation** of participants to each condition
  By **matching** the groups on the **DV**, as suggested above.
- Since we need different individuals in each condition, we have to find a **larger number of participants** compared to those required in a repeated measures design.

The repeated measures design

Uses and advantages

- The major advantage of this design is that it **controls for individual differences** between participants
- It requires **fewer participants**.

Problems and disadvantages

- It cannot be used on occasions when the groups must obviously be **different**, as in the case of investigating sex differences, cultural differences or age differences.
- It cannot be used in studies in which participation in one condition will **affect responses in another condition**. For example, if you were investigating whether the number of times a person met another affected the degree to which they liked them, you could not use a repeated measures design.
- It involves problems of **order effects**.
- Since participants take part in all conditions, they are more likely to guess the purpose of the study, hence increasing the effect of **demand characteristics**.

The matched pairs design

This involves matching every participant in one group with a very similar person in the other group. This is different, and more accurate, than simply matching

groups as a whole but it is a difficult design to use because of the obvious **practical problems** involved.

Types of experiments

The laboratory experiment

This enables the experimenter a high degree of control over variables.

Uses and advantages

- As this involves more precise control over variables, it increases the confidence that the **IV**, rather than extraneous variables, has caused any observed effect on the DV.
- It is easier to **replicate** the study and replication is an essential feature of the scientific method, as discussed later
- Variables can be more carefully **observed** and more precisely **measured** than outside the laboratory.

Problems and advantages

- Since behaviour in the laboratory is very narrow in its range and people may well behave very differently in artificial laboratory conditions than they would normally, the method **lacks ecological validity**, that is, it does not sample real-life behaviour
- It increases the likelihood of the results being affected by **demand characteristics**, discussed earlier
- Humanistic psychologists argue that the treatment of participants in psychological experiments **dehumanises** and **depersonalises** them.

The field experiment

This is an experiment carried out in a more natural setting, such as a local street, library or on public transport. The independent variable is still manipulated and behaviour observed by the researcher.

Uses and advantages

- The behaviour sampled has greater **ecological validity**
- It permits study of behaviour which only occurs **outside** the laboratory, such as reaction to a road sign
- It avoids or at least reduces **demand characteristics**.

Problems and disadvantages

- It is not possible to have such **tight control** over variables in the field
- It may raise fewer **ethical problems** than those in the laboratory, but such factors as invasion of privacy, deception and causing people stress and embarrassment are still problematic.

Activity

The Core Study of Piliavin (section 5.5) and the study by Sherif (section 4.5) are useful examples to use in an appropriate essay. In each case, consider:

a What independent variables are being manipulated?

b What important variables are difficult, if not impossible, to control?

c What ethical problems are faced by the researchers?

The natural experiment

This is an experiment in which psychologists investigate the effect of an independent variable which has occurred in a natural situation but has not been directly manipulated by the researcher. For example, a primary school may decide to try out a completely new reading scheme and the effects of this could be compared with a similar school using a different reading scheme. In such a case, the independent variable, that is, the type of reading scheme, exists but has not been manipulated by the experimenter.

This is not a true experiment because the psychologist is unable to manipulate or control variables. For this reason it is sometimes referred to as a **quasi-experiment**. It is possible, though, to compare two groups, the equivalent of an experimental and a control group.

Uses and advantages

- It permits study of aspects of life which could not be deliberately manipulated, often much broader, less specific behaviour than that which is studied by other experimental methods. It therefore has considerable **ecological validity**
- It can be a rich source of data from which to formulate **new hypotheses**
- Participants are usually unaware that they are taking part in a study, thus reducing problems of **demand characteristics**.

Problems and disadvantages

- There is little **control** over any variables, including the independent variable. This means that cause and effect cannot be established with any certainty.
- It cannot be **replicated**. Replication is an important feature of the scientific method, as discussed below.

The scientific method

In order to be **scientific** (or **empirical**) a method should adhere to the following standards:

1. Data should be collected **objectively**. This means that extraneous variables, included those resulting from experimenter bias and demand characteristics should be eliminated.
2. The study should be **replicable**, that is, it should be possible to repeat it and obtain similar results. If a study is not replicable, it cannot be shown to be reliable and the results may be due to the particular conditions of the study rather than the effect of the IV.
3. The measures used must be **valid**. The concept of validity is discussed in section 11.4 on psychological tests.
4. The **theories** generated from the method should be
   - able to explain the findings

- able to be falsified (disproved)
- generate new hypotheses which can also be empirically tested.

The laboratory experiment is generally considered to be the most scientific method because it is the method which most closely satisfies these criteria.

How scientific are psychological studies?

In psychological research no method is likely to be fully scientific because it is very difficult to satisfy all these criteria due to the following considerations:

The sample should be representative

The extent to which this is possible in psychology is constrained by the following considerations:

a Every person is a **unique individual**, so this seriously limits the extent to which we can generalise to a group of other individuals.
b Miller (1967) estimated that 90 per cent of studies conducted in the USA used **college students**. There is no reason to suppose that they are typical of any group in terms of gender, intelligence, age, personality, social class or culture.
c Many major studies, regardless of whether or not they are conducted with college students, use **male** participants
d Many studies use **volunteers**. Ora (1965) stated that volunteers tend to be insecure, dependent, easily influenced, aggressive, neurotic and introverted.
e Some studies use **animals** and therefore their findings are not strictly generalisable to humans.

Activity

Think of some major psychological studies, including some of the Core Studies in this book, which use students, volunteers, and male only participants. Use these to illustrate an essay which discusses how representative samples of participants in psychological studies really are.

Psychological studies should sample real-life behaviour

We have considered the problems of laboratory studies with respect to the type of behaviour it samples. **Heather (1976)** complains that behaviour in the laboratory is 'unrecognisably different from its naturally occurring form'. Other experimental arrangements, such as field studies, do help to overcome this problem. Even though they are not as precisely controlled, many psychologists consider this a small price to pay to obtain a more realistic sample of everyday behaviour.

Extraneous variables should be carefully controlled

Again there are several problems to consider:

a We return to the **variability** of humans: participant variables are impossible to control as no two people will approach the situation or respond in the same way
b **Experimenter bias**, as discussed earlier, prevents objectivity
c **Demand characteristics**, also mentioned earlier, constitute uncontrolled confounding factors
d It is obviously impossible to control every feature of a situation and many would argue that the greater the control, the more **artificial** the situation becomes and the less likely it is to sample real-life behaviour.

11.2 Hypotheses

The formulation of a **hypothesis** is the starting point for any psychological study. Initially, a hypothesis may be stated in general terms, for example, students perform better on an empty stomach than on a full stomach. But before research is conducted, the variables must be precisely defined and **operationalised**; for example, students will perform significantly better on a mental arithmetic test in the half hour before lunch that in the half hour after lunch. The hypothesis then becomes a precise formulation of what will happen in a particular situation. Before a study is conducted, the investigator formulates **two** hypotheses:

- The **null hypothesis** states that there will be no effect and that observed differences will be due to chance factors
- The **alternative hypothesis** states that any differences between conditions, or relationships between variables, will be significant.

In our example, the null hypothesis would be 'Students will not perform significantly better on a mental arithmetic test in the half hour directly before they eat lunch than in the half hour directly after lunch; any differences will be due to chance factors.'

The alternative (or experimental) hypothesis would be 'Students will perform significantly better on a mental arithmetic test in the half hour directly before they eat lunch than in the half hour directly after lunch.'

These hypotheses clearly state, in exact terms, what the two variables are: the independent variable is the exact **timing** of the test: the half hour before lunch or the half hour after lunch. The dependent variable is **performance** on a mental arithmetic test.

The word 'significantly' is essential because we are only interested in a difference which is large enough not likely to have been caused by chance.

After carrying out the study, we can decide which of the two hypotheses is supported and which is disconfirmed.

One tailed and two tailed hypotheses

The hypothesis above is one tailed because we have stated that we expect people to perform **better** before lunch than after lunch. If we had said that we just expected a **difference** between prelunch and postlunch performance the hypothesis would have been two tailed because prelunch performance could have been better or worse than that after lunch.

One tailed hypotheses predict the **direction** of the effect one variable will have on another – better, worse, faster, slower – and are sometimes called **directional** hypotheses. (They are **one** tailed because the results are expected to go in **one** direction.)

Two tailed hypotheses (sometimes called **non-directional** hypotheses) make less specific predictions about the relationship between variables – perhaps stating that a variable will affect or influence another

or predicting that there will be a difference between two conditions.

How to formulate hypotheses

1. Decide whether the alternative hypothesis should be one or two tailed, and word accordingly.
2. Decide whether you are looking for a **difference** or a **relationship**. In other words, is the design an experiment or a correlation?
3. Do not be vague. Decide how the variables were operationalised and use these exact terms. Make sure that your hypothesis includes **both variables**: the independent and dependent if it's an experiment; the two variables which are expected to show a relationship if it's a correlation.
4. The alternative hypothesis should refer to a **significant** difference or correlation.

11.3 Sampling

The target population

In any investigation, the target population is every member of the group we are studying and therefore, to whom our hypothesis may apply. It may be all nuns, doctors or A level psychology students.

If we are interested in the effect of room temperature on exam performance then our target population is all people taking exams. As it is impossible to study all people taking exams we have to choose a **sample** that, we hope, will be **representative** (typical) of the entire population of examinees. If our sample is not representative of the population then we will not be in a position to make generalisations about how temperature affects exam performance. A **biased** sample is one that is not typical of the rest of the population.

There are several ways of selecting a sample but, as we will see, not all the methods are likely to produce a sample which is representative of the target population.

Random sampling

In a random sample **every** member of the target population has an **equal chance** of being selected. A random sample can be obtained by putting all names of people in the population in to a hat and drawing a sample, or by giving everyone in the target population a number and using random number tables or a computer to generate a random list.

Random sampling is excellent in theory but in practice it is rarely possible since we do not have access to all the members of the target population and, even if we did, those chosen may not wish to participate.

Stratified sampling

A stratified sample is one in which there is the **same proportion** of members of subgroups in the sample as in the target population.

If different subgroups within a population can be identified, then a sample can be selected which reflects those subgroups. For example if the population is all people taking exams we can identify subgroups based on subjects. So, if 10 per cent of students are doing exams in French, 30 per cent are doing them in physics and so on, then our sample should consist of 10 per cent French students, 30 per cent physics students and so on.

Gathering a sample in this way is often complicated and time consuming and for these reasons it is rarely used in psychology.

Opportunity sampling

Opportunity sampling involves using people who are readily available. Psychology students usually use an opportunity sample for their coursework: that is, a sample comprising friends, relatives and anyone else mug enough not to refuse! Opportunity sampling is not likely to be representative of the population and is mainly used for the sake of convenience.

Self-selected samples

Sometimes psychologists advertise for people to take part in studies, and these volunteers make up the sample. Such a method provides willing participants but is extremely unlikely to produce a representative sample.

Sample size

The size of a sample depends upon a number of factors:

1. The larger the size of the target population, the larger the sample ought to be, in order to be **representative**
2. The greater the variability within a target population, the larger the sample should be in order to **reflect this variability**
3. The constraints of **time** and **money** limit the size of a sample.

A general rule is that a sample should be sufficiently large to be representative but not so large that the study becomes too expensive or time consuming to be manageable.

11.4 Psychological tests

A good test meets **three** criteria:

1. Reliability
2. Validity
3. Discriminatory power and standardisation.

Reliability

Reliability refers to how **consistently** a test measures what it claims to measure. A tape measure would not be reliable if it gave different readings when measuring the same object. Similarly, an IQ test is not reliable if it yields different scores with the same population each time it is used. There are several ways in which consistency can be measured.

Split-half reliability

Scores on half the test items are correlated with scores on the other half. Since items on some tests get progressively more difficult, it is usual to correlate scores on even numbered items with scores on odd numbered items. High split-half reliability means that the test is **internally consistent**.

Test–retest reliability

The same group is tested on two separate occasions and the two scores are correlated. This can be problematic because people may remember the test items. This is overcome by the next method.

Equivalent forms reliability

Different tests, of equivalent difficulty, are given to the same group on two separate occasions.

The above methods measure how reliable **the test itself is**. Another form of reliability which is important is:

Scorer reliability

This is a measure of how similar the results of a test (or performance) are between the different people who are scoring. On tests which have only a limited number of answers, then agreement is likely to be high. However, on tests, observations or interviews in which there are no standardised responses, then scorer reliability is more problematic and much training may be required in order to establish an acceptable level of scorer reliability.

Validity

Validity refers to the extent to which a test measures what it claims to be measuring. For example, a test claiming to measure general intelligence would NOT be valid if it consisted only of a series of mathematical exercises and nothing else.

There are several of ways of establishing whether or not a test is valid:

Face or content validity

This simply refers to whether the test seems, on the face of it, to be measuring what it is supposed to measure. In the previous example, if all items on the test seem to be measuring numeracy and nothing else, it does not **look** valid.

Concurrent validity

This involves correlating test scores with another independent measure of the same psychological variable. For example, a new personality test may be compared with results on a previously validated test.

Predictive validity

This involves correlating the results of a test with future performance. The results of many tests are used to predict future behaviour. Examination results are used as a measure of how competent a person may be at performing a certain job or studying at a higher level. If it transpires that these tests are not predictive of future performance, then their predictive validity is low and they are not a great deal of use.

Construct validity

This refers to the extent to which our common sense notions and psychological knowledge indicate that a test is measuring what it purports to measure. For instance, a test of anxiety should show high scores when people are tested just prior to an important interview or a parachute jump and comparatively low scores when people are in a relaxed situation.

Activity

Many students use the terms 'reliability' and 'validity' as if they were interchangeable but they are clearly very different.

Remember:

• A test is **valid** if it measures what it is supposed to measure

• A test is **reliable** if the same results are obtained when the test is used again in similar circumstances.

Make sure you know the difference between 'scorer reliability' and 'test reliability' and that, when answering structured questions, you take note of which type of reliability is being referred to.

Finally, note that this chapter includes a worked exam structured question in which the concepts of reliability and validity are involved.

Discriminatory power and standardisation

A good test must be able to **discriminate** between the individuals taking it. For example, the purpose of an intelligence test is to reveal differences in levels of intelligence. If all items are extremely easy or exceptionally difficult, these differences will not be revealed. In order to be discriminative, tests are standardised by administering them to a large and representative sample of the population and then making adjustments so that the range of scores is **normally distributed** (see section 11.5).

Preparing for the exam

Key terms

alternate hypothesis

biased sample

case study

clinical interview

concurrent validity

confounding variable

constant error

construct validity

controlled observation

correlational study

counterbalancing

demand characteristic

dependent variable

directional hypothesis

discriminatory power

double blind

ecological validity

equivalent forms reliability

experimental hypothesis

experimenter bias

extraneous variables

face validity

field experiment

independent group design

independent variable

informal interview

inter-rater reliability

laboratory experiment

matched pairs design

natural experiment

naturalistic observation

non-directional hypothesis

normal distribution

null hypothesis

objectivity

observer bias

one tailed hypothesis

opportunity sample

order effect

participant observation

predictive validity

quasi-experiment

questionnaire

random error

random sample

repeated measures design

replication

representative sample

scorer reliability

self-selected sample

semi-structured interview

single blind

social desirability

split-half reliability

standardisation

standardised procedures

stratified sample

structured interview

target population

test–retest reliability

two tailed hypothesis

Types of exam questions

1. In the AEB syllabus, there is a compulsory question on Paper 2, consisting of a study followed by questions concerning that study. This is known as the structured question (it is identical on the AS paper) and there are three fully answered ones at the end of this chapter.

2. As far as the NEAB is concerned, there is a compulsory structured question on both Paper 1 and Paper 2.

3. Description and evaluation of the different methods. There will be an essay question on the Perspectives section of the AEB. On the Oxford and Cambridge and NEAB, these questions are integrated into all the papers

and may appear as complete questions or parts of questions.

No matter which exam board you are sitting, you will have to answer questions on methodology and statistics.

Self-test questions

1. Name *three* non-experimental methods.
2. What are the advantages and disadvantages of the methods you have named?
3. What is ecological validity, and which methods are likely to lack it?
4. What is meant by the term 'demand characteristics'?
5. What is the difference between a negative and a positive correlation?
6. How can correlations be used to establish the reliability and validity of psychological tests?
7. When carrying out an experiment, what design options are available? Outline an advantage and a disadvantage of each design.
8. What is meant by standardised procedures, and why is it important to use them?
9. The scientific method requires that certain standards must be met. What are these?
10. To what extent do methods used in psychology meet these requirements?

Exam questions with guidance notes

1. a **Describe** *two* **non-laboratory methods used in psychological research**.

   (10 marks)

   b **Discuss the desirability of studying behaviour away from the constraints of the psychology laboratory.** **(15 marks)**

   AEB (1993)

This is fairly straightforward, provided you answer the question.

- In **a**, you are asked to *describe* the methods – in other words say what each involves – *not* to discuss them. Use examples, but *not* instead of a description. So if, for example, one of your choices is the method of observation, describe all the different types of observation such as naturalistic, controlled and participant, mentioning uses and problems as an integral part of the description.
  (Notice that you are not restricted to non-experimental methods for your choice; you can use experiments, or quasi-experiments, which take place outside of the laboratory.)
- In **b**, you need to discuss the *difficulties/limitations* as well as the *advantages* of working outside the laboratory.
- The main *advantage* is the increase in ecological validity – discuss this in some detail.
- The main *disadvantage* is the lack of ability to control all types of variables, and therefore the inability to accurately establish cause and effect.

- A suitable *conclusion* would be that both laboratory and non-laboratory studies are useful, depending on the exact nature of what is being investigated and that, given the complex nature of humans and the circumstances of their lives, psychologists should not confine their studies to those conducted in the laboratory nor to those conducted outside it.

2. **Describe what is involved in the experimental method as it is used in psychology and discuss its limitations.** **(25 marks)**
AEB (1989)

- Describe the essentials of the laboratory experiment, as is done in the test, explaining such terms as *independent* and *dependent variable*.
- Do the same for the less scientific but nevertheless still experimental methods of *field studies* and *natural experiments*.
- Discuss the *limitations* (problems and disadvantages) of each of these with special emphasis on lack of ecological validity, the need for control of extraneous variables including experimenter bias and demand characteristics, and the problems of ethics (discussed in Chapter 10).
- Balance the disadvantages and problems against the *advantages,* with emphasis on the value of the experimental method in establishing *cause* and *effect*.
- Mention the particular problems which psychological research has in using the experimental method; those mentioned in section 11.4 under 'The scientific method' and 'How scientific are psychological studies?'.
- Discuss the humanistic view that experiments *dehumanise* and *depersonalise*.
- *Conclude* with reference to the fact that, depending on the exact nature of the behaviour being investigated and the specific *aims* of the investigator, the experimental method can be extremely useful or totally inappropriate.

Additional exam questions

1. Critically discuss the use of the scientific method in psychology.
(25 marks)
AEB (1988)

2. There are several alternatives to the experimental method in pursuing psychological investigations. Describe and discuss *two* such alternatives.
(25 marks)
AEB (1991)

3. Among the Core Studies there are several that use the case study method or some method that is similar to a case study. Included in this group are Hodges and Tizard, Sperry, Thigpen and Cleckley, and Freud. Using these studies to illustrate your essay, evaluate the use of the case study method in psychology.
Oxford and Cambridge Specimen Paper

4. The experimental method is seen by some psychologists as the best possible method for scientific investigation. However, an alternative

viewpoint sees the experimental method as inappropriate for investigations of human behaviour and experience.

Take any *two* of the following studies presented in the core syllabus and answer the following questions about *both* of your chosen studies.

    a Piliavin, Rodin and Piliavin (subway Samaritans)

    b Festinger and Carlsmith (forced compliance)

    c Schachter and Singer (emotion)

    d Dement and Kleitman (dreaming)

Write down the names of the two you have chosen.)

Read parts i to v before you start writing.

  i   What are the general aims of the two studies?   **(4 marks)**

  ii   Briefly outline the experimental procedure in each of your chosen studies.   **(4 marks)**

  iii What are the advantages and disadvantages in the use of the experimental method to study these two topics?   **(8 marks)**

  iv Describe how you could use *one* other method (for example, observation, case study, psychometrics, interview, etc.) for *each* of the two topics instead of the experimental method.   **(6 marks)**

  v   Evaluate the advantages and disadvantages of the alternative methods you have suggested for the two topics.   **(8 marks)**

Oxford and Cambridge (1994)

11.5 Statistics

Descriptive statistics

All research inevitably produces results that need to be **understood** and **interpreted**. Inferential statistics (described in the next subsection) allow us to make inferences and draw conclusions; descriptive statistics merely allow us to describe and summarise data.

Measures of central tendency

The mean

The mean is calculated by adding all the scores together and then dividing by the number of scores.

The mean of 16, 16, 17, 18, 18, 29 is **19**

The mean is a useful statistic, as it takes all the scores into account, but it can be misleading if there are one or more extreme scores all in the same direction.

The median

The median is the halfway point that separates the higher 50 per cent of scores from the lower 50 per cent of scores. This is more useful than the mean when there are extreme scores or a skewed distribution.

The median of 16, 16, 17, 18, 18, 18, 29 is **18**

The mode

The mode is the score that occurs most often. It is possible to have more than one mode. If a set of data has two modes it is called **bimodal**. The mode is useful in cases when other scores may be meaningless. For example, in Milgram's study of obedience, it is useful to know the highest voltage value which most participants would administer rather than a mean voltage value.

The mode of 16, 16, 17, 18, 18, 18, 21, 29 is **18**

Measures of variability or dispersion

The range

The range is simply the distance between the **smallest** and **largest** number in a set of scores. It is a fairly crude measure of variability since it only takes account of the highest and the lowest scores, and one very high or low score can distort the data.

The standard deviation (SD)

The standard deviation is a statistical measure of dispersion of a set of scores and tells us how much, on average, scores **differ from the mean**. A large SD tells us that the spread of scores is wide, a small SD tells us that all the scores are clustered together around the mean.

Frequency distribution curves

A frequency distribution curve gives us a pictorial view of variability and tells us how **frequently** each score occurs.

Normal distribution

Some frequency distributions produce a symmetrical, bell-shaped curve known as a **normal distribution**. Such a distribution has three main properties:

1. The mean, median and mode occur at the same mid-point
2. The distribution of scores is identical either side of the mean
3. The curve never actually reaches the horizontal axis but trails away into infinity on either side.

A normal distribution tells us what proportion of scores falls within **certain limits**:

a   The proportion of scores falling between the mean and one standard deviation above or below the mean is **34 per cent**.

b   The proportion between 1 and 2 standard deviations above or below the mean is **13.6 per cent**.

c   The proportion of scores 2 standard deviations above or below the mean is **2.4 per cent**.

(These percentages are approximate.) Figure 11.1 shows these percentages on a frequency distribution curve.

All these percentages may appear confusing, but the concept of standard deviation is very simple and very useful. Suppose we have a huge number of scores on a personality test measuring extraversion–introversion and these scores are normally distributed. The mean is 15 and the standard deviation is 3. This means that:

34 per cent of people score between **15 and 18** (between the mean and 1 SD above the mean)

34 per cent of people score between **15 and 12** (between the mean and 1 SD below the mean)

13.6 per cent of people score between **18 and 21** (between 1 and 2 SDs above the mean)

13.6 per cent of people score between **12 and 9** (between 1 and 2 SDs below the mean)

2.4 per cent of people score below **9**

2.4 per cent of people score above **21**

A score of 18 is **one standard deviation** above the mean

A score of 21 is **two standard deviations** above the mean and so on.

This gives us a great deal of useful information when we obtain scores for individuals. High scores are extrovert, low scores introvert. We know that a person who scores 22 is highly extrovert, more extrovert than 97.6 per cent of the population. Someone with a score of 14 is moderately introvert, but not extremely so, and so on.

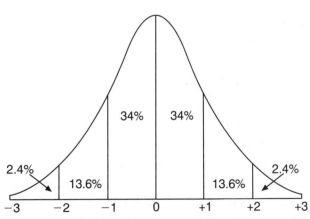

Figure 11.1 Normal distribution curve showing standard deviations from the mean

Skewed distributions

Not all sets of scores are normally distributed. Sometimes distributions are **skewed**, negatively or positively. A positive skew occurs when most the scores fall **below** the mean. A negative skew occurs when most of the scores fall **above** the mean. Figure 11.2 shows the appearance of skewed distributions.

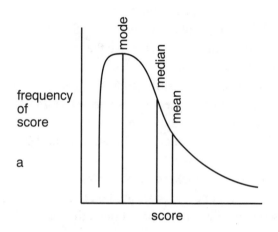

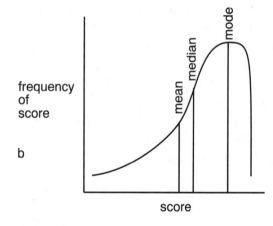

Figure 11.2 Skewed distributions
a Positive skew
b Negative skew

Correlational statistics

Correlational statistics allow us to express the strength of a relationship between two variables as a number between 0 and 1, or between 0 and −1. This number is known as a **correlation coefficient**. A correlation coefficient of +1.00 would indicate a perfect position correlation between two variables, that is, as one variable increases so the other does in exact proportion. For example, the number of heads in a room is usually in direct proportion to the number of arms in a room, provided no one has one arm or two heads. Perfect correlations are very rare in psychological variables, but the nearer a correlation is to +1.00 or −1.00, the stronger is the relationship. A correlation coefficient of −0.9 suggests a strong negative correlation. A correlation coefficient of 0 or near 0 indicates little or no correlation at all. (Correlational statistics are unusual in that they can be descriptive or inferential).

Scattergrams

Scattergrams are ways of illustrating correlational data. All correlational data deals with a set of paired scores and each of these pairs can be plotted on the scattergram. One variable goes on the x axis and the other on the y axis (it does not matter which way round). Each pair will have a number which can be located on the x axis and a number on the y axis and a cross is made at the point on the diagram where they meet. The shape of the scattergram indicates the **type** and **strength** of the correlation, as shown in Figure 11.3.

Inferential statistics

Inferential statistics enable us to reach a decision about whether results obtained are due to the variable we are investigating, or due to chance factors. The purpose of **statistical tests** is to enable us to estimate the extent to which the results could have occurred by chance. This tells us the extent to which it is safe to infer that the results from a particular sample of people are **valid for the whole target population**.

We can never be 100 per cent sure that results are not due to chance factors but tests allow us to establish the probability that results are due to chance.

Levels of significance

If we can never be 100 per cent sure that our results are not due to chance, what percentage of 'sureness' will we settle for?

For most research in psychology we settle for being 95 per cent sure that results are not due to chance before we accept the alternative hypothesis. This

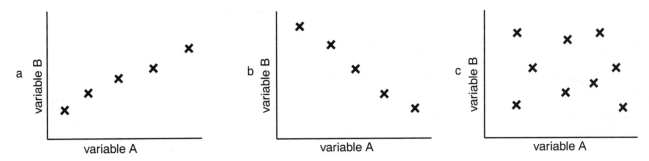

Figure 11.3 Scattergrams showing type and strength of the correlation
a Positive correlation
b Negative correlation
c No correlation

means that we use a **0.05** level of significance, and we reject the null hypothesis when there is a 1 in 20 or 5 per cent probability or less that our results are due to chance factors.

A **0.01** level, that is a more **stringent** level of significance, is used if erroneously accepting the alternative hypothesis could cause serious problems, such as health problems. This now means that the chances of accepting the alternative hypothesis due to a fluke occurrence is now at most 1 in a 100.

The following abbreviations are commonly used to express probability:

p = the probability that the results occurred due to **chance**.

P > 0.05 = the probability of the results being due to chance is **greater than 5 per cent**. This statement would be used if we carried out a statistical test on our data and found our result was not significant at the 0.05 level.

p ≤ 0.05 = the probability of the results being due to chance is **less than or equal to 5 per cent**. This statement would be used if we carried out a statistical test and found that our results were significant at the 0.05 level.

Type 1 and type 2 errors

We can never be 100 per cent certain that results are not due to chance. If we use a 0.05 level of significance and get a significant result, we must accept that there is a 5 per cent probability that our results are due to accidental factors and not to the independent variable or the strength of the relationship as we have claimed.

- A **Type 1 error** occurs if we reject the null hypothesis when the results are due to chance.
- A **Type 2 error** occurs if we retain the null hypothesis and claim that results are due to chance factors when they are not.

The more stringent the level of significance, the more likely we are to make a Type 2 error. For example the 0.01 level of significance states that we can only accept the alternative hypothesis if there is equal to or less than a 1 in 100 probability that results are due to chance.

If we use a stringent level of significance in order to try and avoid making a Type 1 error, we automatically increase the likelihood of making a Type 2 error. Conversely, if we use a more lenient level of probability (say, 10 per cent), we reduce the chances of making a Type 2 error but increase the probability of making a Type 1 error.

The 0.05 level of significance is popularly used by psychologists because it offers the best balance between the risk of making a Type 1 and the risk of making a Type 2 error.

Levels of measurement

Raw data comes in a variety of different forms. The three we are concerned with are:

1. **Nominal or frequency data**
    The nominal scale involves putting data into categories and counting the **frequency** of occurrence. Nominal data is the least sophisticated way of recording results.
2. **Ordinal or ranked data**
    The ordinal level allows us to put data into an

Table 11.1 Choosing a test

Design	Level of data		
	Nominal	Ordinal	Interval or ratio
Repeated measures	Sign test	Wilcoxon sign test	Related *t* test (parametric)
Matched pairs	Sign test	Wilcoxon sign test	Related *t* test (parametric)
Independent measures	Chi Squared	Mann–Whitney '*U*'	Unrelated *t* test (parametric)
Correlation	Chi Squared	Spearman rho	Pearson moment (parametric)

order: first, second, third and so on. Ordinal data gives us more information than nominal data but it is still limited because we do not know how large the gap is between the first and second or between the second and third scores and so on.

3. **Interval and ratio data**

    Interval and ratio level data are data measured on an objective scale which has **equal intervals**, for example, measuring reaction time, temperature or length.

    Ratio data is very similar to interval data but has the added property of having an **absolute zero point** and includes **no minus numbers**. In the analysis of psychological studies at A level standard, we are rarely called upon to distinguish between interval and ratio data.

Suppose we carry out a study which involves using reaction time as the dependent variable.

*   If we use the actual measure in milliseconds then this is **ratio level** measurement
*   If we express the scores by saying 'Participant number 3 was fastest, participant number 56 was second fastest' and so on, this is **ordinal level** measurement
*   If we simply count how many participants reacted more quickly than 0.5 seconds as opposed to those who took 0.5 seconds or longer to react, then this is **nominal level** data.

Choosing a test

Not all statistical tests can be used on all types of data. In order to decide which one to use, we need to know the **level** of data and the **design** of the study. Once we know this we refer to a table like that in Table 11.1 for the appropriate test.

Parametric tests

The related *t* test, the unrelated *t* test and Pearson's product moment are all **parametric tests**. Parametric tests are often described as being more sensitive or more **powerful** than non-parametric tests. This means that they are more likely to detect **statistically significant effects**.

When we can use parametric tests

Parametric tests can only be used when our data meets **three** requirements:

1. The level of data must be **interval or ratio**.
2. Scores must be drawn from a **normally distributed population**. Note that it is the **population** that should be normally distributed rather than the sample chosen.
3. There should be **homogeneity of variance**. This means that the variability of the two sets of scores being compared must be similar. This can be done by working out the variance (which is the standard deviation squared) for both sets of scores.

Preparing for the exam

Key terms

bimodal
central tendency
correlational coefficient
dispersion
frequency distribution
homogeneity of variance
inferential statistics
interval data
mean
median
mode

nominal data
normal distribution
ordinal data
parametric test
range
significance level
skewed distribution
standard deviation
Type 1 error
Type 2 error

Types of exam questions

See the notes under 'Types of Exam Questions' at the end of the last section (on methods).

Structured questions with answers
Question 1 (AEB 1987)

Read carefully the details below of an investigation. Answer each of the questions that follow.

Many GCE A level candidates claim that they are able to work more effectively when they have music as a background noise. Other candidates argue that silence is a more effective background for study purposes.

An experimenter decides to investigate these claims. An independent measures design is used on a group of 40 subjects who are randomly selected from a college population of A level students. The test comprises of a list of 30 carefully chosen 7 letter anagrams, which the subjects have to try to solve in 15 minutes. The experimental group of subjects is allocated to a noise condition; they wear headphones which are attached separately to a central tape recorder that plays popular music to each subject. The control group also wears headphones, but the silence condition is maintained by not having a tape on the tape recorder. When the results are collected for each condition, showing the number of correct solutions, they display homogeneity of variance and exhibit near normal distributions.

a   What advantage would there be in using a repeated measures design?

(1 mark)

b   What would *two* of the disadvantages be if a repeated measures design were to be used? **(2 marks)**

c   Write down a null hypothesis for this experiment. **(2 marks)**

d   Explain why the experimental hypothesis should be two tailed **(1 mark)**

e State an alternative sampling technique to random sampling that might give a more representative sample of A level students. Briefly explain why your alternative method may be more advantageous for this experiment.

(3 marks)

f State briefly why 40 is a reasonable number of subjects for this experiment. **(2 marks)**

g The list of anagrams was made from 7 letter words which were 'carefully chosen'. Identify *two* variables which the experimenter should have taken into account in making this choice. **(2 marks)**

h Write down brief instructions that the experimenter might give to the subject. **(2 marks)**

i Give an example of a random error that may confound the experiment.

(1 mark)

j Briefly describe what is meant by 'demand characteristics'. How may they be shown by subjects in this case? **(2 marks)**

k Explain why the control group also needs to wear headphones. **(1 mark)**

l What criteria should be met before a parametric test is applied? **(3 marks)**

m Assuming that all these criteria are all met, what statistical test would you use in this experiment? **(1 mark)**

n A 0.001 level of significance was proposed in order to judge the difference in results. Discuss briefly why this proposal may lead to a Type 2 error.

(2 marks)

Student answers with tutors' marks and answers

SA = student answer **TC** = tutors comments **TA** = tutors' answers

SA a A repeated measures design may have given us more of a comparison. **0/1**

TC The student may well have the right idea, in that it is better to compare the same individuals in two different conditions than to use different individuals, but it is not at all clear from this answer if that is what is meant.

TA A repeated measured design, by using the same participants in each condition, controls for individual differences between participants.

SA b Two disadvantages of a repeated measures design is that the subject may suffer from fatigue, can practice. **2/2**

TC A good answer.

SA c Null hypothesis is that there will be no difference in the standard of results whether the subjects work with noise or in silence. **1/2**

TC A null hypothesis should say that there will be no **significant** difference (after all, the two sets of results are hardly likely to be identical). The dependent variable could be more precisely expressed, although the student was not penalised for this. A null hypothesis should state that any differences will be due to chance or random factors.

TA Any difference in the number of anagrams solved when listening to music as compared to listening in silence will be due to chance factors.

Equally suitable: There will be no significant difference in the number of anagrams solved when listening to music as compared to listening in silence and any differences will be due to random factors.

SA d   The experimental hypothesis should be two tailed as we are not looking for a specific prediction and therefore need a more general approach. **1/1**

TC   Although this answer would probably gain a mark, it could be improved.

TA   Since the purpose of the study is to ascertain whether music improves *or* impairs performance, then the experimental hypothesis cannot predict a direction in which the results are expected to go, simply that a difference is expected. The key word to include is *direction*.

SA e   An alternative sampling technique which might be more representative is if the subjects were matched for sex and ability, then a matched pairs design was used with counterbalancing.   **0/3**

TC   This student has made a fundamental but not uncommon error. The question does not ask for an alternative **design** but for an alternative **sampling technique**.

TA   A better method than random sampling would be **stratified** sampling with the same percentage of students from each subject area (maths, English, sociology, etc.) and sex in the sample as in the population from which the sample is selected.

SA f   This is enough to work out statistically whether the result are significant and is enough to give a wide variety of subjects.   **1/2**

TC   The first part is correct but 'a wide variety of subjects' is rather vague. It is advisable to include the reason why using more subjects may be impractical.

TA   40 subjects is sufficient to provide a reasonably representative sample and to carry out statistical analysis. It is not too many to make the study too time consuming or expensive.

SA g   The experimenter should firstly take account of the past experience of the subjects of doing anagrams and secondly that some anagrams may be more difficult than others.   **1/2**

TC   The first part of this answer is incorrect since the question does not ask about selection of subjects but about selection of anagrams. The second part may just score a mark but is rather vague.

TA   Any two variables from: word frequency should be the same (how common the words are in the English language); no repeated letters (since this makes the anagram easier); no proper nouns. Any other sensible suggestion would do.

SA h   'You will be given 15 minutes in which to solve as many of the 30 anagrams I shall give you.'   **1/2**

TC   Mention the headphones and be friendly and polite.

TA   'Thank you for taking part in the study. You will be required to solve as many anagrams as possible from the list provided, in 15 minutes. We would like you to wear headphones while you are doing this. Please put the headphones on now and, when given the signal to start, turn over the paper. Is that clear?'

SA i A random error could be that some students do not like the music. **1/1**

TC Fine. Your answer will probably be different, but any variable which is likely to have a random (rather than a constant) effect would be suitable.

SA j 'Demand characteristics' are the effect produced on the subject because of the experimenter; they may manipulate the results to give the answer the experimenter wants. **1/2**

TC This answers the first part of the question but not the second.

TA Demand characteristics are any cues in the experimental situation which are likely to make a participant behave in an unusual way, such as in the way they think the experimenter would like.

In this case, they may have guessed the purpose of the study and if, for example, several participants already believe that music helps them work, participants in the music condition may try harder than those in the silence condition.

SA k The control group should wear headphones so that they have the same pressure on their heads as the experimental group. It may also prevent uncontrolled outside noise from affecting the results. **1/1**

TC Excellent.

SA l You need 1. interval or ratio data
                        2. normal distribution
                        3. roughly equal standard deviation **3/3**

TC Fine

SA m An unrelated 't' test (interval data with an unrelated design). **1/1**

TC Correct.

SA n This is a very high level of significance so that the experimenter may reject his null or experimental hypothesis because the results did not seem significant enough when they might well have been. **0/2**

TC Unfortunately the student has said 'the experimenter may reject his null *or* experimental hypothesis', thus making the answer meaningless. If he or she had simply said the experimenter may reject the experimental hypothesis because the results did not seem significant enough and so on, the answer would be fair.

TA The level of significance is so stringent that unless the probability of the results being due to chance is less than 1 in 1000, then the experimental hypothesis will be rejected. This is therefore liable to lead to a Type 2 error which is rejecting the experimental (alternative) hypothesis when the results are not due to chance but (in an experimental design) due to the independent variable.

Question 2 (AEB 1991)

A psychotherapist wanted to asses the effectiveness of a technique for treating people suffering from animal phobias.

Research into reaction-time had already shown that phobics took longer to

respond to words related to their phobia than to neutral words. In view if this, the psychotherapist reasoned that effective therapy should result in a reduction of reaction-time to phobia-related words.

To test this idea, the psychotherapist selected 10 clients who had phobias about animals whose skin was covered in hair or fur. Reaction times of each client were tested by asking them to read aloud two lists of words. One list (the experimental list) contained both neutral and phobia-related words, for example:

record	apple	monkey
window	table	candle
rainbow	hamster	curtain
rabbit	picture	paper

The list was extended to 40 words in total. The other list (the control list) consisted of 40 neutral words.

Before therapy began, the 10 clients were given standardised instructions in which they were asked to read aloud the two lists as quickly as possible. The time taken to complete each list was recorded. Half the clients read the experimental list first and then the control list, the other half read the control list first followed by the experimental list.

When the course of psychotherapy was completed, the reaction-times of the 10 clients to the two lists were tested in the same way as before. The psychotherapist was then able to compare reaction-times measured before and after treatment. Since the data met the requirements for a parametric test, it was decided to use a related t test to analyse the results. The significance level chosen was $p \leq 0.05$.

a The psychotherapist was confident enough to use a one-tailed hypothesis for this investigation. What is meant by a 'one tailed hypothesis'?

(**1 mark**)

b In this study:
   i name *one* independent variable. (**1 mark**)
   ii what is the dependent variable? (**1 mark**)

c Had the data not filled the criteria for a parametric test, what non-parametric test of differences could be used in this investigation? (**1 mark**)

d One of the criteria that data need to fulfil before a parametric t test is employed is that both sets of data to be compared should have 'similar variance'. Suggest *one* way in which you would check if both sets of data had a similar variance. (**1 mark**)

e Suggest *one* way in which it can be established whether or not a sample of data is normally distributed. (**1 mark**)

f Half the clients read the experimental list first and then the control list, the other half read the control list first and followed by the experimental list. What is the reason for this procedure? (**1 mark**)

g The control lists used in this investigation may appear to be redundant. However, there are good reasons for their inclusion. Briefly explain *one* such reason. (**2 marks**)

h Comparing clients' reaction-times for the control list and the experimental list, would you expect these reaction-times to be:

    i The same or different before the course of psychotherapy? **(1 mark)**

    ii The same of different after the course of psychotherapy? **(1 mark)**

i The psychotherapist decided to use the $p \leq 0.05$ level of significance for this investigation.

    What is meant by the expression '$p \leq 0.05$ level of significance'? **(1 mark)**

j Explain why a 0.05 rather than a 0.01 level of significance was chosen as an appropriate level in this investigation. **(1 mark)**

k The psychotherapist ensured that all the words chosen for this study were of two syllables and of similar length.

    Suggest *one* reason why this was done in this investigation. **(2 marks)**

l In the example from the experimental list you will see that the phobia-related words such as 'rabbit' or 'hamster' do not appear at the top of the list. What would be wrong with putting phobia-related words at the top of the list? **(2 marks)**

m Each client received standardised instructions before their reaction-times were tested.

    i What is meant by the term 'standardised instructions'? **(1 mark)**

    ii Briefly explain why standardised instructions were used. **(1 mark)**

n It is important that the control lists used before and after the course of psychotherapy show reliability.

    i What is meant by 'reliability' in this context? **(2 marks)**

    ii How would you test for reliability in this investigation? **(2 marks)**

o The measurements employed in this investigation could be challenged as lacking in validity. What does the term 'validity' mean in this context?

    (2 marks)

Answers

a A one tailed hypothesis predicts the direction in which the results will occur.

b **i** The independent variables are:

    1. The time the clients were assessed: either before or after therapy.

    2. The nature of the list: whether or not it contained phobia-related words.

  ii The dependent variable is the clients' reaction-times to the lists.

c The Wilcoxon test or the sign test.

d The similarity of variance could be established by:

    i working out and comparing the standard deviations or variances, or

    ii comparing the sketches of distributions of data.

e Normal distribution can be established by:

    i drawing a frequency distribution chart to see if a normal curve is achieved

    ii working out the mean, median and mode – if they are all similar, normal distribution is indicated.

f This procedure is known as counterbalancing and is undertaken to avoid order effects, such as practice or fatigue.

g The list of neutral words act as a baseline or comparison with which reaction times to the phobia-related list can be compared.

h **i** different
　　ii the same.

i If the probability of the results being due to chance is equal or less than 5 per cent, then the null hypothesis can be rejected (or the alternative hypothesis can be accepted). *Take careful note of this answer.* Many students write that this means 'the probability that the results occurred by chance is equal to or less than 5 per cent (one in 20)'. BUT you have not been given a **result**; you have been asked what a particular *level* of significance means. These are two very different concepts.

j The 0.01 level is too stringent for this type of investigation since there would be an unacceptably high risk of making a Type 2 error, that is, rejecting the experimental hypothesis when the results are due to the independent variable.

k All words chosen had to be of a similar length and have the same number of syllables, otherwise these factors may have affected the response time which would not, then, have been due only to the independent variable. Such factors would have represented a confounding variable.

l The appearance of phobia-related words at the top of the list might have been so disturbing for the client that they would not have been able to continue; or, the purpose of the test would have been better disguised by beginning the list with neutral words.

m **i** Standardised instructions mean that all participants receive the same instructions.
　　ii They were used to ensure that all participants had a similar understanding and experience of the experiment – to minimise the possibility of confounding variables.

n **i** 'Reliability' in this context is indicated by the reaction-times to the control lists being similar before and after therapy.
　　ii Reliability could be tested by seeing if there was a significant positive correlation between reaction-times before and after therapy.

o In order for this investigation to be valid, it must be the case that, when testing phobic people, the reaction-time to phobia-related words is longer than the reaction time to neutral words.

Question 3 (JMB 1989)

Psychologists were interested in discovering whether memory is affected by fatigue. Twenty people, ten male and ten female, were recruited and each person was read a series of seven digit numbers by an experimenter. Each person was instructed to repeat aloud, in reverse order, each seven digit number after it had been presented. Hence, if the seven digit sequence of 5–2–3–8–9–7–1 was read by the experimenter, the correct response from the person would be 1–7–9–8–3–2–5. From the responses the experimenter calculated the number of digits recalled, in their correct positions, for each person. The people were then deprived of sleep for 48 hours; after this period each person was given a similar series of seven digit numbers to recall in reverse order.

a   What is the independent variable in the experiment?   **(1 mark)**
b   What is the dependent variable in the experiment?   **(1 mark)**
c   Using the same data describe an alternative method for calculating people's accuracy of response.   **(2 marks)**
d   Name *one* controlled variable in the experiment.   **(1 mark)**
e   Name *one* other variable in the experiment that could have been controlled. Why might it be important to treat the variable you have named as a controlled variable?   **(4 marks)**
f   State the one tailed alternative to the null hypothesis for this experiment.   **(2 marks)**
g   Justifying your choice, state what statistical test would be used to discover whether fatigue affected memory.   **(3 marks)**
h   Describe a procedure, other than digit recall, for measuring the effects of fatigue on memory.   **(4 marks)**
i   Outline an alternative method for producing fatigue.   **(2 marks)**

Answers

a   The independent variable was whether or not people were deprived of sleep for 48 hours.
b   The dependent variable was the number of digits recalled in the correct position.
c   An alternative method for calculating people's accuracy of response would be to calculate the number of incorrect responses that were made (the number of wrong digits or right ones in the wrong place).
d   One controlled variable in the experiment was the sex of the participants.
e   A variable that should have been controlled was the practice effect. All participants did the exercise under normal conditions and then after sleep deprivation. They were therefore used to the exercise and may have found it easier the second time. Counterbalancing should have been done to eliminate this effect.
f   People who are deprived of sleep for 48 hours will remember significantly fewer digits than those who have not been deprived of sleep.
g   The design is repeated measures (related) and a non-parametric test is appropriate with only 20 sets of scores, so a Wilcoxon sign test should be used.
h   Participants could be asked to remember a list of names and faces, a number of objects, an account of an incident, and so on. The design could be the same as the one described in the source.
i   An alternative method of producing fatigue would be to require participants to carry out mental or physical exercises for a prolonged period of time.

Index

Macmillan Work Out Series

For GCSE examinations
Accounting
Biology
Business Studies
Chemistry
Computer Studies
English Key Stage 4
French (cassette and pack available)
Geography
German (cassette and pack available)
Modern World History
Human Biology
Core Maths Key Stage 4
Revise Mathematics to further level
Physics
Religious Studies
Science
Social and Economic History
Spanish (cassette and pack available)
Statistics

For A Level examinations
Accounting
Biology
Business Studies
Chemistry
Economics
English
French (cassette and pack available)
Mathematics
Physics
Psychology
Sociology
Statistics